W9-DAY-538

The Impossible Presidency
Illusions and Realities
of E

22.556

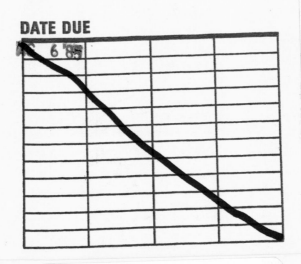

The Impossible Presidency
Illusions and Realities of Executive Power

Harold M. Barger
Trinity University

Scott, Foresman and Company   Glenview, Illinois
Dallas, Tex.   Oakland, N.J.   Palo Alto, Cal.
Tucker, Ga.   London, England

Library of Congress Cataloging in Publication Data

Barger, Harold M.
  The impossible presidency.
  Bibliography: p. 428.
  Includes index.
  1. Presidents—United States.   2. Executive power—
United States.   I. Title.
JK516.B38   1984   353.03'1   83-20374
ISBN 0-673-15576-5

Pp. 250, 252, 253. Quotations from Jonathan Schell, *The Time of Illusion* (New York:
Alfred A. Knopf, Vintage Books, 1975), 367, 368, 376, 382. Used with permission of
Alfred A. Knopf, Inc.

Pp. 300–301. Quotations from Theodore J. Lowi, *The End of Liberalism* (New York:
W. W. Norton & Company, 1979), 278–79. Used with permission of W. W. Norton &
Company, Inc.

12345678-RRC-9190898887868584

For Carol, Jennifer, and Sarah

Preface

The study of the presidency that follows attempts to distinguish images that are mostly illusory from those that have some basis of realism. Chapter 1 explores the importance of the presidency as a popularized leadership role by examining how much the relationship between the people and their president is based on substantive knowledge and how much on myths and illusions. It explores ways in which the president fulfills important psychological and political needs, and how this leads to certain expectations for presidential performance and to the development of a set of popular images and illusions of what presidents are or should be.

Chapter 2 examines the myths and illusions surrounding the political leadership role of the president, which are a major source of current misperceptions and unrealistic expectations.

Chapter 3 analyzes the role of the president as legislative leader, a role surrounded by the illusion that the American chief executive should be able to function as effectively in the legislative arena as a prime minister.

Chapter 4 examines the illusion that presidents direct the Executive Branch. Every new chief executive is optimistic that *he* will succeed, where others have failed, in organizing the federal government so that it will be responsible and accountable to White House management. Every president inevitably is disappointed, however, because his expectations for success and the public's expectations for results are based on a model of executive leadership more appropriate to a prime minister–cabinet system of government than to our own system of separated and fragmented power and responsibility.

Chapter 5 deals with the White House office, the mirror-image machine which instinctively tries to protect the president, but which invariably ends up complicating his problems. The illusion is that the White House staff is an extension of the president, that it provides essential help by acting as a palace guard, preserving his privacy, and handling the countless details of his administration. The reality of the White House staff is that it has become a key part of the president's policy-making apparatus, in the process sealing presidents off hermetically from the give-and-take of politics, from Congress, the cabinet, and other political leaders.

Chapter 6 considers the long-held perception of the "imperial presidency" in foreign affairs and military leadership. Of all the popular images that surround the presidency, that which suggests he single-handedly directs and gives shape to American global policies is the most honest. The international position of the United States has changed dramatically during the past four decades, however, and American power increasingly has been circumscribed by the proliferation of nuclear arms, a changing global economic environment, and political and social forces beyond the control of any single nation or leader.

Chapter 7 explores the impact of popular myths and illusions on presidential power in the domestic-policy arena. During the 1960s and 1970s the United States began to undergo important social, economic, and political changes that led inevitably to increased expectations for government assistance at the same time as the capacity of the nation to satisfy demands slowed down or was reversed. Presidents gradually were forced to act more Scrooge-like, to resist expansion of the federal government in domestic-policy areas. As a result, the presidency increasingly became a "no-win" proposition as one group after another perceived itself as suffering from the declining ability of the government to satisfy its particular demands or needs.

Chapter 8 examines the myths and illusions surrounding the economic powers of the president. The public's notion of presidential control over the federal budget and the American economy is contrasted with the realities of today's uncertain economic conditions. Although the president possesses considerable power to shape overall economic policy, he lacks the ability to affect the outcomes.

Chapter 9 is an overview of the key role the mass media play in perpetuating popular images, illusions, and myths about the presidency. Today the mass media are a major, if not the leading, cause in making the presidency an impossible challenge.

The final chapter discusses the significance of the popularization of presidential power for the future of the presidency and suggests ways of demythologizing the office without destroying its public support. After examining the present system of recruiting presidents, we consider improvements in the system that might result in better-qualified chief executives.

Basic to this book's approach is the firm belief that we need to become more realistic about the powers of the presidency. Although we recommend a critical view of the office, this does not mean that we should become cynical about the heroic traditions of the presidency. Nor do we think that sweeping Constitutional changes are necessary to make the presidency work better, even though such changes might be desirable. We do suggest, however, that a better understanding of the real condition of the presidency would help reduce our present dependency on symbols, myths, and illusions. If such a goal could be achieved, we should then be able to relate to the presidency as responsible citizens rather than as manipulated bystanders.

Acknowledgments

I am grateful to many individuals who supported me with editorial advice and encouragement, since there were times when *The Impossible Presidency* felt like an impossible task. I am grateful first of all to Greg Odjakjian and Bob Johnson, who encouraged me to sign on with Scott, Foresman, and to Christine Silvestri, who was supportive throughout the process of polishing the manuscript for publication. Robert Cunningham was an especially helpful and courteous editor. His judicious, talented assistance with the final copy helped me to produce a tighter manuscript and, I hope, a more readable one.

Professor Arthur Levy of the University of South Florida was helpful in reading my original draft and in making important suggestions for improving it. Professor Levy's detailed and incisive comments were of incalculable value to me in refining the book's general perspectives as well as many key points.

I am grateful to my colleagues in the Department of Political Science at Trinity University for their helpful suggestions, especially Professors Ton DeVos, John Stoessinger, and Mary Weaver. Dottie Grigsby provided both moral support and considerable assistance with manuscript preparation. Professor Gail Myers, Dean Tom Greaves, and Professor Norman Parmer also provided encouragement, and the University helped with a summer stipend that enabled me to devote full-time attention at a critical point in the book's development.

I appreciate the intellectual assistance and encouragement I have received from other students of the presidency, especially Tom Cronin of Colorado College; Louis Koenig of New York University; Margaret Wyszomirski of Rutgers; and Robert Locander of North Harris County College.

Contents

Introduction

The inauguration of Ronald Wilson Reagan on January 20, 1981, as the fortieth president of the United States could not have been more dramatic than if one of Reagan's Hollywood friends carefully staged it. Just as the new president was taking the oath of office, the nation's television news media had one camera eye focused on Reagan and the other on the freeing of fifty-two American hostages who had been held captives for 444 days in Iran. Excitement over the takeoff from Teheran of the jet carrying the hostages mounted at the very moment that the new president was forcefully asserting a new beginning for the nation. Reagan vowed that he would preside over a reawakening of our national power. He proclaimed that never again would terrorists or adversaries humiliate our national pride. As bells pealed across the country to signal freedom for the hostages, many Americans could not help but feel that a new and glorious day had indeed dawned for them, and it coincided with the accession to power of the new president.

Reagan symbolically began his administration on an upbeat tempo, giving a masterful performance to insure the American people that once again the presidency had fallen to the hands of a man of strength, a leader who could restore to our nation's highest office the respect and influence that had seemed to dribble away during a series of presidents since the mid-1960s. His first day as president was perhaps unmatched for the good feelings, the joy that seemed to pass like a tidal wave across the breadth of the land.

Americans hungered for a return to the kind of powerful presidency they had always believed in, but somehow had not had for many years. Not only did Reagan promise to restore American prestige and credibility to our foreign affairs, he vowed also to cut taxes, balance the federal budget, stop inflation, get Americans back to work, and reduce the federal budget. He was, in short, acting exactly as had all of his predecessors, each of whom found that the goodwill and high hopes of inauguration day are unfortunately as ephemeral as many vows exchanged on a wedding day.

Americans are forever seeking the perfect president, not unlike the way they pursue perfect mates, jobs, or any of the other aspects of the good life that is believed to belong by natural right to citizens of the United States. The failure rate in presidents may, however, exceed that for many of our other expectations. Usually a new president can hope to enjoy a honeymoon of about six months to a year with the electorate before the ardor cools. Reagan's administration was no different than any others. Within a year of his promising beginning, the administration was in trouble. Public-opinion polls reflected a steady but pro-

1

nounced downturn in support for his policies, and his leadership over foreign affairs was under attack at home and abroad. While inflation appeared to be momentarily arrested, it came at an immense cost in unemployment. Reagan succeeded in getting Congress to cut taxes, but the shortfall to the federal treasury led to heavy government borrowing, causing interest rates to remain at disastrously high levels and causing millions to worry about the threat of a chronic economic recession. As yet another presidential election loomed, it appeared as if Reagan too might be heading for a single term in the White House.

We live in a time of disposable presidents. Some might insist that this is not so unusual because our society is a disposable society. But presidents were not always so dispensable, and the reasons why the White House, which once symbolized stability and continuity, has lately become a revolving door for incumbents is only partly answered by our nation's tendency to consume and then discard. Americans dispose of one president after another because no recent incumbent has been able to measure up to the office. No incumbent measures up because an immense gulf has opened between what people have come to expect and what presidents can realistically deliver.

It should not be surprising that the presidency has become de-stabilized, for authority at all levels of our society and throughout the world has come under challenge or attack. Parents often seek to fix the blame on teachers or on schools when their children fail to learn, even though the problems may stem from within the family. In the same way voters may attempt to pin the blame for a wide range of societal failures and problems on elected officials, of whom the president is the most visible and handy target. Americans for many years have believed that their presidents should provide leadership in solving many of the problems that threaten us at home and abroad, even though the real powers of the office have never actually justified such optimism.

EFFECTS OF NEW FORCES ON THE PRESIDENCY

This study holds the view that the presidency not only has begun a period of decline but that the office is becoming increasingly unworkable as a result of a number of emerging forces in the domestic and international political environments. The presidency of the 1980s is in fundamental ways a poor reflection of the office that appeared to be extraordinarily powerful from the early 1930s until the end of the 1960s. If the *imperial presidency* was the proper metaphor for that period, the fitting catchword for today might well be the *impossible presidency*.

The presidency has grown impossible because of important changes in American life and because of dramatic alterations in the political and economic balance of power and influence globally. Americans traditionally believed themselves to be an exceptional people, and the presidency symbolized for many years what was supposed to be the best in us. Power appeared to flow almost without interruption to the White House, although institutional or Constitutional changes to formalize such power were rare. During the post–World War II era, presidential authority over domestic and foreign policy making increased, but forces leading to fragmentation in American politics already were beginning to chip away at the two-party system that had enabled presidents to govern with a limited success through coalitions forged with Congress and other politicians. During the same period several nations joined the United States as possessors of nuclear power, and a host of emerging new nations began to demand a share in the world's resources and economic prosperity. By the beginning of the 1970s, it began to dawn on many Americans that there could be limits to our nation's power and prosperity. The Vietnam War, Watergate, energy shortages, rampant inflation, chronic unemployment, and declining productivity all shook the self-confidence of the majority of Americans. Although people continued instinctively to look to the White House for direction in an increasingly confusing and uncertain world, what they saw there were scandals, indecisiveness, and mostly lackluster or incompetent leadership. Four presidents occupied the White House within the space of six and one-half years, from 1974 to 1981, and none seemed capable of providing the public with the kind of leadership normally expected from the nation's most esteemed role.

Some students of the presidency see the problems of the office as stemming from a long series of abuses of power. Others see the office's downturn as originating in the long-range decline in the economic and political strength of the United States. Another view holds that we have politically reformed ourselves to such an extent that political amateurs lacking political party ties now play key roles in selecting presidents; those who are selected now share this amateur status. Still another view holds that we expect too much from a single executive role to begin with, and that we need to look for leadership in alternative centers of decision making rather than to focus all of our hopes on the White House. Some observers insist that the mass media have so commercialized the presidency that what we get now is an oversold, packaged product that resembles the entertainment world more than the political world. An extreme perspective holds that nation-states have become obsolete in today's world, and that governments have failed to deal with fundamental human and societal needs. As a consequence, political leadership universally is more and more discredited.[1]

TRADITIONALISTS VERSUS REVISIONISTS

Those who study the presidency reflect disagreement or confusion over what troubles the office. One major school of research and analysis sees a powerful presidency as inevitable and desirable; anything that threatens such a model is an anomaly or a threat to the nation. Often referred to as *traditionalists*, these analysts believe that the presidency itself is a marvelously flexible institution, one that works well if the "right person" occupies the White House.[2] A *revisionist* school of presidential observers reflects more the disillusionment of recent years, asserting that too much is expected of the office, and that reestablishment of Constitutional checks and balances not only was overdue but imperative if the nation was to avoid any repetition of the abuses and scandals that rocked the White House between the mid-1960s and mid-1970s.[3]

This study may appear to be one more revisionist view of the American presidency. Only in part is this true. The perspective that follows takes issue with several fundamental assumptions of presidential revisionists, and with many of the views offered by more traditional adherents of the strong presidency thesis.

Presidential revisionists suggest that the powers of the office frequently have been abused or misused as a result of inferior presidents, poor policy decisions, mismanagement of the Executive Branch, or personality problems in certain incumbents.[4] Revisionism was a countermovement to more than twenty-five years of what can best be described as academic adulation of the Rooseveltian presidency. From Franklin Delano Roosevelt to John F. Kennedy, students of the office almost unanimously were of the opinion that American government was, indeed, a presidential government, and that the imperial powers that were increasingly attributed to the White House were either too great—or not great enough. Revisionism surfaced widely during the late 1960s and early 1970s as political scientists, historians, and journalists soured on what they saw as abuses of power, first by Lyndon B. Johnson, and later by Richard M. Nixon. Scholars who, as recently as Kennedy, waxed rhapsodical about the benefits of strong-willed presidents began to qualify their evaluations and expectations. The feeling began to emerge that as long as the president was a man of strong character and healthy ego, no powers were excessive. It was the negative presidential personality that bore watching, and if possible the public ought to try to avoid electing such an individual.[5]

For all their apparent criticism of the office, however, revisionists are genuinely sanguine about the possibilities of presidential leadership—*in the right hands*. As Bruce Miroff has noted in *Pragmatic Illusions*, a critical study of the Kennedy years, mixed in "with the [revisionist's] ringing criticisms and elaborate analysis of recent presidential abuses are some barely hidden, nostalgic yearnings for presidential power."[6] Many, if not most, of the revisionists are still enamored of the presidency as an imperial office, even if they avoid the negative interpretation associated with that term. They do not conceal their hope that someday the office will be restored to the illustrious status it enjoyed under certain previous incumbents.

In the view offered in this book, such expectations mirror similar hopes in the public at large, and in both cases the expectations are more illusory than practical. While the presidency has been imperial at times, its powers were never institutionalized, nor did they ever match what scholars, journalists, presidents or the public attributed to the office. The unrealistic images that have come to pervade the role of president in recent years have caused Americans to grow increasingly frustrated. Furthermore, these images are major factors in undermining the office, for they lead to considerable instability and frequent turnovers in administrations. The nation appears to be in a perpetual quest for a new, improved president even before an incumbent has had time to acquaint himself with the layout of the White House.

Each president falls victim to a Sisyphean quest: the more he tries to live up to what the public wants or expects, the more he fails. And the more he fails, the greater the public demand that the president try even harder, or that a new president be given the chance. Whatever influence presidents once gained through the majesty of their office is weakened today by the need to appeal constantly to public opinion.

A major flaw in both the revisionist and traditionalist views of the White House is that neither has fully grasped as yet the critical changes in the global political arena as well as within the United States itself, changes that have dramatically restructured the president's decision-making capacities. Most of our assumptions and expectations about how presidents can and should act derive from a period in which American power and influence made us the most powerful nation on the face of the earth, a beacon of inspiration and hope for millions. Most of the forces for change that have had an impact globally as well as on the United States have served to reduce the American capacity to act or to lead, and the president has symbolized this decline in our national position.

INFLUENCE OF THE MASS MEDIA

This study holds that as the forces for change were diminishing the power and resources of the president, the mass media were encouraging a widespread popular conception of the office that diverged considerably from reality. The president in the past two decades has been refashioned into a national media celebrity who is as dependent as any film star on the arts, skills, and techniques of press agents and entertainment producers. If our newest president has any success, it may well be because he is a consummate political performer, a man who had been training for the role for nearly sixteen years.

Mass-media professionals, as well as image makers and public-opinion pollsters, are the technicians who have replaced the cigar-smoking party professionals of yesterday. Presidents once gained power through an intricate but informal process of coalition building, "wheeling-and-dealing in smoke-filled rooms." Today a president makes his appeal for national support from television studios in New York, Los Angeles, or Washington, buttressed with great quantities of computer data showing where the voters are. The new politics involves a considerable amount of slick selling of the president as candidate or incumbent. The danger is that the slick selling of the president produces product expectations in the consumer public that rarely can be satisfied by any incumbent of the presidency as it now exists. As the process of selling the president increases in sophistication, the public expects still more, and as each president fails to live up to advance billing, a vicious cycle of expectation-frustration ensues.

What is disturbing about all of this is the extent to which the office of the presidency has become vulnerable to forces divorced from politics or political responsibility. Politics is the art of brokering among many conflicting and competing interests. At a time when the capacity of existing institutions to deal with political demands is shrinking, Americans are losing political control over the selection and functioning of the nation's most important political office. Public images of the presidency now owe their shape and texture as much to Madison Avenue as to Pennsylvania Avenue.

Illusions are important to every nation and its people. They help provide a sense of community, and are often self-fulfilling. Perceptions may lead to actions, and images may contribute to shaping reality. As Americans venerated great presidents of the past, they came to embrace illusions and myths about the office that contributed substantially to each incumbent's resources and exercise of power. These popular conceptions fulfilled important emotional needs, just as they encouraged some presidents to push far beyond the Constitution their personal prerogatives and authority.

When people begin to substitute illusions and myths for reality, leadership is jeopardized, for it invariably creates the potential for failure. Popular illusions are poor foundations on which to build political power of an enduring or pragmatic nature. They lead to the danger of manipulation by a president skilled in the techniques or arts of modern communications, or to the risk of a president being manipulated or "designed" by image makers.

Robert E. Denton, Jr., writes that the central dilemma confronting the presidency today is "how to cultivate an active, democratic citizenry with highly inflated visions of presidential grandeur, greatness, and salvation."[7] Presidents dominate not only the news media, they also monopolize the public's political space to the extent that *all* policy-making public administrations and national politics are perceived as resulting from the White House. Americans live in a symbolic world over which the president has unparalleled power, according to the American political philosopher Michael Novak:

> *His idiosyncrasies, ambitions, and failures dominate more conversations than those of any other citizen—as truly if he is unpopular as if he is popular. . . . To cease believing in his power will not make it go away. To say we must not vest our hopes or fears in him runs counter to the plain fact that he has nuclear power at his fingertips, more police power than any sovereign in history, more power to dominate the organs of public opinion than any other human, more power in defining who are the nation's enemies, more power over the military and the making (if not the declaring) of war than any citizen or group of citizens.*[8]

The presidency consequently may exist mostly as an illusory office, but the truth of the matter is that Americans *do* depend on the office. For all of the myths and images that have come to enhance the symbolic and mystical qualities of the role, there is just enough reality behind each to sustain the expectation that a more perfect president can be found if the present incumbent is found wanting. The presidency has grown impossible because the gap between public illusions and reality as well as between expectations and performance is now so massive that no one can bridge it any longer.

NOTES

1. A good overview of various perspectives of the presidency is in Richard A. Watson and Norman C. Thomas, *The Politics of the Presidency* (New York: John Wiley & Sons, 1983), 1–18.

2. See, for example, Louis Koenig, *The Chief Executive*, 4th Ed. (New York: Harcourt, Brace Jovanovich, 1981); Richard E. Neustadt, *Presidential Power: The Politics of Leadership from FDR to Carter* (New York: John Wiley & Sons, 1980); and Clinton Rossiter, *The American Presidency* (New York: Harvest Books, 1960).

3. The best overall treatment of the revisionist perspective is offered by Thomas E. Cronin, *The State of the Presidency*, 2d Ed. (Boston: Little, Brown and Company, 1980).

4. James David Barber, *The Presidential Character: Predicting Performance in the White House* (Englewood Cliffs, N.J.: Prentice-Hall, 1972); Thomas E. Cronin, *The State of the Presidency* (New York: Alfred A. Knopf, 1974); George Reedy, *The*

Twilight of the Presidency (New York: Mentor Books, 1970); and Arthur Schlesinger, Jr., *The Imperial Presidency* (Boston: Houghton Mifflin Company, 1973).

5. Barber's book is the most important recent work about the presidential personality. See also: David Abrahamsen, *Nixon v. Nixon: An Emotional Tragedy* (New York: New American Library, 1976): Alexander and Juliette George, *Woodrow Wilson and Colonel House* (New York: Dover Publications, 1964); Doris Kearns, *Lyndon Johnson and the American Dream* (New York: Harper & Row, Publishers, 1976); and Bruce Mazlish, *In Search of Nixon: A Psychological Inquiry* (Baltimore: Penguin Books, 1972).

6. Bruce Miroff, *Pragmatic Illusions: The Presidential Politics of John F. Kennedy* (New York: David McKay Co., 1976).

7. Robert E. Denton, Jr., *The Symbolic Dimensions of the American Presidency* (Prospect Heights, Ill.: Waveland Press, 1982), 135.

8. Michael Novak, *Choosing Our King* (New York: Macmillan, 1974), 10.

Chapter 1

The Impossible Presidency
Illusions Versus Realities

Nowadays everybody tells us that what we need is more belief, a stronger and deeper and more encompassing faith. A faith in America and what we are doing. That may be true in the long run. What we need first and now is to disillusion ourselves. What ails us most is not what we have done with America. We suffer primarily not from our vices or our weaknesses, but from our illusions. We are haunted, not by reality, but by the images put in place of reality.

   Daniel J. Boorstin, *The Image: Or What Happened to the American Dream*

I believe this generation of Americans today has a rendezvous with destiny. . . . [L]et us dedicate ourselves to renewing the American compact. I ask you not simply to "Trust me," but to trust your values—our values . . . . We have it in our power to begin the world over again.

   Ronald Reagan, Acceptance Speech at the Republican National Convention, 1980

No illusion haunts Americans as persistently as the illusion that the president of the United States is an all-powerful, all-knowing, one-man government. We suffer from continual disappointment with our chief executive because we hold images of the presidency that seldom match reality. Our nation is said to be in the throes of a crisis in public authority, primarily due to a sharp downturn in public confidence and support of a series of recent presidents. The real crisis, however, may stem from our refusal to view the presidency for what it really is: an executive role the powers of which are seriously limited and checked, except during brief periods of national emergency or when national security is threatened. The failures of the presidency in recent years are less the fault of individual presidents than the result of excessively unrealistic public expectations. The inadequacies of successive incumbents are not so much proof of mediocre presidents as of serious imbalances between the actual powers of the office and what people have come to expect the president to accomplish.

Throughout much of our history this imbalance between what people imagined the president to be and what he actually was did not cause widespread frustration or anguish because the federal government played a far less visible or meaningful role in the lives of most people. The president was mostly a figurehead or chief of state, a position hardly designed to disappoint or to earn him widespread ill will. On rare occasions well-marked by history, a president would perform an act of great importance or courage, but much of the time he presided over a system characterized by many as congressional government and by others as ordered anarchy.

The gigantic expansion of the federal government into all aspects of American life and the emergence of American economic and military power as the leading force in the twentieth century changed not only the presidency but also the expectations that Americans and people worldwide held of the office. The emergence of modern mass-communications technology also worked to dramatically alter public perceptions of the president. First newspapers, then radio, and ultimately television discovered the presidency to be a source of infinite public curiosity and fascination. The president simplified the complexities of national politics for the mass public. He and his family provided human interest and drama equalled only by soap operas. And he had the potential power to make life-and-death decisions in a world marked by increasing tension, conflict, and nuclear danger. Historians and political scientists were generally in agreement: the nation's leading political office justified high expectations, for it was an office of ever increasing authority and potential. Clinton Rossiter, author of the classic *The American Presidency*, wrote at the close of the 1950s:

> *All the great political and social forces that brought the presidency to its present state of power and glory will continue to work in the future. Our economy and society will grow more rather than less interdependent, and we will turn to the president ... for help in solving the problems that fall thickly upon us.*[1]

Rossiter was correct in predicting that we would turn increasingly to the president for answers, but he was overly sanguine in implying that solutions would be forthcoming. Few if any observers of the presidency are as hopeful today. Political experts who only a few years ago fretted over the abuse of power by zealous presidents now lament the seeming impotence of all incumbents. The presidency is a troubled institution as it approaches its two-hundredth birthday. Marked by personal tragedy and plagued by scandals and policy failures, the White House has seen six presidents come and go between 1960 and 1980. During this period the office has suffered a downturn in public affection, esteem, and confidence unprecedented in this century.

Presidents almost appear now to be as disposable as beverage containers or spouses in our consumer-oriented, success-driven culture. No president since Eisenhower has served two full terms. Except for Eisenhower and Kennedy, every incumbent since Franklin D. Roosevelt has left the White House in relative public disgrace or political defeat. Gallup polls from Eisenhower to Reagan show a persistent erosion in the public popularity of all presidents. Public approval of the six presidents who preceded Reagan steadily declined from the point when each took office to the midway point of his administration. The indispensable president has become the impossible president.

A handy explanation for what ails the presidency is to blame everything on recent incumbents with poor track records. The failures of presidents' policies in Vietnam and revelations of immoral and criminal conduct in the Watergate scandal were major blows to presidential influence and prestige. So too have been years of drift in the White House when critically needed leadership and policies to deal with energy shortages, inflation, unemployment, and international unrest were either lacking or fell short of public expectations.

Congress appeared to share much of the blame for drift and mistakes, and Congress had its share of scandals. By the beginning of the 1980s, both the legislative and executive branches seemed unable to generate any sustained public confidence in national government, but it was the president who received most of the attention and who paid the severest penalty.

This study contends that the major failures in the presidency are much more profound than individual acts of wrongdoing or institutional failures in public policy. The fundamental problem with the presidency is the growing gap between what the public expects presidents should accomplish and what the office is functionally capable of achieving. There is a massive misperception on the part of the American public as to the nature of executive authority in our fragmented and limited political system. There is likewise a somewhat romanticized view of presidential power in today's global arena. It holds that the president who carries a big stick can preserve American prestige abroad, but paradoxically it also holds that he ought to be able to do so without a military draft or an increased defense budget.

Ironically, these same popular misconceptions often are held by candidates for the presidency and even by incumbent chief executives themselves. Nor are members of Congress, journalists, presidential scholars, or other world leaders immune from unrealistic expectations about the power of the White House. All share the quest for a standard of executive performance and accomplishment that is highly improbable if not impossible.

THE IMPOSSIBLE PRESIDENCY

The impossible presidency is the imperial presidency turned upside down.* The imperial presidency was feared for what seemed to be unbridled powers over American military and foreign policy, as well as for a frequently callous disregard for the will of Congress. The impossible presidency is a matter of concern because of its seeming inability to exert American power convincingly anywhere in the world, as well as for its incapacity to provide leadership in domestic policymaking. Imperial presidents had a reputation for secrecy, clandestine operations, and manipulation. Impossible presidents are unable to hide their weaknesses, to cover up their errors, or to cloak the dissension that appears widespread among White House advisers and other federal officials. Imperial presidents are alleged to have either adroitly used or abused the mass media, while impossible presidents in attempting to use the media often find themselves used and abused. The image of the more powerful presidency was based on the United States's unparalleled global dominance economically, militarily, and politically. The more troubled presidency is a by-product of a diminished American status abroad and at home.

American presidents, however, are not the only political executives to find political success, much less survival, increasingly difficult. Leaders throughout the world have found the political arena to be more and more difficult to master, and authority in a variety of nongovernmental contexts likewise has begun to confront challenges from many sources.

Americans have expectations for presidential performance that in no way match the real powers of the office. We are far more emotional

---

*The term *imperial presidency* came into widespread usage after publication of Arthur M. Schlesinger's book, *The Imperial Presidency* (Boston: Houghton Mifflin Company, 1973).

about presidents—who lack formal authority—while Europeans are much less idealistic about prime ministers or presidents who *do* have substantial political powers.[2]

American presidents depend mostly on reputation and personal skill to influence public opinion rather than on institutional powers. Although the presidency's powers have never been as great as they seemed, all the same forces that test the mettle of other national leaders whose powers are institutionalized have come to increasingly challenge the White House. Consequently, Americans may expect more of their presidents than other peoples do of their elected executives, but the ability of American presidents to deliver is far less certain.

Related to this mismatch between perception and performance is the fact than an American president must fill paradoxical roles. He is both the ceremonial head of state and also the nation's chief politician. The result is an office that is ambivalently expected to be above politics, even though it is mired in politics.

The impossible presidency results from the tensions generated by the office's strong symbolic position in American life and its inability to respond to economic, social, and political forces with any degree of predictable success. The presidency increasingly appears to be occupied by failures when the real problem is the job description does not fit the resources available to the incumbent. Beginning in Chapter 2, we will examine the gap between expectations and reality in the president's performance as a political leader. Successive chapters will consider the lack of fit between popular expectations for his performance in all the various responsibilities with which he is publicly charged: legislative leadership, administration of both the government and his own White House, and formulation of domestic, foreign, and economic policies. In this chapter we will consider how the public regards the presidency, and what this leads to in terms of expectations of individual presidents. A review of findings from political socialization research will suggest important psychological functions served by the role, and a number of expectations that emerge from the public's images of the presidency will be examined. Let us begin by considering the unique status the presidency enjoys in our culture.

EXCEPTIONAL AMERICA: EXCEPTIONAL PRESIDENTS

Americans appear to be obsessed with the presidency. Often the fascination is focused on personal details of the president's daily life and on his family, but in terms of substantive politics the president ranks

far in front in news media attention and public interest.[3] This popular
interest may reflect a latent need for many individuals to identify with
a great and powerful personage, and through him to participate vicari-
ously in momentous, exciting, and heroic deeds and events.[4] In many
ways this fascination parallels and sometimes exceeds that shown by
the majority of the British toward their monarch and the royal family.

Whatever its latent psychological functions, the office of the president does reflect the central position the role occupies in our national
political system. The president is the nation's only elected official who
represents all the people. As chief of state he represents the United
States before other nations and the international community. In a
system marked by great social, economic, geographic, and cultural
diversity, his is the only voice that can begin to assert with any claim
to validity the sound of collective authority and national purpose. In
times of crisis the president is the only political leader with the
potential to overcome the fragmentation that characterizes American
society or to move quickly and forcefully, in spite of the built-in limits
of our system, to preserve order or protect national security. No other
individual has as much opportunity to influence or lead public opinion
or to shape the public agenda. Our obsession with the presidency,
consequently, is easy to understand, for in many ways he represents
whatever collective power exists in the United States.

Our propensity to want to believe great things about the office is
not surprising either. Immigrants to the United States found an absence of the symbols of national community that are taken for granted
in other countries: a monarch and the royal family, centuries of tradition, and unique cultural characteristics. As a people we have always
had to turn to more pragmatic political manifestations of our nation to
find the symbols, myths, and rituals that bind other peoples to their
nation. The U.S. Constitution has served such a purpose from the start,
as has the American flag. But it was the president who became the
living embodiment of the nation as he became our surrogate king, the
symbol of our past and greatness. The role thus serves a vital function
in linking to the national political community all newcomers, whether
immigrants or native-born children.

When Richard M. Nixon was seeking the Republican nomination
in 1968, one of his advisers described the public relationship to the
president in the following way:

> *People identify with a president in a way they do with no other*
> *public figure. Potential presidents are measured against an ideal*
> *that's a combination of leading man, God, father, hero, Pope,*
> *king, with maybe just a touch of the avenging furies thrown in.*
> *They want him to be larger than life, a living legend, and yet*
> *quintessentially human.*[5]

Americans regard their presidents with a mixture of awe, deep affection, and religious reverence, although of late with increasing frustration and disappointment. Some presidents are folk heroes whose exploits rival the deeds of kings or knights. The visages of past presidents grace our currency and are carved into the side of a mountain. The lives of some provide grist for myths and legends. The death of a president in office occasions the kind of grief normally reserved for a family member or close loved one. Every new president automatically inherits a legacy of goodwill and high expectations that he too will reveal heroic attributes once he settles into the White House.

This tendency to make heroes out of presidents is curiously countered by an equally strong streak of political cynicism. We dislike political authority and are distrustful of anyone immoral enough to engage in politics. We are not sure whether politicians really belong on pedestals or shackled to a stock. The reverence for presidents is never too far above the surface of its opposite emotions of disdain, distrust, and disappointment. Even our most heroic presidents have at times stirred negative emotions and endured outright hostility from substantial numbers of citizens.

Nonetheless, cynicism toward a president causes a rather unsettling feeling in most Americans, who prefer to believe their presidents are cut from noble cloth. The notion that the presidency is an extraordinary office which functions admirably when great men are presidents is, as political scientist H. Mark Roelofs suggests, a myth that gives rise to all the symbolism, rhetoric, and legends that surround the nation's memory of great presidents.[6] Americans wish to believe that because a few outstanding incumbents were able to accomplish great things as president, the office ought to function with greatness as a matter of course, although the evidence against such a course of successes is substantial.

This view of the presidency parallels the idea that the United States of America is itself an exceptional society, that "self-evident" principles of nature have inevitably directed our nation to an unparalleled success as an economic giant, a world power, a moral exemplar, and as "the last great hope for mankind." Rossiter wrote, "No president can fail to realize that all of his powers are invigorated, indeed are given a new dimension of authority, because he is the symbol of our sovereignty, continuity, and grandeur. . . ."[7]

Rossiter, in fact, saw the president as "a moral spokesman for us all," a challenge that prompted British critic Henry Fairlie to ask, how can a mere politician be a *moral* spokesman as well as a *symbol* of the *nation*?[8] Political scientist W. Wayne Shannon believes the answer is that the presidency is a unique office in a unique nation. Presidents are expected to symbolize not only a nation but also the American democratic idea:

> *[T]here can be no doubt that we have sought reification of the nation's meaning in the lives of hero-presidents—in Washington's patriotism and rectitude, Jefferson's democratic faith, Lincoln's martyrdom for liberty and union, and Franklin D. Roosevelt's compassion and soldiership for freedom.*[9]

American exceptionalism is a product of the particular American historical experience, and it is manifested in what the historians Daniel Boorstin and Louis Hartz have called a belief in "givenness" which holds that, in the beginning and once and for all, the Founding Fathers gave us a political theory, a set of values, and a philosophy of government which are continually reaffirmed by present experience and which can guide our future behavior.[10]

Boorstin argues that the unique role our national past has played in constructing our image of ourselves and our standards of American life has made us hypersensitive about our past. Consequently, whereas other cultures regard history as a prologue to the present, Americans tend to see theirs as providing immutable givens, or as natural laws from which our institutions and processes invariably evolved. In this view the presidency is a reflection of "the genius of American politics," as Boorstin titled his study.[11] It is represented by those who were best able to personify the development of such cherished American ideals as liberty, equality, or a rags-to-riches life story.

Shannon suggests there is a unique sense of an "American way of life" implicit in such a perspective. Americans look back across their nation's history with a sense of continuity that is "truly amazing by the standards of other nations." We seek the guidance of our national heroes as if they were contemporaries, and refer to the Constitution as if it were chiseled in granite, an updated version of the Ten Commandments. All the while we constantly reassure ourselves that we cannot go wrong if we do not stray from the course of Americanism set for us by history and our earlier heroes.[12]

The image of what a "good" president is is mostly shaped by our experience with past presidents, according to Michael Novak's study of the symbolism of the presidency. The American president functions as king, prophet, and priest because the United States functions as a kind of secular religion. "Americanism" involves a belief in both stability and progress, in the promise of an American dream that opens unparalleled possibilities to everyone. It values equality of opportunity while at the same time permitting vast inequalities of wealth and status. It sees our country as "the greatest" and our way of life as a moral inspiration for others.[13]

Exceptionalism helps explain why we tend to conceptualize the presidency in terms of the greats, and to ignore or pass over the many who were average or substandard. The presidency for most Americans is thought of as the office of Washington, Lincoln, and Franklin D. Roosevelt. Rarely does anyone bring up Franklin Pierce or Millard Fillmore, and many would like to forget that such presidents as Ulysses S. Grant, Warren G. Harding, Calvin Coolidge, Richard M. Nixon—and perhaps even Jimmy Carter—ever occupied the White House.

It is the greats who shaped American history and politics for years to come, or so many of us believe. It is they who provided their successors with a strong base of legitimacy and goodwill on which to begin each new administration. Presidents who follow in the footsteps of the greats are also expected therefore to be men of extraordinary achievement, ability, and morality. Those who fail to measure up are usually regarded as deviant cases, aberrations in the normal course of American history.

Washington, of course, holds the supreme symbolic position as the "father of his country," but it is Lincoln who represents the supreme national myth, the rich symbol of the man of humble origins who made good, the leader whose life was sacrificed on behalf of his followers. Rossiter admiringly noted:

> *He is . . . the martyred Christ of democracy's passion play. And who, then, can measure the strength that is given to the president because he holds Lincoln's office, lives in Lincoln's house, and walks in Lincoln's way! The final greatness of the presidency lies in the truth that it is not just an office of incredible power but a breeding ground of indestructible myths.*[14]

Lincoln showed to what extent a president could push his limited authority during times of national crisis. Franklin D. Roosevelt, however, is the exemplar of the all-powerful and compassionate president of modern times. FDR is credited with gathering into the White House a great range of powers over foreign and domestic policymaking. In attempting to counter the effects of the depression, Roosevelt is widely held to have shifted the balance of policy initiative from Congress—where it had rested throughout most of our history—to the presidency. FDR proved that a skilled popular leader could be a major force for social, political, and economic change.

World War ii and the emergence of the United States as the world's leading industrial and military power further solidified Roosevelt's grip on national power, and led to a vigorous executive-centered authority over foreign policy and the war. Roosevelt's flamboyant personality, his uncanny instinct for using the radio to go directly to the people, and his sharp sense of timing in dealing with news reporters helped heighten public awareness of his leadership. Before long, FDR had earned the reputation of being America's great educator, a position he used so well that he convinced millions he was a one-man government.

After FDR's inauguration in 1933, the Executive Branch did, in fact, take on additional major responsibilities and powers which affected every American and which made the national government increasingly more important and visible than ever before. Elected with a mandate for action, Roosevelt wasted little time in pushing through Congress emergency measures to ease the nation's crippling economic crisis. During his first administration sixty new governmental agencies came into being in the Executive Branch. Federal spending increased from nearly $3 billion in 1925 to $6½ billion in 1935. The buildup of the presidency was so extensive and rapid during the 1930s that the Executive Office was created in 1939 to give Roosevelt much-needed help.

World War II contributed to an even faster growth in government spending and an expansion of presidential power. By 1945 federal expenditures had jumped to nearly $93 billion, some fourteen times greater than ten years earlier.[15] The war concentrated defense and foreign policy authority in the Executive Office. At war's end the federal government had become a far more complex, powerful, centralized, and expensive entity than ever before. More significant was the fact that the focus of power had shifted dramatically from Congress to the White House. With the shift an image of the president as the omnipotent and omniscient leader came to be widely shared, an image reflected admirably by a leader of considerable charisma, a man who possessed an instinctive flair for dramatic leadership.

Political power gravitated to Roosevelt during twelve of the most threatening and crisis-filled years in American history, and he used all the influence available and more to provide dynamic leadership to a nation frightened by economic depression and threatened by aggression. More than any president before or since, FDR came to symbolize the nation, making the president an everyday, familiar figure. British journalist Godfrey Hodgson notes that Roosevelt "thus decisively enhanced the identification between the presidency and the nation that is one of the essential traits of the modern presidency."[16]

Roosevelt well understood the function of nation's teacher, and he became tutor to millions, instructing them in basic economics, foreign policy, and politics—FDR-style. His personal success in welding together a coalition of Southern whites, blacks, labor, intellectuals, urbanites, ethnic minorities, and farmers gave him strong influence over the newly resurgent Democratic party and provided him with the influence necessary to rally party leadership and support in Congress for much of the legislation that came out of Washington between 1933 and the end of World War II.

FDR's success gave rise to many of the myths and illusions that serve both as a source of great influence as well as of misery to contemporary presidents. Roosevelt made an office that was designed to be neither politically responsible to the masses nor dominant among the institutions of the national government. Some argue that it was a fortuitous conjunction of the right man meshing with the times that enabled FDR to deal with the triple threats of depression, war, and social reform. His achievements nurtured the expectation that all future presidents ought to be able to function with the same success. Furthermore, he weakened the two-party system even as he was playing political father to the strong, new Democratic party. By excessively personalizing his power in the Executive Branch and his leadership of the party, he signalled to future presidents the pattern of setting the president above and independent from the party. Roosevelt thus laid the groundwork for future difficulties in rallying party support in policymaking by presidents who were so independent of the party that they no longer had a lifeline to Congress. Only a generation later did it become clear that when Roosevelt cut the president loose from the party, he had deprived his successors of the "ballast and tackle needed to steer the ship." Hodgson notes:

> . . . [H]e personalized the presidency more than ever before, and so encouraged a double identification of the president with the presidency, and the presidency with the nation, so that the president became for most Americans the living symbol of the nation in a direct and personally and emotionally vivid way as not even Washington or Lincoln had ever been.[17]

Roosevelt's success actually prevented major structural changes in the presidency that might have occurred had a lesser leader been in office during the depression and the war. Because FDR was able to achieve significant changes in the structure of the economy and to garner sufficient authority to lead the United States into a position of global prominence, he deflated pressures that might have otherwise built up for changes needed in the relationship between the executive and legislative branches.

If Roosevelt's administration was the source of rising public expectations for an all-powerful presidency, John F. Kennedy's became the model for dramatizing and glamorizing the presidency. The Kennedy name still evokes a nostalgia in many Americans some twenty years after his assassination. Next to portraits of Lincoln or Washington, no other president's countenance adorns as many school classroom walls, or hangs in as many public buildings or private homes. A survey by Louis Harris in 1977 revealed that Kennedy was rated far above any other president on a range of desirable leadership qualities, and a Gallup poll in 1979 confirmed that the memory of JFK still burns brightly: Kennedy was rated by a two-to-one margin over FDR, his nearest rival, as the most competent president to deal with the problems of today by a nationwide sample.[18]

Kennedy's popularity is traceable to his inheritance of the support of presidential scholars who had extolled Roosevelt's activist, dynamic presidency. Arthur M. Schlesinger, Jr., chronicled Roosevelt's life in a three-volume biography in which the lesson was drawn that all successful future presidents would pattern themselves on the Rooseveltian model. Schlesinger saw Kennedy as a youthful successor to FDR, as did Richard E. Neustadt, whose *Presidential Power* served as a manual to Kennedy when the new president entered the White House in 1961.[19] Both academicians were representative of a majority of observers of the post-Eisenhower presidency who argued that what the United States most needed was a virile, progressive leader, one who could resume the centralization of power in the White House begun by Roosevelt, but interrupted during the Eisenhower years. Kennedy's brash vigor, his "can-do" spirit—whether directed toward developing a Peace Corps to spread American technology and goodwill to underprivileged countries, standing up to the communists, or sending a man to the moon—charmed these students of the presidency whose eye-teeth had been cut during Roosevelt's time. Erwin C. Hargrove, in *The Power of the Modern Presidency*, described Kennedy's style of leadership as one based on strong personal idealism. He is, Hargrove wrote, "more nearly the kind of man we can expect and hope to find in the presidency most of the time—a democratic character who is a political man by virtue of role as much as personality."[20]

Much of Kennedy's continued mass popularity derives less from scholarly admiration than from the fact that he was the quintessential telegenic leader, the first president to be genuinely successful in appealing to the public via television. Kennedy came across as handsome and "cool" in the best sense of the term, as used by the communications specialist Marshall McLuhan. Moreover, Kennedy was able to inspire people with his rhetoric. JFK, his beautiful wife, Jacqueline, their children, and the entire Kennedy clan—all of them were able to dominate the nation's attention more than any other first family. Because of America's fascination with its new hero, the national television networks adopted in 1963 a new half-hour format for the evening news programs. Even the most trivial details about life in the Kennedy White House seemed newsworthy. Although American journalists, scholars, and politicians of the time were critical of the growth of the Mao Zedong personality cult in China, our own mass media were then creating a Kennedy cult at home! Kennedy's assassination and its aftermath—the official mourning ceremonies and funeral—became events of monumental proportions. Few Americans old enough to recall that period will ever forget it.

Theodore H. White, the leading chronicler of our presidents, played a role in creating the romantic myth of the slain president. After the assassination White was invited to the Kennedy family compound on Cape Cod and asked to write a public epitaph for JFK. Jacqueline Kennedy recalled her husband's fondness for "Camelot," the title song of a popular Broadway musical. That was how she wanted Americans to remember JFK and the magic time and place of his brief presidency.[21] White's account of this incident in *Life* magazine helped create one of the most enduring myths about JFK.*

UNEXCEPTIONAL PRESIDENTS: THE NOT-SO-GREATS

Many if not most presidents have failed to live up to the FDR-JFK model. In large measure this is because they lacked that poorly defined quality known as "charisma," and partly it is because president-watchers have found them wanting in certain qualities associated with great presidents.

Harry S. Truman was seriously handicapped because he succeeded Roosevelt. Truman was generally portrayed by the press as a small-time machine politician, a haberdasher, or (according to his mother-in-law) a dirt farmer. Outspoken, highly partisan, short-tempered, and no stranger to profanity or earthy expressions, Truman was the very antithesis of the sophisticated and smooth Roosevelt. Ironically, Truman's candor—which got him into so much trouble while he was president—made him something of a folk hero after his death. A Broadway play, a book, and an award-winning television production during the mid-1970s sharply contrasted Truman with Lyndon B. Johnson and Richard M. Nixon. New generations of Americans know Truman as the plain-speaking president whose portrait Jerry Ford chose to hang in the Oval Office on assuming the presidency in 1974.[22] Historians too have treated Truman more generously in recent years, rating him as one of America's near-great presidents on the basis of his foreign-policy leadership and efforts to carry out most of the social programs begun under FDR.[23]

Dwight D. Eisenhower was another president who missed the mark of exceptionalism, even though he was unique among postwar presidents in that he not only lasted two full terms but also enjoyed widespread popularity throughout his eight years in office. But his reputation has long suffered from the judgment of president-watchers who saw in him a bumbling, inarticulate, and largely ineffective chief executive. A more recent analysis of his two terms by political scientist Fred I. Greenstein gives quite a different picture of Eisenhower as

---

* In a conversation with the author in 1980, Roger Hillsman, Kennedy's adviser on Far Eastern policy, remarked that JFK had an intense dislike of sentimentalism and any maudlin displays of emotion. Hillsman insisted, "He [JFK] would have thrown up if he'd heard that Camelot story!"

an intelligent, politically astute leader who was quite successful in obtaining what he wanted from Congress and his own subordinates.[24]

Like Truman, Lyndon B. Johnson found it difficult to overcome the glamorous image of his predecessor. For Johnson the Kennedy myth was a curse that seemed to haunt his presidency. Kennedy had style, but Johnson had political skill and substance, one observer noted.[25] Johnson's vice-president, Hubert H. Humphrey, once suggested that "Kennedy became much more of a hero as he became much more of a martyr. . . . His weakness and flaws were quickly forgotten. Johnson was constantly compared to Kennedy, and that was like comparing a heavyweight boxer to a ballet dancer."[26]

The romanticizing of the slain Kennedy clouded for some time his lack of substantive achievements. In office only 1008 days, Kennedy was largely remembered for his promise to bring about a change rather than for any solid legislative accomplishments. His successor, Lyndon B. Johnson, succeeded with most of Kennedy's agenda, carrying through Congress bills concerned with civil rights, an income-tax cut, medical-care insurance for the elderly, and assistance to the poor. But Johnson, like many presidents, failed to live up to public expectations. Within a year of his landslide election victory over Barry M. Goldwater in 1964, Johnson began to suffer a sharp decline in the public-opinion polls. This trend proved irreversible.

Johnson had hoped the electorate would see him as another FDR—perhaps as someone even greater. During his early months in office, LBJ carried the latest public-opinion polls with him wherever he went, and would pull them out to show how popular he was. The war in Vietnam, however, soon began to weigh heavily on the White House as the conflict widened and grew increasingly more frustrating. While Johnson and his military leaders kept promising the "light at the end of the tunnel" and a victory soon to come, the news media portrayed a war that had become a quagmire in which more and more American lives and resources were swallowed up. Before long, a credibility gap developed, and Johnson found it difficult if not impossible to sell his policies to an electorate which was beginning to equate the president with a snake-oil salesman. By early 1968, his popularity reeling as a result of continued bad news from Vietnam, LBJ could no longer appear in public without confronting masses of antiwar demonstrators.

Swept into office largely because of public dissatisfaction with Johnson's Vietnam policies, Richard M. Nixon declared he had a secret plan to end American involvement in Southeast Asia. Nixon's election was no triumph of image over substance. In fact, the public's image of the man was not much more flattering than its perception of LBJ. For years Nixon's nickname of "Tricky Dick" reflected his long-standing reputation as a ruthless political gut-fighter. Yet few presidents entered office with as established a reputation for experience in foreign affairs or political skills as Nixon.

He was perennially plagued by another equally unflattering public image: he was known as a colossal "square." A campaign consultant in 1968 graphically described Nixon's lack of public appeal:

> *[A] lot of people think Nixon is dull. Think he's a bore, a pain in the ass. They look at him as the kind of kid who always carried a bookbag. Who was forty-two years old the day he was born. They figure other kids got footballs for Christmas, Nixon got a briefcase and he loved it. He'd always have his homework done and he'd never let you copy.*[27]

The lack of a popular public image did not prevent Nixon from winning election to the presidency twice. Nor did it stop him from continuing the war in Vietnam or from expanding the conflict into Cambodia and Laos in the face of growing opposition. Nixon's reputation for political ruthlessness was confirmed when he and the White House staff attempted to eliminate opposition to his foreign policy and to silence those regarded as threats to the nation's security or to the political security of the administration. Nixon and his assistants attempted to intimidate, harass, or destroy the reputations of those who stood in their way. In June 1972 agents of the Committee for the Re-election of the President were caught bugging the Democratic National Committee's headquarters in the Watergate apartment complex in Washington, D.C. This incident began a long chain of events that led to Nixon's forced resignation in August 1974. As Watergate unravelled, a host of other criminal or questionable activities in the Nixon administration became known: dirty tricks aimed at discrediting political rivals; questionable ethics in appointments to the federal bench and diplomatic posts; misuse of personnel in the Central Intelligence Agency, the Federal Bureau of Investigation, and the Internal Revenue Service; and fraudulent income-tax returns prepared on behalf of the president.

Many of these criminal actions were symptomatic of one president's weak character and personality problems. But other aspects of Watergate pointed to serious inadequacies in the presidency itself, which had come to a boiling point during the late 1960s and early 1970s. The Constitution's grant of authority to the president is filled with ambiguity and vagueness, but it had permitted over the years the evolution of a highly personalized and at times dictatorial office. So long as these informal powers were held by an incumbent of proven ability and character or by one acceptable to the legions of president-watchers in academia or the press, the inadequacies were either ignored or overlooked, for the Constitution also is flexible enough to permit the growth of countervailing forces. But the Vietnam War raised questions as to just how far individualized exercises of power should be allowed to go. For advocates of the powerful FDR model, what had previously been a much valued imperial presidency suddenly became a threat when its power was in the hands of a politician many if not most of them detested: Nixon.

"JUST PLAIN FOLKS" PRESIDENTS

Did Vietnam and Watergate *cause* the downturn in presidential influence and authority, or were they symptomatic of other forces at work that led two presidents to sorely overreach their power? Certainly both presidents took extraordinary measures to demonstrate their authority and to prove their credibility to their own people and to other nations. In Johnson's case, unable to sustain the impression of his authority and facing a widespread loss of legitimacy with the public, he decided to step down. For Nixon, the threat to his power was answered by the Watergate-related activities. Unable to measure up fully to public expectations or demands, Nixon responded by trying to totally manipulate the political environment. He tried to destroy the opposition political party and to restructure reality on his own terms. He used the agencies of the federal government to punish adversaries, and he placed himself above the law and the Constitution.

Has the presidency reached a point that in order to live up to popular illusions an incumbent must subvert the institutions and processes of government to succeed? Both Presidents Ford and Carter valiantly attempted to prove such is not the case. Both de-imperialized the trappings of the White House and attempted to reduce some of the public's unrealistic expectations as to what the presidency could achieve during a decade of increasing uncertainty at home and abroad.

Ford assumed office as the nation's first unelected president from the position of our first unelected vice-president. His claim to the Oval Office itself was tenuous, but a public and capital exhausted by Watergate responded quickly and positively to the new president's first words after being sworn in: "Our long national nightmare is over. Let the healing begin."[28] A month later Ford's own nightmare began when he reopened the festering wound of Watergate. Pardoning former President Nixon for any past crimes for which he might be charged, Ford opened himself to the charge of making a political payoff to Nixon.

Equally damaging to Ford was a public image that suggested that while he might be trustworthy and a "nice guy," he was not sufficiently strong or tough at handling foreign affairs. He also was frequently at loggerheads with the Democratic Congress, giving the impression of a lack of skill in domestic-policy leadership. Anything but imperial, Ford often appeared more like a president of the Grand Rapids Rotary Club than of the United States. His deliberate manner of public speaking tended to suggest that he was not the brightest man ever to occupy the White House.

When Ford sent the Marines into Cambodia to recover the crew of the merchant ship *Mayaguez*, his rating briefly shot up eleven points in the polls. But it gradually began to slip once more as the perception began to settle in that he was indeed an "accidental president." A national television comedian, Chevy Chase, enjoyed great success by imitating a clumsy President Ford tripping over his own legs, bumping his head on doors, and causing a shambles of state papers every time he sat down at his desk. According to White House Press Secretary Ron Nessen, Ford personally enjoyed Chase's parodies, but the image of a stumblebum did little to enhance Ford's stature or reputation.[29]

Ford's definition of the office was as much the result of his personal style as of any methodical scheme. But when Jimmy Carter came to the White House, he had a deliberate plan to get rid of the last vestiges of the imperial presidency that had fallen into such disrepute under LBJ and Nixon. Running a remarkably brilliant campaign to wrest the Democratic party nomination away from better-known party hopefuls, Carter portrayed himself as an anti-establishment candidate, a nonpolitician, and an outsider to Washington. He promised to create a government "as good as the American people," and he chose his notion of what a president should be from images rooted in the populist and reform movements that have rocked American politics sporadically since the beginning of this century. Exalting the common man, these reformers favored governmental leadership that was nonpolitical, rational, scientific, and professional. The root of many evils in politics was found in political parties, strong interest groups, and the lure of power. Populism and reform led to a number of important changes in local and state politics, including nonpartisan elections, the council-manager form of city government, and the direct primary, initiative, referendum, and recall. The most significant impact on the presidency stemmed from the direct primary nominating system. Candidate Carter believed that the decade from 1965 to 1975 had paved the way for a new period of national reform, particularly in terms of the presidency. He shaped his campaign accordingly, representing himself as a professional administrator above politics.

Carter's own self-description in his autobiography is revealing:

> I am a farmer . . . a businessman . . . almost a professional planner. . . . I'm an engineer. . . . When I was elected governor of Georgia, I went to the office not as a politician, although I don't apologize for that word, but . . . as a planner, as a businessman, as a scientist.[30]

The image of a president of the people, of a leader above the give-and-take of politics, served Carter well during his first few months in office. A national news magazine not known for its Democratic sympathies noted during this honeymoon period that "the campaign to polish the presidential image is a smashing success." The president was responsive to ordinary people, and he was a natural performer in public. The magazine continued:

> *Standing sweating in shirt sleeves in a humid auditorium in Yazoo City, Miss., he is humble. ("I don't have all the answers; I've got a lot to learn.") . . . Staying overnight at a private home, the president never fails to carry his own luggage, make his own bed, write an excuse if his presence makes the family's children late for school, and kiss the hostess at the door on leaving.*[31]

Public-opinion polls after Carter's first six months showed high ratings for his performance, although the president was beginning to act more and more political as he dealt with Congress, the bureaucracy, and party leaders, and as he began to confront various interest groups opposed to his goals in domestic and foreign policy. A scandal involving his close friend, Bert Lance, head of the Office of Management and Budget, tarnished the image somewhat, and the escapades of Brother Billy, swilling beer and trading on his president-brother's position during a series of tasteless public appearances, further damaged Carter. By the end of his first year in office, Carter's honeymoon was over. Polls showed that a favorable rating of 75 percent in the early spring of 1977 had sharply declined by November to 56 percent, the fastest fall from grace of any previous president except for Ford, whose sharp decline in the early fall of 1974 was directly attributable to his pardon of Nixon.[32]

Part of the explanation for Carter's precipitous drop obviously included his confrontations with various interests over budget priorities, negotiations for a SALT II disarmament treaty with the Soviet Union, a proposed Panama Canal treaty, and changing policy in the Middle East that appeared at times to be more favorable to the Arabs than to the Israelis. Many White House observers, however, saw the president's problems as more symbolic than imbedded in policy conflicts or failures. A *Newsweek* columnist observed that Carter had "reversed course so dramatically and demystified the office so utterly that he is now having trouble projecting presidential authority—both in Washington and in the country at large."[33]

Carter's deliberate desymbolizing of the presidency made it difficult for increasing numbers of Americans to accept him as the legitimate heir to the office of Lincoln, FDR, and JFK. He alienated many reporters who saw his folksy image as sham and hypocrisy. And what started out as public affection for a folksy leader gradually began to turn to doubt about his capabilities and stature. Traveling with the president during a swing through the farm belt in 1977, *Newsweek's* Meg Greenfield wrote:

> *I was continually struck by the contrast between the imposing paraphernalia of the office and the deliberately unimposing style of Carter. People pressed up against airport fences and barriers . . . seemed genuinely wowed by the approach of Air Force One. It looms especially large on airfields that have been cleared of other traffic, its huge jets whining and screeching as it wheels up toward the waiting greeters and microphones. But the magic of the moment tends to be dispelled by a hail-to-the-chiefless chief who skips nimbly down the steps looking frail and unattended, dwarfed by the giant aircraft, a simple, normal person—just like you and me.*[34]

Carter's anti-elitist image extended to his insistence that the Washington social register carry his name as Jimmy Carter and not as James Earl Carter. He wore a cardigan sweater while sitting in front of a fireplace during an address to the American people on energy conservation. (The fire in the fireplace crackled so loudly it sounded to television viewers as if the president might be enveloped in flames before he could finish his talk!) News photographers showed the president padding around the White House in jeans. In 1977 he had the dubious distinction of being one of the few presidents not to be listed on the Custom Tailors Guild's list of the ten best-dressed men in America. The Guild cryptically noted that Carter's indifferent and careless fashion "may adversely affect his image among other world leaders, and might generally encourage similar sloppiness among American men."[35] (The day that Candidate Carter learned he had garnered sufficient delegates to win the nomination on the first ballot, he called a group of reporters to a news conference in his Plains, Georgia, home. But first he changed from a suit into freshly pressed denim jeans with matching denim jacket, to carefully show he was definitely *not* an establishment candidate.[36])

Not until his presidency was on the verge of a breakdown in the summer of 1979 did Carter begin to consider that one of the problems might be his leadership style. Calling on the assistance of an Atlanta media adviser, Gerald Rafshoon, to help construct a new Carter persona, the president began to wrap himself more in the trappings of the presidency. He dismissed several cabinet members who were at odds with some of his policies. He attempted to rally the public by scolding it for not making the sacrifices the country needed to curtail energy usage. And he began to engage in more global summitry in an effort to show Americans he was acceptable to other world leaders. Unfortunately, not even his successes—including the Camp David peace accord between Egypt and Israel, the Panama Canal treaties, his establishment of formal diplomatic relations with the People's Republic of China, or his deregulation of the airlines, trucking, and rail industries—overcame the impression that Carter was unpresidential.

Carter's experience verified that the image of power is power, and the illusion of strength equals strength. So successful was he in de-imperializing the presidency that he delegitimated his own claim to the office. Carter was elected because of the decade of presidential abuses of power that had caused widespread public cynicism. But public disenchantment with the presidency was never due to the *use* of power but to its *abuse* or *inept use*. Carter reduced public expectations by being a president who was smaller rather than larger than life. He reduced the stature of his own power by appearing never to measure up to it. He made Americans feel two things that they are not used to feeling and will not abide, *Time* magazine noted after his election defeat by Reagan. Carter made them feel puny, and he made them feel insecure.[37]

Carter's failure as a public leader contrasted with Kennedy's success, although historians might well argue that Carter actually achieved more substantial results than Kennedy. While Kennedy consistently exhorted the people to dedicate themselves to improving the nation and the world, Carter kept rebuking them for suffering from malaise and for being soft. Kennedy declared that Americans could accomplish any goal if they set their sights high and made the effort. Carter proclaimed that events were beyond our control, and that Americans needed to get used to sacrifice and a limited life-style. Carter's leadership might well have been more realistic, but it was far less popular.

AMERICAN EXCEPTIONALISM REVISITED: THE REAGAN ADMINISTRATION

Reagan's victory in 1980 was less a personal triumph than a public rejection of Carter's scaled-down presidency and portrayal of a nation past its prime. Reagan's campaign pitched its main theme on the charge that it was Carter's personal failure as president that had led to America's problems. Our humiliation at the hands of Iranian militants holding U.S. embassy personnel hostages, the skyrocketing inflation rate, the sluggish economy, and our faltering prestige among our allies and adversaries—all were laid on the shoulders of the Carter administration.

Reagan resurrected the image of a powerful president, implying that he would solve America's woes and reassert American leadership in the world at the same time that he would get the federal government off our backs. Nevada Senator Paul Laxalt's nomination speech on behalf of Reagan at the Republican National Convention declared that Reagan would restore the American dream and help each American to realize it once more. Reagan, meanwhile, was able to overcome negative images suggesting he was nothing more than an aging Grade B movie actor, and a trigger-happy right-wing warrior. He projected the personality of a calm, affable, and—in spite of his sixty-nine years— boyish candidate, whose ideals fit neatly with those of millions of everyday American citizens. He generated a nostalgia and yearning for the mythical good old days, when the American dollar was the standard currency around the world, and Americans could travel the globe with their heads held high. His victory might well have been a rejection of Carter's uninspiring leadership, but it was also an indication that the public still believed that a president could reaffirm its faith in American exceptionalism.

In a study of Reagan's rhetoric prior to the 1980 election and during the first few months of the new administration, Shannon found the president to be a true believer in American exceptionalism. A recurrent theme in Reagan's acceptance speech at the Republican convention, in his inaugural address, and in other major speeches held that current problems were the result of the nation's having strayed from "given" American principles to which it must now return. These principles included belief in freedom, individualism, limited government, free enterprise, localism, and divine providence. "[W]e can and will resolve the problems which now confront us. . . . And after all, why shouldn't we believe that? We *are* Americans."[38]

The real culprit in undermining the American way of life, Reagan insisted, was the growth of big government. In his inaugural address, he declared:

> *It is no coincidence that our present troubles paralleled and are proportionate to the intervention and intrusion in our lives that result from the unnecessary growth of government.*
>
> *We are a nation that has a government—not the other way around. And that makes us special among the nations of the earth.*[39]

Such an appeal is a clear-cut argument to return to first principles, to some kind of pristine beginning in which truth and logic were merged into a political theory of immutable validity by the Founding Fathers. Shannon suggests that the symbolism employed by the president at the end of his inaugural address was nothing short of remarkable in its declaration of American exceptionalism:

> *In the course of a few hundred words the president invokes our sense of divine providence and mission, the view from the west face of the Capitol to the "shrines to the giants on whose shoul-*

ders we stand. . . ." Washington, Jefferson, and Lincoln are shown
as personifiers of the nation and its ideals. . . . "Whoever would
understand in his heart the meaning of American, will find it in
the life of Abraham Lincoln. . . ." All told the passage is ex-
tremely moving. And clearly, it is meant to teach us. The example
of American heroes—great and small—must give us the strength
to face current problems.[40]

During the early months of the Reagan administration, public-
opinion polls reflected a renewed sense of optimism and buoyancy in
the electorate as hopes for an economic revival with decreasing inflation, and of a forceful new foreign policy, created an atmosphere of
expectation and a new spirit of trust. By the end of Reagan's first six
months, it appeared as if the United States had another FDR in the
White House, although one of conservative persuasion. With his triumphs in winning massive budget and tax cuts, Reagan succeeded in
reversing the unbridled growth of federal government that had continued ever since the early days of Roosevelt. Reagan's skill in dealing
with Congress drew praise even from those who disagreed with his
conservative policies, and his warmth, charm, and charisma made him
personally popular with the public. His tough approach in dealing with
the Soviet Union was applauded by many who felt the United States
once again had a president who would not let our adversaries walk all
over us.

Before long, however, all of Reagan's good fortune seemed to turn
on him. The massive budget cuts he orchestrated through Congress
began to take a toll on all elements of society, particularly on the poor,
unemployed, youths, and minority groups. The image of a disarmingly
charming, warm leader began to turn into one of a slick Scrooge who
favored the rich and cared little for the unfortunate.

Reagan suffered also from a growing public perception that he was
not fully in control of his administration. He frequently appeared
uninformed about major issues, and he often gave glib responses to
reporters' questions, suggesting that he was still more the entertainer
than the nation's chief executive. The financial community cooled
toward Reagan's economic program as the massive tax cuts pointed to
gigantic budget deficits and the economy seemed to stagnate. His
foreign policies began to appear belligerent and poorly coordinated as
the administration became poised for another Vietnam-styled intervention in El Salvador. As the threat of a new nuclear arms race
loomed, considerable opposition to his defense policies emerged. Eventually, loyal Republican supporters in Congress began to waver in their
support of the administration, and the media increasingly portrayed
Reagan as stubborn, superficial, and incompetent.

As Reagan's promises to restore the United States to its former greatness began to run up against reality, the public's sense of frustration and disappointment with the presidency once again was reflected in declining public support for the incumbent. Candidates began to gear up for yet another presidential election, encouraged by the prospects that one more president was eminently defeatable. Americans for their part seemed poised to seek once more a new exceptional president—someone who would rekindle the myth of the FDR-JFK presidencies.

THE NEED TO BELIEVE IN PRESIDENTS

Why do people persist in believing presidents are capable of being all things to all people? Why, indeed, do presidents and candidates for the office continue to repeat all the old promises and bromides in the face of repeated failures and one-term administrations? Our past tradition of venerating presidents inevitably means that we will continue to expect great things from contemporary executives. That a few past presidents performed heroically during national crises does not diminish the expectation that all presidents ought to be successful all the time.

The mass public holds opinions about the presidency that are more emotional than rational, personal and glamorous rather than substantive and cognitive. Our expectations for the presidency consequently bear little congruence to its actual Constitutional powers or to its capacity to function in a system of checks and balances and limited government. The capability of any incumbent to measure up inevitably falls far short of what is actually possible. Our images of the presidency have come to be mostly illusions.

Very few Americans have ever seen a president up close in person. Fewer still have actually met or had any direct communication with a president. The role is one that is learned second-hand through intermediaries. Public-opinion polls and voting studies confirm that the vast majority of people have little substantive knowledge about what a president actually does, what decisions he makes, or what policies he advocates. For most people, knowledge about the president is almost totally based on *images* developed through various processes of political socialization.

A substantial body of political socialization research has established the central importance of the presidency in fulfilling emotional and cognitive needs. The president stands supreme and almost alone in the American public's conception of the national government. He not only links individuals to their government, he is also the major source for the development of positive, affective bonds of attachment to political authority. No other role fulfills as critical a function in unifying the nation or providing a symbol for the national government.

Learning theory helps to explain how the presidency accomplishes these functions. The late Swiss educational psychologist Jean Piaget, for example, found that children learn to relate cognitively to government and political authority through stages predetermined by innate physiological capabilities.[41] Up to the age of seven or eight, a child usually has only vague, highly personalized images of the political world, derived mainly from experiences with authority figures and rules within the family. From age eight to twelve, the child is receptive to filling in this emotional content with more substantive knowledge, such as how institutions work or why rules are necessary. In early adolescence and beyond, the child grows increasingly capable of using reasoning and logic to make comparative judgments and value decisions about the goodness or badness of his or her political environment. The president ideally serves as *the* key agent in each of these learning stages because of his great visibility and prominence, as well as because of the highly personal nature of the role.

From birth until about age six or seven, a child's relationship to authority is largely family-centered; it is emotional, affective, and highly personalized. The father and mother symbolize security, affection, and the source of rules. Slowly the child becomes aware of political authority beyond the family in the roles of the president and the police officer, the former because of his great visibility and power, the latter because of frequent direct contact and experience. A study in the early 1960s found that 86 percent of a second grade subsample of elementary school children chose either George Washington or John F. Kennedy's picture as the one best representing what government meant.[42] Not only did the president dominate the political vision of young children, he was also seen as benign, friendly, and nurturant. Political scientists David Easton and Jack Dennis noted in their study *Children in the Political System* that from the earliest grade, the child "sees the president as on a commanding height, far above adults as well as children. The president flies in on angel's wings, smiling, beneficent, powerful almost beyond the realm of mere mortals."[43]

The president is believed to serve as a surrogate for parental authority, a father writ large. His image is all-powerful, warm, helpful, nurturant, kind and all-knowing because children need to feel that those in charge of them are benign. Imaginative stories or anecdotes reflecting the colorful imagery of the world of children help in developing such a conception. For example, one of the most enduring myths in American culture is that of Washington and the cherry tree. Through it, Parson Weems has given generations of American children the notion that presidents are extraordinarily honest.

As children slowly begin to fill in this affective and symbolic image at around age seven, the regime or structure and functions of the presidency in the context of Constitutional government begins to form, but it never diminishes the warm regard with which the children began their image of the president. Perceptions up until the eighth grade are so overwhelmingly positive toward the president that Easton and Dennis were unable to find in all their sampling "a child who did not express the highest esteem for the president." Children viewed the president through "rose-colored glasses, with no taint of criticism, mistrust, or indifference creeping into the picture."[44]

Nonetheless, by the eighth grade, President Washington and the incumbent president drop to a much lower level of importance as textbooks and curricula emphasize institutions and processes above unique personalities, and such symbols of government as the Congress and elections loom larger. Still the president comes across as almost a superman among political mortals, particularly in textbook treatments of the role. Formal political education has generally been found to reinforce mostly positive images of the president.

Most of the political socialization research that found an almost universally positive regard for the president was produced at the same time as American textbooks were reflecting a general idealization of the presidency. This was during the popular administrations of Eisenhower and Kennedy. There is substantial evidence that Presidents Johnson and Nixon were viewed much less positively, and samples of children from such subcultures as Appalachia, the black ghettoes, and the Mexican-American community of the Southwest did not share as benevolent an image as middle-class white children. Watergate itself profoundly altered the image of at least President Nixon for middle-class white children, several studies indicate.[45] This growing disaffection among younger children since Watergate parallels the decline in adult confidence and esteem detected by public opinion polls since the mid-1960s.

The development of negative images toward the president runs counter to the traditionally enduring, diffused support and positive feelings most Americans have felt toward their chief executive. Although adult assessments may have fluctuated from time to time, and varied from group to group, the prevailing view was usually positive. A president could normally count on a reasonably solid base of respect and goodwill because the public held the office in such high regard. The public might lose confidence in an incumbent's policies, qualifications, or performance, but he could carry on by trading off the basic regard and respect extended to the role he occupied. This was evident even in 1973 when a substantial majority of the public continued to believe President Nixon's version of his lack of involvement in Watergate, even as one revelation after another of his duplicity became public knowledge. Not until the House Judicial Committee voted articles of impeachment did a majority of the people finally reject the president's version of events.

The diffused support for the role found in adults is believed to be a carry-over from our childhood socialization. There is little research that systematically examines how adults feel about the presidency, but public-opinion polls and voting-behavior research suggest that much of the electorate reacts positively or negatively to the president on the basis of personalized, emotional, and symbolic images rather than from any knowledge or understanding about the president's accomplishments, policy positions, or capabilities.

The personal nature of the role, so important to young children, remains important to adults. Fred I. Greenstein observed that when people were asked to indicate what they liked or disliked about a president, the most commonly mentioned aspects involved personal characteristics: sincerity, integrity, warmth or coldness, candor, and whether the president seemed concerned about people or not.[46] This personal dimension enabled people to identify with the president as they could with no other political figure, empathizing with him when things were not going well and feeling pride at his accomplishments when he was successful.

There are obvious dangers to a democratic nation in which citizens relate to the chief executive role more emotionally than cognitively. An emphasis on personal characteristics negates far more important aspects of the role, and it minimizes the development of a broader understanding of other political roles and complex political relationships. There also is a serious threat to the legitimacy of the office if and when the public's diffused support is altered by a long-term decline in presidential performance. Dennis suggests that if positive diffuse support is the consequence of previous accumulations of experience with a series of popular, successful presidents, the opposite experience—a run of ne'er-do-wells—might result in a collapse of presidential authority:

> [T]he process of presidential institution building . . . is clearly reversible, and . . . the actions of an incumbent can be significant for public support for the presidential institution. Thus the performance of presidents and the resulting public image have determinant effects on the authority they leave their successors.[47]

IMAGES VERSUS POLITICAL REALITIES

Images of the presidency thus represent a role that is complex, remote, and vaguely understood. It is a role that is particularly difficult to comprehend because very few people ever have the experience of direct learning. Virtually all sources for learning about the presidency emphasize the more affective, emotional, symbolic, and personal characteristics, and present the office in an oversimplified form. Furthermore, the models on which the office is based are mostly heroic, exceptional presidents from a past that is overromanticized.

The day-to-day operation of the Executive Branch involves such a bewildering array of events, decisions, communications, and other roles and personalities that conceptualizing it in terms of heroic, one-man dimensions not only grossly oversimplifies but distorts it as well. The presidency is shrouded in all kinds of myths and illusions fostered not only by scholars in textbooks but also by the mass media, and even by incumbents as well.

The only way most people are able to make sense out of this confusing but central political role is through images. Images are mental constructs formed from the raw material in the world around us. They are molded by personal experience, emotions, and psychological needs. Boorstin in *The Image: Or What Happened to the American Dream* defines an image as "an imitation or representation of the external form of any object, especially a person."[48] Kenneth Boulding in *The Image* argues that an image is our store of subjective knowledge of the world, of things we believe to be true. Images of the president may only provide rough summations or indices of the vast complexity of the institution, but they are important because most people cannot tolerate ambiguity or uncertainty.[49]

Images are important in understanding how people relate to the president because most individuals perceive and interpret facts in accord with their images and with the way such facts are represented through symbols. Symbols too stand for things that are acknowledged but not actually encountered. The flag, for example, represents love of country and patriotism, two emotions that while not empirically verifiable, nonetheless are meaningful to the person reacting to that particular symbol. Symbols of the presidency such as the White House, the presidential seal, or the executive jet, Air Force One, give identification to the individual who gains possession of them, legitimizing the transfer of the role from one incumbent to the next.

Every president needs the support, or at least the passive acceptance, of a majority of citizens if government is to function without constant interruption or upheaval. All presidents must persuade the American people of at least two things: (1) the people and their chief executive constitute a political community; and (2) the present incumbent is the legitimate governing authority. Any president needs to legitimize not only the institutional role but also his right to be there. Presidents thus need to explain

> . . . to the populace what they are doing and how their activities conform to the community's developing sense of itself. Even in the best circumstances, this explanation cannot be continuous, direct and complete. . . . [A president] will resort to simplified

> *explanations and more or less straight-forward or devious rationalizations. To insure that these arguments are persuasive and generate awe, they will be decked out with all kinds of traditional symbols, folktale references, and other legendary allusions.*[50]

One means by which a president tries to legitimize his authority is myths. Anthropologists find myths surrounding national leaders prevalent in all cultures, advanced as well as primitive. Myths are supposed truths about a society that are taken for granted. They help a people become aware of themselves as members of a political community. A myth is both a people's legend and their hope. Myths convey images and symbols through the examples of individuals. The myth of Horatio Alger, for example, reifies the American dream so well that virtually every president or candidate feels constrained to prove that he has raised himself up by the bootstraps from poverty to the White House. If, unfortunately, the president is a rich man, he must prove how empathetic he is with those who have yet to make it.

Rituals also help give meaning to images by involving leaders and followers in a common symbolic enterprise, reminding people in vivid, expressive and dramatic fashion of their communality and joint interests. The presidential campaign and election as well as the inauguration are rituals that legitimate presidential authority and give meaning to images. So does the playing of "Hail to the Chief," or having the president make the first pitch that opens the baseball season. Rituals are reminders of the continuity and grandeur of a nation. There is a clear parallel, for example, to be drawn between the coronation of the British monarch and our presidential inauguration.

Whether images are expressed symbolically—through myths or in rituals—if they are reasonable reflections of reality, they can be educative, helping people to adapt their behavior to changing conditions or to different personalities. The remarkable ease with which we make transitions between presidents has always amazed nations where transfers occur only through bloodshed or Machiavellian intrigue. Images can also be educative if they enable people to act in their own best interests. For example, the image of a president or candidate as a strong supporter of civil rights may, if accurate, enable blacks or minorities to make important judgments about whether to support him or not.

Whenever images are merely fiction or fantasy, they become illusions. They may be exciting or entertaining, reassuring or promising, but they do little to help people understand or cope with reality. An illusion is, in fact, an image confused with reality. Illusions are prevalent in any culture where people find it uncomfortable if not impossible to accept facts. Americans are vulnerable to illusions, Boorstin argues, because we have a tendency to consider the impossible to be only slightly less attainable than the difficult. Our unlimited opportunities have always nurtured the American dream because many of us actually could achieve it. But a new menace of unreality caused by our success in making illusions so vivid and realistic that they became credible has made us come to believe in images that are themselves unreal.[51]

The greatest threat to the contemporary presidency—the reason it has become such an impossible role and a graveyard for those with unlimited aspirations for power—lies in the fact that the gap between realistic images and illusions about the presidency has virtually disappeared. The forces that now surround and impinge on the institution—television, professional image makers, campaign experts, narrow interest groups, and White House "palace flacks"—are all bent on perpetuating images that are far more illusory than real. Unfortunately, each president cooperates in fostering such illusions, believing that what's up front is more important to his success than what is inside.

Images are important in linking citizens to the president because they can be accurate, in which case they provide meaningful glimpses into the strengths and weaknesses of a president's character, qualifications, and style. It is not easy to hide one's true personality after countless daily appearances on television or frequent public appearances. President Johnson gave people the impression of a stubborn, domineering egotist, a wheeler-dealer who was skilled at arm-twisting but not adept at appearing credible. According to those who worked with him and knew him, that image fitted. Nixon's paranoid personality, his slashing, no-holes-barred, win-at-any-cost image reflected his real character and political style. Ford's nice-guy but awkward demeanor and Carter's image of the Washington outsider were also close to the mark.

It is not so much that image politics is bad, but that images lend themselves to considerable distortion by the image makers, whether in the media, the professional campaign manager's world, or the White House. A national bestseller that satirically examines bureaucracy, *The Peter Principle*, suggested that "an ounce of image is worth a pound of performance."[52]

An adviser to candidate Nixon wrote in a 1968 memo:

People vote more for a chief of state—and this is primarily an emotional identification. . . . The response is to the image, not to the man, since 99 percent of the voters have no contact with the man. It's not what's there that counts, it's what's projected.[53]

PRESIDENTIAL ILLUSIONS

Mass communications scholar Dan Nimmo observes in his *Popular Images of Politics* that many of our political images are illusions.[54] A major illusion holds that people know what is going on in politics, despite the fact that most of us do not experience politics directly or concretely but rather through a filtered re-creation in the mass media. Another prominent illusion is that the public can participate in government by choosing politicians to represent them. The reality, Nimmo writes, is this may be the case with a few public officials, but even then, public influence is limited almost exclusively to election seasons. Many other political decision makers are not subject to popular election, and thus are beyond the control of a democratic polity. Finally, people believe that elected politicians are the real decision makers, ignoring the actual involvement and dominance of technicians, professionals, and bureaucrats in influencing if not making decisions.

Many of the political images that once facilitated our adaptation to the political world are no longer functional. "There are many images that bind us affectively to the political environment, but there is a poverty of images that contribute to popular cognitive understanding and control over politics," according to Nimmo.[55] Nowhere is this more obvious than with the presidency. Tempted by the tremendous potential of the mass media and by awareness of how important traditional presidential images are in eliciting and sustaining popular support, no president or candidate can resist identification with images whether they fit or not. Convinced by scholars and textbooks, prodded by the press, a president believes he *must* promise people he will succeed where all others have failed, that *he* will live up to their expectations. At this point the president challenges the realities of American politics—particularly the politics of the last quarter century—and links himself to a set of illusions that persist in spite of experience.

Illusions could not exist for long if they were completely incredible or beyond any belief. Illusions must have *some* truth or validity; otherwise few people would be tempted to believe in them or to hold on to them in the light of everyday experience. Presidential illusions persist and guide public images of the presidency as well as the behavior of presidents because presidents in the past have occasionally achieved remarkable results. Whenever presidential power is contemplated, we naturally think about those who were able to use the office to affect the nation's destiny, to commit the nation to war, or to steer it through troubled times.

When the exceptional president or the extraordinary accomplishment becomes the benchmark against which all chief executives are judged, the end result is bound to be disappointment, frustration, and cynicism. Consequently, each presidential candidate or incumbent feels compelled to attempt more than is possible, or to distort his accomplishments and to deny his inadequacies or mistakes. This significantly widens the gap between what people expect and what they get, and it also leads to a vicious cycle in which every president, finding himself unable to measure up to unrealistic standards, tries to compensate with still more promises or exaggerated claims.

Illusions about the presidency thus survive because the White House is so inextricably entwined with myths, symbols, rituals, and public expectations that no one risks demolishing them. Ray Price, Nixon's speech writer, realized this better than most when he wrote that politics is more emotional than rational, particularly where presidents are concerned:

> *[People want the president to be] someone to be held up to their children as a model; someone to be cherished by themselves as a revered member of the family, in somewhat the same way in which peasant families pray to the icon in the corner. Reverence goes where power is; it's no coincidence that there's such persistent confusion between love and fear in the whole history of man's relationship to his gods. Awe enters into it.*[56]

It is this extraordinary need or wish to see the president in exceptional dimensions that leads the White House to perpetuate so many unrealistic expectations and illusions, thereby keeping alive the public's images of the presidency despite reality. We revere the presidency not because of what it actually *is* but for *what we want it to be*, and what we want of presidents is that they embody popular images.

The most shopworn illusion surrounding the office holds that a president can be successful without being a politician. Our veneration of past presidents means that every president has to play a charade in which he tries to act nonpolitical—like a saint—while trying to make the political system respond to his leadership. This illusion stems from our very beginnings, and it reflects President Washington's view that the office should be more statesmanlike than partisan. It also reflects our cultural biases about politics and politicians.

In actual practice, of course, the presidency is the most politicized role in our nation, for only through political maneuvering can anyone win the office, much less make it function. Presidential scholar Thomas E. Cronin has argued that our most effective presidents in the past were in fact highly political. "[T]hey understood the importance of political parties . . . and did not condescendingly view the American common man as childlike and dependent on an omniscient president."[57]

Another deeply rooted illusion—but one that has developed largely since Woodrow Wilson—suggests that presidents dominate, or should dominate, the legislative process. National policies are seen as presidential policies, and if a president does not succeed in achieving promises made during the campaign to satisfy public needs or expectations, he is held personally accountable. The illusion is that presidents "initiate" and Congress "legislates." But the reality is that the policy process is far more complicated, and involves much more interplay among key institutions and individuals than a simple White House–Capitol Hill relationship suggests.

The illusion that presidents ought to be successful in making the Executive Branch function responsively and responsibly likewise flies in the face of experience. A popular myth suggests that skilled management can make bureaucracies accountable, and if our nation's chief executive fails to get a handle on government, that is evidence of his own administrative incompetence and lack of experience. In truth, all presidents have complained about their inability to get the federal bureaucracy to carry out directives, and every president attempts to shake up what has come to be an increasingly unaccountable and unmanageable federal bureaucracy. Federal executives resist the White House because they are beyond dismissal or punishment, and almost all have staying power that far exceeds any administration.

Every president succumbs to the illusion that the disloyalty of the executive branch can be countered by a loyal White House staff. The White House office has grown virtually into a "corporate presidency" with hundreds of individuals acting in the name of the president. To the public, such staffs are seen as well-organized establishments that significantly ease the awesome burdens of the presidency. There is considerable truth to such a perception, for the White House office has in fact rescued presidents from the trivia and tedium of everyday decision making. On the other hand, such staffs have themselves become one more bureaucratic level with which a president must contend, and in many ways the most troublesome of all, because of the distortion they encourage in the president's perceptions of the world and the public's image of the president. White House assistants increasingly are tempted to try to isolate the president from the unpleasantries of politics. They are prone to oversell the president in order to compensate for the setbacks the administration faces from every corner of the real political world. As a result, White House assistants contribute significantly to raising false expectations about the presidency, and increase the president's widening credibility gap by exaggerating his accomplishments while minimizing his shortcomings.

The most tenable illusion about presidential power is that which suggests he has immense power and resources in foreign policymaking and national defense. A modern president prefers foreign policymaking over domestic decision making, a popular thesis proclaims, because global affairs afford him the opportunity to make decisions with much less opposition from Congress, the public, interest groups, or the press.[58] Furthermore, the president can avoid the cumbersome and unresponsive federal bureaucracy in foreign affairs by acting unilaterally or through his national security adviser and secretary of state.

A president appears more presidential, it is argued, when he is dealing with other heads of state or foreign dignitaries, or when he makes critical decisions about the nation's security. The formal power to order a nuclear attack or counterattack adds a frightening but convincing dimension to his role as foreign policymaker and commander in chief.

There is, however, far less than meets the eye to the president's much vaunted global and military authority. In a nuclear era in which the great powers have each other checkmated by mutual destructive military force, illusions take on a vital significance all their own. Power and influence are no longer automatically related to the *amount* of power possessed by a nation, but to its willingness to employ power under varying circumstances. More critical than ever is the *credibility* of a nation's foreign-policy leadership.

The decline of American strength and prestige globally have also added to the president's problems of foreign-policy leadership. No longer does the United States monopolize nuclear power, and no longer is its economy strong enough to permit us to stand as the world's chief peacekeepers. The emergence of a host of new independent nations, along with shifting balances of power among the older nations, has ended the days of presidential domination over global policy.

Not only is the president supposed to represent the United States as a virtuous and great power among nations, but he is also supposed to be the great provider at home as well. President Truman once observed that the president must be the lobbyist for all the American people. The illusion is that the president is chiefly responsible for adjusting inequities and righting wrongs because no other political leader in fact *can* assume the interests and ethical imperatives of the nation as a whole. His domination of our political consciousness automatically ensures that the president will be the reference point for every major domestic issue or problem. Minorities look to him for leadership in civil rights. He is expected to champion the causes of the aged, the young, women, and groups that would even change the Constitution to permit school prayers or to ban abortions. The president is held personally responsible by Michigan auto workers or Pennsylvania steel workers who have lost their jobs because of low-cost Japanese imports, or by the young couple unable to buy their first home because of high mortgage interest rates. He is, in short, all things to all people.

Not only is the president's capacity far more limited than popular images suggest, but the demands on the president have grown far more pressing and specific from an electorate that itself is growing more and more fragmented and diverse. The policy environment has changed remarkably in terms of population trends, work patterns, personal and societal values, and life-styles. Yet high expectations remain the most distinctive characteristic of the American people.

Most of our illusions about the central role of the White House in domestic affairs are tied to economic expectations. No single factor in politics correlates as strongly with presidential popularity as good economic times, yet presidents invariably find themselves victimized by popular illusions about their economic power. The United States's economy is gigantic, diversified, and incredibly complex. Furthermore, it has become inextricably entwined with the global economy since the 1950s. Decisions affecting the economy are made by huge corporations (many of which are multinationals), and by labor unions, bankers, investors, and individual consumers who are beyond the president's influence, much less control. American business only grudgingly permits government interference, yet corporations, industry, and workers have all come to depend upon governmental outlays as much as any social security recipient or army veteran receiving a disability check. Big government and big business have become hopelessly interdependent, and the president's desk is widely held to be where the buck stops.

As long as the American economy towered over the economies of all other nations, our presidents reaped political benefits. American presidents received the credit in good times, for the dominant illusion was that a president could fine-tune the economy by encouraging an expansive federal fiscal policy during downturns and by putting on the brakes on spending during economic booms.

Beginning in the late 1960s, however, the American economy began to lose ground in the global economic system. Increased competition for resources and markets by other industrialized nations as well as by newer developing countries led to greater competition for American businesses. It also led to inflation, increased costs in energy, and an eventual decline in our nation's productivity. No matter how much presidents attempted to fine-tune it, the economy seemed to be permanently mired in troubles. Instead of an almost certain guarantee of reelection, it became an almost certain guarantee of only one term in the White House.

What is unusual about these illusions is that experience has yet to be proven a good teacher. Although most of the president's vaunted powers have been revealed to be chimeras, each candidate and each new president continue to insist that the office will work and that promises can be kept. The mass media persist in treating every president as if he indeed could or should exercise extraordinary leadership, and that the political universe turns on his orders.

Consequently, there persists in the public imagination, in the mass media, and in politicians who covet the White House the grandest illusion of all: that the problems of the office can be corrected by the right person, or by rearrangement of existing structures in the

Executive Branch. A few voices from time to time may suggest that the problems of the office stem from serious institutional weaknesses in its Constitutional position. But such arguments are readily dismissed by the declaration that the presidency is so uniquely an American invention that no one really wants to change it. Most if not all of the reforms suggested for improving the office or the recruitment system seldom address the fundamental question of whether or not the public's expectations now far exceed the present office's capacity to perform.

The real powers of the presidency thus are considerably less than the illusions that dominate the office. Popular images of the role primarily stem from myths about past "greats" as well as from current mass media portrayals of the office and its relative position in the national government. Popular images presuppose the presidency capable of generating a kind of political power which it never really possessed, and which is historically alien to the American political experience. According to Roelofs, presidential powers are mostly personal, episodic, and negative. The idea that a president achieved major national priorities, that he acted as a tribune of the people, or that he led the country by means of a New Deal across a New Frontier to a Great Society is largely mythmaking.[59] A Napoleon, a Lenin, or a Mao Zedong might have achieved such sweeping results, but American presidents have never possessed the raw authority to match such political leaders. Given the dispersed nature of our politics, no president can build up or extend his authority into systematic patterns of sustained control.

The myth of presidential greatness—the main source of our many illusions about the presidency—persists because so much of our political socialization and our mass communications technology continues to foster it. Our propensity to hang onto the American dream and to the belief in an American exceptionalism prevents such illusions from dying. The myth of presidential greatness thus is essential to covering up our own weaknesses and national political inequities. In the face of our widespread cultural egotism and fragmentation, the presidency *is* the one hope for overcoming irresponsibility and narrow, selfish parochialism, and for marshalling people behind worthy national goals and purposes.

Unfortunately, in an attempt to measure up to images that are unrealistic, presidents are constantly under pressure to promise and attempt more than they can ever realistically hope to accomplish, and thus to overreach themselves. When they fail or fall short—as they invariably do most of the time—they try to substitute rhetoric and to beef up the presidential image with public-relations gimmickry, replacing style for substance. Instead of solving the presidential dilemma, however, this usually only worsens it because public expectations are further distorted, and the disappointment usually only serves to alienate people from the president who "misled" them.

DISILLUSIONING OURSELVES ABOUT PRESIDENTS

The ideal representative government is one in which reasonably informed citizens participate rationally in choosing and evaluating their leaders. Leaders legitimate their positions and powers on the basis of how well they meet the wishes of the majority. Few governments, of course, ever live up to the ideal because most people lack the knowledge, skills, or motivation to make rational judgments about those who rule them. Most people do, however, react when the political system seems to be failing, and when private concerns are threatened by or frustrated by political decisions. Images provide the means by which most citizens are able to understand complex, remote, and powerful institutions, and they enable people to evaluate governmental performance in at least a rudimentary manner.

Citizens ought to act more rationally and realistically, but we might just as well argue that sin or greed should be eradicated from human nature. People will always depend on images in relating to presidents because there is no other practical means to enable the great majority of Americans to gain knowledge or experience about the role. At best all we can develop is a representation of the role and the person occupying it.

Illusions likewise will always surround the presidency because our mass-media–dominated culture is particularly susceptible to oversimplification, dramatization, and romanticization. We are a people in perpetual search of fulfillment and perfection. We are believers in a Manifest Destiny that promises life can only get better, more pleasurable, and more personally rewarding. The president personifies this American dream and American positivism, and as long as the economy and society reflected opportunity and real growth, he was the major beneficiary of illusions stemming from the dream. When American economic and political power began to be challenged or matched by those of other nations, and limits to our expectations began to cramp our nation's life-style, it was the president who suffered the most from the weaknesses and inadequacies of our illusions.

It is not so much that images or illusions of the presidency are themselves confusing or especially dangerous. The image of presidential power often means real power. The image of strength or trustworthiness often translates into public confidence that provides a president with the strength and loyalty necessary to lead. The illusion that a president is in control of the economy may be just the thing to calm a jittery stock market, to make the dollar appear more stable on foreign money market exchanges, or to encourage business and consumer confidence. What is disturbing about our "fix" on images, particularly those that are obviously illusions, is that it lends our nation's most important political role to considerable distortion by mass-media professionals, image merchants, and White House staffs, and it encourages presidents to try to "give the public what it wants."

Popular rule must involve substance as well as image and illusion. Our political fortunes clearly are well served by dealing with the problems of our nation and the world as they really are rather than by what we think they are or wish they were. It is a debasement of democracy to suggest that presidents must play to the popular passions of the mass electorate in order to govern with some degree of effectiveness. Such a trend would be dangerous if not self-defeating for presidents as well as for the nation. Images that reasonably reflect the real world are helpful in enabling millions of otherwise nonpolitical citizens to judge candidates for the presidency or to evaluate incumbent presidents and their performances. Images that misrepresent the role or the incumbent are illusory, and frequently lead to frustration and instability in our nation's leading political institution.

NOTES

1. Clinton Rossiter, *The American Presidency* (New York: Harvest Books, 1960), 237.

2. See, for example, the essays in Richard Rose and Ezra Suleiman, eds., *Presidents and Prime Ministers* (Washington, D.C.: American Enterprise Institute, 1980).

3. Herbert Gans, *Deciding What's News* (New York: Pantheon Books, 1979), 162.

4. Fred I. Greenstein, "Popular Images of the President," *American Journal of Psychiatry* 122 (November 1965): 523–29.

5. Quoted in Joe McGinnis, *The Selling of the President, 1968* (New York: Pocket Books, 1969), 204–5.

6. H. Mark Roelofs, *Ideology and Myth in American Politics* (Boston: Little, Brown and Company, 1976), 165–71.

7. Rossiter, 18.

8. Henry Fairlie, "Thoughts on the Presidency," reprinted in Lewis Lipsitz, ed., *The Confused Eagle* (Boston: Allyn & Bacon, 1973), 216–27.

9. W. Wayne Shannon, "Mr. Reagan Goes to Washington: Teaching Exceptional America," *Public Opinion*, December-January 1982, 13.

10. Daniel J. Boorstin, *The Genius of American Politics* (Chicago: Phoenix Books, 1958), 9; and Louis Hartz, *The Liberal Tradition in America* (New York: Harcourt, Brace and World, 1955), 58.

11. Boorstin, 9.

12. Shannon, 13.

13. Michael Novak, *Choosing Our King* (New York: Macmillan, 1974).

14. Rossiter, 108.

15. Lance T. LeLoup, *Budgetary Politics: Dollars, Deficits, Decisions* (Brunswick, Ohio: King's Court Communications, 1977), 35.

16. Godfrey Hodgson, *All Things to All Men* (New York: Simon & Schuster, 1980), 65.

17. Ibid.

18. Louis Harris and Associates Survey, 1977; and the Gallup Organization, 1979 (commissioned by WHYY-TV-TV, Philadelphia).

19. For current edition of Neustadt's book, see Richard Neustadt, *Presidential Power: The Politics of Leadership From FDR to Carter* (New York: John Wiley & Sons, 1980).

20. Erwin C. Hargrove, *The Power of the Modern Presidency* (New York: Alfred A. Knopf, 1974), 74.

21. Theodore White, *In Search of History: A Personal Adventure* (New York: Harper & Row, Publishers, 1979), 517-25.

22. Merle Miller, *Plain Speaking: An Oral Biography of Harry S. Truman* (New York: Berkely Medallion Books, 1974); "Plain Speaking," a television special starring Ed Flanders (WQED, P.B.S., Pittsburgh, 1975); and "Give 'Em Hell Harry" (New York: Avon Books, 1976).

23. Arthur M. Schlesinger, Jr., "Our Presidents: A Rating by 75 Historians," *New York Times Magazine*, July 29, 1962; and *San Antonio Express*, February 21, 1983, 2-D.

24. Fred I. Greenstein, *The Hidden Hand Presidency: Eisenhower as Leader* (New York: Basic Books, 1982).

25. Merle Miller, *Lyndon: An Oral Biography* (New York: G. P. Putnam's Sons, 1982), 342.

26. Ibid., 345-46.

27. McGinnis, 103-4.

28. *Time*, August 19, 1974.

29. Personal communication from Ron Nessen, April 12, 1975.

30. Jimmy Carter, *A Government As Good As Its People* (New York: Simon & Schuster, 1977), 53-54.

31. *U.S. News & World Report*, August 8, 1977, 15.

32. The Gallup Poll, *Public Opinion 1978* (Wilmington, Del.: Scholarly Resources, 1979), 26-27.

33. Meg Greenfield, "Hail to the Chiefless-Chief," *Newsweek*, November 7, 1977, 116.

34. Ibid.

35. *New York Times*, November 21, 1977, 36.

36. Martin Schramm, *Running for President* (New York: Pocket Books, 1977), 59-60.

37. *Time*, January 5, 1981, 13.

38. Quoted in Shannon, 16.

39. Ronald Reagan, "Inaugural Address," reprinted in Robert S. Hirschfield, ed., *The Power of the Presidency* (Hawthorne, N.Y.: Aldine Publishing Co., 1982), 209.

40. Shannon, 13.

41. Jean Piaget, *The Origins of Intelligence in Children* (New York: W. W. Norton & Company, 1952); and *The Construction of Reality in the Child* (New York: Free Press, 1969).

42. Robert D. Hess and Judith V. Torney, *The Development of Political Attitudes in Children* (Garden City, N.Y.: Doubleday & Company, Anchor Books, 1967), 41.

43. David Easton and Jack Dennis, *Children in the Political System* (New York: McGraw-Hill, 1968), 171.

44. Ibid., 177.

45. See, for example, F. Christopher Arterton, "The Impact of Watergate on Children's Attitudes Toward Political Authority," *Political Science Quarterly* 89 (June 1974): 269, 288; Harold M. Barger "Demythologizing the Textbook Presidency: Teaching About the President After Watergate," *Theory and Research in Social Education* 4 (Spring 1976): 51–65; and Majorie R. Hershey and D. Hill, "Watergate and Pre-adults' Attitudes Toward the President," *American Journal of Political Science* 19 (November 1975): 703–26; on the Appalachian children's images, see Dean Jaros, H. Hirsch, and F. Fleron, Jr., "The Malevolent Leader: Political Socialization in American Subculture," *American Political Science Review* 62 (March 1968): 64–75.

46. Greenstein, 526–29.

47. Jack Dennis, "Who Supports the Presidency?", *Society* 13 (July-August 1976): 53.

48. Daniel J. Boorstin, *The Image: Or What Happened to the American Dream* (New York: Atheneum Publishers, 1962), 197.

49. Kenneth Boulding, *The Image: Knowledge in Life and Society* (Ann Arbor, Mich.: University of Michigan Press, 1956), 7.

50. Roelofs, 39.

51. Boorstin, *The Image*, 240.

52. Laurence J. Peter and Raymond Hull, *The Peter Principle* (New York: Bantam Books, 1968), 121.

53. McGinnis, 204.

54. Dan Nimmo, *Popular Images of Politics* (Englewood Cliffs, N.J.: Prentice-Hall, 1975).

55. Ibid., 148.

56. McGinnis, 204–5.

57. Thomas E. Cronin, "Putting the President Back Into Politics," *Washington Monthly*, September 1973, 12.

58. See Aaron Wildavsky, "The Two Presidencies," in A. Wildavsky, ed., *Perspectives on the Presidency* (Boston: Little, Brown and Company, 1975), 447–61.

59. Roelofs, 169–70.

Chapter **2**

The People's Choice
The Myth of the Nonpolitical President

No president . . . can escape politics. He has not only been chosen by the nation—he has been chosen by his party. And if he insists that he is the "President of all the people" and should therefore offend none of them—if he blurs the issues and differences between the parties—if he neglects the party machinery and avoids his party's leadership—then he has not only weakened the political party as an instrument of the democratic process—he has dealt a blow to the democratic process itself.

John F. Kennedy, quoted in David Broder, *The Party's Over* (New York: Harper Colophon, 1972, 34).

The most misleading illusion surrounding the president suggests that he is "president of all the people," and that because of his unique position as our popularly chosen head of state, he is or should be above politics. Although he wins office as the candidate of one of the two major political parties, a president tries to act more like a statesman than a party politician because that is what Americans expect.

Politics implies wheeling and dealing in smoke-filled rooms among cigar-chomping politicians with few scruples. It suggests grubby, under-the-counter deals and trade-offs in which votes are exchanged for specific benefits or rewards. The illusion is that the man chosen to lead our nation is cut from nobler cloth. Presidents are supposed to be pristine, pure, and unsullied by such "dirty" activities.

This illusion is mostly based on a deeply rooted belief that a president should avoid politics because he is the head of state. A president can appear "presidential" only if he ignores party politics. For the traditional American distrust of government pins most of its ills or shortcomings on political partisanship.

Candidates for the presidency are forced into the awkward position of campaigning as if they are unaffiliated with a political party while seeking to attract the vote of regular party supporters. Presidential hopefuls must campaign as if they are running *against* rather than *for* government. An incumbent president seeking reelection must strive to appear *above* rather than *immersed in* politics. By remaining in the Oval Office where the nightly newscasts show him hard at work making important decisions, or by holding court in the White House rose garden, a president signals to the electorate that *he* is not going to lower himself into the election fray. He will remain on the job to which the voters have elected him while others engage in the frivolity of shopping-center appearances, television talk shows, and the "fried-chicken" circuit. His campaign may even go so far as to not identify the president's name with a political party, emphasizing instead that voters have an opportunity to "reelect the president,"or to keep whatever-his-name-is at the helm for "four more years."

The image of the nonpolitical president is patently false because there is no way that the nation's chief executive can develop the coalitions necessary to govern without political parties or political maneuvering. The illusion of the nonpolitician president is reinforced every time a presidential election is held because today's recruitment system encourages candidates or incumbent presidents to virtually sidestep political party organizations and to use their own personal organizations to make direct appeals to the electorate. The contemporary presidential candidate or incumbent is a "party of one." He wins a national party's nomination and campaigns as the top of its ticket, to be sure, but his victory is almost completely personal. His run for the White House or for reelection is directed by a band of personal loyalists and campaign professionals whose commitment is to the candidate and not to any political party. Once elected, the new president forms a White House organization which is a carbon copy of his successful campaign staff but which typically excludes party leaders.

In a purely descriptive sense presidents nowadays *are* nonpartisan. Some would argue that Eisenhower was the first nonpolitician president, for he never lost his view of himself as standing apart from politics generally or from his own political party in particular.[1] The ties a nonpolitical president has with his political party are the result of a shotgun marriage arranged by his faithful supporters holding the gun on party professionals. Often unwillingly, party leaders and party supporters have little choice than to accept the candidacy of the man who successfully wooed the public and gained favorable mass media coverage. Party regulars find themselves excluded from the inner circle of presidential assistants after inauguration, but once the new president attempts to build a consensus that will enable him to govern, he finds his lack of ties to the party a serious handicap.

Political parties served for more than 150 years as intermediaries among the mass electorate, the president, and Congress, but neither of the two major parties is capable any longer of fulfilling such a function. As a result, it is the president who suffers the most.

Many of the political party's functions have been assumed by mass-media and mass-communications technologists. The media, particularly television, are the new intermediaries linking the mass electorate to presidents or presidential candidates. The pervasiveness of mass media and communications technology in our society have accentuated the growing separation of the presidency from political parties, and made the office the world's greatest plebiscitary leadership role.

The decline of the president's party relationship and the emergence of a personalized presidency began, however, before television or new campaign technology became dominant forces in American politics. The public's ambivalent image of the president as more statesman than politician is deeply rooted in our political culture, and it stems from our persistent distrust of government and politicians matched with our need to perceive presidents as exceptional or heroic.

Our image of the president is also based on a misperception of many Americans that direct democracy is inherently superior to representative government. The belief that the people's judgment is preferable to smaller bodies of individuals acting as trustees was not held by the Founding Fathers. But it has been an important element of every reform movement in our nation from the Jacksonian democracy of the 1830s to the Progressives of early in this century, and more recently in the reforms of the political parties themselves.

In this chapter we will examine the illusion of the nonpolitical president, considering what the decline in the presidency's relationship to political parties means both in terms of recruitment and the functioning of the office. We will begin with a brief review of what the founders had in mind when they designed the original presidential recruitment system, for the idea of separating the office from politics began with them. We will then examine the changing role parties play in nominating presidents, and the impact that mass media and mass communications have on presidential recruitment today. The chapter concludes with a discussion of what has happened to the president's position as titular leader of his political party.

STATESMAN-KING OR PARTISAN POLITICIAN?

The founders' conception of the presidency as a nonpartisan position modeled after the British Whig king is well known.[2] So too are President Washington's efforts to put the stamp of nonpartisan statesmanship on the office during the nation's first administration. The problem of reconciling a powerful legitimate political leadership with democratic ideals has wracked the presidency since the office was first debated at the Constitutional Convention. When the founders combined the head-of-state role with the political role, they had no idea that the office would quickly evolve into an elective position that would fuel the development of two major national parties.

The founders wanted a process that would promote statesmen as candidates, for they feared direct popular election would encourage demagogues to compete for the office, which might lead to dictatorship. If candidates for the nation's highest office had to strike popular poses, they would be tempted to make rash promises, to flatter the public, or to generate unrealistic expectations of what they would do if elected.[3]

Walter Bagehot, the British Constitutional scholar, once argued that the British royalty provided a disguise that enabled the nation's "real rulers to change without heedless people knowing it."[4] The monarch provided a *dignified* element of government which excited and preserved the reverence of the public, while the prime minister, Parliament, and cabinet constituted an *efficient* part by which government was given its force and legitimacy so its powers could be employed.

The founders believed that symbolic leadership could be combined with political leadership by leaving the selection to elites in an electoral college consisting of the "better sorts." A popular election would reduce the president to the status of a politician competing with other politicians to gain office.

The creators of the presidency also believed they were inventing a system of separate institutions modeled after the British parliamentary monarchy. But by the 1780s the distinction between administration centered in the crown and legislation reserved for Parliament had ended. The two functions had been fused in the parliamentary cabinet system, an arrangement which continuously legislated, seated, and unseated ministers, bringing cohesion to the making and carrying out of public policy. Bagehot observed that a parliament is the ideal body for selecting national executives because of its closeness to political affairs and its experience in governing. He suggested that the original electoral college designed as the recruitment process for American presidents was intended to be exactly such a selection system even if it was located outside the Congress.[5]

It was the consensus of the Constitutional Convention that the legislatively based selection of the chief executive would be a form of executive weakness, for it would tie the executive to the lawmakers. Its members did not foresee the opposite possibility: a ministry could be chosen from the legislature, and this ministry, by controlling the time and life of the legislature with the help of party discipline, could remain relatively independent and powerful.

The founders' solution—the electoral college—delegated responsibility for presidential recruitment to state legislatures, which were to choose electors equal to the states' congressional delegations. These electors were expected to be individuals of capability and merit, somewhat removed from the passions of the masses. Such electors would be more likely than the untutored citizen to seek as president an individual of strong character, experience, or proven statesmanship, rather than someone skilled at arousing popular emotions. Such an approach would "insure that formal or constitutional authority would not be overwhelmed by informal or extra-constitutional authority, by power based on 'charisma' or assertions of some kind of claim to the popular will," according to political scientist James Ceaser in his book *Presidential Selection*.[6]

Ceaser believes that by institutionalizing executive authority in the Constitution, the founders thought they were eliminating the need for a popularly based leader. Institutionalized leadership would result from elevating men to the presidency on the basis of distinguished public service or national reputation:

> *The winner in such a process, no matter what his margin of victory, can . . . legitimately assert the claim to be president of all the people, and his election would not divide the populace into such strongly antagonistic parts.*[7]

The electoral college initially served as both a nominating and electing body. But it functioned well only as long as Washington, whose statesmanship and reputation influenced the design of the system, was available. By 1796 it was clear the college was headed for failure, as political parties emerged over the policy differences between the Federalists and anti-Federalists. Both parties concentrated their efforts on behalf of specific candidates. As a result, by 1800 the Congressional caucus in which party members gathered to select the party's presidential candidate had assumed the nomination function.

"King Caucus" approximated a parliamentary selection system from 1800 until 1824, when the Republican caucus was unable to agree on a successor to James Monroe and balloting was split among five contenders. Andrew Jackson, the popular favorite, lost to John Quincy Adams, and pressure began to build for reforming the party selection system. The result was the national party convention, which came into being in 1832 as a method of opening up the nomination process to more people and of democratizing the parties. But national conventions proved to be even less representative than the caucus because they were dominated by party bosses, and no attempt was made to appeal to the mass electorate.[8]

Nonetheless, the national convention system, like the caucus, was a reasonable facsimile to the system originally intended by the founders. The choice of a presidential candidate was reserved to an elite council of politicians. A presidential aspirant presented his credentials to party leaders, or waited to be asked to run. He would be judged on the basis of his potential for building a national constituency that could win the White House, as well as for his political and leadership skills.

Political wheeling and dealing among party leaders over who would make the best candidate typically took place over a period of months prior to the party's national convention. Often there were frantic last-minute sessions in smoke-filled rooms as party bosses brokered among themselves to cut deals favorable to their interests. Such party councils generally included elected public officials, big-city machine bosses, party professionals, and leaders of interest groups affiliated with the party. Many of these power brokers had known the candidates for a period of time, and they possessed the political acumen to make reasonably good assessments of qualifications and likelihood for success in the general election.

Delegates to the national convention were chosen through a mixture of state party caucuses, and after 1900 of a few state primaries. But most were chosen on the basis of how well they could be controlled by party leaders. (Primary results were usually ignored if they favored a candidate opposed by the party's leaders.) Assembled at the national convention, such delegates were expected to nominate the candidate the party had anointed, and to make independent judgments on their own.

After nomination, the party served as the candidate's main campaign organization, providing professional politicians to help in raising money and mobilizing voters. The party was reasonably successful in co-opting organized interest groups, partly because such groups were represented on party councils, and partly because the candidate and party platform were pledged to reward these groups should the prize be won. This saved the candidate from having to barter personally with groups for their electoral support; instead, it made various interest groups part of the party's national consensus even if some groups were less than enthusiastic about certain policies or goals of the party.

The political party also energized public opinion and extended institutional responsiveness by making elected officials collectively responsible to the electorate, since most politicians running for Congress also had to subordinate their interests to the national party. Political scientist Everett Carll Ladd, Jr., suggests that the overall impact of parties when they were stronger meant an enormously expanded level of public control over government.[9] Parties aggregated "the preferences of the mass public for political leadership and policy choice, . . . converting what was incoherent and diffuse to specific, responsive public decisions."[10]

THE DECLINE OF THE PARTY IN THE ELECTORATE

A responsible party system provides a critical linkage between the mass population and governmental institutions, for as Ladd has noted, only parties can organize the issues so that mass publics can effectively act on them. "[Parties] make elected officials in some sense collectively—rather than individually—responsible to the electorate."[11] There is no way an electorate as large as ours can achieve the kind of participation and control that democracy presupposes without some kind of linkage institution that distills and translates. A party traditionally was "asked to engage in an extraordinary narrowing of the alternatives in the democratic struggle for public office," and to come up with "candidates broadly representative of the wishes of those voters making up its regular expected majority."[12]

Americans have always been ambivalent about political parties, although a majority of the electorate depends on them to help make sense out of elections. Many voters nonetheless feel uneasy about admitting they hold partisan attachments, believing that ideally one ought to vote for the best candidate and not because of party.

A popular myth holds that when there is more democracy in politics, corruption is less likely and electoral outcomes are more representative of the people's best interests. This, however, confuses participation with representation. Candidates for high national office in most parliamentary democracies are nominated by party leaders or party conventions restricted to party members. The nation's electorate is limited to ratifying or rejecting the choice of candidates offered by each party in the general election. Our own system operated in a similar manner until the beginning of this century, after which voters gradually began to take part in nominating various state and national party candidates in direct primaries. The nomination of the American president remained, however, beyond the influence of the people until the end of the 1960s.

A number of powerful social movements emerged as national political forces during the 1960s. The civil rights movement was the first, and it ultimately resulted in the passage of federal laws guaranteeing the right of blacks to vote and providing protection for the exercise of the franchise. A massive protest movement against the Vietnam War followed; this movement involved millions of young people who eventually were enfranchised by the Twenty-sixth Amendment that gave eighteen-year-olds the right to vote.

The outcome of all this was an expansion of the electoral system that increased the opportunities for many more Americans to express a variety of political demands, although there was little if any change in the government's capacity to act on these demands or to produce tangible policy results. Political parties attempted to adjust to the demands of this expanded and sometimes volatile electorate by opening their nomination procedures for the presidency to more and more voters.

Popular involvement, however, did not make the selection system more responsive to some form of collective democratic will; instead it led to greater fragmentation in political parties and national politics. Nominations became free-for-alls in which an increasing number of self-anointed candidates competed for the vote of an expanded electorate, much the way American businesses competed for shelf space and sales.

The impact of increased public participation and weakened national parties made public-opinion polling and the mass media more important in building a winning coalition and in campaigns for nomination. But the weakening of ties to political parties left the individual candidate or incumbent somewhat isolated, without the traditional political loyalties or affiliations which contributed to national consensus building.

The presidential candidate cut loose from party must build his own government coalition from the base up. This coalition has to be constructed out of many different elements, all of which will later lay claim on the president's favor since they will claim it was *their* support that helped him win. Such a coalition may not be difficult to build, but it is virtually impossible to hold together.

PARTY FAILURE TO DEAL WITH CHANGE

Walter Dean Burnham, one of our leading students of the party system, has suggested that parties have lost influence because the nation's socioeconomic system developed and transformed itself with an energy and thrust unparalleled in modern history while "the nation's political system, from parties to policy structures, [saw] no such development."[13]

The American electorate since World War II has been marked by much higher levels of formal education and mobility. It has been increasingly more open and eclectic in its life-styles, and has been more dependent on national mass media for information than were earlier generations. All these changes have paralleled increasing demands on the national government for services and new programs as well as remedies for socioeconomic and political injustices. Political parties have been slow to respond to these pressures and changes. But when they finally responded with attempts to reform party procedures, the results were debilitating to regular party organizations. This was inevitable since several important functions that had traditionally made for party influence in government were being eroded by change.

Parties were weakened by the federal government's gradual assumption of many services formerly provided by local party organizations to the needy. The power of big-city political machines was based on their ability to deliver goods, social services, and jobs to large numbers of people. But from the New Deal on, these functions increasingly became the responsibility of the welfare state and nonpartisan government bureaucracies.

Partisan ties were also weakened by a general increase in the voting public's formal education. Parties have traditionally simplified politics for the average citizen, serving as a convenient handle to the bewildering world of elections. But as the proportion of Americans completing high school or college increased after World War II, levels of political information also expanded, and the reliance on parties to present potential candidates and to define issues declined.

Other important changes occurred in the American family, usually the single most important source for the development of party attachment.[14] Families have increasingly been marked by rising rates of divorce, single-parent households, job mobility, and new moral standards. Until the 1950s most Americans were born, married, lived, and died in the same geographical region or community as their parents. Today many families are scattered across the country (even across the globe) by changing employment patterns, jet travel, and new opportunities for self-fulfillment and development.

Since socialization to parties begins early in life and the attachment once formed is strongly resistant to change, partisan identification has often been compared to religious socialization.[15] But the evidence is strong that such partisan transferrals are being weakened along with families, and that personal identification with a political party is less common and less important as a predictor of voting than in the past.

Data collected by the Center for Political Studies at the Institute for Social Research of the University of Michigan confirm the erosion in partisanship. Table 2-1 below shows that attachment has declined in proportion of identifiers as well as in their intensity of commitment since the 1950s.

TABLE 2-1 Party Identification 1954–1980

							YEAR						
	1954	1956	1958	1960	1962	1964	1966	1968	1970	1972	1974	1976	1980
Strong Democrat	22%	21%	23%	21%	23%	26%	18%	20%	20%	15%	17%	15%	18%
Weak Democrat	25	23	24	25	23	25	27	25	23	25	21	25	23
Independent Democrat	9	7	7	8	8	9	9	10	10	11	13	12	11
Independent	7	9	8	8	8	8	12	11	13	13	15	14	13
Independent Republican	6	8	4	7	6	6	7	9	8	11	9	10	10
Weak Republican	14	14	16	13	16	13	15	14	15	13	14	14	14
Strong Republican	13	15	13	14	12	11	10	10	10	10	8	9	8
Apoliticals: Don't Know	4	3	5	4	4	2	2	1	1	2	3	1	2
	100%	100%	100%	100%	100%	100%	100%	100%	100%	100%	100%	100%	100%

Source: From William J. Crotty and Gary C. Jacobson, *American Parties in Decline*, p. 29. Copyright © 1980 by William J. Crotty and Gary C. Jacobson. Reprinted by permission of Little, Brown and Company. Data supplied by the Center for Political Studies.

Younger voters between eighteen and thirty-five years of age are far more willing to identify themselves as independents than voters over forty. Data from a 1976 election study showed, for example, that half of the voters under thirty claimed independent status of one form or another, while only 17 percent described themselves as strong Democrats or Republicans. Among the oldest voters—age sixty-one and over—78 percent identified with a political party, 40 percent of them strongly.

At the same time that people have become less partisan, increasing numbers of them have split their vote between the presidential candidate and candidates for other offices on the basis of personalities and issues. This phenomenon is particularly characteristic of younger and better-educated voters, and it gives rise to a considerable amount of single-issue voting or voting on the basis of the candidate's image. Ironically, it was precisely this kind of specific voting which led the Democratic party to initiate a series of reforms that further weakened the party's control over candidate-selection procedures.

PARTY REFORM—AND RETRENCHMENT

The presidential campaign of 1968 stirred millions of normally apolitical youths and others to political activism, mostly because of opposition to President Johnson's Vietnam War policies. Some turned to radical politics and violence, but most attempted to work within the system to effect change. Opposition first coalesced around the self-proclaimed candidacy of Minnesota Senator Eugene McCarthy, who mounted a challenge to Johnson's renomination. In the New Hampshire primary, the nation's first, McCarthy cut deeply into LBJ's support, raising serious doubts as to whether the president could win reelection in November. New York Senator Robert F. Kennedy entered the Democratic race on the heels of McCarthy's New Hampshire triumph. By late March, facing an internal party uprising, Johnson announced he would not be a candidate for renomination. Several months later Kennedy's assassination after the California primary left McCarthy as the chief alternative to the Johnson administration's policies.

When the Democrats convened in Chicago in late August, antiwar opposition centered on the party platform and on LBJ's hand-picked successor, Vice-President Hubert H. Humphrey, who was in the untenable position of having to support Johnson's policies. Humphrey refused to enter a single primary for fear that he would be humiliated by voters rejecting the Johnson administration (or his own candidacy). Instead, Humphrey relied on the support of party leaders who had long held him in high regard. Since these party bosses controlled the majority of delegates, no matter what the primaries signalled, Humphrey would get the party's nod.

Thousands of antiwar protestors, ranging from well-intentioned citizens to political activists, gathered in Chicago to confront the Democratic party's old guard and Chicago Mayor Richard J. Daley, boss of the last powerful big-city political machine. Daley was determined that protestors would not disrupt the convention. As a mob of demonstrators gathered in the streets outside convention hotels on the night of Humphrey's nomination, the Chicago police—armed with night sticks and tear gas—brutally waded into the crowds. Thousands chanted, "The whole world's watching! . . . the whole world's watching!" as television recorded the mayhem in the streets. Humphrey's nomination proceeded inside the convention hall, but it was clear he had inherited a badly divided and battered party.

Many delegates believed that the violence reflected the legitimate frustrations of individuals long ignored by the Democratic party. Stunned by the conflict in the streets and by the bitterness that divided delegate from delegate, the Democratic party appointed a commission to come up with reforms that would open up the party and bring dissident factions into it.

This commission, headed by Senator George McGovern and later by Congressman Donald Fraser, took the approach that the more people participating, the stronger the party. Citing the old adage that the "cure for the ills of democracy is more democracy," the commission provided a series of far-reaching reforms that turned the Democratic party upside down. Many of the party's key political officeholders and leaders were driven out by a rule forbidding the appointment of such individuals by virtue of their official positions. Another rule encouraged wider participation by political amateurs and individuals committed to a particular candidate or issue. The most controversial provision called for a quota system to insure in state delegations to the national convention a "reasonable" representation of women, youth, and minority groups in proportion to their size in the population.

McGovern successfully turned the rules to his advantage in winning the 1972 nomination, and his triumph clarified what the changes meant to the nominating process. Pro-McGovern delegations were chosen by procedures that allowed thousands of normally apolitical, inactive citizens to seize control of state Democratic parties in party caucuses across the nation. A similar result occurred in states with primaries, as people opposed to the Vietnam War stormed primary after primary, winning pluralities for McGovern and confirming that single-issue voters can overwhelm candidates of the middle simply through the sheer force of commitment. By convention time McGovern had enough delegates to win on the first ballot, although his candidacy was viewed with alarm by a majority of regular Democratic party identifiers.

Television cameras scanning the sea of delegates on the floor of Miami's Convention Hall found instead of the middle-aged, mostly white and male party professionals of past years many more women, members of minorities, and young people. Some delegates were long-haired young men, scarcely old enough to vote, while others were college teachers, students, civil rights activists, and a variety of people with deep commitments to social or political change in one form or another. Most were amateurs—first-time participants in the nominating process.

Conspicuously missing as a delegate was Mayor Daley of Chicago, who had been the single most powerful political broker in the party prior to 1972, as well as party officials who had dominated earlier Democratic national conventions. The bizarre gathering in Miami was far from representative of the party's rank-and-file voters, much less of its leadership. Political scientist Jeane J. Kirkpatrick's study of Democratic party delegates in 1972 found that the differences between them and Democratic party regulars were so great that the policy preferences of ordinary Democratic party supporters were better represented by Republican delegates than by Democratic delegates![16] McGovern, in fact, was the first choice of only 30 percent of the nation's Democrats.

Many of McGovern's more zealous supporters eventually turned against him when he reached out for support to old-line elements of the party, including not only the hated Daley but also labor leaders and party chieftains who had earlier supported Johnson's Vietnam policies. Many Democrats, however, could not forgive McGovern for the take-over of their party by individuals whose life-styles and political values were so at variance with theirs. As a result, many Democratic party identifiers either sat out the election or voted for Nixon.*

After McGovern's defeat the Democratic National Commitee appointed a commission headed by Baltimore city council member Barbara Mikulski to draw up another set of rules. This time state delegations were merely urged to "encourage" minority members, women, and youth to participate so that they would be fairly represented at all levels of the national party's deliberations. Party elites dumped by the 1972 rules were encouraged to return to the fold by a provision requiring at least 10 percent of a state's delegation to be chosen at large, and to include public officials, party leaders, and members of such recently underrepresented Democratic constituen-

---

* Nixon attempted to appeal to dissident Democrats by running outside the Republican party. The Committee for the Re-election of the President (CREEP) was Nixon's campaign organization. It is significant that Nixon ran for reelection largely divorced from the Republican party, but it was CREEP's activities, bankrolled by a huge campaign war chest, that led to Watergate and all its related crimes.

cies as labor unions. Winner-take-all primaries were eliminated, and state delegations were required to represent voting strength of candidates polling at least 15 percent of a state's primary or caucus-convention vote. These actions reduced intraparty conflict and resulted in a reasonably harmonious convention in 1976. But they clearly did not prevent another outsider from winning enough delegate support to score a smashing first-ballot victory again, sweeping all the party's "favorites" out of his path by convention time.[17]

The nomination of Jimmy Carter in 1976 was the ultimate triumph of the nonpolitician working completely within party rules. If McGovern's nomination was an example of the new power that issues had over partisanship, Carter's symbolized the triumph of style over party. Carter snatched the Democratic nomination from the reluctant fingers of party regulars through a clever appeal to that old American prejudice: dislike and distrust of politicians. He was understandably encouraged by the mood of the electorate after Watergate. His campaign game plan, drawn up even before the end of the 1972 election, pinpointed that the leading national concern in 1976 would be to restore confidence in government. The candidate who could project most convincingly the image of the political outsider, the quintessential nonpolitician, would have the best chance by far to win the nomination and perhaps the election.

Carter's aides advised him to make a major effort in the Iowa state party caucuses, the first real test of candidate strength and to win big in the first primaries—New Hampshire and Florida—so he could become an overnight celebrity with the national media. (Carter was virtually unknown to an audience on a nationally televised quiz show the year before the primaries.) Early successes would then provide momentum for subsequent victories in primaries and caucuses.[18]

Instead of going after party leaders who would probably consider the candidacy of a Georgia peanut farmer somewhat of a joke, Carter sought out private citizens in the living rooms of their homes. He carefully built a network of personal acquaintances who were flattered to be approached for help by a man who might become president of the United States. Carter accepted the hospitality of hundreds of families, often spending the night in their homes.

The tactics that won Carter the nomination against other Democratic stalwarts did not serve him well, however, once the election campaign began. Party regulars did not trust him since he was an outsider. (Many of his supporters had been McGovernites in 1972, and still were not fully accepted by the party faithful.) From an overwhelming lead in the public-opinion polls after his nomination, Carter saw his popularity drop sharply until election day when he managed to squeak through to a narrow victory over Ford.

In the 1980 election the Democrats operated under another set of rules that favored the renomination of the incumbent Carter. A commission headed by the Michigan state chairman, Morley Winograd, provided that each state should establish a proportional representation plan for delegate selection, with a minimum cutoff of 15 to 20 percent below which any candidate would be denied delegates. This not only discouraged the proliferation of candidates to challenge the incumbent, it also reduced the danger that delegates would be divided among a number of candidates in such a way as to deny Carter renomination on the first ballot.

The Winograd rules shortened the delegate selection season from six to three months. The rules also required the state parties to hold closed rather than open primaries; the delegations were to be evenly balanced between men and women; and the primary-selected delegates were to vote their original candidate preference on the first ballot at the national convention.[19]

Whether the rules changes meant a genuine democratization of party participation is quite another matter. The 1980 national convention included 15 percent blacks, about 50 percent women, and 11 percent under the age of thirty. But more than 40 percent of the delegates were public officeholders or government employees, compared to only about 7 percent of the population normally employed in public service. Ten percent were public school teachers, far more than the 2 percent of the normal population in public education. Austin Ranney, a student of conventions, observed that "one of the great reasons for reform from the very beginning was to get away from patronage, so delegates would not be beholden to bosses."[20] The delegates at the 1980 convention revealed that an incumbent administration could become a new kind of political boss: big government, with its programs of financial support and its vast potential for employment, could be used by a president to sway delegates just as convincingly as any political boss of the past.

Democratic party regulars have been less than ecstatic about the outcomes of their reforms of the past fifteen years. Grass-roots control has led to two defeats (1972 and 1980), and to a less than satisfactory nominee in 1976. Party rulemakers thus struggle every four years to come up with a new formula to restore greater party influence in the candidate selection process. The 1982 formula was the most ambitious yet in trying to increase the power of party leaders, elected officials, and big-state delegations. A commission headed by North Carolina Governor James B. Hunt recommended that more than four hundred unpledged delegate slots be apportioned among the states on the basis of their delegation size and number of Democratic party officeholders. These uncommitted delegates were to include up to two thirds of the Democrats serving in the House and Senate. The remainder would be distributed by state party committees to Democratic governors, big-city mayors, and other elected and party officials. Each state Democratic chairman and vice-chairman would also be among the unpledged delegates, bringing the total to about 550 out of the approximately 3,800 delegates to the convention.[21]

The Republican party has not quite equalled the Democrats in the urge to reform. The GOP, for example, has never been as zealous in pursuing quotas. Although it has undertaken a few rules changes, they have occurred more as a reaction to Democratic reforms than as a result of any intense pressure from the party ranks. The GOP has largely remained middle- to upper-middle class, white, Anglo-Saxon, Protestant, and suburban; it has kept a decidedly pro-business outlook.

Ironically, Republicans were tugged into the direct primary route more by the Democratic party's actions than by any ground swell within the GOP. But by the 1980 convention the Republicans had surpassed Democrats in the proportion of delegates chosen by primaries. Democrats chose 61.6 percent of their delegates through direct, binding primary elections in 1980, a reversal in the party's trend toward direct primaries caused by the fact that Texas Democrats dropped the system. Another 28.6 percent were chosen by party caucuses, and 9.8 percent were party officeholders selected as a result of the Winograd commission. The Republican party selected 75.5 percent of its delegates through primaries and 24.5 percent in caucuses. Unlike the Democrats, the Republicans made no provision for including a percentage of party or political leaders as additional delegates, since the GOP had rarely excluded party elites from its national delegations.

Whether the latest changes by the Democratic party will result in a return to more party-based nominations or not remains to be seen, but the likelihood is that they will not. There are a number of forces at work in the recruitment today which are impervious to party influence, not the least of which is the president's own relationship to the electorate and to other political institutions. Parties have lost control over presidential selection because they are weak. The notion that political parties can mandate a return to some earlier halcyon period in which they controlled presidential recruitment is about as logical as expecting that the president or Congress can restore American dominance in the world simply by proclaiming it. The Republican party's own experience shows that the outcome is the same, no matter how much participation there is by party leaders and political elites in the selection process. Politicians who stand out from the party mainstream by their ideological or narrow appeal, issue-oriented candidates, or celebrities who offer instant recognition or a new, improved personality—all are advantaged in today's democratized system. This is not only because the parties are weak but also because changes in campaign finance laws, the growing influence of mass media, and the changing nature of the American electorate favor candidates who are outside the party mainstream.

PUBLIC FINANCING OF
PRESIDENTIAL CAMPAIGNS

Many of the Watergate crimes originated within the Committee for the Re-election of the President. The Republican party was not involved since it had nothing to do with the president's campaign. CREEP collected almost all the money spent for the reelection, while the Republican party was left with reduced financial resources for party candidates seeking congressional or state offices. More than 150 individuals alone contributed some $20 million to Nixon's campaign chest, much of which was "laundered" through Mexican banks.[22]

There is a perverse kind of irony in the response by Congress to the abuses of CREEP, for reforms targeted at shifting the funding of presidential campaigns from the wealthy and powerful interest groups to the public ended up weakening the two parties even further.

In the Federal Campaign Act of 1974 Congress rejected the opportunity to channel funds through parties; instead, it gave money directly to the candidates, putting a premium on the ability of a candidate to generate a large number of small contributions, mostly through direct-mail appeals. The legislation thus had the effect of encouraging candidates whose strength lay in ideological or issue-based appeals, or who were adept at making personalized appeals to a nationwide electorate. The 1974 reforms provided federal subsidies of up to $5 million to any candidate who accepted limits on campaign spending. To qualify, a candidate had to raise $5,000 in each of twenty states for a total of $100,000. The following limits were imposed on candidates in the 1980 election:

1. Only $10 million could be spent for preconvention campaigning, including party caucuses and primaries, plus an inflationary allowance that amounted to $4.7 million;
2. Each of the parties was limited to $4.5 million, plus an inflation allowance for its national conventions, and to $4.8 million for the presidential campaign;
3. Each party nominee was allotted up to nearly $30 million in federal funds for the election campaign staff.

Taxpayers could contribute to the system through a voluntary $1 checkoff on their federal income tax forms. Parties were allowed to contribute additional funds for the nominee's support. But presidential campaign managers are so fearful of exceeding the legal spending ceiling that they have discouraged the establishment of local campaign headquarters, further undercutting grass-roots party support. State and local party committees were prohibited by the law from giving direct support to presidential candidates.

A major result of these provisions is that most candidate organizations allocate a greater share of their budgets to television spot advertisements and to candidate-paid appearances on five-, ten-, or fifteen-minute programs. This tends to enhance the importance of media consultants, advertising professionals, and campaign managers.

A loophole in the federal law was discovered in 1980 when federal courts ruled that individuals or groups could not be prevented from spending money on a candidate's campaign as long as there was no direct collaboration between the fund-raising organization and the candidate. In the 1980 election political action committees (PACs) collected and spent nearly $15 million on behalf of Ronald Reagan, while the Democrats received $15 million from organized labor alone.[23] As a result, campaign spending reforms in the future may largely serve to deter parties from active fund raising, but encourage contributions from narrowly based issue-oriented supporters.

POPULARIZING THE NOMINATION PROCESS

The most important result of party reforms since 1968 is that parties have surrendered their control over the choice of presidential candidates to the mass electorate. The nomination of a presidential candidate is no longer a representative process in which delegates and party leaders decide who will head the party's ticket; it is now a process of direct democracy.

It is an illusion to assume that a presidential candidate chosen by direct nominations is necessarily the people's choice, or that he is more representative of the electorate's wishes than a candidate chosen by party bosses. Reforms seem to have democratized the nominating process in party caucus systems as well as in primaries. But in fact they have shifted participation from a small party elite to unrepresentative samples of the mass electorate. The outcome of such "open procedures" usually is nowhere near as reflective of the policy preferences of the general electorate as was the former party-dominated system. An examination of direct primaries and party caucuses reveals just how much they fall short of representing the national electorate.

DIRECT PRIMARIES

On the surface the direct primary election appears to be the most democratic of all nominating procedures. Progressive reformers early in this century claimed such a system would eliminate the corruption of political party bosses, and would lead to candidates who would be more responsive to the people than to party elites.

Florida held the first presidential primary in 1904, and Wisconsin followed in 1905. By 1916 twenty-six states held primaries of one kind or another, but in most states party leaders bent primary results to their advantage and delegate commitments frequently were meaningless. After World War I the primary movement declined to such a degree that for the next forty years only slightly more than a third of the delegates to the national conventions were chosen by primary vote.

Primaries were generally seen as a testing ground for newcomers to the presidential sweepstakes who hoped to gain the attention of party regulars. A front-runner occasionally entered the primaries to show his popularity, but no candidate could hope to *win* the nomination simply by entering primaries. Senator Estes Kefauver won thirteen of seventeen primaries in 1952, but failed to win the Democratic party nomination because the party leaders opposed him. The choice of party regulars, Adlai E. Stevenson, was nominated even though he did not enter a single primary.

Kefauver's efforts signaled a trend party leaders could not long ignore. Even as early as the 1940s, party officials had begun to see increasing numbers of candidates striking out independently of party organizations to gain primary victories for a number of national posts. At the same time primary-selected delegates to the national convention began to exert a growing influence in the brokering that went on in convention back rooms. With the advent of television coverage in 1952, the potential for individual candidacies improved greatly because candidates could make themselves visible directly to the electorate through advertisements or by making news.

John F. Kennedy's nomination in 1960 proved a decisive turning point in the importance of primaries. He had a superbly trained campaign staff that was professionally managed, well-financed, and attuned to television. In key primaries in West Virginia and Wisconsin, he defeated the more popular party candidates, proving that not only could a Catholic win in a conservative Bible Belt state but that success in early primaries could help propel an outsider into the thick of the party's deliberations.

Although Kennedy's success highlighted a new importance for primaries, they alone were still not sufficient to win the nomination without broader party backing. Even as late as 1968, primaries were more important in confirming the status of the front-runner than in establishing the candidate as the winner. In fact, the candidate leading in the Gallup poll *before* the first primary was held won the nomination seventeen of nineteen times between 1936 and 1968.[24]

All of this changed, however, after the McGovern-Fraser Commission reforms. In a number of states, parties elected to hold primaries rather than to try to conform to the labyrinthian rules covering quotas. The 1972 Democratic convention became the first in which a majority of delegates were selected by primaries. By 1976, still more states moved to the primary system and in each party convention close to three quarters of the delegates were selected through primaries. In 1980, thirty-five states plus Puerto Rico and the District of Columbia held direct primaries.

An optimistic view of primaries holds that they genuinely reflect the will of the various state electorates, and that they encourage an open field of entrants who must prove their mettle in a series of diverse and challenging tests to win nomination. The long primary season builds voter interest and awareness, supporters argue, while it mercilessly exposes those incapable of measuring up to pressure and pushes to the forefront those who can appeal to a varied electorate's image of leadership. Election analyst Richard Scammon, for example, argues, "If a man can't get through those primaries, maybe he can't handle the job in the White House. And I'd rather know about it in advance before he's elected than six months after he's elected."[25]

Critics argue that turnout in primaries is so low that a minority of voters selects party nominees, and the choice is often based less on party loyalty than on superficial impressions of the candidate's image or his stance on a narrow range of issues. In eleven state primaries contested by both parties between 1948 and 1968, the average turnout was 39 percent, compared to 69 percent turnout in the national elections in the same states.[26]

Table 2-2 displays the voting turnout in the 1980 presidential primaries compared to the general election. The data confirm that participation is sharply lower for primaries, revealing that there is far less democracy involved in direct primaries than the idea suggests.

Primary electorates are highly unrepresentative of many state electorates, a risk noted by political scientist V. O. Key. The effective primary constituency may consist predominantly of people in certain sections, of ethnic or religious groups, or of individuals "responsive to certain styles of political leadership or shades of ideology, or of other groups markedly unrepresentative in one way or another of the party following."[27]

Direct primaries open up the nomination system to disruptive forces which threaten to fragment an already weak national party consensus. Delegates chosen in primaries often are selected simply because of their attachment to a candidate and not because they have any abiding interest in the party. This capacity to appeal directly to voters provides ideological candidates—those from the political right or left—with a much better chance of winning delegates and even the nomination, since the appeal of such candidates is usually beyond the party's mainstream. The candidate may appeal to only a fringe group, but the turnout rate for that group may well exceed that of the regular party electorate for a state. Because fringe or extreme candidates are

TABLE 2-2   **Voter Turnout in the 1980 Presidential Primaries, Compared to Turnout in the General Election**

State	Total Voting Age Population	Votes Cast In 1980 Primaries	Percentage Turnout: Primaries	Votes Cast In 1980 Presidential Election	Percentage Turnout In Election
Alabama	2,729,000	442,311	16	1,283,399	47
California	17,281,000	5,765,150	33	8,215,737	48
Florida	7,381,000	1,587,940	22	3,481,645	47
Georgia	3,818,000	584,951	15	1,535,795	40
Idaho	637,000	184,989	29	426,593	67
Illinois	8,178,000	2,281,169	28	4,637,242	57
Indiana	3,872,000	1,146,062	30	2,173,926	56
Kansas	1,714,000	474,818	28	955,357	56
Kentucky	2,579,000	334,722	13	1,265,350	49
Louisiana	2,874,000	400,743	14	1,530,419	53
Maryland	3,049,000	632,152	21	1,476,034	48
Massachusetts	4,247,000	1,296,487	31	2,484,825	59
Montana	555,000	201,718	36	328,640	59
Nebraska	1,123,000	352,532	32	621,623	55
Nevada	584,000	114,342	20	238,618	41
New Hampshire	663,000	257,380	45	380,146	67
New Jersey	5,374,000	833,338	16	2,850,186	53
New Mexico	884,000	216,600	25	438,385	50
North Carolina	4,219,000	913,691	22	1,842,271	44
Ohio	7,703,000	2,037,083	27	4,201,993	55
Oregon	1,910,000	647,968	34	1,110,574	58
Pennsylvania	8,742,000	2,791,187	32	4,468,544	51
Rhode Island	704,000	43,165	6	387,108	55
South Dakota	485,000	155,996	32	323,353	67
Tennessee	3,292,000	479,564	15	1,604,547	49
Vermont	366,000	109,136	30	206,522	56
West Virginia	1,390,000	448,674	32	710,652	51
Wisconsin	3,347,000	1,522,649	45	2,237,798	67

Source: 1980 presidential election data were compiled by the author from the *Statistical Abstract of the United States*. Primary turnout data are from *Congressional Quarterly Weekly Report*, July 5, 1980, p. 1874. Reprinted with the permission of Congressional Quarterly Inc.

encouraged, primaries frequently focus public attention on differences and disagreements within the party, further weakening any chances of building a broad coalition for the election.

Primaries, with their candidate-centered bias, may be a form of plebiscitary democracy, but they distort the preferences of the minority and ignore the wishes of the broader electorate. Front-runners such as Eisenhower, Kennedy, or Nixon, as well as outsiders such as McGovern and Carter, used primary victories to convince rivals and uncommitted delegates they were the choice of the nation's electorate. But as James Davis has noted in his study of presidential primaries:

> *This transmutation of the presidential primary into a gigantic popularity contest is a far cry from the original plan of the progressives to take the convention decision-making out of the hands of political bosses and put it into the hands of the people, acting through their popularly elected delegates.*[28]

The upshot of all this is that since the 1960s, party leaders have had to stand by helplessly as their power and influence in the nomination of the presidency were gradually nibbled away in state after state. "No longer can the party insiders' hand-picked choice, a favorite son, or a 'dark horse' expect to receive the nomination," Davis notes. "These marginal candidates have been swept aside by candidates who have demonstrated their vote-getting strength and personal popularity in the primaries."[29]

PARTY CAUCUSES

The precinct caucus system for selecting delegates was still used in twenty-one states by the Democrats in 1980, and in eighteen by the Republican party. At first glance this process appears to favor party regulars since party bosses have controlled the presidential selection system throughout most of our history under this system. But even the party caucus has been democratized by reforms to the extent that, as the Winograd Commission reported in 1978, "there are no significant differences between delegates from caucuses and primary states."[30] The new rules requiring public notice of caucuses and encouraging quotas and representation of minority views, combined with an increased national media attention to party caucuses, have dramatically opened up to amateurs and newcomers what once was mostly an exclusive gathering of the party faithful; the results have been much the same as for the primaries.

The typical caucus-convention process begins at the precinct level where delegates are selected to attend a district or county party convention. From there, a slate of delegates is chosen for the state convention where the final selection of the state's delegates to the national convention is made. The precinct is the key to the caucus, however, for it is at this level that the people are chosen who affect the selection processes the rest of the way to the final balloting at the national convention.

Party caucuses in the 1970s and in 1980 differed significantly from those of the past because in a number of states a fierce struggle in the local precinct meetings often resulted in individuals dedicated to an issue or a single candidate packing the caucus. Frequently, the outcome of the caucus bore little similarity to the actual party voter preference in the precinct. Zealous conservatives dedicated to Senator Barry Goldwater swamped Republican precinct caucuses in 1964 and won him a majority of the party's delegates long before the national convention. But an overwhelming majority of regular Republican identifiers were opposed to Goldwater's candidacy. McGovern likewise won in nonprimary states by a similar series of packed caucuses as tens of thousands of participants bound together by their opposition to the Vietnam War overwhelmed party regulars. The caucus system may, in fact, be even more vulnerable to nonparty candidate take-overs than primaries because traditionally few party regulars attend precinct meetings and any well-organized candidate with the backing of a corps of true believers can easily overwhelm a party's normal turnout. Carter and Reagan both organized their campaigns to turn out their supporters to precinct meetings in the 1976 and 1980 nomination campaigns.

Precinct caucuses failed to receive the same publicity as primaries in the first election after the rules changes, mostly because such gatherings took longer to resolve in favor of a candidate; they also lacked the immediate news appeal a primary provided. But Jimmy Carter carefully plotted to storm the Iowa caucuses—the first major nomination test in the country in 1976—to establish himself as the front-runner even before the first highly publicized primary in New Hampshire. His success led to nationwide attention and was followed by a victory in New Hampshire. Carter became an overnight news sensation: the new face leading the pack of familiar old politicians.

By 1980 early caucuses began to capture some of the national media attention formerly enjoyed by the first primaries. In turn, this generated a significantly heightened interest in the voters in such early caucus states as Iowa and Maine. The network news media trained their big guns on Iowa weeks before the 1980 caucuses, and the massive publicity resulted in an estimated 215,000 voters turning out— almost five times as many as in 1976![31] Despite the high voter interest in the 1980 Iowa caucus, the overall turnout rate for caucuses is quite poor. *Congressional Quarterly* collected reports from Democratic state party organizations in 1976 in states with caucuses. Table 2-3 shows the percentage of voting-age residents participating in Democratic first-level precinct caucuses that year.

The party caucus remains a somewhat confusing process to many rank-and-file voters, but the evidence from Iowa and other caucus states suggests that voters are learning quickly. Although caucuses take longer to organize, they are less expensive than primaries because caucuses require less television advertising.

By 1984, states seemed to be considering a return to the party

TABLE 2-3 **Estimated Participation in Democratic Precinct Caucuses, First-Level, 1976.**

| | | ESTIMATED ATTENDANCE AT CAUCUSES | |
	ESTIMATED VOTERS	ESTIMATED TURNOUT	% ELIGIBLE VOTERS
Alaska	231,000	1,000	0.4
Arizona	1,555,000	26,700	1.7
Colorado	1,773,000	30,000	1.7
Connecticut	2,211,000	106,600	4.8
Hawaii	600,000	3,000	0.5
Iowa	2,010,000	45,000	2.2
Louisiana	2,532,000	120,000	4.7
Maine	741,000	6,500	0.9
Minnesota	2,721,000	58,000	2.1
Mississippi	1,544,000	60,000	3.9
Missouri	3,348,000	20,000	0.6
New Mexico	771,000	10,000	1.3
North Dakota	432,000	3,000	0.7
Oklahoma	1,937,000	65,000	3.3
South Carolina	1,933,000	63,000	3.2
Utah	783,000	16,300	2.1
Vermont	327,000	2,500	0.8
Virginia	3,528,000	20,000	0.6
Washington	2,536,000	60,000	2.4
Wyoming	266,000	600	0.2

Source: Voting population is taken from Bureau of the Census, *Population Estimates and Projections,* Series P-25, No. 626, May, 1976. Democratic precinct caucus attendance is taken from estimates published in various issues of *Congressional Quarterly Weekly Report* between January 24, 1976, and May 15, 1976. Reprinted with permission of Congressional Quarterly, Inc.

caucus system in an attempt to rebuild party strength at the precinct and state levels and to regain party leverage over the nomination. Whether a return to caucuses would actually result in a rebirth of parties or in improved candidates is questionable, however. For one thing, it is an illusion that caucuses have become too responsive to the public at large. The low turnout rate suggests otherwise: a tiny minority of voters make the decisions that a larger electorate makes in primaries, but those who turn out for caucuses generally resemble demographically the same kinds of voters who participate in primaries. Caucuses are thus equally vulnerable to voters attracted to specific personalities or narrow issues, only on a smaller scale than for primaries. Indeed, the Goldwater nomination in 1964, McGovern's triumph in 1972, and Carter's campaign in 1976 all revealed how easily party regulars can be sidetracked in party caucuses by amateurs.

Our system of presidential selection leaves the United States as the only major democratic political system in the world—with the

"BUT I DON'T THINK I KNOW HIM"

DEM. '76

©1976 HERBLOCK

From *Herblock On All Fronts* (New American Library, 1980)

possible exception of France—without a *representative* element in the choice of its chief executive.[32] No other nation has ever copied our direct primary process or opened up party procedures to as broad an electorate, although other American political practices have served as models to the world. Our recruitment system for presidents clearly is not one of them.[33]

NATIONAL CONVENTIONS

National party conventions are now rituals of confirmation rather than genuine nominating assemblies. The national convention ends up as a personal celebration of the winning candidate and his legions rather than a serious forum for deliberating over the qualities of the candidate who seeks to lead the nation for the next four years. Not since 1952 has a convention required more than one ballot to pick a candidate. Since World War II, only Thomas E. Dewey in 1948 and Adlai E. Stevenson in 1952 failed to win nomination on the first ballot.

The national convention remains the supreme decision-making body of the political party. But when it is dominated by delegates with little or no party commitment, the convention may end up as a catalyst for further splintering or fragmenting the party. The party suffers by seeing its nomination go to an outsider. In addition, the national convention becomes the source for the party's policy agenda for the next four years, and it may become the source for new reforms in party selection procedures. As a result, the convention appears on the surface to be a gigantic unification party between the candidate's supporters and party regulars. Typically it launches the presidential campaign in an atmosphere of cosmetic brotherhood; the forces of the victor try to adopt the party and seek to be adopted by the party. For their candidate will need the party's help to win the election.

Ironically, the qualifications important for winning the party's nomination now have little or nothing to do with the qualities required for winning a national election. Nor are the criteria for winning the nomination genuinely related to the skills or qualifications needed to govern. Instead, the present system of presidential selection establishes a new breed of political boss—Madison Avenue–types who can help maverick candidates appeal to various coalitions of voters while the hucksters attempt to rally more traditional elements of the party behind their candidate-celebrity.

THE NEW POLITICS

The demise of political parties has created a vacuum into which have poured the energies, expertise, and financial resources of new presidential kingmakers. Richard L. Rubin has observed of this development:

> . . . as nomination success becomes based increasingly on the candidate's personal resources, campaigning skills, and ability to attract the notice of the mass media . . . candidates are drawn away from links with established party leaders toward their own personal followings.[34]

These personal followings are, however, characterized by highly tenuous bonds. Single-issue groups narrowly focused on such issues as abortion, nuclear energy, consumer protection, civil rights, or Constitutional amendments on behalf of specific groups seek to rally voters who have lost their party attachment. Such groups—and they are increasing in number and strength with each election—try to capture the national party for a personality or cause in order to advance narrow policy goals in spite of widespread public opposition or indifference. Whether such coalitions succeed or not, once an election is over they fall by the wayside in terms of party activity. If their presidential candidate wins, he frequently ignores the party whose organization and machinery he briefly used to win the nomination and the election. He proceeds to act presidential—that is, above partisan politics. This stance, however, inevitably serves to alienate groups which make up his presidential coalition. Some eventually turn against the president and begin to search for another candidate on whom to pin their expectations. If a coalition's candidate loses, various segments usually break off, perhaps to gather again in another four years with the same candidate. Or they may seek a new face that can help them try once again to obtain their narrow policy goals.

Single-issue groups not only fragment any chance of political consensus but they "whipsaw conscientious public officials with non-negotiable demands, and generally [play] havoc with responsible government and politics," according to David Broder, a long-time observer of presidential politics.[35] Issue-concerned voters, like presidential candidates, learn they can bypass the party structure and "take their case directly to the people." Broder notes:

> The result is that independent autonomous office holders are confronting independent, autonomous interest groups in a kind of unmediated power struggle that leaves the national interest in shreds and helps persuade voters to express their dissatisfaction in the most dramatic way possible—by not voting.[36]

Those with ambitions for the White House no longer must serve a long apprenticeship in various party positions or in public office. With the support of enough groups, with sufficient money, and with highly skilled campaign specialists, they can mount a frontal assault on the White House.

Parties have not adapted well to the changes in mass communications technology. Television particularly has diminished the party's influence over candidate recruitment and its ability to mobilize a mass electorate. In the past our parties functioned primarily as electoral organizations rather than policy organizations, although the ability to control the former often meant some influence over the latter. The mass media, however, have grown far more successful at organizing information, attracting voter attention, and recruiting potential candidates. The media are not the sole cause of party troubles, but the growing pervasiveness of television and of professionals skilled in utilizing mass communications has accelerated the rate of party decline.

THE MAKING . . . AND MAKING . . .
AND MAKING OF THE MEDIA
PRESIDENT

By 1980, television had changed the way presidents campaigned so dramatically that reporters of the campaigns of the 1960s and 1970s felt like relics of the past. Journalist Joel Swerdlow wrote of the 1980 election:

> *Gone were the days when a candidate's chief goal was meeting people. Gone were pre-dawn hand-shaking at factory gates and the post-midnight meetings with campaign volunteers in store-front headquarters. Gone were the exhausted, bleary-eyed report-ers, struggling to make just one more early morning baggage call before their flesh gave out. . . . The cold essence of presidential campaigning has become the television camera lens. Campaigns are organized for pictures, not words or ideas.*[37]

Campaigns for the presidency today are almost totally mass-media campaigns. For the vast majority of voters, the primaries, party cau-cuses, conventions, and general election have little meaning or reality outside what is pictured on TV or communicated by slickly designed and executed political ads. The long nomination and election process comes to focus less on the candidate's policy positions or experience than on the excitement of the competition—the "horse race." The public is encouraged to seek a "new and improved" president by the techniques used to peddle soap, liquor, or automobiles.

The mass media share the president's obsession with the non-political presidency. The media delight in trying to spotlight the candi-date who fits preconceived notions about what a president should be. They equally relish deflating front-runners and in pointing out the political motivations behind every action of a candidate or president. Candidates and incumbent presidents counter by attempting to turn every campaign maneuver into "hard news" that reveals statesmanlike qualities.

Mass-merchandizing techniques were first employed extensively in Nixon's 1968 presidential campaign. Experts from television, pub-lic-opinion polling, advertising, and a host of other mass-communica-tions fields were marshalled to reshape a "new" Nixon. In reality, they were trying to hermetically seal off the old Nixon by carefully limiting his public exposure and by designing, packaging, and merchandizing him as a calm, experienced statesman rather than a battle-hardened politician.

The packaging and selling of Nixon were a foretaste of future campaigns. By the 1970s no presidential hopeful could mount a credi-ble campaign without the professional assistance of mass communications. TV advertising has become the single most expensive item in contemporary presidential campaigns because more people can be reached for less money by TV than by any other medium. Carter and Reagan, for example, spent over half their total 1980 campaign funds on media advertising.

While many lament this trend toward selling presidents as if they were commodities, others argue that there is a limit to how much a candidate can be packaged. There has to be *something* up front with the candidate, for Americans are sophisticated consumers, and are not tempted to buy obviously shoddy products. A media-shaped candidate cannot win simply on the basis of his appearances, the argument runs, but a good candidate cannot win *without* television.

The new media-centered politics inundates the electorate with words and pictures, with a constant barrage of "pseudo-events"— staged events and carefully arranged video appearances. Instead of providing the electorate with valuable information or drama, such campaigns turn the entire process from nomination to election into a predictable, antiseptic, and frequently boring experience. The president or candidate becomes a homogenized personality. Serious domestic or foreign policy questions are answered with thirty- or sixty-second pronouncements which appear spontaneous but which often are carefully rehearsed and coached. To show one's real self or to reveal anger or any human frailty, to express one's real political views or plans is to risk alienating the national mass audience.

During the 1968 nomination season Michigan Governor George Romney admitted on nationwide television that American military officials had "brainwashed" him during a fact-finding tour of Vietnam; his candor resulted in his decline as a viable candidate. In the 1972 race Democratic front-runner Edmund Muskie was caught by television as he momentarily broke into sobs and became speechless with anger after berating New Hampshire newspaper publisher William Loeb for publishing ugly stories about Muskie's wife. The press widely interpreted Muskie's behavior as evidence he lacked stability or control. When Muskie fared less well in the New Hampshire primary than the media had predicted, they proclaimed his campaign on the skids. Six weeks later Muskie dropped out of the race.

In the past the media did not hold such power over presidential candidates, few of whom were subject to the kind of intense media and public scrutiny that is the lot of candidates today. Television especially exerts a new kind of tyranny over the selection process, demolishing values that functioned for more than 170 years of a two-party system. Communications expert Marshall McLuhan commented that television has caused the party system to fold like an organizational chart in all countries. This is because politics and issues have become useless for election purposes since they are too specialized and "hot"; the shaping of a candidate's image has taken the place of discussing conflicting points of view.[38]

Television demands excitement, conflict, immediacy, and personalization because the medium has mostly evolved as a mass-entertainment system. As a result, television concentrates excessively on the "horse-race" aspect of presidential politics—the competition and personalities in the race for the White House—rather than on substantive policy differences. It is impossible to separate the presidential race from the functioning of the office itself. Even before a new president takes office, the press begins to speculate like Las Vegas bookmakers as to who the nominees will be four years into the future. Every act or decision of an incumbent is measured by the press against a yardstick with political calibrations.

Media coverage of presidential elections before the TV era was reasonably straightforward and far less concerned with the horse-race aspect of who was in front and who was bringing up the rear. Paul Lazarsfeld and associates found in a study of the 1940 presidential election that 50 percent of all the news coverage dealt with policy matters or presidential leadership qualifications. Only 35 percent focused on the race itself.[39] What the candidates said about their own qualifications and how they would handle policy was newsworthy because the 1940 election was much shorter than present-day campaigns and elections.

By 1972, with television dominating election coverage, Thomas Patterson and Robert McClure found content overwhelmingly centered on rallies, motorcades, polls, campaign tactics, and other pseudo-events aimed at injecting color, movement, and the impression of excitement. Television abhorred "talking head" shots—filmed sequences showing a candidate talking about an issue. What was needed were pictures showing a flurry of activity, the image that more was happening than was really the case. Important questions about candidate qualifications or public issues totalled only 3 percent of all available news time on the major networks from September 18 to November 6, 1972. "Steady viewers of the nightly network newscasts learn almost nothing of importance about a presidential election," Patterson and McClure concluded.[40]

Newspapers, by contrast, were somewhat more effective in covering the issues. Yet candidate television commercials proved to be the most substantive source of information about candidate positions on issues, according to Patterson and McClure. They concluded:

The three main factors of television's issue coverage—the infrequent mention, then only fleeting references, plus films showing

> *unrelated and distracting "action" while the audio gives a glancing blow to an issue—all create an impossible learning situation that adds nothing of substance to the voters' civic education.*[41]

Coverage remained in the same rut in 1976, Patterson found, as the networks again concentrated on the race at the expense of questions of national policy or leadership. Winning and losing, strategy and organization, appearances and tactics were the dominant themes of day-to-day election news. What news coverage existed of issues centered on clear-cut issues that were controversial or colorful, neatly divided the candidates, provoked conflict, or could be stated in simplistic terms.[42]

The print press has tended to follow television's style of coverage, partly because television sets the agenda and partly to emulate the most successful of the news media. A study by the *Washington Journalism Review* of the 1980 nomination season confirmed earlier findings of the trivialized content now common to election coverage. Stories in the *Washington Post, New York Times,* and *Chicago Tribune* revealed not only an addiction to forecasting outcomes of primaries and caucuses but also a tendency to hype events and manufacture issues, to overcover the campaign with hundreds of unnewsworthy stories and cavalier treatment of minor candidates.[43]

If the race is the most important story of today's media-sized presidential campaigns, the candidate's image is the most important measure for predicting the outcome. The cool image projected by a Kennedy or Reagan may eventually become *de rigueur* for anyone hoping to win the White House. The candidate skilled in the art of dramatic communication or persuasion and favored with a pleasing face or personality will always have an edge over the more experienced politician or statesman who may appear dull or colorless.

Mass-media campaigns favor candidates with financial resources to buy media time and to hire the professionals who can develop a marketable image. Unemployed politicians are advantaged because they can afford to spend month after month on the campaign trail, negotiating the tortuous maze of primaries, caucuses, and staged events. Conscientious office-holders who are attentive to public service cannot spare the time now needed to mount a credible campaign. Senator Howard H. Baker, Jr., minority leader of the U.S. Senate and a candidate in the 1980 sweepstakes, had to drop out of contention early because his duties in the Senate kept him from devoting enough time to the campaign. Serious campaigns begin two years or more before an election, and some candidates are perennial candidates. (Reagan began to run for the White House in 1968.) Today's media campaigns thus are tilted toward the compulsively ambitious, hyperactive breed of personality. Such people are not necessarily well qualified for the presidency but are perhaps the only ones who can survive the present system.

TV and other media directly influence the mechanics of the nominating and election process. Party caucuses and primaries are scheduled so as to attract national media attention to a state. A candidate arranges his day to fit the deadlines and needs of the major networks. A swollen press entourage accompanies the candidate as he moves from one televised appearance to another across the country. Our presidential recruitment system has begun to resemble the professional football season. After countless primaries, caucuses, and straw polls, the satiated fans sit back to watch the superbowl of politics—the election itself, a contest which seems almost anticlimactic and which millions are relieved to see finally end.

Fascinated more by the race than the issues at stake, the media turn early nomination tests in states like New Hampshire and Iowa into exaggerated political events. Less than one half of 1 percent of the Democratic party's convention delegates and only slightly over 1 percent of the Republican party's are chosen in New Hampshire's kickoff primary. But the state has an importance that overshadows much larger states like New York and Ohio that hold primaries later. "As goes New Hampshire, so goes the nomination." The winner of that state's primaries has won nomination nine out of twelve times between 1960 and 1980, and since 1976 New Hampshire has been exactly on target. The Granite State is not a microcosm of the American electorate. Its predictive genius is mostly the result of the media's proclaiming the winner of its primary the candidate to beat, thereby setting the course for upcoming primaries and caucuses. The media thus provide a significant bonus to the candidate who prevails in the snowy hamlets of New Hampshire, in effect pushing him several furlongs in front of other less successful but perhaps viable candidates.

According to a study by Michael Robinson and Karen McPherson, in 1976 New Hampshire received one third of all network television coverage on the nominations between November 24, 1975, and April 9, 1976. During the two and a half months preceding the New Hampshire primary, 54 percent of the campaign news on television and 34 percent of the campaign stories were mostly or entirely focused on New Hampshire.[44] New Hampshire received 2.6 TV stories for each of the thirty-eight delegates it elected to the two national conventions. The next two primary states, Massachusetts and Florida—which together chose seven times as many delegates as New Hampshire—received less TV coverage than the Granite State. Robinson and McPherson also found a total of 616 news stories on delegate selection appeared on the three major networks and in three major daily newspapers; of this number, New Hampshire alone received 250, or 41 percent of all coverage.[45] "[W]inning New Hampshire and one of the two big communication states (Massachusetts and Florida) is tantamount to winning the nomination," they conclude.

The coverage of the mass media thus becomes a form of self-fulfilling prophecy. As a result, participation is often discouraged in successive, more important primaries that follow. If the press declares the race all but over after the first few primaries, voters begin to feel as if their participation is hardly worth the effort. Participation in the first quarter of primaries in 1980 revealed participation to be up 28 to 35 percent over 1976 as a heavy media blitz focused on an intense race among Reagan, Bush, Anderson, and other Republican candidates, as well as on the feud between Kennedy and Carter. A record 52 percent of New Hampshire's registered voters, for example, turned out in both party primaries under the intense media coverage. Few New Hampshire residents failed to meet a candidate, or to be interviewed by a news reporter, or to be swept up in the excitement of the nation's earliest media primary. Later in the season, however, participation slacked off sharply compared to 1976 levels as many voters in the middle cycle of primaries (Pennsylvania, Illinois, and Indiana) accepted the media's assessment that the earlier races had all but settled the nomination.[46]

In 1984 all states, including New Hampshire, have to hold their Democratic party primaries or caucuses within a three-month "window"—between early March and early June—to diminish the impact of early, media-concocted primaries. The Republican party is expected to follow suit.

Chief Presidential Election Dramatist

The mass-media decision to dramatize the presidential selection process can be traced to the success of a new form of political journalism that treated the race for the White House like the plot of a gripping novel or a form of high drama. Chief architect of this new journalism was Theodore White, former *Time* correspondent and free-lance journalist who wrote *The Making of the President, 1960*. Several publishers had turned White's book down on the assumption that *no one* was interested in reading about a presidential election after it was over. White's book, however, was not the traditional reporter's account of politics. Filled with dialogue, crisp personality sketches, and anecdotes, it left readers feeling as if they had shared the confidences and campaign trails with the candidates. It became an instant best-seller and won a Pulitzer prize.

White wrote sequels in 1964, 1968, 1972, and 1980. His success suggested that the public had an insatiable appetite for trivial details about presidential candidates. Editors began to push reporters and correspondents to come up with similar material to make their reporting more colorful and appealing. By 1972 White himself was uncomfortable over what his approach had wrought in presidential election coverage. White had watched the 1960 Wisconsin primary returns with Kennedy and only one other person, another journalist, in a Milwaukee hotel room. But twelve years later when McGovern won his party's nomination in Miami, a reporter compared the nominee in his hotel suite to a "fish in a goldfish bowl":

> *There were three different network crews at different times. The still photographers kept coming in in groups of five. And there were at least six writers sitting in the corner. . . . We're all sitting there watching him work on his acceptance speech. . . . He tries to go into the bedroom with [an advisor] to go over the list of Vice Presidents . . . and all of us are observing him, taking notes like mad, getting all the little details.*[47]

The Prime-Time Convention

The old-style party nominating conventions filled with long-winded oratory, interminably drawn-out floor demonstrations, and rambling debates on the floor have also faded into history. Today the prime-time needs of network TV have a higher priority with party convention planners than the delegates themselves. As a party official explained in 1980, "The most important thing we can get out of a convention is television coverage. Our own delegates are not the people we should be talking to, we want the T.V. audience."[48]

Television first broadcast nominating conventions in 1952, and from the start attracted sizeable audiences, particularly during important sessions such as the balloting for president or the nominees' acceptance speeches. Gradually parties shifted convention scheduling to prime-time hours to maximize audiences. Convention business is streamlined or conducted off camera to avoid boring national audiences, wasting valuable network time, or embarrassing the party by airing troubles before the mass public. Tedious committee reports, roll calls, and general sessions have been shortened. Politicians at the 1980 Republican convention were asked to limit their speeches to eight minutes, and the top GOP stars—former President Ford, Henry A. Kissinger, and John Connally—were scheduled during prime-time slots in the evening.

Well-known entertainment stars now perform on the convention program, taking up time once left to party oratory or floor demonstrations. Even so, network television frequently ignores what is going on at the rostrum to create its own news or excitement. News anchors interview prominent party politicians, delegates, or celebrities in an attempt to inject drama, conflict, or human interest into what is normally dull television fare.

The three networks spent more than $40 million to cover the 1980 conventions, while each of the parties, by comparison, spent only $4 million to hold the conventions. Today's conventions appear more as huge gatherings of media personnel than party convocations aimed at nominating presidential candidates. Press representatives outnumbered delegates by more than three to one at the 1980 conventions as hordes of network correspondents and TV crews, local TV reporters, and newspaper, magazine, and free-lance journalists from all over the nation competed for the attention of delegates and politicians. An ironic twist to recent conventions finds some national television correspondents as much targets of attention for delegates as the delegates are for correspondents!

The net impact of all of this media attention is that conventions have become staged extravaganzas with little political purpose other than to rally the party faithful and to appeal to independent voters or wavering supporters of the opposition party. The limits to which a candidate's organization will go to make sure that no hitches occur in the big show were revealed by the Nixon forces in 1972. A minute-by-minute script was provided to speakers and floor leaders instructing speakers when to pause, nod, and accept "spontaneous" cheers. The script stipulated when a "demonstration" would interrupt the convention secretary in mid-sentence!

The Republican convention in 1980 ran afoul of the media for quite a different reason: the party's nominee almost lost control over his choice of a vice-presidential running mate to the news media. Polls before the convention suggested a "dream" ticket matching Reagan with Ex-President Gerald Ford as his running mate. Negotiations were under way to explore the remote possibilities of such a ticket when reporters found out. A televised interview with Ford on the CBS Evening News while negotiations were continuing revealed that Ford was demanding almost an equal share in executive power with the president, a position that had already caused Reagan and his advisers to back off from Ford. So anxious to cover the story were the networks, however, that they proceeded to pour fuel on the fires of rumor. Responsible sources on the floor confirmed that the deal had been struck when in actuality they were reporting rumors they had heard from the media. The dean of anchors, CBS's Walter Cronkite, reported late in the evening that "Gerald Ford will be [Reagan's] selection as his vice presidential running mate. . . . They are going to come to this convention hall tonight to appear together on this platform . . . to announce that Ford will run with him."[49] In the meantime Reagan had asked George Bush to be his running mate. So confused was the convention hall that Reagan was forced to make a late-night appearance to announce his choice and to silence the rumors.

The networks find TV coverage an untenable damned-if-they-do, damned-if-they-don't proposition. Ratings have dropped appreciably in the last several conventions, but the networks cannot afford to skip coverage because the conventions give them an opportunity to parade their news network celebrities before the nation in our most important political rite. It is also a convenient time to advertise the new fall season of entertainment programs. Network officials justify gavel-to-gavel coverage on the basis that they are providing a public service with in-depth coverage of candidates, issues, and party positions lacking during the rest of the long nomination and election season.

In fact, the media may provide a bit more substance during the convention. But once the election campaign begins, it is back to business as usual. The election campaign typically involves a monotonous series of stories almost identical to those from the primary and caucus season, focusing on staged events, candidate blunders, conflict, controversy, and campaign hoopla or color.

In 1976 and 1980 the highlight of media coverage was the presidential debates: three in 1976 and two in 1980. Meticulously planned and staged for the maximum visual impact, the debates were less the substantive discussions of issues and qualifications of the candidates than campaign appeals uttered by performers aware that *how* they looked and acted meant more than *what* they had to say.

The media, particularly TV, have so intruded into presidential elections that network commentators now project who the winner will be before millions of American voters have even had a chance to vote. Election night coverage in 1980 scarcely had begun before computers projected Reagan the winner, even in states where voters were still casting ballots! Carter was quoted as being ready to concede before hundreds of thousands of voters had reached the polls on the West Coast and in Hawaii and Alaska.

PUBLIC-OPINION POLLING

The move from a party-based elite to a popularized system for choosing presidents has shifted attention of the mass media to public-opinion polls, which provide a steady stream of data showing what the public thinks about candidates and the president. In fact, polls create the presidential images and illusions they seek to measure. Boorstin has argued that as polls become increasingly more accurate, they begin to influence what people think and know. "The more confidence pollsters can inspire in their power to offer us an image of what we will really believe or will choose at some future time, the more blurred becomes our notion of what is our own real preference as voters."[50] Polls offer images of public opinion that are "synthetic, believable, passive, vivid, concrete, simplified, and ambiguous as never before":

> *Having been polled as a representative of the public, [the citizen] can then read reports and see how he looks. As polls become more scientific and detailed—broken down into occupations, counties, income groups, religious denominations, etc.—the citizen can discover himself (and the opinions which he "ought" to have or is likely to have). . . . Public opinion—once the public's expression—becomes more and more an image into which the public fits its expression. . . . It is the people looking into the mirror.*[51]

Polls directly contribute to the detachment of presidents and presidential candidates from political parties and other political actors because polls encourage a direct dialogue between the candidate (or leader) and the electorate. They enable politicians to develop positions without the time-consuming effort of utilizing the party to build a coalition, for there is an almost instant feedback on just how well one is "playing in Peoria" or anywhere else in the country.

Polls are pseudo-events because they create public reactions. Pollsters then measure the impact of such concerns in poll results which are analyzed by the media for clues to the dynamics of the electorate.[52] Public-opinion analyst Irving Crespi claims this linkage between polls and the media constitutes a feedback loop: definitions of *what* is news determine the content of polling, which in turn affects the political process and results in news.[53]

Public-opinion polls did not play a meaningful role in presidential politics until the late 1930s. FDR used them to obtain data he needed in guiding public attitudes on aid to Britain. As he gradually brought the United States closer to the British, he usually was able to stay just a step ahead of public opinion.[54] Roosevelt did not use polls to promote policies that would make him more popular but as an important resource in leading the people.

Truman distrusted polls after the 1948 elections when all the pollsters wrongly predicted his defeat. Eisenhower made only limited use of polls, but Kennedy avidly followed polling results. He remained a skeptic, however, as to their accuracy in reflecting public attitudes. Johnson carried the latest polls in his pocket and would show them to everyone within reach when the polls were favorable to him. But he condemned polls as inaccurate when they indicated a sharp slippage in his approval rating. Johnson's surprise announcement in March 1968 that he would not seek reelection was probably due to polls showing that less than a third of the electorate supported him.

Since LBJ, presidents have turned the use of polls inside out. They have used them to improve their image rather than to develop an understanding of public reaction to their policies. The danger of this new use of the polls is that the president who tries to alter his image on the basis of polls may become the led rather than the leader.

When Nixon's public image declined as a result of Watergate, the White House pulled every stop in an attempt to turn the polls around. Nixon took to nationwide television several times, appeared before news reporters, and tried to divert attention from Watergate by state visits abroad. All the same, his rating continued to decline with each new revelation.

Carter was even more addicted than Nixon to using polls to prop up a sagging image. When a temporary fuel shortage plagued the nation in June 1979, he announced he would make a public speech. But when he found that he had nothing to say, he had to abruptly cancel the address. Before several key primaries in 1980 he issued optimistic statements about the situation of the American captives in Iran. Such statements were designed to shoot his rating up and thus salvage the primaries.

Reagan had a similar preoccupation with polls. When public opinion strongly opposed the buildup of U.S. military strength in El Salvador, he briefly dropped this issue until he could achieve his first-year budget and tax-cut programs. When polls showed a big slump for him with Catholic voters, he flew to Chicago—home of the nation's largest Catholic school system—and proposed tuition tax credits for families with children in nonpublic schools. A low rating with blacks prompted the president's visit to a black family in whose front yard the Ku Klux Klan had burned a cross. After a decline in popularity with conservatives because of his slowness to act on the school-prayer and abortion issues, Reagan suddenly appeared at conferences of some ultraright groups.

There is little research to support a linkage between public opinion on specific issues and the popularity of a candidate or president. But there is overwhelming evidence that public opinion on highly visible issues can be the determining factor in a president's decision. Perhaps as the presidency becomes increasingly less stable for an incumbent, public opinion will seem more and more threatening.

Because polls have become, in fact, continuous mini-elections, they fulfill important needs of parties and politicians. They are an important source of data needed to run an election campaign because they accurately predict primary and national election outcomes. In a study of presidential nominations between 1936 and 1972, political scientist James R. Beniger found a strong correlation between a candidate's standing in the polls and his ability to win the nomination.[55]

Since polls add to the horse-race atmosphere, national TV networks, national news magazine, and big-city dailies have developed their own polls. Thus the polling results that cascade out of computers every presidential election year are increasing. In addition to providing a steady source of sportslike data, polls are logical extensions of a candidate-centered election process. A self-announced candidate with resources to mount a costly media campaign or with celebrity status can use polls to claim viability as a presidential prospect. Polls helped propel Wendell Willkie from political obscurity in 1940 into the Republican nomination. They also helped advance the candidacies of Eisenhower, Kennedy, Eugene McCarthy, McGovern, Nixon, Carter, and John Anderson.

Critics charge that at best polls are only superficial glimpses into the voters' complex world. Frequent simplistic surveys of the public may do less to illuminate public opinion than to tip off candidates as to what kind of presidential images the people are seeking. Some polls can be misleading in view of the volatility of the political scene and the public's lack of understanding of issues, policies, or candidate qualifications. For example, Senator Edward Kennedy's decision to challenge Carter for the Democratic nomination in 1979 was based on polls that asked voters to choose between Kennedy and Carter. Kennedy's wide margin of support was more a sign of disenchantment with Carter than of preference for Kennedy.

Polls are less useful in dictating what positions a politician should take than in showing how to use positions already taken and which issues to avoid. Polls can also help pinpoint opponent strength that needs to be countered. They may have more impact on candidates, campaign organizations and their workers and contributors, and the media than on the average voter. When Carter's personal pollster, Patrick Caddell, informed the president two days before the 1980 election that the final poll showed the president well behind Reagan, Carter did not dispute the finding. Returning from a final day of campaigning in the Pacific Northwest, Carter and his wife wept in the privacy of their cabin on Air Force One when they learned of Caddell's poll.

PRESIDENTIAL IMAGE BUILDERS

Prior to 1900, a presidential candidate was supposed to act more like a reluctant groom than an ardent suitor. It was unseemly to seek the nomination. Instead, the candidate was expected to wait for a group of party leaders to pay a call and advise him of his selection. After nomination, the candidate kept a low profile while awaiting the electoral judgment. Seeking votes in an active way was thought unfitting for a future president.

Formerly voters received most of their information about a candidate from the parties or from their friends, fellow workers, or family members. Today's voters, however, are saturated with information by the mass media and by the candidate's staff. Since the candidate's main goal is to capture the attention of voters and the media, images and illusions are more important than policies or political ideas. The candidate has to convince the media and the electorate that he is a legitimate heir to the office, and that he reflects the people's expectations.

As a result, the candidates have turned from the party professionals of yesterday to a new breed of experts—professional campaign managers. These people are media technicians who are skilled in public-opinion polls, advertising, and direct-mail solicitations. They can turn an unknown but ambitious and financially well-provided aspirant into a national political celebrity—but at considerable expense. The old-fashioned party professionals are shunted to the sidelines until after the nominating convention. Then they are called on to rally the party faithful behind the professional juggernaut that spearheads the candidate's campaign.

The first campaign management organization was born in California, a state with a history of weak political parties. Reformers have found a fertile soil among the state's rootless new immigrants for such antiparty devices as the referendum and initiative. In the absence of a strong party tradition, Whitaker and Baxter, the first professional campaign management firm, won seventy of the seventy-five campaigns it handled from the late 1930s on. Many of the techniques they pioneered are still used today.[56]

Presidential campaigns are the World Series of campaign consultants. The overall direction of a campaign remains with the candidate's own staff. But his assistants must work with the campaign's chief management organization and with countless other organizations that raise funds, prepare speeches, do scheduling, and coach the candidate for media appearances. Included is an army of specialists: psychologists, political scientists, radio and TV writers, media space buyers, telephone organizers, statisticians, demographers, and computer analysts.

All these specialists have the same goal as the political party: to win. In the past the party used to seek victory by appealing to voters through a broad coalition. Instead, today's campaign specialists package and market the candidate, exaggerating his good qualities and minimizing or hiding his flaws. Marketing involves finding out what the public wants and making it appear that the candidate has it. As a prominent campaign specialist conceded, "I'm not in the business of *educating* voters. I'm out to reinforce their biases and prejudices, to win at least 50 percent of the vote for my candidate. I'm in it to make money."[57]

A major goal is favorable coverage for the candidate on prime-time national TV, especially the evening news. Since the professionals realize that the national media can be both a threat and a boon, they also attempt to project favorable images of the candidate through costly paid ads. Commercials, it is hoped, will overcome any negative images of the candidate that appear in the national media.

Professional campaign managers must also attract a great many contributors around the nation through a process political scientist Larry Sabato calls "the poisoned pen of politics"—direct mailings. Sabato condemns this process because it creates a false illusion of intimacy between the candidate and the citizen. Some direct-mail appeals use fear tactics and highly emotional arguments to stir reactions in groups known to hold ideologically far-out views. Usually there is little contact between the candidate and the direct-mail consultant, who deals only with members of the candidate's staff. Rarely is the candidate involved in developing a mailing that goes out over his name and contains "personal" statements on the issues.[58]

In addition to an appeal for contributions, most mailings contain simplified statements of a negative or gimmicky nature. They are produced by computers and machine-signed to look as if they came from the candidate to the recipient. Incumbent presidents' letters are mass-produced on high-grade White House stationery and signed by a "mechanical" president. Mail appeals are carefully targeted to sympathetic groups or to those most likely to make a contribution. Occasional snafus occur, however. In 1972 Nixon's White House staff was furious when one of his reelection direct-mail appeals was sent to Hubert H. Humphrey—an unavoidable risk in any operation involving millions of pieces of mail.[59]

Because the GOP first took up direct mail on a large scale, the Republicans have benefited from it more than the Democrats. Between the early 1970s and 1980, thanks to direct-mail appeals, the Republican party base increased from 34,000 contributors to 870,000.[60] So far the most successful direct-mail consultant has been Richard A. Viguerie, an ultraconservative who helped raise a considerable share of Reagan's campaign war chest in 1980.

The new consultants not only profit by their efforts but often join the White House ruling elite. H. R. Haldeman, a California ad executive and creator of the Un-cola ads for 7-Up, became Nixon's chief of staff. Ron Ziegler, a California public-relations executive, was named press secretary. When Carter came to power, Hamilton Jordan, architect of the president's progress from Plains, Georgia, to the White House, became chief of staff; Jody Powell, another key figure in the

Carter campaign, became press secretary. The record of these media professionals in the White House was disastrous in Nixon's case and not much better in Carter's. Despite their skill in image building and campaign management, such individuals are usually woefully inexperienced or incompetent in government.

There is little evidence that the image makers have had a positive impact on voting behavior or turnout. In fact, voter participation has declined steadily since TV became a dominant force in national politics. Some voting analysts believe that the constant bombardment of voters with ads, election results, and pseudo-events may confuse and bore the electorate. As with public-opinion polling, media politics may have more impact on candidates and professionals than on the voters who are their targets. In giving the people "what they want," candidates and media experts may seriously overestimate the impact of the "big pitch" or underestimate the voters' common sense.

On one point there is general agreement: the new media politics has not produced better candidates or presidents than the old party elite system it replaced.[61] Moreover, it results in a weaker president who, after the election, must form an administration mostly on his own.

THE PARTY CHIEF

In Europe the political party makes the prime minister. But in the United States a politician wins the White House through a divide-and-conquer strategy against fellow partisans. As political scientist Richard Rose noted:

> *The European system of selecting leaders by party caucuses strengthens party unity, and this in turn strengthens the collective authority of government. . . . The position of a European party leader is that of a politician subject to party discipline as well as using party discipline to sustain collective direction of the government.*[62]

Since World War II the average British prime minister has been a member of Parliament for a quarter century before entering No. 10 Downing Street. Thanks to years of working within the party, he or she has a broad understanding of how colleagues think and what is necessary to gain their support. But a candidate for the presidency often boasts of being a *stranger* to Washington and a party *outsider*.

A newly elected prime minister enters office with a government already in place. But a new president has to create an administration in his own image. As the president reinvents the wheel, so to speak, he has to appear above partisanship while appealing for support from both sides of the party spectrum and from the electorate. The Carter administration provided a vivid object lesson of this point.

Through such tactics as town meetings, a nationwide telephone call-in, and direct TV appeals for support, Carter tried to have a direct relationship with the people. But he rarely followed through on such approaches. Apparently regarding them merely as symbolic gestures of goodwill, he soon returned to his managerial style, and concern for details. He failed to see that he could not succeed without securing the support of the Democratic majority in Congress.

Although Carter scorned the party, he failed to persuade voters to light fires under the Democrats in Congress who were reluctant to pass his measures. He did not understand that it is more effective for a president to go directly to the public as an *exception* to following a party strategy; he wanted to make such appeals a *replacement* for such a strategy.

Reagan seemed more sensitive to the need for party government than Carter. Yet he was willing to use public appeals when necessary to achieve his goals. At first he did so with greater success than Carter. He showed how powerful a personal approach can be in obtaining party backing when the president has public opinion on his side. But if this situation changes, party cohesion will be short-lived. When Reagan's economic and foreign policies proved unpopular with many voters, Republicans who had at first firmly backed the president grew less supportive.

In fact, presidential leadership over political parties has always been uncertain and subject to the ups and downs of popularity. Which of our presidents has really measured up to the ideal of a party leader proposed by some political analysts? (Was FDR a powerful party leader, or was the Democratic party mainly an extension of Roosevelt as a "party of one"?) The president's resources as party leader are more illusionary than real, and they carried more weight in the past than today.

As titular head of the party, the president appoints its national chairperson. But most recent presidents have ignored both the chairperson and the national committee. No president wants the party national committee to function as an independent political base. Unless he plans to use the national committee in his reelection plans, he is apt to eliminate the committee as a factor in his political maneuvering.[63]

JFK relied on an organization top-heavy with family members and close associates. LBJ had his Texas "gang," and Nixon his advertising and public relations people. Under Carter the Democratic National Committee was controlled almost directly from the White House by people who had masterminded Carter's victory in 1976. Reagan's staff consisted mainly of old associates from his time as governor of California, although he added to his staff individuals who had served in previous Republican administrations. As a rule, campaign professionals and personal loyalists have little regard for party officials. As we shall see in Chapter 5, members of the president's staff isolate him from frequent contacts with party leaders.

As party chief, the president is expected to help party candidates campaigning for Congress or high state offices. But in recent years the presidential coattails seem more a threat than a blessing. The president's popularity is almost always on a downward slide when off-year races are held, and many party candidates try to avoid too close an identification with the president.

An illusion persists that a president is entitled to compliance from party officials and officeholders, but there are limits to such power. Carter, for example, tried to punish Chicago Mayor Jane Byrne for endorsing Senator Edward Kennedy for the Democratic nomination in 1979. When Carter withheld federal funds from the city, however, press headlines about Carter's punitive acts made him look no better than any ordinary machine boss.

Today the pressures that weigh most heavily on a president do not come from the party but from special-interest groups. Such groups or issue-constituencies have often played a role in the president's electoral coalition. Every administration has an in-house staff set up especially to deal with these groups (see Chapter 5 for fuller information on this topic).

CONCLUSION

The myth of the nonpolitician as president is not only a very misleading image about the presidency but it is also symptomatic of what is wrong with the office. Americans expect their president to be a pristine, godlike figure untouched by the uglier aspects of politics. Yet we are consistently disappointed when the lack of political skill or the weaknesses of the political system prevent him from acting decisively and efficiently.

The presidency is our *most* political office. It has grown increasingly impossible not because presidents have acted too much like politicians, but because they have found that the fragile political coalitions of which they once were a part have almost collapsed. National politics today involves free-floating groups and technicians motivated more by their own spoils than by any collective spirit. Today's president must be a consummate politician if he hopes to survive, but the coalitions he builds bear little resemblance to the traditional party coalitions that in the past served to guide (and occasionally to assist) administrations.

The question today is not whether a president can be above politics. Can he be a "party of one" and hope to develop a consensus on the major problems confronting the nation without the assistance of strong political parties? Parties may be almost anachronisms in today's media-centered society, but the president suffers as much or more than anyone from their decline. As a one-man distillation of government, every new president is under immense pressure to succeed, but not likely to do so.

Current candidates or incumbents are strongly tempted to play off the strong antipolitician sentiments of the American people, particularly at a time when political parties have little influence in the recruitment or governing process. Every president inevitably pays the price for his independence, first when his policy agenda becomes mired in a partyless and leaderless Congress, and later when another self-anointed candidate decides to challenge his renomination.

There is, however, little likelihood that political parties will ever recapture the influence they once enjoyed in national government. No matter how many times they reform themselves, the forces of fragmentation are greater. TV and campaign professionals have made parties almost superfluous to the presidential nomination process. Too many other sources of power with strong claims on the politicians are tied into the national government. It is unlikely that the parties will ever be able to absorb these sources of power and shape them into a truly strong party coalition.

The result is *not* a people's president—a nonpolitician—but a president beholden to narrow interests and issue groups and to Madison Avenue professionals. What is disturbing about this situation is that the illusion of a nonpolitical executive is totally inconsistent with what Americans really want from their presidents. Michael Novak put it most succinctly:

> *What a good American is seldom free to desire openly is authority or power. These must always be disguised. . . . Demands of power must always be made to seem demands of reason. We fancy political leaders who are not or do not seem to be political. . . . So vastly out of tune with reality are these pretenses that we impose on politicians the unconscionable task of disguising their main business.*[64]

NOTES

1. Emmet John Hughes, *The Ordeal of Power: A Political Memoir of the Eisenhower Years* (New York: Atheneum Publishers, 1963), 194.

2. Ralph M. Goldman, "Titular Leadership of the Presidential Parties," in Aaron Wildavsky, ed., *The Presidency* (Boston: Little, Brown and Company, 1969), 307.

3. See James Ceaser, *Presidential Selection* (Princeton, N.J.: Princeton University Press, 1979). Much of the discussion of presidential recruitment here derives from Ceaser's excellent discussion.

4. Walter Bagehot, *The English Constitution* (New York: Anchor Doubleday Books, 1957), 106.

5. Bagehot, 83.

6. Ceaser, 50–58.

7. Ibid., 59.

8. Terry Sanford, *A Danger of Democracy* (Boulder, Colo.: Westview Press, 1981), 29–35.

9. Everett Carll Ladd, Jr., *Where Have All the Voters Gone?* (New York: W. W. Norton & Company, 1978), xxv.

10. Ibid., xvii.

11. Ibid., xxi.

12. Ibid., xiv.

13. Walter Dean Burnham, "The End of American Party Politics," in Peter Woll, ed., *American Government: Reading and Cases*, 6th ed. (Boston: Little, Brown and Company, 1978), 261.

14. See, for example, W. Miller et al., *The American Voter* (New York: John Wiley & Sons, 1960); and Norman Nie, Sidney Verba, and J. Petrocik, *The Changing American Voter* (Cambridge, Mass.: Harvard University Press, 1976).

15. William J. Crotty and Gary C. Jacobson, *American Parties in Decline* (Boston: Little, Brown and Company, 1980), 26.

16. Jeane J. Kirkpatrick, *The New Presidential Elite* (New York: Russell Sage Foundation and Twentieth Century Fund, 1976), Chap. 10.

17. *Delegate Selection Rules for the 1976 Democratic National Convention* (Washington, D.C.: Democratic National Committee, 1974).

18. For an excellent account of Carter's campaign, see Martin Schramm, *Running for President: The Carter Campaign* (New York: Pocket Books, 1977).

19. *Delegate Selection Rules for the 1980 Democratic National Convention* (Washington, D.C.: Democratic National Committee, 1978).

20. *Time*, August 25, 1980, 13.

21. *Delegate Selection Rules for the 1984 Democratic National Convention* (Washington, D.C.: Democratic National Committee, 1982).

22. Ruth K. Scott and Ronald J. Hrebenar, *Parties in Crisis: Party Politics in America* (New York: John Wiley & Sons, 1979).

23. *Today, Journal of Political News and Analysis*, September 26, 1980, B-17.

24. James W. Davis, *Presidential Primaries: Road to the White House* (Westport, Conn.: Greenwood Press, 1980), 114–132.

25. *U.S. News & World Report*, November 19, 1979, 37.

26. Ladd, 61

27. V. O. Key, *American State Politics* (New York: Alfred A. Knopf, 1965), 153.

28. Davis, 8

29. Ibid.

30. *Openness, Participation and Party Building: Reforms for a Stronger Democratic Party*, Morley Winograd, Chairman, Commission on Presidential Nomination and Party Structure (Washington, D.C.: Democratic National Committee, 1978), 29.

31. *New York Times*, August 9, 1980, 33.

32. James W. Ceaser, "Direct Participation in Politics," in Richard M. Pious, ed., *The Power to Govern* (Proceedings of the Academy of Political Science, 1981).

33. Scott and Hrebenar, 124.

34. Richard L. Rubin "Presidency in an Age of Television," in Pious, *The Power to Govern*, 143.

35. David S. Broder, "Let 100 Single-Issue Groups Bloom," reprinted from the *Washington Post*, January 7, 1979, by Robert A. Taft Institute of Government, New York, N.Y., 1.

36. Ibid., 2.

37. Joel Swerdlow, "The Decline of the Boys on the Bus," *Washington Journalism Review* (January-February, 1981).

38. Quoted in Joe McGinnis, *The Selling of the President, 1968* (New York: Pocket Books, 1970), 20.

39. Paul Lazarsfeld, Bernard Berelson, and H. Gaudet, *The People's Choice* (New York: Columbia University Press, 1968), 115-119.

40. Thomas E. Patterson and Robert D. McClure, *The Unseeing Eye: The Myth of Television in National Elections* (New York: G.P. Putnam's Sons, 1976), 58.

41. Ibid.

42. See Thomas E. Patterson, *The Mass Media Election* (New York: Praeger Publishers, 1980), Chaps. 4 and 5.

43. Douglas Lowenstein, "Covering the Primaries," *Washington Journalism Review* (September-October, 1980): 38.

44. Michael J. Robinson and Karen A. McPherson, "Television News and the Presidential Nominating Process: The Case of Spring, 1976," (Washington, D.C.: Department of Politics, Catholic University).

45. Ibid.

46. *New York Times*, June 8, 1980, E-5.

47. Timothy Crouse, *The Boys on the Bus* (New York: Ballantine Books, 1973), 33.

48. *U.S. News & World Report*, July 14, 1980, 28.

49. *Time*, July 28, 1980, 54.

50. Daniel J. Boorstin, *The Image: Or What Happened to the American Dream* (New York: Atheneum Publishers, 1962), 238.

51. Ibid.

52. C. Anthony Broh, "Horse-Race Journalism: Reporting the Polls in the 1976 Presidential Election," *Public Opinion Quarterly* 44 (Winter 1980): 528.

53. Irving Crespi, "Polls as Journalism," *Public Opinion Quarterly* 44 (Winter 1980): 466.

54. Seymour Sudman, "The Presidents and the Polls," *Public Opinion Quarterly* (Fall 1982): 301-10.

55. James R. Beniger, "Winning the Presidential Nomination: National and State Primary Elections, 1936-72," *Public Opinion Quarterly* 40 (Spring 1976).

56. See Larry J. Sabato, *The Rise of Political Consultants* (New York: Basic Books, 1981).

57. Personal communication from George Shipley of Shipley and Associates, a Texas-based campaign consulting firm, July 9, 1980.

58. L. Sabato, *The Rise of Political Consultants* (New York: Basic Books, 1981), 220-255.

59. Ibid., 221.

60. Ibid., 224.

61. Harold Mendelsohn and Irving Crespi, *Polls, Television and the New Politics* (Scranton, Penna.: Chandler Publishing Co., 1970), 265.

62. Richard Rose, "Government Against Sub-governments," in Richard Rose and Ezra Suleiman, eds., *Presidents and Prime Ministers* (Washington, D.C.: American Enterprise Institute, 1980), 316.

63. Joseph Califano, Jr., *A Presidential Nation* (New York: W. W. Norton & Company, 1975), 146-53.

64. Michael Novak, *Choosing Our King* (New York: Macmillan, 1974), 281-82.

Chapter 3

The Grand Legislator

*Oh, if I could only be President and Congress too
for just ten minutes!*

Theodore Roosevelt

*I have the greatest respect for Congress, but I
don't consider the Congress to be inherently
capable of leadership. I think the Founding
Fathers expected the president to be the leader
of the country.*

Jimmy Carter

One of the more curious notions Americans have about the presidency
is that it ought to function with the same kind of collective authority
over the policy process that a prime ministry does in a parliamentary
system. True, "Congress now awaits the president's legislative proposals for it is he who establishes much of the legislative agenda and
sets priorities."[1] But the image of the American president as a powerful
chief legislator on the order of a British prime minister is as much an
illusion as the idea that a president is above politics. Historically,
Congress has exhibited as much or more leadership over policymaking
as the presidency, and constitutionally Congress has many substantial
advantages over the executive.

Only on infrequent occasions have presidents measured up to the
mythical "grand legislator" suggested by the mass media and textbooks. The evidence is that Congress is far underrated as a legislative
innovator. But our fascination with the presidency invariably leads us
to attribute monumental policy changes to him and to deny the central
role of Congress. Congress is held to be congenitally incapable of

formulating and pushing through a comprehensive legislative program without the president. When we think back to major legislative accomplishments of the past, we almost always see them as the personal triumphs of presidents. This perspective may enhance the symbolic importance of the office, but it puts every president on the spot when it comes to *his* legislative feats.

The leading source of exaggerated images of presidential policymaking power stems from our tendency to overemphasize the personal contribution of presidents to sweeping policy changes. We then infer that every president ought to be able to ram important legislation through Congress whenever there is a pressing national need. We mythologize Franklin D. Roosevelt for his single-handed accomplishment of the New Deal during the dark days of the Great Depression. The Great Society belongs as exclusively to Lyndon B. Johnson in the public mind as the Emancipation Proclamation to Lincoln. These are norms of legislative leadership to which every president is expected to ascribe. Such expectations gloss over the key but complex role Congress played in both the New Deal and the Great Society programs. They also ignore the more frequent failures or inadequate executive-legislative dealings which traditionally characterize relations between Capitol Hill and the White House.

Americans want their president to function like a prime minister in a collectively responsible parliamentary government, but the president possesses neither the Constitutional authority nor sufficient resources to make government function efficiently or with accountability. Responsible government means a fusion of powers between the executive and legislature rather than a separation. It requires members of the government—the prime minister and the cabinet—to present a united front to the legislature. And if the legislature refuses to support the government on important policy matters, the prime minister can immediately dissolve parliament or resign along with all the other cabinet ministers, necessitating a new election which could jeopardize the political careers of individual members of the parliament.[2]

Such a system provides important channels of communication between those who govern and those who are governed, for it emphasizes leadership, party loyalty, and accountability between members of the legislature and members of the ministry or executive branch. Former British Prime Minister Harold Wilson once observed that a British prime minister lives far more dangerously than an American president because Parliament can remove a PM by refusing to supply, sustain, or support a cabinet.[3] Wilson exaggerated, however, because rarely do backbenchers—members of Parliament who do not hold posts in the government—refuse to support the cabinet on major tests. In contrast, an American president—virtually unremovable by Congress save for impeachment for treason, bribery, or high crimes and misdemeanors—is usually frustrated by an inability to get legislation through Congress, even when his own party controls a substantial majority. Congressional expert Norman Ornstein comments, "We have never had sustained congressional-presidential unity for even one full term."[4]

Presidential success or failure in the legislative arena is as much a matter of illusion as actual results. John F. Kennedy, who had a relatively dismal record with Congress, is still rated by the public as our most effective modern president while Jimmy Carter, who is considered a failure, achieved a number of his leading policy objectives.[5] The mismatch between expectations for presidential leadership and actual legislative accomplishment has become increasingly more damaging to recent administrations because there is much more at stake for more people in governmental programs today than during Kennedy's time.

The United States lacks a single institution that can effectively assert collective authority on major issues of the day. As British political scientist Richard Rose noted:

> *The fundamental point is that American government is not meant to be managed or led by one person. . . . The president has a hard time getting a handle on government because there is no handle there. . . . There are few occasions when the president enjoys a monopoly of power in government.*[6]

Americans persist in looking to the president for policy leadership because he is their only nationally elected representative, and his claim to represent the national interest takes precedence over any other's. The national legislative agenda is, in fact, the product of the Executive Branch and Congress, but the president plays the leading role in giving it shape, content, and public visibility. Consequently his responsibility as chief legislator is both logical and legitimate in the public's eyes, even if it is unsupported by formal Constitutional grants of authority. This misconception persists even though his efforts are marked with frequent failure.

The president's leadership over national policymaking is fraught with uncertainty, and stymied by roadblocks, delays, and rejections. No other presidential task is as vulnerable to the wishes or whims of so many others or as subject to breakdown or failure. The gap between the promise of legislative leadership and what can realistically be achieved has grown wider in the past decade as a result of powerful counterpressures from Congress and other political forces. Presidential misjudgments in Vietnam prompted counterreactions by Congress against the president's foreign-policy authority, and the domestic-policy environment has grown increasingly hostile to collective direction.

Basic changes in how Congress functions as well as in the outlook of its newer members toward their institution and their constituencies have made Congress less amenable to collective persuasion. The decline of political party influence has contributed to a dispersion of power inside Congress, making it more difficult for the White House to work through party leaders to develop and steer a president's legislative agenda through the labyrinthian legislative process. The policy agenda itself has changed dramatically as the United States faced declining prosperity at home and a dwindling monopoly over economic and military power abroad. Demands for new programs ran up against pressures to hold the line on governmental spending. In the aftermath of Watergate, suspicion of the White House led to increased congressional surveillance.

This chapter contrasts the illusion of the president as a powerful legislative leader with the realities of his dealings with Congress. It examines how that myth derives from an exaggerated perception of the role that several modern presidents have played in developing major political changes. The chapter also examines the powers and resources available to the White House, contrasting them with the growing number of constraints facing every new administration in recent years. The chapter concludes with a consideration of the impact that recent changes in Congress and reforms of the legislative process have had on the president's role as chief legislator.

THE MYTH OF THE SUPERLEGISLATOR

The belief that individual presidents have achieved remarkable results in policy leadership fits neatly and tidily with our need to see the presidency as an exceptional role. But it clashes with the real world of national politics, for rarely is collective authority achieved in our system. Only occasionally have presidents been superachievers in the policy process because fragmentation is more common than cooperation. Strong presidential leadership over Congress is the exception rather than the rule, and conflict between the two branches is as American as apple pie.

At the same time that presidents are overrated, Congress is underrated as a policy innovator. Political scientists Ronald C. Moe and Steven C. Teel argue that Congress has exhibited more initiative and leadership in policymaking than the presidency, and that Congress frequently has spurred the White House into action or has itself taken action without the president's support.[7] It is difficult to assign credit for an idea, however, and since the presidential policy agenda is always treated much more conspicuously in the national news media, it is widely assumed that the White House or the Executive Branch is responsible for major policy proposals. Textbook treatments of important legislative periods or major policies generally attribute to presidents both the idea and the successful legislating of significant programs, and Congress is typically relegated to a subordinate "helping- (or hindering-) hand" role.

The image of the president as a strong legislator mostly stems from four chief executives of the twentieth century: Theodore Roosevelt, Woodrow Wilson, Franklin D. Roosevelt, and Lyndon B. Johnson, each of whom is credited with achieving landmark legislation and giving new direction to national policy. Each was in office at a time when the demand for collective national leadership was great. But the notion that each achieved almost single-handedly remarkable legislative records—through skillful manipulation of Congress or by sheer weight of their dynamic personalities—greatly oversimplifies rather complex political interactions between the executive and legislative branches.

Theodore Roosevelt is remembered for defining his authority so broadly as to imply a *duty* to be the nation's chief policymaker. TR claimed to be the steward for the American people, bound not only by the right but the obligation to "do anything that the needs of the nation demanded, unless such action was forbidden by the Constitution or the laws."[8] Roosevelt used his authority to initiate and to push through Congress several major pieces of legislation, including the Hepburn Act that gave the Interstate Commerce Commission power to regulate interstate utility and railroad rates; laws protecting workers; and conservation measures that set aside vast areas of land as national parks. He was unsuccessful, however, in obtaining a number of other proposals, including relief for labor and regulation of business. Many other Rooseveltian reforms were gradually enacted in the Taft and Wilson administrations. Business leaders pressured conservatives in Roosevelt's own party to resist his ambitious reforms, and TR was frequently at blows with a recalcitrant Congress. (He is once said to have become so exasperated with Congress that he declared to an aide that he wished he "could turn 16 lions loose on the Congress." But, the aide warned, the lions might make a mistake. "Not if they stay there long enough!" Roosevelt shot back.[9])

It is frequently claimed that Wilson conducted our only parliamentary-cabinet government. Viewing his powers as analogous to the British prime minister's, Wilson frequently addressed Congress in person and often appeared on Capitol Hill to intervene directly at various stages of the legislative process. He even maintained a President's Room at the Capitol, where he consulted with congressional leaders on pending administration bills. Wilson was committed to restructuring the economy and completing many of the progressive reforms begun earlier under Roosevelt. His involvement contributed to legislation establishing the Federal Trade Commission as well as historic measures such as the Clayton Antitrust Act and the Federal Reserve Act. Wilson also engineered passage of the income-tax amendment, legislation limiting child labor in factories, and measures reducing tariffs. He was less successful in winning other major legislative goals, including the most important goal of his political career: ratification of U.S. membership in the League of Nations. The U.S. Supreme Court overturned the child labor law, and Congress resisted other progressive proposals with increasing success. Wilson's efforts on behalf of Democratic candidates running for Congress in 1918 mostly failed, and his party lost both houses. By the time he left office, Wilson's relationships with Congress were openly and mutually hostile.[10]

The most dramatic transformation in the relationship between the presidency and Congress occurred during the first two terms of Franklin D. Roosevelt. FDR changed the power ratio between Congress and the White House, publicly taking it upon himself to act as the leader of Congress at a time of deepening crisis in the nation.[11] More than any other president, FDR established the model of the powerful legislative presidency on which the public's expectations still are anchored. Roosevelt's first hundred days in office have become part of American political folklore. Within hours of assuming the presidency, he called a special session of Congress, declared a bank holiday, initiated measures to stop the nation's economic hemorrhaging, and was responsible for a series of bills which radically restructured and expanded the role of the federal government in the nation's economy.

The popular view of this remarkable period holds that FDR and his New Deal brain trust of bright, young, progressive advisers rammed one piece of legislation after another through a rubber-stamp Congress. While Roosevelt unquestionably was the major force behind the social and economic changes of this period, the essential role of Congress in initiating and carrying through much of the New Deal agenda is usually ignored or minimized. "Most of the New Deal legislation for which F.D.R. has been given recognition had a well-defined prenatal history extending back several years before it was espoused by the Roosevelt administration," according to Moe and Teel.[12] The historian Arthur M. Schlesinger, Jr., has written that far from being a tame and servile body, Congress "played a vital and consistently underestimated role in shaping the New Deal"—sometimes in the face of a lack of enthusiasm if not outright opposition by the White House.[13]

A member of the New Deal brain trust, Leon H. Keyserling, claims that FDR—far from being the great catalyst behind the measures commonly regarded as the heart of the New Deal—was at best only remotely involved.[14] As an assistant to New York Senator Robert F.

Wagner, Keyserling was involved with several groups developing the National Industrial Recovery Act (NIRA), the cornerstone of the New Deal, which provided for federal supervision over industry as well as a massive public works program. Roosevelt was cool to the idea of public works until Secretary of Labor Frances Perkins, Senator Wagner, and others finally succeeded in having this program incorporated into the bill. The public works provision ultimately led to a number of other public employment measures. Wage-and-hour provisions in the NIRA were forerunners to the Fair Labor Standards Act of 1938. Section 7(a) of this act, which provided for collective bargaining, maximum working hours, and minimum wages, evolved into the Wagner Act of 1935 that created the National Labor Relations Board.

Keyserling drafted the National Labor Relations Act (the Wagner Act)—often called organized labor's Magna Carta—but Roosevelt declined to support it. In fact, he placed a number of stumbling blocks in front of the bill until a revised version passed the Senate. Schlesinger concedes that Roosevelt took a hands-off attitude toward the historic measure strengthening the rights of labor in collective bargaining and providing widely expanded civilian public works projects. But historically it is Roosevelt who is remembered for these acts.[15]

Other key New Deal programs also originated in Congress, and often were either not supported or only lukewarmly endorsed by Roosevelt. The Tennessee Valley Act of 1933 had its origins in the efforts of Senator George Norris during the Coolidge and Hoover administrations. The Agricultural Adjustment Act was not a White House creation, but stemmed from farm relief proposals of the 1920s and early 1930s. The U.S. Housing Act of 1937, which established the original nationwide program of low-rent housing and slum clearance, was not actively supported by Roosevelt. Neither was an employment act originally drafted in 1944 that later became the 1946 Employment Act charging the president with responsibility for achieving high levels of employment and a stable economy.

Most of Roosevelt's reputation stemmed from the Seventy-third Congress. By 1935, when the Seventy-fourth Congress convened, his influence began to decline. A conservative coalition gradually emerged to thwart many of Roosevelt's programs, most notably his plan to pack the U.S. Supreme Court by adding six additional members to bolster the New Deal majority on the court. FDR's attempt to purge his party of wayward Democrats during the 1938 off-year elections likewise failed. From 1938 on, Roosevelt achieved only modest success with his legislative proposals while he increasingly relied on vetoes to block Congress.

Unlike Roosevelt—who had to be sold on many of the historic measures later credited to him—Lyndon B. Johnson was a supersalesman for the programs that collectively became known as the Great

Society. Years of experience—first as a congressman, later as a Senator, and finally as Senate majority leader—honed Lyndon Johnson's political sensitivities and legislative skills to a fine edge. In 1963 he assumed a largely unfulfilled legislative agenda from the assassinated John F. Kennedy which included a broad range of social and economic programs. LBJ was not content with merely fulfilling Kennedy's agenda, he wanted to leave his own mark on history—perhaps to even equal Roosevelt's reputation. Johnson pushed through Congress many of the key elements of Kennedy's programs, including the 1964 Civil Rights Act, a tax cut, aid to education, and Medicare. Johnson also proposed a number of measures of his own, including the 1965 Voting Rights Act, the war on poverty, and a rent subsidy measure.

The popular impression of Johnson is that he was one of the greatest masters of the legislative art to ever inhabit the White House, and that his unique skills enabled him to achieve so much so quickly. A prevalent image of Johnson suggested a tall Texan looming over the shoulders of a member of Congress, arms draped in a stranglehold around the legislator's neck, as Johnson horse-traded for his vote. Johnson focused on legislators who might be "swing" voters on an issue. Familiarizing himself with their reasons for opposing his legislation, he would study detailed memoranda or dig into his personal recollections about them to try to find what it would take to convert them. Johnson would appeal first to their loyalty to the nation, to posterity, and—ultimately—to Lyndon Johnson. He would make them feel as if their votes were the most important and courageous acts of their distinguished public lives. He might imply—but rarely directly threaten—a cooling-off of the legislators' "special" relationship to the president. But he rarely offered a direct trade because if word got out that he was trading for votes, every member of Congress would try to hold out for a favorable deal with the White House.[16]

Johnson knew committee leaders intimately. He was close to party chieftains, and he enjoyed the company of members of Congress—whether it was swapping yarns or drinking bourbon. He frequently telephoned legislators to wish them a happy birthday, and invited them on the spur of the moment for a walk around the White House grounds. He called members of Congress who were important in winning a legislative victory to thank them for their support.

Recent scholarly assessments of Johnson's legislative accomplishments, however, question whether his mastery over Congress was as important to the legislation of the Great Society as popular accounts suggest. LBJ may have been the beneficiary of a legislative agenda whose time had come. Several observers of the period believe that had Kennedy lived, he might have gotten through Congress most of the same programs for which Johnson received credit. Senate Minority Leader Everett Dirksen and House Majority Leader Carl Albert claimed that Kennedy's program "was on its way before November 22, 1963 (the day he was assassinated). Its time had come."[17] Lawrence F. O'Brien, who served as chief congressional liaison aide to both Kennedy and Johnson, suggested that legislative breakthroughs already had taken place with such measures as Medicare and civil rights before Kennedy's death.[18] Political scientist Paul Light insists that much of the image of LBJ's extraordinary prowess with Congress is a myth— that his success was closely tied to the massive Democratic majorities which swept into Congress in 1964 on Johnson's coattails.[19]

Certainly Johnson's mastery over Congress was as short-lived as Roosevelt's in the 1930s. LBJ's magic had begun to wane as early as 1966 when Vietnam started to cut into his support in Congress. After the extraordinary burst of legislation in 1965, his batting average began to drop with each successive year until his last year when he barely gained a third of his proposals sent to the Hill.

The personal roles FDR and LBJ played in the legislative achievements of their time might be exaggerated, but the fact remains that each played an important part in shaping the environment and agenda in which the various policies of the New Deal and Great Society were achieved. Subsequent presidents suffer in comparison, however, because not only were the images of Roosevelt and Johnson overdrawn but the political environment itself has become less amenable to the exercise of policy leadership. Now it appears as if each president is a legislative bumbler—a chronic underachiever.

CHIEF LEGISLATORS OF A LESSER STRIPE

Roosevelt and Johnson earned their legislative reputations at a time when conditions were ripe for new policies and programs benefitting many segments of American society. Beginning with the late 1960s, however, the need to constrain the growth of new federal programs and to control the rapidly rising costs of existing ones began to loom as an unavoidable challenge. The White House had been the obvious source for daring new policy innovations from the New Deal to the Great Society. Thus Congress looked to the president for leadership even as Senators and Representatives provided much of the substance for the legislation that poured out of Washington. The election in 1968 of a conservative president, along with a declining capacity of the federal government to meet rapidly rising costs of programs, signalled the start of a new presidential-congressional relationship in policymaking. The White House increasingly became a force of resistance to policy innovation; Congress increasingly assumed the role of protector of the public interest as Richard M. Nixon sought to reverse or to slow down social legislation. Johnson gained his Great Society agenda by working with Congress; Nixon sought his goals by virtually ignoring Congress.

Nixon interpreted his election as a mandate to challenge the free-spending ways of a Democratic-controlled Congress. His landslide reelection in 1972 reinforced this view as Nixon saw his victory "conferring not only an extraordinary measure of legitimacy on him, but also a kind of illegitimacy upon . . . Congress."[20]

Nixon's ties with members of Congress consequently were distant, frequently hostile, and devoid of any trust or candor essential for cooperation. Congressional expert Ralph K. Huitt suggests that Nixon did not seem to want anything from Congress, and although he initiated domestic programs and proclaimed priorities, he seemed to lose interest in them quickly. "Congress found itself upbraiding him for not really trying to get what he said he wanted, which many members wanted more than he did."[21] Opposing Nixon on domestic programs was like "pushing on a string," according to some members of Congress. There simply was no resistance. "Instead, Nixon tried to run things without Congress. Impounding funds, deferring the spending of them, shifting money from one purpose to another . . . gave him control of what really mattered, the allocation of government resources."[22]

Gerald R. Ford enjoyed better personal rapport with members of Congress because of his long association with the House, especially as minority leader. But he was so invariably at odds with a Democratic-controlled Congress out to reduce the White House to a coequal if not subservient status in the policy process that he had limited success. Like Nixon, Ford was not bent on pursuing any well-developed domestic agenda, but was determined to regain control over the federal budget with a "no-new-spending rule" which precluded substantial policy initiatives. The few major policy proposals advanced during his abbreviated term were mostly holdovers from the Nixon agenda, and they were concentrated on the twin problems of inflation and energy.

Ford's relationship will best be remembered for his resistance to Congress rather than for his leadership. In two and a half years he vetoed sixty-six measures, compared to Nixon's forty-three vetoes in five and a half years. The fact that Ford had not been elected either to the vice-presidency or the presidency further reduced whatever political capital he might have otherwise held because of his friendly personal ties with individual members of Congress.

A massive backlog of legislation as far as the Democratic majority in Congress was concerned had built up by 1977 as a result of the Nixon-Ford years of retrenchment, vetoes, and limited initiatives. Jimmy Carter inherited this situation, and as one Carter official described it, Congress had its own priorities with precious little room left over for Carter's own initiatives. Hundreds of bills were left over from the Ford administration. Ford's veto of so many bills left Congress desperate for a number of new programs.[23]

The expectation for Carter to perform magnificently as legislative leader was strong, given the substantial Democratic majorities that swept into office along with him in 1976. But many new legislators had run better in their districts or states than Carter had as the presidential nominee; thus there was little or no question of any coattail effect. Many of the newer, younger members of Congress were fiercely independent, reform-minded, and less susceptible to presidential persuasion than at any time in the past century.

Whatever chance there might have been for Carter to establish himself as a chief legislator was dashed by his clumsy dealings with Congress. During his first year in office, he sent to Congress eighty legislative proposals, but quickly discovered that a shotgun approach to drafting and then firing off bills at Capitol Hill was no way to win legislative goals. Bills were submitted which contained provisions already written into law or which were part of pending legislation without recognizing the prior contributions of members of Congress. Many bills were hastily and poorly drafted by White House and departmental aides without prior consultation with congressional leaders. The White House seemed anxious to overwhelm Congress with good intentions rather than to systematically follow through with what had already been introduced. Congressmen, for example, were persuaded to support an administration plan for a $50 tax rebate, only to find the proposal dumped without any advance warning from the White House.[24]

Representatives and Senators complained of never having telephone calls returned by the Carter staff. Some were angry at having to pay for their own meals when invited to the infrequent White House breakfast meetings with the president. Carter and his aides—known unaffectionately as the Georgia Mafia—rarely attempted to socialize with congressmen or to get to know key legislative leaders. Carter seemed as reclusive, distrustful, and combative toward Capitol Hill as Nixon. Carter's legislative assistants were woefully inexperienced in the ways of Washington or congressional politics, and many lacked the contacts vital to good liaison with Congress.

Congressional leaders asked Carter at the end of his first year to slow down the legislative assault, to do his homework, and to pay greater attention to establishing liaison with Congress. Legislative committees tried to sort out from the flood of legislation those bills most worthy of consideration and to rewrite many others. Carter reacted by criticizing Congress in public and by threatening to take his legislative agenda to the public if legislators refused to go along with him. He resisted compromises on many bills, and accused legislators of being pawns of special interests. When a bill was finally passed, Carter took credit even when it bore little resemblance to the original administration proposal. He claimed credit, for example, for the deregulation of the price of crude oil even though he had little to do with the bill.[25]

Carter tried to revise his congressional strategy in 1979, but it was too late to establish leadership over Congress. By then his image as a bumbling chief legislator had become well established on Capitol Hill and in the nation's press. A special White House executive management committee headed by Vice-President Walter F. Mondale was established to set priorities and to find a basic legislative direction for the floundering administration. Task forces were created to help coordinate congressional and media strategies, and attempts were made to improve communications between the White House and Congress. Tighter coordination between departmental lobbyists and White House legislative officials was stressed, and cabinet officials were ordered to work more for the president's initiatives than their own. An effort was also made to reach out to constituent groups favorable to administration legislation in the earlier stages of development. Most important, the president agreed not to back new legislative proposals until the proper spadework in Congress had been accomplished. The White House legislative agenda was pared down considerably from the ambitious but largely unsuccessful first two years when more than a hundred proposals were dispatched to Congress.[26]

The success of a president's legislative leadership is as much a matter of perceptions as of actual policy accomplishments. Polls show the public evaluates a president's performance of his job without having much substantive information on which to base its judgment. This is particularly true of knowledge about a wide range of policy initiatives which are not especially played up in the press. The media emphasize the more controversial and newsworthy initiatives, that is, those with significant impact on many individuals or groups, or initiatives generating a great deal of conflict among the branches of government. A president's reputation consequently tends to ride most heavily on policies which present the greatest hazard and least likelihood of success.

Carter was frequently portrayed as inept in his dealings with Congress (and he was). But he was given consistently low marks for his legislative accomplishments by both the press and Congress in spite of the fact that his overall record compared favorably to LBJ's. Carter's problems stemmed from the kinds of legislative initiatives he undertook. Many involved issues for which there was no easy answer or consensus; indeed they were issues in which the outcomes inevitably meant a reduction in benefits or increased costs to taxpayers. His energy plan, for example, provided for conservation and ultimately higher fuel costs with the goal of making the United States self-sufficient in energy. The elimination of pork-barrel water projects, the

Panama Canal treaties, and civil service reforms all alienated large numbers of Americans and seemingly benefited no large constituency. There was no great ground swell of popular support for a comprehensive energy program, particularly if it meant higher gasoline and fuel prices. Nor was there a great base of support for welfare reform, hospital-cost containment, or reversing U.S. policy toward Taiwan. Few Carter proposals promised the kind of national assistance that FDR's New Deal or LBJ's Great Society agenda offered.

A Carter domestic-policy staff aide interviewed by Light in his study of the president's domestic policy agenda commented:

> *We are entering a period of very difficult choices for the president and Congress. The issues we have to deal with are no longer as easy to support as they used to be. We have entered a period of resource shortages which require a firm governmental response. Gas rationing is not exactly the kind of issue to ride to reelection, but the president has to take it on. We are also in a period of extreme pressure on federal funding; of choices between B-1 bombers and hospital equipment, between an MX missile and inner-city redevelopment. We have to make very hard choices now. Maybe we are also in a period of one-term presidents. There were very few issues that we could have selected that would have helped us in the campaign. Most have involved some level of public sacrifice, and all we see ahead of us is more of the same.[27]*

During his first few months in office, Ronald Reagan made it appear that he would succeed in making such tough choices, and that he would convince not only the public to buy his proposals but the Congress as well. Tagged as the Great Persuader, Reagan won massive budget cuts alongside the largest tax cut in history from a Democratic-controlled House and a Republican Senate. He followed these twin triumphs with a much publicized victory when the Senate refused to halt the administration's proposed sale of $8.5 billion in AWACS radar planes and military gear to Saudi Arabia. The press hailed Reagan as an FDR of the right, and his legislative tactics as the most skilled and successful since LBJ.

But Reagan's triumph was short-lived, and within weeks Congress began to pull away from the administration. Shortly after the 1982–83 fiscal year began, stories began to appear in the national media about the impact of nearly $40 billion in budget cuts on the needy, minority groups, college students, education, and just about any group or individual dependent on federal outlays. Senate and House Republicans became anxious, and Democrats rebelled against Reagan's proposed 1984 federal budget because of deficits of close to $200 billion projected as a result of the shortfall from the tax cut, compounded by a recession that was reducing revenues to the federal treasury (see Chapter 8 for a fuller discussion of Reagan's economic program). As the recession grew deeper, Congress prepared to do battle with Reagan over the question of making further cuts in the domestic budget or in military expenditures, and what if any new taxes should be levied to make up some of the immense shortfall to the Treasury.

Reagan was out in front of Congress in 1981, but by 1983 the new Ninety-eighth Congress appeared to be pulling a reluctant president behind its policies. Soaring federal deficits, high unemployment in a stagnant economy, scandals in the expenditure of funds by the Environmental Protection Agency, and growing opposition to a new nuclear arms race with the Soviets all weakened Reagan's position. The White House was forced to support legislation developed by a coalition of Democrats and Republicans in both houses. This legislation extended jobless benefits and provided for new public-works and job-retraining programs and for limited reductions in defense budget requests. The 1982 midterm elections substantially cut into Reagan's support in Congress. Voters produced eighty-one new members in the House, fifty-seven of them Democrats, who were mostly lined up against further administration cuts in social programs and opposed to sharp increases in the defense budget. Reagan too appeared in danger of becoming another victim of what Light has characterized as the "no-win" presidency, a string of one-term chief executives increasingly caught up in a political vise, cross-pressured from a number of angles with little opportunity for release.[28]

FORMAL PRESIDENTIAL POWERS

Presidential scholar Richard E. Neustadt suggests that the Constitution created a government of separated institutions sharing powers. The formal powers of the presidency and Congress are "so intertwined that neither will accomplish very much, for very long, without the acquiescence of the other."[29] The president's capacity to lead legislatively stems as much from a variety of informal personal and political resources as from any institutionalized or Constitutional grants of authority, for every president enters office with the same formal powers. What distinguishes one president from another are the resources available to activate his leadership, the skill or success with which he employs these resources, and the willingness of Congress to accept his direction.

The most obvious handicap to presidential leadership over Congress is the fact that he has limited authority in the legislative process. Article I of the Constitution clearly intended for Congress to be preeminent in the policy process. The presidency moved to center stage because the public gradually came to expect him to lead legislatively and Congress accepted his primacy, granting him additional powers above and beyond the Constitution's narrow grants of authority. But many of these powers are more ephemeral than reliable, for they depend on congressional acquiescence. Legally the president has only the power to veto legislation, to make recommendations to Congress, to call and adjourn special sessions, to make treaties and appointments subject to Senate confirmation, and to conduct foreign policy.

The Veto

The authority to veto acts of Congress is the only formal power delegated by the Constitution's legislative grant in Article I, and that power is limited by the ability of Congress to override by a two-thirds vote in both chambers. The president can exercise a pocket veto by withholding his signature on bills delivered to his desk after Congress has adjourned its regular session. But he cannot extend the pocket veto when Congress is on temporary recess, as both Nixon and Ford tried to do during congressional breaks. The federal courts ruled that pocket vetoes can be used only when Congress has adjourned for the session.

Often the threat of a presidential veto is sufficient to cause Congress to tailor a bill more to the liking of the White House. As Table 3-1 shows, it is difficult to override a veto. Consequently Congress usually will think twice before it passes legislation clearly offensive to the White House. The president must make the veto threat credible, however, and he must not threaten lightly lest he appear to be bluffing. Reagan's threat to veto a critically needed jobs and recession-relief bill in 1983 prompted Congress to eliminate provisions for $1.2 billion in revenue sharing as well as a totally unrelated amendment repealing a new withholding tax on interest and dividend income.

The amendment to cut withholding was illustrative of a growing practice of legislators to try to finesse the president's veto power by attaching riders to critical bills in the hope he cannot afford to veto the main legislation. Riders are irrelevant provisions targeted at advancing an individual member's personal policy goal or benefitting special constituencies. A perennial rider that troubled the Carter administration involved cutting off federal funding for abortions.

Despite congressional efforts to force the president's hand on essential legislation, he does enjoy a substantial advantage in the legislative process not only because the threat to veto influences the outcome of measures but also because the veto itself is overridden only with great effort. Some indication of just how difficult it is to override is provided by the example of President Nixon's 1973 veto of the War Powers Act (see pp. 137–38). Nixon's veto came right after the "Saturday night massacre" when Nixon fired Watergate Special Prosecutor

TABLE 3-1 **Presidential Vetoes, 1933–1980**

	REGULAR VETOES	POCKET VETOES	TOTAL	OVERRIDDEN
Roosevelt	372	261	633	9
Truman	180	70	250	12
Eisenhower	73	108	181	2
Kennedy	12	9	21	–
Johnson	16	14	30	–
Nixon	24	19	43	5
Ford	44	22	66	12
Carter	13	16	29	2

SOURCE: U.S. Senate Library, *Presidential Vetoes, 1787–1976* (Washington, D.C.: Government Printing Office, 1978); Carter's record was updated with data in *Congressional Quarterly Almanac*, 1980, 5. Reprinted with the permission of Congressional Quarterly, Inc.

Archibald Cox for his persistence in trying to obtain Nixon's Oval Office tape recordings. Controversy over Nixon's refusal to cooperate with the investigation seriously undermined his public-opinion polls and damaged his credibility, but his veto was overridden by a cliff-hanging margin of 284–135 in the House—just four votes over the two-thirds majority required by the Constitution.[30]

The president is constantly besieged with advice over whether or not to veto legislation that runs counter to White House priorities or in which various provisions, amendments, or riders conflict with administration policy. Frequently the conflict is between a cabinet secretary whose department is principally affected and who wants the president to sign in spite of objectionable provisions, and members of the White House staff or Office of Management and Budget who urge him to veto. When the OMB recommends that the president should sign, he usually does. If the OMB advises against, however, the results are less predictable. Nixon and Ford faced numerous bills the OMB recommended them to veto, even though cabinet or agency officials urged approval. Usually the president went along with the cabinet or departmental advice because, as political scientist Stephen J. Wayne noted, "once Congress has passed the legislation [the] pressures are normally for the president to approve."[31] Aware of the political implications and eventual fallout from his veto or approval of legislation benefitting certain groups, the president may decide the path of least political resistance is to heed the pressure to assent, particularly during an election year.

Initiation of Legislation

The president's personal role in developing and pushing legislation through Congress may often be exaggerated, but the executive initiation of legislation *is* one of the hallmarks of the modern presidency. The idea that the White House would try to tell Congress what to legislate was grounds for impeachment a century ago. But today members of Congress routinely expect the president rather than their own leaders to be the source of new programs and policies that deal with the complex problems of the nation.[32]

The practice of the president sending a comprehensive legislative blueprint to Congress began in 1948 when President Truman sought to establish a legislative record on which to campaign. He used his State of the Union address, budget message, and economic report to present a comprehensive legislative agenda. Each of his messages was followed up by specific proposals—most of which were ignored by the Republican Congress.

The two most important sources of presidential policy initiatives are the White House staff and the Office of Management and Budget. The White House staff attempts to impose the president's personal wishes and goals on policies, and it plans political strategies for getting his proposals through Congress. The OMB is responsible for coordinating policy initiatives from various federal departments and agencies through a process of central clearance. But all too frequently the OMB becomes involved in a major way in program planning. (The role of the White House staff in lobbying for the president's programs will be examined later in this chapter.)

Central clearance involves OMB review of all legislative proposals originating in departments and agencies of the Executive Branch. This task initially fell to the Bureau of the Budget, the forerunner to OMB—and over time it came to include managing Executive Branch legislative efforts, coordinating policy efforts among units, and communicating to Congress the president's position and intentions on pending measures.[33]

Because of its deep involvement in legislative programming and its authority to examine legislation passed by Congress and awaiting the president's signature, the OMB soon was seen as a politicized version of the former Bureau of the Budget. Departments and agencies viewed the OMB as a threat to their budgetary needs while Congress resented the OMB's attempt to use budgetary tactics to circumvent congressional policy goals.

Nixon's reorganization plan creating the OMB also created a council to plan domestic legislation. The council would decide "what we do" while the OMB would determine "how we do it," and "how well we do it," according to Nixon.[34] The Domestic Council, as it was called during the Nixon administration, was composed of the president, vice-president, attorney general, secretaries of most cabinet departments, as well as the director and deputy director of OMB. Nixon envisioned the council as the domestic policy equivalent to the National Security Council, which provided advice on foreign-policy and national security matters. John Ehrlichman, a White House assistant, headed the council, which dominated Nixon's domestic-policy process for the next several years.

The Domestic Council prepared working papers for Nixon, evaluated agency proposals for legislation, helped draft presidential messages to Congress, and prepared supportive data for specific administration legislative measures. One of its major goals, however, was to make certain that presidential interests dominated over the interests of the departments and agencies.[35]

The council was quickly mired in political wrangling among the White House, cabinet departments, and career civil service executives. This was because, under Ehrlichman's direction, it spent much of its time trying to undermine cabinet secretaries and intimidating officials in federal agencies who were at odds with the president's policy goals or philosophy. Domestic Council staff members seemed to be constantly involved in putting out brush fires instead of developing or coordinating policies or shaping strategies. A unit of the council nicknamed the "Plumbers" served as a White House secret political unit. The Plumbers were involved in criminal break-ins and a variety of felonies, including the attempt to bug the Democratic National Committee's headquarters in the Watergate complex.

Carter replaced the council with a unit known as the Domestic Policy Staff. Later Reagan reduced the size of this unit and renamed it the Office of Policy Development. The OPD was to coordinate five cabinet councils and to develop policy recommendations on issues that affected various domestic departments and agencies. Reagan's OPD was designed to function as a White House support system, facilitating discussions and policy planning by the cabinet instead of competing with other organizations for the power to shape policy. Under Reagan the Office of Management and Budget (OMB) has proved more influential on policy matters than the Office of Policy Development. The relative importance of both these organizations has varied with the presidents' personal style of administration.

While presidents utilize their domestic-policy unit along with the OMB to develop key proposals for the legislative agenda, it is misleading to credit the White House as the sole originator of bills. According to Moe and Teel, "The ideas germinating in Congress are like a shopping list to presidential assistants from which they select those ideas most appropriate for presidential cooptation. . . . It is difficult to determine the exact point at which modification of executive proposals becomes genuine legislative initiative."[36]

Several studies suggest that Congress has been the source of many more legislative innovations or changes than the presidency, largely because of Congress's sensitivity to smaller, localized constituencies.[37] By serving as a "safety valve" for the discontented, Congress is able to move from the parochial to the patriotic policy goal, from the specific to the general, while presidents assume the perspective from the "top down."

Presidential Success

How successful are presidents as legislative initiators? Some have been more successful than we credit them—Carter, for example—whereas most of them seldom accomplish what is expected of them. More than half the legislation sought by presidents never makes it out of Congress, and those initiatives that do pull through are often altered substantially from the original intention of the White House.

The *Congressional Quarterly* calculated a presidential boxscore of successes for presidential legislative initiatives between 1954 and 1975. The index was based on final bills in general accord with the initial White House proposal, even though specific details or aspects might have differed from the original provisions in the presidents' proposals. The index included only initiatives emanating from the White House and excluded legislation from executive agencies or sources outside the presidents' immediate staff. Table 3-2 shows that the presidential batting average varied considerably during the twenty-one-year period; the success rate has declined sharply since 1968. The table does not distinguish between "major" and "minor" policies nor between domestic and foreign or defense policies. Most major bills are products of considerable compromising between Congress and the Executive Branch as well as within each branch.

Aaron Wildavsky has suggested that presidents are generally more successful with foreign and military policies than with domestic issues because Congress is responsive to a greater range of interest groups in the domestic arena than in international policymaking. Congress and the public may be more willing to defer to executive leadership over foreign and military policies because opponents of such policies normally are less organized, weaker, and provided with fewer resources to challenge an administration. Wildavsky's thesis of the "two presidencies" is supported by data from 1948 to 1964 showing that Congress approved 73 percent of all White House initiatives in defense and 59 percent of all foreign policy measures, but only 40 percent of presidential domestic proposals.[38]

Lance LeLoup and Steven Shull compared Wildavsky's findings with data from 1965 to 1975 and found that while presidential initiatives continued to fare better in military and foreign policymaking, the gap between the domestic and international presidencies had nar-

Table 3-2 **Boxscore of Presidential Initiatives**

YEAR	NO. SUBMITTED	NO. APPROVED	% APPROVED
1954	232	150	65
1955	207	96	46
1956	225	103	46
1957	206	76	37
1958	234	110	47
1959	228	93	41
1960	183	56	31
1961	355	172	48
1962	298	132	44
1963	401	109	27
1964	217	125	58
1965	469	323	69
1966	371	207	56
1967	431	205	48
1968	414	231	56
1969	171	55	32
1970	210	97	46
1971	202	40	20
1972	116	51	44
1973	183	57	31
1974 (Nixon)	97	33	34
1974 (Ford)	64	23	36
1975	156	45	29

SOURCE: George C. Edwards III, *Presidential Influence in Congress* (San Francisco: W. H. Freeman and Company, 1980), 14. Based on data in *Congressional Quarterly*. Used with permission of W. H. Freeman and Company Publishers.

rowed. During this ten-year period presidents were successful 61 percent of the time in defense initiatives, half the time in foreign policy, and 46 percent in domestic legislation.[39] The increase in success with domestic policies reflects the 1965–66 highwater mark of the Johnson administration's Great Society agenda. The LeLoup-Shull data suggest that presidents are not consistently successful in obtaining results from Congress, and that the approval rate since 1965 clearly has been declining.

Congressional Delegation of Authority

The U.S. Supreme Court has held that Congress cannot delegate legislative authority to the president. But this has not prevented Congress from delegating to the White House administrative and executive powers that are tantamount to legislative authority. Presidential legislative initiatives generally seek broad authority for Executive Branch officials, and federal executives are usually given flexibility in "legislating" the finer parts of a law through issuing regulations.

What Congress can give to presidents it can also take away or significantly restrict. Many legislative measures provide narrow statutory authority to the Executive Branch and include specific prohibitions and limitations on how policies are to be carried out. (We will examine in more detail later in this chapter two such legislative checks on the White House: the legislative veto and congressional oversight.) Congress frequently rewrites or revises the statutory bases of agencies, statutorily prescribes agency rules and guidelines, interprets and monitors agency regulations and directives, delegates authority directly to certain officials, and limits the president's authority to set policy for his agencies. Authority may be restricted for one or two years, and may be delegated to personnel outside the control of the president, such as regulatory commissioners or autonomous officials in agencies that function as commissions or public corporations.[40]

On occasion Congress has contributed to strengthening the president's hand by providing him with broad grants of authority to interpret legislation. For example, the Economic Stabilization Act of 1970 gave the president standby authority to impose wage and price controls, even though President Nixon at the time opposed the measure because he was against controls. (He surprised everyone by imposing wage and price controls on the economy a year later.)

Congress also has added to the president's powers by granting the Executive Branch clear-cut authority over new policy areas. The Atomic Energy Act, for example, placed responsibility for nuclear armaments and the peaceful development of nuclear energy under the president's jurisdiction. Congress enhanced the policy planning capability of the White House when it approved Nixon's 1971 reorganization converting the Bureau of the Budget into the Office of Management and Budget. (Presidents, in fact, became chief program planners and managers of the government as a result of congressional passage of the Budget and Accounting Act of 1921, which placed the federal budget process directly under the president's control and provided him with the capability of planning and administering broad programs of national policy.)

It is not unusual for presidents to ignore or to violate provisions of legislation passed by Congress. Nixon conducted clandestine military operations in Laos in 1971 in violation of the Cooper-Church Amendment forbidding the use of American ground forces in that country or in Thailand. And the Environmental Protection Agency interpreted Reagan's apparent lack of commitment to environmental safeguards as justification for not properly carrying out programs for cleaning up hazardous-waste landfills or in spending funds appropriated by Congress for various environmental projects.

Executive Orders

Presidents often issue on their own authority executive orders which have the impact of legislation or which later on may lead to congressional action. Such orders are issued in the course of administering the day-to-day operations of the government, but they frequently are used to establish new policies which go beyond implementation of existing statutes. For example, Kennedy issued an executive order requiring integration of public housing and elimination of discrimination in the sale of homes financed by the Veterans Administration or by Federal Housing Authority–backed loans. Johnson issued an executive order banning sex discrimination in federal employment or by federal contractors and subcontractors. Both orders were later incorporated into laws by Congress in the Civil Rights Acts of 1964 and 1968.

Treaty Power

If there is one formal power which provides the president with a considerable advantage over Congress, it is the treaty-making authority vested in the executive by the Constitution. Although subject to a two-thirds approval by the Senate, the treaty-making power enhances the president's overall influence over foreign policy, for it makes him a one-man distillation of national policy toward other political regimes.

The Executive Branch dominates the treaty-making process from initial negotiations to final drafting and submission to the Senate—a singular monopoly that stems from a precedent set by President Washington. He sought the Senate's advice on treaty negotiations with Indian tribes, but the Senate reacted by trying to monopolize the deliberations on the treaty, thus alienating Washington and causing him to withdraw in "sullen dignity."[41] Presidents have kept the power mostly to themselves ever since.

Political scientist Louis Fisher, who studied the legal and constitutional tensions between Congress and the presidency, insists that the framers of the Constitution never intended the treaty-making power to become a monopoly of presidents. The two branches were supposed to be inextricably linked by the declaration in the Constitution that the president "shall have power by and with the advice and consent of the Senate, to make treaties. . . ." Little advising takes place today before Congress is supposed to assent. Fisher believes the power never was intended to be divided into two distinct and sequential stages: the first involving unilateral executive negotiations and the second, Senate consideration.[42]

The Senate may refuse to ratify a treaty, as happened with the Treaty of Versailles formally ending World War I. The president may not even submit a treaty if chances for approval appear dim, as was the case with Carter's Strategic Arms Limitation Treaty (SALT-ii) signed in 1979 with Soviet President Leonid Brezhnev. Or the Senate may require considerable lobbying by the White House to obtain approval, as happened in 1978 with two treaties turning the Panama Canal over to Panama. Months of political bargaining and negotiating with Senators finally won Carter a narrow ratification victory, but the House came close to refusing to appropriate funds needed to carry out the treaties' provisions.

Executive Agreements

Presidents have increasingly turned to executive agreements instead of treaties to accomplish their foreign-policy objectives. Such agreements are made by presidents with other heads of state or national governments. Although the agreements do not require any kind of congressional assent, they usually require appropriations to be implemented. Roosevelt's brazen destroyers-for-bases deal with the British prior to American entry into World War ii is one of the more famous executive agreements. Others include the Yalta and Potsdam accords between the allies at the end of the war, the Vietnam peace agreement, Nixon's grain-sales deal with the Soviet Union in 1972, and Carter's Camp David peace accord between Egypt and Israel in 1978. The deal between the United States and Iran that ultimately secured release of fifty-two American hostages from Tehran in 1981 was an executive agreement negotiated by the Carter administration.

Executive agreements evolved out of simple expediency in dealing with other nations. Between 1789 and 1976 the United States entered into 1202 treaties and 8473 executive agreements.[43] Although the president in this way sidesteps Senate approval, he runs the risk that Congress may refuse to appropriate funds to carry out the agreement. Congress, however, does not lightly reject executive agreements. To do so impugns the reputation of the United States, or at least raises serious doubts about the authority of the president over his own government.

There is another element of risk in forsaking the treaty process for executive agreements. Such agreements are binding only on the administration making them, and once a president leaves office, agreements which he has entered into may be ignored by his successor. Reagan, for example, hesitated for several weeks before deciding to honor provisions of the agreement Carter made with Iran to secure freedom for the U.S. embassy hostages.

To ward off strong opposition later, presidents often consult with Congress prior to making an executive agreement. The president may even submit an executive agreement to Congress, as Nixon did in 1972 for his trade agreement with the Soviet Union because congressional approval was required for credits and tariff concessions needed to carry out provisions of the accord. The Senate served notice it would block legislation to implement the trade pact if the Soviet Union did not lift oppressive exit fees for Jews and others seeking to emigrate from the Soviet Union.[44]

Presidents claim their authority to make executive agreements has a constitutional basis, and federal courts have upheld the authority although limiting it in certain cases.[45] Typically, a president often turns to existing statutes to provide justification. For example, many of the agreements between the United States and South Vietnam from 1965 to 1974 were justified under the authority granted to the president by the Gulf of Tonkin resolution. Passed by both houses, this resolution provided the president with "all necessary measures to repeal any armed attack against the forces of the United States . . . [and] to assist any member or . . . state of the Southeast Asia Collective Defense Treaty requesting assistance. . . ."[46]

Impoundments

Presidents may try to weaken or destroy the intent of Congress by impounding funds appropriated through legislation. Presidents as far back as Jefferson claimed a constitutional basis for the authority to impound, either by rescinding or canceling funds appropriated by Congress, or by deferring spending to some future date. Such power traditionally was used cautiously to avoid a confrontation with Congress or the federal courts. Many impoundments were only temporary, ordered because of improprieties in a program's administration; usually the funds were later released. Congress provided presidents with the statutory authority to impound funds in cases where recipients of federal funds, such as school districts or state and local governments, failed to comply with federal laws, guidelines, or court rulings. Truman, Eisenhower, and Kennedy all impounded additional defense funds added to their budgets by Congress, while Johnson impounded funds added to an agricultural appropriations measure.

Nixon, however, used impoundments to terminate close to $19 billion worth of programs mandated by Congress for urban needs, social welfare, health care, and poverty programs. Nixon claimed a right to *not* spend funds he had not requested from Congress! Other impoundments were justified on the basis that his budget contained requests to cancel or rescind funds, and he should not be required to spend appropriations until Congress had considered his rescissions. Federal courts found his position untenable in almost every one of the cases brought by groups seeking a release of the funds, and in several decisions, the courts ruled the president's budget had no constitutional or statutory standing but was merely a recommendation.[47]

Executive Privilege

Congress has the constitutional authority to oversee implementation of legislation and to make certain the Executive Branch is carrying out statutes according to the intent of Congress. This requires that Congress be able to obtain information from the executive. Although the Constitution does not formally provide for the power of investigation, the Supreme Court has upheld such authority whenever Congress attempted to obtain information needed to legislate or to oversee the administration of statutes.[48]

Presidents for their part often decline to provide information to Congress on the grounds that their authority to act in the nation's interest, to conduct foreign affairs, or to serve as commander in chief gives them the right to withhold certain kinds of information. Thus have presidents since Washington invoked executive privilege by refusing to divulge a wide range of information upon request of Congress. Washington refused to honor congressional requests for his private papers touching on foreign policy or treaty negotiations. Claiming executive privilege, Jefferson declined to appear in person at Aaron Burr's trial. Up until 1973 the doctrine prevailed that the president was personally immune from judicial procedures unless impeached and convicted, although his subordinates were not.[49]

Normally, however, when conflict arose between the two branches over the disclosure of information, negotiations resolved the differences and the doctrine enjoyed a kind of common-law status. But a serious constitutional conflict arose over executive privilege during Nixon's Watergate problems, and the crisis was solved only with the president's resignation in August 1974. Testimony at the Senate Watergate hearings in the summer of 1973 revealed that Nixon had secretly tape-recorded conversations in the Oval Office since 1971. A special Select Senate Committee on Presidential Campaign Practices investigating Watergate, as well as Special Prosecutor Archibald Cox, who had been appointed independent investigator into the crime and its alleged coverup, both sought the president's tapes as evidence. Nixon claimed executive privilege, arguing that he alone had the right to decide what information would be turned over to either the Senate committee or the federal prosecutor.

A federal Court of Appeals rejected the president's claim of total immunity on the basis that the impeachment clause of the Constitution provided the only legal means for investigating a president; when a strong case could be made, such as the one made by the special prosecutor, that criminal evidence might be involved, the president must provide the evidence to the court. The decision recognized the existence of executive privilege for certain kinds of information, but took the position that such claims are testable in court. After the president failed to convince the special prosecutor to give way on his demands, Nixon fired Cox. But the U.S. Supreme Court upheld the Court of Appeals ruling in July 1974 in the case *U.S.* v. *Nixon;* two weeks later the president was compelled to resign because certain tapes revealed proof of his involvement in efforts to cover up the Watergate crimes.

Presidential use of executive privilege against requests by Congress or federal courts for information were relatively rare before the Nixon administration. Kennedy and Johnson each invoked executive privilege only twice. Nixon personally claimed it four times between 1969 and 1973; his subordinates in the Executive Branch used the claim more than two hundred times in refusing to provide Congress with requested information. Nixon held that the doctrine even extended to his right to refuse to permit his White House aides or any individual in the Executive Branch to testify before Congress. This was a potentially serious problem since White House staffs and executive personnel have been heavily involved in policymaking in recent years.

The *U.S.* v. *Nixon* decision provided the first constitutional recognition of the right of executive privilege, but the right was not so absolute as Nixon had maintained. The ruling left standing an as yet undefined but potentially large area of presidential confidentiality in military, foreign-policy, or national security matters; this provides the White House with a strong lever in dealing with congressional requests for information. Whether or not the president enjoys such privileged immunity from congressional investigations was not fully clarified in the Watergate tapes case, but remains an important constitutional question.

Appointment and Removal Powers

The president has broad powers to appoint officials to top executive posts in the federal government, but many of these appointments require confirmation by the Senate. Congress decides by law which positions aside from those explicitly established by the Constitution, such as federal court judges, ambassadors, and consuls, require senatorial confirmation. The director and deputy director of the Office of Management and Budget, for example, were made subject to confirmation from 1974 on, even though confirmation had never been required for the director of the forerunner to OMB, the Bureau of the Budget.

The Senate is normally receptive to most presidential appointments, holding that a chief executive ought to be allowed to have his own choices in the matter of who will serve him. A study by political scientist Donald C. Tannenbaum showed that from 1945 to 1975 only 30 of 4284 presidential nominations to top federal government, military, and judicial posts were not confirmed. Only one cabinet-level appointment out of 107 was turned down, and one sub-cabinet appointment out of 1024.[50]

The Senate, however, occasionally can act tough on nominations to controversial or sensitive posts. For example, Carter tried to make Theodore Sorensen director of the Central Intelligence Agency. But the nomination met with resistance in the Senate because Sorensen had lifted confidential records from the White House after Kennedy's assassination in order to make use of them without proper clearance in his book about Kennedy. Eventually Carter had to withdraw Sorensen's nomination and replace him with someone more acceptable to the intelligence community. Reagan's nomination of Ernest Lefever to be assistant secretary of state for human rights also foundered when there surfaced in the nation's press statements and writings by Lefever indicating he was willing to support regimes that had violated human rights. (Lefever suggested during the hearings that communists were behind the opposition to his appointment.)

The Senate has grown uneasy at times about the rubber-stamp reputation of its confirmation procedures, particularly in the aftermath of the Bert Lance affair. Lance was approved without much questioning as Carter's director of OMB in 1977; six months after the perfunctory Senate hearings, he was discovered to have been involved in questionable, if not illegal, banking practices in Georgia. Lance resigned, but not without leaving the Senate's reputation for careful consideration of presidential appointments about as tarnished as his own banking record.

Appointments to the federal judiciary receive more rigorous hearings by the Senate. Of twenty nominations for justice of the Supreme Court during the thirty years studied by Tannenbaum, three were turned down, two of them consecutively. The Senate refused to confirm Judge Clement Haynesworth of the U.S. Fourth Circuit Court of Appeals in 1969 following his appointment by Nixon. A few months later the Senate rejected even more roundly Judge G. Harrold Carswell of the Fifth Circuit Court of Appeals, this time on the grounds that he was not qualified to sit on the High Court because of racist statements in public.

Supreme Court nominees receive tougher scrutiny from the Senate today because the court realizes that a justice will be around long after the president has left office, and that the future course of legislation may well be affected by the appointment of justices with well-formed ideological or policy outlooks.

PRESIDENTIAL RESOURCES AND TACTICS

Formal powers and statutory expansion of the president's legislative role count for less than the resources a president can bring to bear on the legislative process. Formal powers guarantee certain advantages, but they do not explain why some presidents are successful legislative leaders and others are not. According to Light, many students of the presidency confuse formal powers with influence, blurring distinctions between a president's prerogatives and the intangible factors that determine how well he does with Congress.[51]

The resources available to a president are his personality, his political skill and experience, his ability to communicate, his popularity, and his party ties. The president's unique status provides him with yet another resource that affects his ability to establish the national agenda, to control the timing of policy initiatives, and to dominate the national political news or consciousness. All of these resources, however, work both ways. While they may add immensely to his authority, they may just as well detract from it, for there is no guarantee that becoming president automatically improves the quality of any one or several of the resources or his ability to employ them.

Personality

Presidential personality has been a subject of immense fascination for scholars and the public, especially since Nixon. Does an understanding of an incumbent's personality offer clues as to how successful he will be as president? Are there certain traits that correlate with legislative legerdemain? A leading proponent of the thesis that personality is the key to presidential performance is political scientist James David Barber, whose *Presidential Character: Predicting Presidential Performance* has been a popular classic since it appeared in 1969.[52]

Barber's argument holds that the kind of president a person becomes depends on important early character traits, his outlook toward others, and the style in which he handles his duties. The ideal president is one who has a secure ego, who can relate to others with some degree of trust and understanding, and who relishes power not to enhance his ego but for what it can produce. Such a personality—an "active-positive" type—is far preferable to the "active-negative" type—who is compulsive about activity and needs power to compensate for ego anxieties. The latter type is ambitious but unsure, and views life as a struggle to seize and hold power against countless enemies who are out to "get" him.

Barber's model does not help explain presidential success with Congress. Several presidents have accomplished far-reaching legislative programs of reform, even though they were classified as active-negatives in his book—for example, Wilson and Johnson. Two presidents who were active-positives—Truman and Kennedy—did not enjoy tremendous luck with Congress, although FDR, an outstanding example of the strong personality, did. Nonetheless, a personality explanation may be more valid than Barber's own evidence suggests. Both Nixon and Carter disdained Congress, and were suspicious of legislators. The president who is self-assured yet friendly and open to others, who is capable of extending trust and consideration, probably will enjoy better relations with Congress than one who isolates himself imperiously behind the White House walls.

Much of Reagan's remarkable success with Congress during his first few months was due to his personality. Meeting frequently with members of both parties, he proved a sharp contrast to his predecessor as he charmed Representatives and Senators with his warmth and sense of humor. Even his chief protagonist, Democratic House Speaker Tip O'Neill, admitted, "I *like* the guy. He's got a lot of class." Other legislators admitted that it was hard to resist Reagan's entreaties because he was so genuinely personable, even though concern over Reagan's domestic spending cutbacks and demands for increased defense spending generated considerable opposition after his first eight months in office.

Public Prominence

Perhaps the greatest resource available to a president is his standing with the American public. Members of Congress must constantly be concerned with the president's current status in the polls. Political scientist George Edwards has argued that members of Congress anticipate the public's reactions to their behavior toward the president and his policies.[53] Members of Congress defeated in 1974 had supported Richard Nixon significantly more than did those who won reelection, according to one study. Other researchers have found that the public assesses Congress in terms of the public's evaluation of the president, while Edwards reports that still other findings show a direct connection between the president's popularity and public voting for Congress.[54]

Whenever congressional opposition to White House legislative initiatives hardens, a president today heads for a TV studio in the White House to take his case directly to the American electorate (see Chapter 9). Television provides the president with a substantial advantage over Congress, for major policy speeches may be witnessed by upward of 75 million viewers. But the use of television to advance the president's legislative agenda or to rally public support can be a two-edged sword. When the president goes public, he literally puts his neck on the public chopping block by identifying himself squarely with an issue or bill that usually has stirred vigorous opposition in Congress. His appeal may gain a flood of letters, telephone calls, and telegrams to members of Congress urging them to back the president. But if he fails to win his program or if it does not work, he has focused full responsibility on himself.

The margin of a president's electoral victory usually has only a slight impact on congressional support. The president elected by a narrow margin will have a hard time convincing Congress he possesses much support for his programs. Yet one who wins in a landslide may enjoy only marginal advantages if his victory is not paralleled by a corresponding sweep by his party of seats in Congress, as Nixon's massive victory in 1972 proved. Public support and electoral margin may best be understood in terms of a threshold effect. As long as a president remains at a specific level of public approval—50 percent or more—public support has only a slight effect on congressional responsiveness. If he drops below that threshold, public opinion begins to have a significant impact in eroding support. Because huge electoral margins do not necessarily result in additional party strength in Congress, the effects cannot be measured, although it is known that the lower the margin of victory and the less the opportunity for party changes in seats, the less political influence will there be for the president.[55]

Most members of Congress respond to the president's prestige, however, particularly among voters in their respective districts or states. A president who wants to increase congressional support for his programs is dependent on his popularity with the electorate, but the lack of presidential popularity significantly reduces his influence among legislators.[56] The support of a member of Congress is mostly dependent on whether both the legislator and the president benefit from a measure. Although public approval of a president may be high, it does not necessarily guarantee support, but an absence of public support can certainly damage the president's influence.[57]

Reputation

Politicians who share power do what they think they must, according to Neustadt. Members of the Washington community are "compelled to watch the president for reasons not of pleasure but vocation." Those whom a president "would persuade must be convinced in their own minds that he has the skill and will enough to *use* his advantages."[58]

Reputation thus becomes another essential resource for any president who would exert influence over the policy process, for reputation is one of the most valued currencies in official Washington.

FDR liked to ask aides for "something I can veto" to impress on members of Congress his power and will.[59] The president's ability to influence Congress depends greatly on maximizing the uncertainty of his opposition. Legislators as well as other political actors must believe that punishment follows from transgressions against the White House, but they must never be allowed to know in advance the nature of that punishment. Uncertainty in the cost-benefits calculation discourages some opposition before it even arises:

> *The greatest danger to a president's potential influence . . . is not the show of incapacity he makes today, but its apparent kinship to what happened yesterday, last month, last year. For if his failures seem to form a pattern, the consequence is bound to be a loss of faith in his effectiveness "next time."*[60]

Presidential reputations once were built up over time, mostly through personal relationshps with legislators and politicians. Now the personal element may be virtually absent and a reputation can be established much more quickly through the use of mass communications. This puts a president at the mercy of forces somewhat beyond his control, for his image becomes as important as his real personality. His image is increasingly dependent on how the national news media view him or how his White House staff projects him through public relations. Reputations formed on the basis of media images are not necessarily inaccurate. Former CBS anchor Walter Cronkite, who knew a number of presidents personally, suggests that the image of a president as projected on television is usually not far from a true reflection of his personality. "Nixon was a political schemer and it showed," Cronkite said. "Johnson was an overbearing man and that came across. Carter was inexperienced and uncomfortable dealing with anyone outside his Georgia circle. And that's the way he came across in the media."[61]

Carter's reputation particularly suffered for, as Neustadt has suggested, nothing is more debilitating to a president than the impression that he is incompetent. Carter's lack of experience in Washington enabled him to win the 1976 election, but his legislative skills were nonexistent. His weaknesses were constantly magnified by the Washington press corps, which quickly adopted the perspective that most policy failures or congressional inactions could be explained by Carter's incompetence and inexperience. The media contributed to a self-fulfilling cycle of executive-legislative hostility and mutual disrespect which only served to further isolate the White House from Capitol Hill. Reports of Carter's fumbling attempts at congressional relations only decreased his influence with both houses and party leaders, adding to the erosion of any influence he might have developed with Congress. As his reputation suffered, the perception of his incompetence increased, leading to greater resistance and stubbornness on the part of Congress. Shortly after Carter's 1980 defeat, *New York Times* veteran columnist James Reston asserted that "without a doubt," the press was primarily responsible for destroying Carter's political reputation.[62]

Legislative Skills

Johnson once explained that there was but one way for a president to deal with Congress:

> . . . and that is continuously, incessantly, and without interruption. If it's really going to work, the relationship between the president and Congress has got to be almost incestuous. He's got to know them even better than they know themselves. And then, on the basis of this knowledge, he's got to build a system that stretches from the cradle to the grave, from the moment a bill is introduced to the moment it is officially enrolled as the law of the land.[63]

Legislative skill involves more than knowing Congress, however. The president who is legislatively skilled senses when the times are ripe for a program. He anticipates problems and needs sufficiently to preempt Congress, and is careful to build a broad base of public support. But he is attentive to working closely with legislative leaders and key committee members to eliminate as many roadblocks as possible before a bill reaches critical stages of consideration. He tries to build a network of support that includes cabinet secretaries, agency officials, and experts, and that involves leaders from interest groups affected by the proposal. Most important, however, he is aware that the success of his efforts rests heavily on reflecting firmness while appearing to be flexible.

John F. Kennedy had served in the House and Senate, but he lacked the skills in dealing with members of Congress that Johnson had developed over the years. JFK had little of LBJ's sense of legislative timing or protocol. Johnson believed that a "measure must be sent to the Hill at exactly the right moment," and that moment depended on momentum, on the availability of sponsors in the right place at the right time, and on opportunities for neutralizing the opposition.[64] Kennedy created a climate of high expectations with his promise to get the country moving again, but he failed to gain many of his legislative proposals because he misread the opposition, was overly cautious when confronting opponents, and failed to line up the support of groups essential to getting his programs through Congress.

Johnson succeeded with the measures which had eluded Kennedy precisely because Johnson judged the political environment to be more responsive to the proposals in 1964 and 1965, and because he worked closely with interest groups and Congress. For example, recognizing that Kennedy had lost a full legislative year in his pursuit of federal aid to education, Johnson refused to let an education bill go to the Hill until the White House had the backing of major interest groups representing public as well as parochial education. Kennedy lost on education because he had refused to include Catholic schools. In this way he alienated the National Catholic Welfare Conference, which was able to prevail on key members of Congress to vote against the administration's measure. (Kennedy may have been concerned that supporting the parochial school position would stir up the old issue of his own Catholicism once more.)[65]

Skill may not always translate directly into policy achievement, but a lack of skill can surely damage the president's public as well as political reputation, in turn creating a widespread and perhaps politically fatal perception that the president is weak or does not know what he is doing. Every president must be concerned with his congressional liaison efforts or what less fastidious observers call "presidential lobbying."

Congressional Liaison

Kennedy may have lacked the legislative skills of a Lyndon Johnson, but he was responsible for shaping a legislative liaison office which under Johnson became the most proficient in modern times. Headed by Lawrence O'Brien, the Office of Congressional Relations was the tip of a White House legislative operation that included liaison staffs in federal departments and major agencies. Johnson viewed these lower-echelon liaison staffs as the most important positions in his government. After the 1964 election he instructed his cabinet chief to select top candidates to handle the liaison between their departments and Congress.[66]

Liaison activities now are fully institutionalized, and members of Congress expect to share in White House policy operations, to receive favors from the president, and to be actively involved in the president's legislative agenda.[67] Liaison, however, is only as good as the president and his closest advisers are willing to make it because the president must back up his legislative assistants and honor their commitments if he is to succeed in working with Congress. Nixon's liaison staff included first-rate professionals, but they were constantly undermined by White House assistants like H. R. Haldeman, Nixon's chief of staff, or by John Ehrlichman and other assistants from the Oval Office. Nixon's first legislative liaison chief, the veteran Bryce Harlow, resigned after two years because of a lack of communication or consultation with Nixon, as well as because of difficulties with Haldeman and Ehrlichman. Clark MacGregor, Harlow's successor, was quickly rendered ineffective by Nixon's vitriolic attacks on the Ninety-first Congress. ("[T]his Congress will be remembered and remarked upon in history not so much for what it did, but for what it failed to do," Nixon once bitterly declared. The nation had watched a body that "seemingly had lost the capacity to decide and the will to act."[68]) MacGregor too departed within two years, to be succeeded by William E. Timmons, who proceeded to denounce Congress as "miserable," "irresponsible," "appalling," and "cynical."[69] After the 1972 election, what was left of Nixon's legislative liaison efforts fell almost exclusively to Haldeman, Ehrlichman, and other top White House aides.

Carter's legislative liaison efforts also left a great deal to be desired. Carter's staff was, like the president, totally inexperienced in congressional matters. Liaison was turned over to Frank Moore, who had been liaison chief with the Georgia legislature when Carter was governor of Georgia. Moore had never worked in Washington or on Capitol Hill. He failed to return telephone calls to members of Congress; he appeared insensitive to the political needs of legislators; and he and his staff virtually ignored the all-important consultations early in the administration when the president was attempting to sell his policy agenda to Congress and the nation.

Reagan's legislative relations were quite successful at first, largely because of Reagan's personal style, but also because of his staff's extensive experience with Congress, the White House, and the Executive Branch. Anxious to avoid the mistakes of Carter's liaison operation, Reagan's staff, under the direction of another veteran, Max Friedersdorf (Ford's liaison chief), held to the lobbyist's maxim that "If you take care of the little things, the big things will take care of themselves."[70] The staff knew what brand of cigars House Speaker Tip O'Neill smoked. They saw that he and other congressional leaders were invited to an "impromptu" seventieth birthday party for Reagan. They did not ask a House member from a "district where cows outnumber people to vote against raising dairy price supports," as one Washington journalist noted.[71] Reagan's staff promptly returned telephone calls, and White House breakfasts for members of Congress were paid for by the president. Aides provided legislators with sets of cuff links bearing the presidential seal (each pair cost about $5), and tickets for the presidential box at the Kennedy Center for the Performing Arts. The most talented liaison staff will not succeed, however, if the president's timing in both formulating and carrying through with his agenda is bad.

Timing

Johnson exhorted his congressional liaison staff shortly after his 1965 inauguration to "get all my legislative proposals during this session, *now!*"

> *Every day that I am in office, I lose part of my power. Every day that I use that power, I have less power left. You must get this legislation through immediately. I want you to go out and work! I want you to bowl with those congressmen. I want you to talk with those congressmen. I want you to sleep with the congressmen if you have to. I want you to get this legislation through now—while I have that power.*[72]

A president is elected for four years. But if he does not establish momentum for his legislative agenda during the first few months while he still enjoys a honeymoon with the public and mass media, he will find his opportunities quickly extinguished as the inevitable policy conflicts begin to fragment his party, Congress, and the executive agencies.

The argument that Kennedy would have eventually achieved his legislative agenda had he had longer than "a thousand days" needs to be considered in the context of timing. It may not be realistic to assume that he would have accomplished more had he lived, given the fact that he lost Congress during the critical early months of his term. Much of Carter's failure with Congress stemmed from his bungling of his legislative agenda during the early months. Reagan's success in achieving the largest budget and tax cuts in history was largely due to his skill and care in handling these policies from the beginning of his administration.

Congress functions with an entirely different political clock than the White House. Many members of Congress are careerists—they have been around for a long time and will probably be around long after a president leaves. The legislative process is ponderous, decentralized, and vulnerable to checkmates and vetoes at nearly every stage of the process. The sluggish pace at which Congress deals with legislation means that many programs on a president's agenda may take a long time to be passed, and that many will never make it through at all. Congress not only disposes, it opposes as well, and its opposition usually increases with the length of time over which legislation moves.

Party Leadership

Party support is the single most important resource a president has going for him in Congress. Whatever influence he might bring to bear on his agenda depends primarily on party ties. But therein lies an important explanation of why the presidency has become a no-win proposition, for as Light suggests, "Parties now provide only a shallow base of influence in the legislative process. Presidents must still turn to parties, but parties no longer supply the whip."[73]

Legislative success is almost totally dependent on keeping members of the president's own party in the fold, while gaining bipartisan support from as many members of the opposition as possible. Although party seats do not guarantee automatic support, they are essential if an administration is to win crucial tests. White House staffs view congressional parties as more stable than public opinion; even when a president is slipping in the polls, he can count on a fairly stable base of party support in Congress. This support, however, generally declines over the course of an administration, paralleling the downward trend in public support for the president, although perhaps not as pronouncedly or as rapidly.[74]

Edwards' study of presidential influence over Congress confirms the importance of party support between 1953 and 1978. Members of the president's own party supported him more than members of the opposition party, with the one exception of foreign policy, for which House Democrats gave more solid support to Republican presidents than Republican Representatives. Republican presidents generally take an activist, internationalist position in foreign policy—an outlook now shared more by House Democrats than Republicans.[75] The presidential party is overall a strong force in foreign policy because members of Congress generally feel free from constituency pressures in global policies, and the president's greater personal responsibility for foreign policy leads them to support him to avoid undermining his influence with other nations.

Presidential party support is less certain in domestic-policy areas, particularly those dealing with civil rights, social welfare spending, agricultural assistance, and energy. A member of Congress is more likely to bow to constituent pressures or interests in these policy areas; when there is a conflict between constituents and administration programs, a legislator invariably goes with his or her voters because the desire to be reelected is usually stronger than the wish to act in the national interest.[76]

Party members in Congress usually agree with the policy stands of their president because no one wants to embarrass the president or jeopardize his or her reelection chances. There may be sufficient partisan loyalty in some members to encourage them to back the president even when they are less than enthusiastic about his programs. Partisanship is encouraged by the fact that no one likes to be cut off from access to White House social life, from access to the president, or from favorable relations with him.

If parties provide such support, why are presidents not more successful as legislative leaders? One obvious explanation is that we have had a divided government for all but four of the twelve years between 1969 and 1983. As a result, several presidents lacked sufficient party strength in Congress to begin with. Even if he has a majority, party leaders in Congress find it increasingly difficult to develop a consensus for administration programs since their power is now mostly limited to coordinating the legislative process. Party-support scores fail to show the significant differences that now disrupt party unity over issues, as a growing number of nonparty actors and forces intrude into the legislative process.

As noted in the preceding chapter, presidents have not been highly successful in helping their party to win congressional seats in midterm elections. Political scientist Walter Dean Burnham suggests that incumbents are now immune from such electoral effects as a presidential landslide because of weakened party identification in the electorate and the significant advantages of incumbency.[77] In seventeen elections between 1946 and 1978, 91 percent of all House incumbents seeking reelection were successful, while success for Senators was only 68 percent.[78] House seats have become much safer as the result of a decline in the percentage of electorally competitive districts since the mid-1950s. Thus the coattails effect has been virtually eliminated. Members of Congress are now more responsive to public opinion and conscious of the need to provide constituent services than they are of a need to back the president. These trends parallel significant changes within Congress itself that affect the president's capacity to lead.

CONGRESSIONAL CONSTRAINTS ON THE CHIEF LEGISLATOR

When the Ninety-third Congress convened in January 1973, there was a widespread fear among its members that the nation faced a constitutional crisis of the first magnitude. Nixon had just won a monumental landslide reelection, which he interpreted as a public mandate for his policies and leadership. The *New York Times* predicted that the administration would move quickly to consolidate its power to threaten what was left of the checks-and-balances system.[79] Nixon refused to consult with Congress before expanding the nation's military commitment from one nation to another in Southeast Asia. His impoundment of billions of dollars appropriated by Congress, his unlimited use of executive privilege to maintain administration secrets, and his attempts to silence opposition by the press and dissidents all pointed ominously to the threat of a presidential dictatorship.

When the Ninety-seventh Congress convened in January 1981, the question no longer was could Congress restrain an imperial president, but could any president muster sufficient authority to make the system work so that Congress and the Executive Branch could tackle the major issues and problems confronting the nation. Congress had changed from a collection of weaklings who let the president kick sand in their faces to a fiercely independent and stubborn-minded gathering of 535 individuals and nearly three hundred committees and subcommittees. The "New Congress" was often openly hostile to the president, and less inclined to accept direction from the White House. At the same time, in both houses the authority of leaders was significantly curbed by reforms aimed at opening up Congress to greater influence by rank-and-file members.

A popular explanation for the renewed vigor of Congress in the 1970s holds that it was a direct result of Watergate and of Nixon's abuses of power. This is an oversimplification, however, because other important developments that predated Nixon's administration also contributed to the changes in Congress. These developments were related to the increasing fragmentation of the political system, to a breakdown in political ties between members in each house, and to a diminished capacity of the Executive Branch to dominate the policy process.

The decline in party strength and changes in the electoral system have been discussed in Chapter 2. Many members of Congress were winning office increasingly without party support by the 1960s, and most felt little loyalty to party or administration. Democratic House Leader Jim Wright described the newer members of Congress in the 1970s as "more concerned about image and less about substance."[80] This might be harsh, however, because members of Congress today increasingly are caught up in their own narrow issue concerns—but on a parochial rather than a national basis.

Issues and problems dominating the nation's agenda in the 1970s and 1980s were different from those of previous decades. They related more to scarcity than abundance, and to insuring fairness in application rather than to the expansion of new programs. Declining federal resources, greater competition for energy supplies and other raw materials, technological and educational disparities in the labor force, and concern over industrial and economic competition among states and entire regions came to preoccupy decision makers and to undermine older party coalitions. (Chapters 6, 7, and 8 will examine these new political challenges in greater detail.)

All of these changes were reflected in Congress by changes that contributed to increasing autonomy within the membership of both houses and decreasing cooperation between the legislative and executive branches.

The Dispersion of Power

Power in Congress in the first two thirds of this century primarily rested with powerful legislative leaders in each house as well as with a number of senior committee chairpersons who possessed virtual life-or-death control over the flow of legislation. The old power configuration was broken during the 1960s, and especially during the 1970s, by the replacement of many of the older members by new "Young Turks," many of whom insisted on a greater individual share of authority. The last five elections have resulted in a sea change in the membership of both houses; the new faces in Congress are today much less amenable to political direction but far more interested in their own policy agendas.

At the same time power in Congress gradually was dispersed from the old committee kingpins of the past to a growing number of subcommittees. Subcommittees first appeared in the Senate as early as 1946, and shortly thereafter in the House. By the mid-1950s, about half of all legislative hearings in both chambers were held by subcommittees. By 1980 that proportion had reached more than 80 percent as the number of subcommittees in Congress exceeded 260. Reforms of the 1970s that undermined the veto power of committee chairpersons provided these subcommittees with independent staffing and funding; the result was that these subcommittees proliferated even faster. The legislative process was marked not only by greater independence in the committee structure but also by much more fragmentation. The power of standing committees was diluted, and subcomittees became "where the action is."[81]

The White House must now confront an incredibly complicated jumble of overlapping jurisdictions and ambitious power brokers in dealing with Congress. In the past a president or his legislative aides knew which committee leaders or key members had to be pampered in order to move the president's agenda along. The president often could rely on influential party leaders in each house to help. Now legislation is typically scattered across a number of jurisdictions, and White House appeals must be directed to the lowliest freshman member in Congress because of the importance of his or her vote in subcommittee; occasionally this is because the neophyte member of Congress may be leading the fight for or against a measure. The *Congressional Quarterly Almanac* observed of this development:

Instead of bargaining with a handful of House and Senate . . . leaders and committee chairmen during a cozy White House luncheon, a president now had to cut a bevy of rival subcommittee chairmen into the deal. And even if an agreement emerged, a president had no guarantee it would not unravel the next day if a few freshmen Democrats joined with the Republicans to oppose it in favor of their own ideas.[82]

Congressional Expertise and Information

Individual members—even freshmen—feel more competent to challenge or battle wits with the White House because of the growth in congressional staffs, both for legislators and for committees and subcommittees. The total number of staff employed by Congress increased from 4300 in 1957 to nearly 12,000 in 1980. Another 20,000 or more work in such legislative service organizations as the Congressional Research Service, the General Accounting Office, and the Congressional Budget Office.

Congress tends to hire generalists who may develop some expertise in particular fields. But compared to their counterparts in the Executive Branch, these generalists are amateurs.[83] Political scientist Hugh Heclo, however, describes them as generally "bright, often remarkably young technocrats who are almost indistinguishable from . . . specialists in the executive branch."[84] Whatever their qualifications, such assistants have encouraged the spirit of independence and brashness of many members of Congress who now feel that they are as well prepared as the president to tackle major policy problems.

Different Constituencies

Another immense handicap to the president is, ironically, his greatest asset as chief legislator: he represents the collective interests of the American people. This may gain him considerable national attention and maybe even public gratitude, but it does not win ball games with Congress. For individual members of Congress are able to resist the collective interest or national consensus and still come out on top.

Americans venerate the presidency, and we are inclined to put a new incumbent briefly on a pedestal. But we turn one after another out of office with predictable regularity. The U.S. Congress, in contrast, enjoys far less public esteem, affection, or attention, but rarely is an incumbent defeated for reelection. Representatives and Senators have been caught in scandals that would destroy the public reputation of many a civic leader, but voters soundly reelect most of them out of appreciation for all they have done for the folks back home. Images of Congress as an institution are typically unflattering. Although public-opinion polls consistently show Congress ranking low in trust and esteem, individual legislators are held in high regard for their constituent services. A typical reelection appeal is "Congressman So-and-So Delivers!"[85] Indeed, members of Congress often run for Congress by running against Congress or the president (a derivation of the current practice of presidential candidates running against government while seeking its highest office).

Samuel Patterson notes that members of Congress run on behalf of:

> . . . *solutions to a host of national problems—solutions for which they cannot be held accountable as merely individual members of a collective body. Incumbents have acquired very handsome resources for use in their districts, and with these they present themselves as helping the district, as responsible for the distributive largesse of the national welfare state, and as struggling faithfully, if helplessly, against great national crises, evils, and policy problems.*[86]

A member of Congress is an obscure figure compared to the president, but the legislator can satisfy many specific needs of his or her constituents and let the chips fall where they may on larger, national issues. In fact, most legislators can usually act without their constituents knowing what they are doing, much less caring. A reason for this is that most people get their information about what is going on in Washington, D.C., through national TV network news, and rarely is an individual legislator spotlighted. We will consider the implications of this more fully in Chapter 9 when we take up the role of the mass media in the presidency. For now, it is enough to say that presidents are constantly in the public limelight on national policy matters. Since the more typical result is failure, compromise, or sluggish action, the White House frequently appears to be "on hold"—in the position of constantly trying but rarely succeeding.

Political commentator Eric L. Davis has found that members of Congress increasingly value the goal of seeking reelection through constituency service. This has an adverse effect on a president's legislative agenda because the congressperson can be reelected primarily on the basis of the benefits provided his or her district, rather than on support offered to the president's programs.[87]

Congressional scholar Richard Fenno believes that members of Congress pursue various goals, but primarily seek to acquire power in the committee system, to make good public policy, and to provide constituency services. The making of policy, however, is a distinctly secondary consideration because the typical member of the House, in particular, must constantly be concerned with reelection prospects. "He first asks himself what his constituents want or what actions on behalf of his constituents will help to reelect him. He then pursues [these] policies—by seeking membership on [a] relevant committee."[88]

A member of Congress in the 1980s can no longer afford to emphasize the development of *new* policies so much as the protection of already existing policies that benefit constituents. The proliferation of subcommittees and greater autonomy from centralized party leadership mean that each legislator now feels freer to subject presidential initiatives to greater scrutiny and criticism.

CONGRESSIONAL COUNTERATTACKS ON EXECUTIVE PREROGATIVES

Since 1972 Congress has attempted to recoup some of the momentum which had shifted from Capitol Hill to 1600 Pennsylvania Avenue with measures designed to limit the president's discretionary authority while increasing Congress's own.

In 1972 Congress passed the Case Act requiring the president to report any executive agreement within sixty days unless national security was involved. The War Powers Act of 1973 attempted to restrain presidents from unilaterally committing armed forces abroad without consulting Congress and obtaining a declaration of war. Should the president actually dispatch troops to foreign soil, he would be required to pull them out within sixty days unless war was declared, and he would have an additional thirty days to complete troop withdrawals.

Congress also challenged the practice of allowing presidents broad discretionary powers whenever a national emergency is declared. The National Emergency Act of 1976 provided a system for presidents to end national emergencies. But any emergency proclamation automatically from now on ends after one year unless the president informs Congress within ninety days before the emergency is due to expire that he needs to continue the declaration. Congress may question the president as to why any state of emergency lasting longer than a year needs to continue, or Congress can terminate the emergency by a concurrent resolution.

During the 1970s and early 1980s Congress increasingly turned to the legislative veto to frustrate presidential policy leadership. The legislative veto permitted one or both houses of Congress to cancel presidential or executive agency actions whenever both or occasionally only one house disapproved of the way a law was being carried out. The legislative veto originated in 1932 when Congress delegated to President Hoover authority to reorganize the government, but retained the right to veto his plan if a majority of legislators objected. It did not become a nuisance to the presidency until Nixon's administration when the device became a major weapon to counter abuses of executive authority.

The War Powers Act was the best-known example of legislation with built-in veto provisions, but congressional vetoes were also included in legislation restricting the president's authority to sell arms to other countries, to restrict exports of American technology as well as nuclear fuel, and to force the president to spend funds on specific programs. The veto also was used liberally to overturn rules or actions by independent regulatory agencies and federal agencies.

Congress relied more and more on the legislative veto as the national government's role in a wide range of programs grew during the 1960s and 1970s. As the policy agenda grew larger and more complex, Congress drafted measures hastily and carelessly at times, delegating sweeping authority to the Executive Branch without guidance on how to properly carry the laws out. The veto provided a means for legislators to later dictate to the Executive Branch how laws should be administered.[89] One member of Congress argued that the legislative veto was "the only vehicle we have to get a handle on the bureaucracy."[90] An opposing view, however, held that the device encouraged the growth and influence of "triple alliances" by which special interest groups working through congressional subcommittees were able to directly influence how programs were administered.

The U.S. Supreme Court in 1983 ruled the legislative veto unconstitutional. The decision came in a narrow case in which Congress overrode a decision of the Immigration and Naturalization Service to allow a foreign student whose visa had expired to remain in this country. Responding to the argument that the veto enabled Congress to deal efficiently with the increasing complexities of modern government, Chief Justice Warren Burger declared that the Founding Fathers ranked other values higher than efficiency. The court's majority held that the Constitution intended for legislation to be achieved through a deliberate process involving both houses of Congress with approval of the president, and that Congress had the opportunity to override a president's veto by a two-thirds vote of each house.

On the surface it would seem that the presidency was significantly strengthened by the High Court's ruling because more than two hundred laws involving a wide range of domestic and foreign policy programs were affected. But Congress cannot be so quickly written off. In fact, the presidency may yet be the real loser in the decision since Congress may now be encouraged to develop more detailed and restrictive legislation, thereby diminishing the president's executive discretion. Or Congress may increasingly resort to using the federal budget to rein in the president.

CONCLUSION

Congress has almost always been unwieldy, agonizingly slow to act, and fragmented. Frequently it has been marked by self-serving behavior of members worried more about their political futures than national leadership and national policies. Only rarely have presidents been successful in mastering Congress, and even then their influence was of short duration and not as overwhelming as popular accounts hold. To expect the system to function otherwise is to ask for the impossible, for the founders intended Congress and the presidency to be independent of each other; each was to be capable of checking and balancing the ambitions of the other.

The cost of separation, however, has grown proportionately with the cost to the nation in political drift, and in the government's inability to respond to seemingly intractable social, economic, and political problems. The system appears designed, in fact, to plug leaks and to patch up minor repairs, but not to provide any form of long-range planning or systematic management for policy needs. Cooperation is essential between Congress and the president. Without cooperation, either is capable of bringing the government to a standstill. We live in a time of declining resources in the federal government and of a reassertion of congressional prerogatives against the White House. Because we as a people continue to expect high levels of performance from the president, widespread public cynicism and frustration are inevitable.

Congress is actually advantaged in the present political situation. Individual members can fight for narrow constituent interests, ignore the greater problems raised by collective policy needs, and still enhance their political powers. But the president ends up paying the supreme price: his political life. This is because only he can represent the national interest. The emphasis on constituency service by members of Congress today means that the American electorate, more than ever before, may be better represented in the halls of Congress in terms of narrow interests, issue groups, regional or parochial political concerns, but much less well served with policies designed to solve national problems. Presidents must now form what one White House veteran has called a "roll your own majority" for every new proposal that is sent to the Hill.[91]

Power in Congress will probably remain dispersed and unresponsive to presidential leadership for some time to come, perhaps permanently, because there is little or no likelihood that political parties will ever again reassert their consensus-building influences in the policy process, or regain their capacity to control recruitment of both legislators and presidents. The issues of the 1980s and beyond will increasingly pit group against group, region and locality against region and locality, as conflict for resources grows even fiercer. Congress will continue to be the central arena for slugging it out. Perhaps that explains the ironic results of our national elections, which appear to favor one party for the legislature and the opposition for the White House. The president is asked to assume the responsibilities of collective policy leadership, which today usually means tightening up the purse strings, while legislators are continually reelected for what they can extract from the federal purse.

Without strong parties the chance of restoring powerful leadership to both houses of Congress is remote. Without strong leaders in the legislative process, no president will ever be able to develop the resources within Congress to provide national direction to policymaking. The ability of presidents to affect the nation's policy agenda has shrunk at a time when the demand for new solutions to the persistent problems that menace the country continues and grows. The political costs and difficulties of pushing an agenda through Congress have multiplied immeasurably in recent years, but public expectations for presidential performance have not abated. In fact, the almost ritualistic rejection of one incumbent after another suggests that the quest has become frantic. The result is an increasingly impossible presidency: damned if it does, and damned if it does not, attempt to direct the nation's legislative agenda.

NOTES

1. Ronald C. Moe and Steven Teel, "Congress as Policy-Maker: A Necessary Reappraisal," *Political Science Quarterly* 85 (September 1970): 444.

2. Stephen T. Early, Jr., and Barbara Knight, *Responsible Government: American and British* (Chicago: Nelson-Hall Publishers, 1981), 235 passim.

3. Ibid., 174.

4. *Time*, April 26, 1982, 14.

5. A conference on the presidency of John F. Kennedy, November 12–14, 1980, at the University of Southern California brought together a number of former Kennedy administration people. They were generally in agreement among themselves that it was JFK who planted the seeds of many of the Great Society programs later passed during Johnson's administration. For a discussion of Carter's legislative accomplishments, see Jimmy Carter, *Keeping Faith* (New York: Bantam Books, 1982).

6. Richard Rose, "Government Against Sub-Governments," in Richard Rose and Ezra Suleiman, eds., *Presidents and Prime Ministers* (Washington, D.C.: American Enterprise Institute, 1980), 297.

7. Moe and Teel, 446.

8. Erwin C. Hargrove and Roy Hoopes, *The Presidency: A Question of Power* (Boston: Little, Brown and Company, 1975), 33.

9. George E. Mowry, *The Era of Theodore Roosevelt* (New York: Harper & Row, Publishers, 1958), 173.

10. Stephen J. Wayne, *The Legislative Presidency* (New York: Harper & Row, Publishers, 1978), 14–15.

11. Godfrey Hodgson, *All Things to All Men* (New York: Simon & Schuster, 1980), 60.

12. Moe and Teel, 447.

13. Arthur M. Schlesinger, Jr., *The Coming of the New Deal*, vol. 2 of *The Age of Roosevelt* (Boston: Houghton Mifflin Company, 1958), 554–55.

14. Personal correspondence with Leon H. Keyserling, November 26, 1982.

15. Ibid.

16. Doris Kearnes, *Lyndon Johnson and the American Dream* (New York: Harper & Row, Publishers, 1976), 236.

17. Eric F. Goldman, *The Tragedy of Lyndon Johnson* (New York: Alfred A. Knopf, 1969), 58.

18. Lawrence F. O'Brien, *No Final Victories: A Life in Politics from John F. Kennedy to Watergate* (New York: Ballantine Books, 1974), 145.

19. Paul C. Light, *The President's Agenda* (Baltimore: Johns Hopkins University Press, 1982), 213.

20. Ibid., 206.

21. Ralph K. Huitt, "White House Channels to the Hill," in Harvey Mansfield, ed., *Congress Against the President* (New York: Praeger Publishers, 1975), 76.

22. Ibid.

23. Nelson W. Polsby, *Congress and the Presidency*, 3rd ed. (Englewood Cliffs, N.J.: Prentice-Hall, 1976), 51.

24. *Congressional Quarterly Almanac, 1980,* 2.

25. Ibid.

26. Dom Bonafede, "The Tough Job of Normalizing Relations with Capitol Hill," *National Journal,* January 13, 1979, 54–56.

27. Light, 215.

28. Ibid., 205.

29. Richard E. Neustadt, *Presidential Power: The Politics of Leadership from F.D.R. to Jimmy Carter* (New York: John Wiley & Sons, 1980), 29.

30. *Congressional Quarterly Almanac, 1973,* 905.

31. Wayne, 85.

32. James L. Sundquist, *The Decline and Resurgence of Congress* (Washington, D.C.: Brookings Institution, 1981), 143.

33. Robert S. Gilmour, "Central Legislative Clearance: A Revised Perspective," *Public Administration Review* 31 (1971).

34. Steven Shull and Lance LeLoup, *The Presidency: Studies in Policy Making* (New Brunswick, Ohio: King's Court, 1979), 144.

35. Richard A. Watson and Norman C. Thomas, *The Politics of the Presidency* (New York: John Wiley & Sons, 1983), 254.

36. Moe and Teel, 448.

37. Ibid., 469.

38. Aaron Wildavsky, "The Two Presidencies," in A. Wildavsky, ed., *Perspectives on the Presidency* (Boston: Little, Brown and Company, 1975), 447–61.

39. Shull and LeLoup, 295–305.

40. Richard M. Pious, *The American Presidency* (New York: Basic Books, 1979), 178.

41. Louis Koenig, *The Invisible Presidency* (New York: Holt, Rinehart and Winston, 1960), 14.

42. Louis Fisher, *The Constitution Between Friends: Congress, the Presidency and the Law* (New York: St. Martin's Press, 1978), 193-94.

43. *Congressional Quarterly, Congress and the Nation,* IV (Washington: Congressional Quarterly, 1978), 865.

44. *New York Times,* October 19, 1972.

45. Fisher, 205-8.

46. Public Law 88-408, August 10, 1964.

47. *Minnesota Chippewa Tribe* v. *Carlucci, Civ. Action No. 628-73* (D.D.C., 1973); *National Association of Collegiate Veterans* v. *Ottina, Civ Action No. 349-73.* (D.D.C., 1973); *National Association of State Universities and Land Grant Colleges* v. *Weinberger, Civ Action No. 1014-73* (D.D.C., 1973).

48. *McGrain* v. *Daugherty,* 273 U.S. 135 (1927).

49. Robert C. Dixon, Jr., "Congress, Shared Administration and Executive Privilege," in Harvey Mansfield, ed. *Congress Against the President* (New York: Praeger Publishers, 1975), 134.

50. Daniel C. Tannenbaum, "Senate Confirmation and Controversial Presidential Nominations: From Truman to Nixon," paper presented at the annual meeting of the American Political Science Association, San Francisco, September 2-5, 1975, 5.

51. Light, 14.

52. James David Barber, *Presidential Character: Predicting Presidential Performance* (Englewood Cliffs, N.J.: Prentice-Hall, 1977).

53. George Edwards III, *Presidential Influence in Congress* (San Francisco: W. H. Freeman and Co., 1980), 89.

54. Ibid., 90.

55. Light, 29.

56. Ibid., 109.

57. Ibid., 86-91.

58. Neustadt, 126.

59. Ibid., 152.

60. Ibid., 129.

61. Personal communication from Walter Cronkite, February 23, 1982.

62. Personal communication from James Reston, November 17, 1980.

63. Kearnes, 226.

64. Ibid.

65. See discussion in Tom Wicker, *JFK and LBJ: The Influence of Personality Upon Politics* (Baltimore: Penguin Books, 1968), 83-148.

66. Abraham Holtzman, *Legislative Liaison* (Indianapolis: Bobbs-Merrill Co., 1973), 1.

67. Watson and Thomas, 267-68.

68. *Public Papers of the Presidents, 1971,* 23-28.

69. Fisher, 48.

70. *San Antonio Express-News,* May 31, 1981.

71. Ibid.

72. Quotation cited by Wilbur Cohen at a symposium, "The Presidency and Congress: A Shifting Balance of Power?", November 15, 1977, Lyndon B. Johnson School of Public Affairs, University of Texas at Austin.

73. Light, 213.

74. Ibid., 27.

75. Edwards, 61–62.

76. John W. Kingdon, *Congressmen's Voting Decisions* (New York: Harper & Row, Publishers, 1973), 110–12; Malcolm Jewell, *Senatorial Politics and Foreign Policy* (Lexington: University of Kentucky Press, 1962), 30–46; and Edwards, 61–66.

77. Walter D. Burnham, "Insulation and Responsiveness in Congressional Elections," *Political Science Quarterly* 90 (Fall 1975): 412–13.

78. Thomas E. Mann, "Elections and Change in Congress," in Thomas E. Mann and Norman J. Ornstein, eds., *The New Congress* (Washington, D.C.: American Enterprise Institute, 1981); and Christopher Buchanan, "Senators Face Tough Reelection Odds," *Congressional Quarterly Weekly Report*, April 5, 1980, 905–9.

79. *New York Times*, March 5, 1973, 20; March 9, 1973, 18; and March 11, 1973, IV–3.

80. *Time*, April 26, 1982, 13.

81. Roger H. Davison, "Subcommittee Government: New Channel for Policy-Making," in Mann and Ornstein, *The New Congress*, 117.

82. *Congressional Quarterly Almanac*, 1980, 5.

83. Edwards, 46.

84. Hugh Heclo, "Issue Networks and the Executive Establishment," in Anthony King, ed., *The New American Political System* (Washington, D.C.: American Enterprise Institute, 1979), 100.

85. Edwards, 38.

86. Samuel Patterson, "The Semi-Sovereign Congress," in King, ed., *The New American Political System*, 149.

87. Eric L. Davis, "The President and Congress," in Arnold J. Meltsner, ed., *Politics and the Oval Office* (San Francisco: Institute for Contemporary Studies, 1981), 113–115.

88. Richard J. Fenno, *Congressmen in Committees* (Boston: Little, Brown and Company, 1973), 55–62.

89. *New York Times*, June 26, 1983, sec. 4, 1.

90. *Congressional Quarterly Weekly Report*, October 30, 1982, 2772.

91. *Newsweek*, January 26, 1981, 41.

Chapter 4

Chief Executive
The Illusion of Bureaucratic Responsibility

I thought I was president. But I couldn't make them do a damn thing.

    Harry S. Truman

[W]e have no discipline in this bureaucracy. We never fire anybody. We never reprimand anybody. We never demote anybody. We always promote the sons-of-bitches that kick us in the ass. That's true in the State Department. It's true in HEW. It's true in OMB, and true for ourselves, and it's got to stop!

    Richard M. Nixon

Shortly after his inauguration Jimmy Carter was preparing for a meeting with Latin American dignitaries when he detected a rotten odor in his office. A mouse had died inside a wall of the Oval Office. With the stench growing unbearable, an emergency call went out to the General Services Administration to remove it. The GSA, the agency responsible for maintenance of federal offices, declined to act because it insisted it had already exterminated all the mice in the White House. The dead mouse obviously was an intruder from *outside*, therefore it was the responsibility of the Interior Department, which is charged with care of the White House grounds. A telephone call to Interior received a similar rebuff: the dead mouse was not its concern since it was now *inside* the White House and Interior was responsible for exterior problems. An angry and exasperated president finally ordered officials from both agencies to his office where he exclaimed, "I can't even get a damn mouse out of my office!" A special task force representing *both* agencies was formed to get rid of the smelly rodent.[1]

Carter's frustration with his lack of power as chief executive is a chronic condition of the presidency. Truman once observed, "They talk about the power of the president, they talk about how I can just push a button to get things done. Why, I spend most of my time kissing somebody's ass."[2] Truman predicted that after Eisenhower became president, he would "sit here . . . and he'll say, 'Do this!' 'Do that!' *And nothing will happen!* Poor Ike—it won't be a bit like the Army. He'll find it very frustrating."[3]

Textbook descriptions and official organization charts place the president atop a massive pyramid of departments, agencies, bureaus, and commissions. He is said to be the boss of approximately 2.8 million federal employees in some 1245 agencies. This huge administrative system is not a single structure, but rather three distinct types of organization, including cabinet departments, independent agencies, and independent regulatory commissions. The size, complexity, and diversity of the executive establishment make it difficult for anyone to administer. The bureaucracy's independence from the president makes it impossible to direct.

As far as every president is concerned, the most frustrating illusion about his office is that which suggests he ought to be able to control this incredibly complex, fragmented, and autonomous system if he is sufficiently clever, determined, and skilled. The discovery that large numbers of people who supposedly work for the president freely ignore his directives and wishes is one of the most unsettling aspects about being president.

There is a simple but appealing logic to the idea that a president ought to be able to master the Executive Branch if only he possesses the magic touch. Article II, Section 3, of the Constitution charges the president with taking "care that the laws be faithfully executed." Section 2 provides him with the authority to appoint, with the advice and consent of the Senate, "all other officers of the United States, whose appointments are not herein otherwise provided for, and which shall be established by law."

In reality, the president's formal authority as head of the Executive Branch is the least substantial of any of the powers associated with the modern presidency, for the overwhelming majority of those who implement the laws of Congress and the president's decisions are beyond his control. Executive Branch personnel are more concerned with their own bureaucratic self-interests than with the president's, and frequently they are lined up in opposition to his policies or directives.

Nonetheless, the belief that the president ought to be able to impose control and to obtain accountability from the federal bureaucracy persists because of a myth that it is possible to have responsible government in the American system. Such a perspective is deceptive because modern administration is complex and dispersed, and it involves an expanding number of actors within government and without. These actors have little reason to be bound to an illusory collective national interest.

The myth that a president can control the Executive Branch also belies the reality that the American government was never intended to be managed or led by one person. "A president can no more manage the whole of government than he could manage a herd of wild horses," Richard Rose has observed.[4] Public policy expert Harold Seidman has suggested that the Executive Branch is a microcosm of American society. "Inevitably it reflects the values, conflicts, and competing forces to be found in a pluralistic society. The ideal of a neatly symmetrical, frictionless organization structure is a dangerous illusion."[5] The toughest job for most presidents is not to persuade Congress to support a legislative program, but to convince the relevant bureaucracy or agency—even when headed by persons of his own choosing—to follow his directions faithfully so that the shadow of policy can be transformed into the substance of the program.[6]

A naive view of how the presidency ought to function vis-à-vis the bureaucracy was offered by John Ehrlichman during the Nixon administration:

> *There shouldn't be a lot of leeway in following the president's policies. It should be like a corporation, where the executive vice presidents (the cabinet officers) are tied closely to the chief executive, or to put it in extreme terms, when he says jump, they only ask how high.*[7]

Even if cabinet secretaries were to jump, there is little likelihood they could make their subordinates respond in kind to the dictates of the White House. Federal bureaucrats are mostly beyond White House control because they are given broad and often independent operational authority by Congress. The allegiance of federal agencies is less to an administration than to Congress or powerful client groups.

This chapter begins by examining the illusion that a president ought to be able to master the federal Executive Branch. It contrasts this illusion with the realities of the working bureaucracy by examining who staffs Executive Branch departments and agencies, to whom they are accountable, and to what extent they can be managed by the president and his political appointees. The myth of responsible government—manifested in the belief that genuine cabinet government is possible in America—is held up against the performance of cabinet secretaries and departments. The chapter concludes by considering various attempts to reorganize the Executive Branch to make it more accountable to the president.

THE MYTH OF RESPONSIBLE PRESIDENTIAL AUTHORITY

The president's constitutional role as chief executive creates the expectation that he ought to be able to get a handle on the federal government's administrative machinery. Our intense public interest in and emotional attachment to the presidential personality intensify that expectation.

We can easily understand the image of a single chief executive entering office to promote his policies through a band of loyal political subordinates because this idea fits in with our preoccupation with the presidential personality. The ideal of undertaking public service at the call of the president still attracts many new political appointees to Washington. But as Heclo has noted, there are no "natural" forces to bolster the expectation that presidential appointees will be able to work together in his behalf:

> *The president's formal power as the single chief executive is often illusory . . . [and] even within his own executive branch he must persuade others and calculate his power stakes rather than cudgel his minions. This . . . has not altered the customary concentration on the president and, like the standard constitutional or party government models, it relegates the bulk of political executives to a secondary, derivative role in the executive branch.*[8]

Expectations for strong collective leadership by the president stem from a widespread misconception that our system can function much like a parliamentary-cabinet government in which there is a fusion of powers between the chief executive, the legislature, and the permanent government.

The British prime minister is the model that most influences American expectations for presidential leadership, but it is inappropriate. A prime minister is chosen by Parliament, thus tying the executive directly to the majority political party within the legislature. Other ministers heading governmental departments likewise are from Parliament, and they owe their appointments to the fact their party controls a majority. Together, the prime minister and other governmental ministers constitute a plural executive—the cabinet, the ultimate decision-making authority in the British government.

The prime minister may be "first among equals"—indeed it is commonly argued that the role has become more "presidential" in recent years. But the collective nature of the cabinet is the real force behind the prime minister's authority as well as for reconciling diverse political pressures on the ministers of the various departments. The cabinet sustains the authority of a minister to direct departmental affairs for as long as the cabinet can hold together as a collective body. As Rose has noted:

> . . . because of a strong bond of party loyalty uniting politicians in the legislature and the executive, the cabinet can be confident that parliament will endorse its actions. . . . [T]he doctrine of collective responsibility . . . requires that every politician in the cabinet accept a decision and not criticize it publicly.[9]

Each minister has considerable personal discretion to make decisions within his or her department's policy areas, but the minister must always accept the decisions and guidelines offered by the cabinet even when they run against the department and its interests. Like his or her counterpart in the United States, a British minister deals with pressure groups but without frequent interference or intimidation from the legislature. The cabinet thus is a "strong political counterweight to the particularistic demands of pressure groups."[10]

Pressure groups are not ignored nor are they especially frustrated, for ministers are politicians and they too must accommodate constituent groups. But groups must deal with the ministries since there is where political power resides. Pressure-group demands which are inconsistent with government policy will fail since all ministers must abide by the collective will of the cabinet.[11]

The spirit of responsibility extends throughout the government civil service as well. Each cabinet member depends on an elite corps of senior civil service professionals who are experienced in government as well as in dealing with interest groups. High-ranking administrators rise through the ranks of the government service to the topmost levels of a department and become assistants or deputies to the cabinet minister. These senior civil service executives neither stall nor try to buck decisions of the government reached through "due form," that is, through consultation between the government and senior civil servants. Once consulted, the career government servant acts without public complaint or personal evasions, even when he or she may have fought the government's position to the very end.[12]

Ministers return the loyalty of government servants in full measure, according to Richard Neustadt.[13] Politicians rarely meddle with official recruitment or promotion, and by and large the bureaucracy administers itself. Ministers may take all the credit for government decisions for themselves, but they also must take the heat. Ministers carefully protect the privacy and status of civil servants but, what is more important, they *lean* on them and *expect* to be advised. They even *follow* their advice.

Strong lines of accountability and responsibility between the executive and legislature as well as with the government bureaucracy may be possible only in a unitary government such as Britain's. Certainly in parliamentary-cabinet governments in federal systems—such as in Canada or West Germany—it is more difficult to develop strong collective authority, and in countries marked by numerous divisions in the electorate, governments frequently require cabinets to bargain away authority in order to sustain a governing coalition. The U.S. system of separation of powers and checks and balances is especially unsuited for the kind of collective authority found in Britain, for strong party discipline would reduce Congress to a rubber stamp when the same party controlled the White House as well as both houses of Congress. On the other hand, whenever party control was divided between the executive and legislative branches—a rather frequent situation in American politics—the government would be virtually stalemated for two to four years.

American presidents achieve their power independently of political parties or of Congress, and this provides presidents with relative freedom from either source. Since members of Congress, like the president, are elected separately and directly by the voters to constitutionally coequal branches of government, neither relies on the support of the other for continuing in office. However, even though the president achieves his authority independently, he is not free to exercise that power personally as head of the government since the bureaucracy itself is dependent on Congress for its resources.

The ties between the American president and his cabinet thus bear little resemblance to the British cabinet system because the cabinet in American government has no legal status, nor are political decisions made by various cabinet secretaries binding on a president or Congress. Cabinet secretaries may be clearly subordinate to the president, but they are far more vulnerable to pressures on their departments.

The president and his cabinet secretaries do not constitute in any meaningful sense a plural executive. Since the president is not directly tied to party or legislature, he can choose individuals to head cabinet departments on the basis of their agreement with his policies or as rewards for political support. Lacking collective responsibility, many cabinet secretaries shift their loyalties toward the departments and their clientele. As a result, the Executive Branch becomes increasingly a "collection of fragmented bureau fiefdoms unable to coordinate with themselves intelligently."[14]

A prime minister works in constant contact with his or her cabinet and legislature. By contrast, a president and his appointees end up going their separate ways, as the president's personal assistants gradually isolate him from direct contacts with cabinet secretaries and others who are seen as "poor team members" or as having sold out to their departments. Meanwhile, the presidency itself begins to assume many characteristics common to large-scale bureaucracies as the White House becomes overspecialized, poorly coordinated with the government, and separated by a communications gap. The White House also begins to "politicize" the upper echelons of the government career civil service with presidentialists who will try to bend the professional bureaucrats to the president's purposes.

Lacking internal cohesiveness provided by a unified party system and a collectively responsible cabinet of ministers, administrative units in the Executive Branch frequently end up unsupported by the White House and left to fend for themselves against the demands of the political environment. In the absence of presidential support and direction, government bureaucrats look elsewhere for their resources, personnel, funds, and authority. Top-ranking government executives end up more responsive to Congress and to clientele interest groups than to the president because Congress is more supportive of their needs. In addition, their interactions with interest groups are more frequent and more intense.

There also is a significant difference between the British and American government services. While British career civil servants may advance to the highest positions in the departments, a newly inaugurated president appoints political officials to positions that are several steps *down* in the cabinet departments.[15] A president can penetrate the government service more deeply, but he creates in this way a buffer zone between civil servants who have experience and expertise and political newcomers who generally only stay for a few years before leaving the government. Prime ministers benefit from continuity and professionalism in the civil service, while in the United States considerable shifting in and out of high government posts results in a lack of consistency and follow-through.

CHARISMATIC ADMINISTRATIVE LEADERSHIP: THE FDR MODEL

The idea that a hybrid form of responsible government is possible in the United States—notwithstanding the inappropriateness of the parliamentary-cabinet model—is based on the example of Franklin D. Roosevelt, who proved it was possible to achieve accountability and efficiency through unorthodox administrative tactics and personal charisma.

Roosevelt believed that formal administrative systems could never sufficiently provide information, ideas, and results, and that a president relying on a single system inevitably became its prisoner. He tried to check and balance information acquired through private, informal, and unorthodox channels and espionage networks with what he received from official government sources.

More than sixty new agencies were created during Roosevelt's first term, and managing the expanding federal bureaucracy was said to be "fun" for the president. He toyed with federal agencies as if "they were pawns in a chess game, moving them wherever it would best strengthen his strategic position."[16] Roosevelt gave cabinet chiefs considerable independence, but at the same time he never hesitated to create ad hoc agencies to deal with problems, leaving the bureaucracy usually responsible in a state of demoralization.[17] "We have new and complex problems," Roosevelt once explained. "Why not establish a new agency to take over the new duty rather than saddle it on an old institution? . . . If it is not permanent, we don't get bad precedents."[18] Roosevelt's creation of unorthodox new structures reflected his personal style of using competition to spur on administrators. By pitting agency against agency he kept final authority in his own hands. Nonetheless, this helter-skelter growth of ad hoc agencies pointed to the need for reorganization, and Roosevelt attempted to restructure the Executive Branch to maximize his control over the many bureaus, agencies, and functions that evolved during his administration.

Roosevelt initially sought to create a European-styled career civil service with a cadre of permanent executives directly accountable to the president, but Congress rejected such a far-reaching reorganization in favor of a much more modest plan in 1939. Congress created the Executive Office of the President (EOP) in which were located the Bureau of the Budget, the National Resources Planning Board, and a new White House office to help the president.* Although he failed to achieve the responsible executive establishment he originally had envisioned, Roosevelt was successful in dominating the reorganized Executive Branch largely through reliance on intensely loyal "in-and-outers"—talented academicians and professionals from outside government who increased his effective control over agencies and programs.

Roosevelt's administrative skills and accomplishments have been widely praised and held up as models to which all subsequent presidents might aspire. But his eclectic, personal approach created an informality and impermanence in the executive bureaucracy that have troubled chief executives ever since.[19]

---

*We will examine in greater detail the EOP and White House offices in the next chapter.

Roosevelt did not create a bureaucracy, but an "inspired mish-mash of programs, agencies, bureaus, and free-lance troubleshooters slapped together so that they would not display the systematic tenacity of a true bureaucracy," according to Godfrey Hodgson, a British observer of American politics. This entire structure was "ingeniously arranged in such a way that the frontiers of every agency's jurisdiction would overlap so that each was in constant competition with its neighbors."[20] Such a system did little to strengthen the status, morale, or training of federal civil servants.

RUNNING AGAINST THE BUREAUCRACY: RECREATING THE FDR MODEL

Every four years presidential candidates promise that they will succeed in revitalizing executive authority through adroit managerial skills and personal approaches, but invariably whoever wins the White House finds the bureaucracy to be even more intractable than his predecessor did. As a result, the gulf between political leadership and the bureaucracy widens and deepens, and successive presidents have grown more and more hostile toward the civil service.

The antigovernmental rhetoric of presidential campaigns almost insures that every new president will begin his administration in an atmosphere of mutual suspicion and perhaps hostility. Alabama's former governor, George Wallace, stirred up voter resentment against federal bureaucrats every time he ran for president by suggesting that "briefcase-toting, pointy-headed bureaucrats" were responsible for a wide assortment of civic dissatisfactions. If elected, Wallace promised to throw the briefcases (which he claimed contained only peanut butter sandwiches) into the Potomac River. Presidents Nixon, Ford, and Carter all criticized the federal bureaucracy for its red tape, "excessive" regulations, and gargantuan growth. Ronald Reagan made the bureaucracy the chief target of his campaign attacks. "Government is not the *solution* to our problems, it is the *cause*," according to one of Reagan's favorite crowd-pleasing lines. He promised to reduce the massively swollen federal bureaucracy and to get it "off the backs of the American taxpayer."

By emphasizing the failures and shortcomings of the Executive Branch and by promising to correct the situation, each new president ironically becomes part of a problem he cannot solve. After raising public expectations that once and for all the government will suddenly start to function effectively and fairly, it is only a matter of time before the president himself becomes identified as responsible for its failure. This is because many Americans begin to believe that he is genuinely in control of its operations.

THE PRESIDENT AS SCAPEGOAT FOR THE BUREAUCRACY

The president monopolizes whatever interest or attention the public devotes to the functioning of the Executive Branch because much of the administrative aspect of the federal government is incomprehensible even to presidents and their White House staffs. "The public is ill-prepared to recognize, much less to hold accountable, what in many cases are the most influential actors and institutions in American politics," according to political scientist Bruce Miroff.[21] Thus bureaucratic power—which frequently circumscribes and surpasses presidential authority—is faulted in the abstract ("pointy-headed bureaucrats" and red tape) while the president—who has put himself on public record as willing and able to do something about the government—is held personally responsible for what is beyond his control. Miroff has suggested:

> *An audience accustomed to seeing one dominant figure in the public space, and habituated to finding its political satisfactions or disappointments through that figure, comes to believe that his are the powers of action that matter the most. But as presidential powers of action stand out, other forms of power are obscured.*[22]

The mass media's compulsion to focus on the presidential personality reinforces the image that he is responsible or *should be* for almost everything that transpires in the Executive Branch. There is even a psychological basis for such a perspective for, as Heclo has noted, in good times and bad the president *is* the center of national political attention. "His popular following and public stature give him resources for bargaining and leadership that no political executive in the departments can hope to match."[23]

The public image of the president as a strong chief executive can be a substantial asset when social, political, and economic indices are in reasonably good order because the president is the beneficiary of prosperity and tranquillity. But when the public agenda is swollen with seemingly unsolvable problems or crises, and candidates become increasingly more vocal about the failures of government bureaucrats, the incumbent president begins to look more and more like an incompetent administrator.

REALITIES OF EXECUTIVE POLITICS

The president's weaknesses as chief executive can be directly traced to the Founding Fathers' obsession with fragmented power. The federal bureaucracy in the Constitution is a joint enterprise of the president and Congress, even though organizationally it is a part of the executive. The bureaucracy nonetheless is not a hapless creature of Congress or the president. Government agencies possess a momentum and inertia all their own as a result of the separation of powers and the checks and balances. It may be difficult to get a new governmental activity started, but once an agency has evolved to manage it, politicians find it difficult to reverse or end the activity.

Paradoxically, the very system the founders designed to limit government has had exactly the opposite effect in terms of the bureaucracy, because fragmentation of executive authority has meant fragmentation of responsibility. Instead of preventing the expansion of government, the lack of collective responsibility has been a major factor in the proliferation of activities and commitments.

The president's inability to exert political control over his "own administration" stems from the misconception of the founders that policy execution is logically distinct from policymaking. The idea that the president would be above politics, that he would primarily serve as an impartial administrator of laws passed by the Congress has proven unworkable from the start because the president is the only political force in our system capable of overcoming fragmentation when the nation's security is threatened or when major changes are critically needed in American society. Since FDR, the expanding involvement of the Executive Branch with a vast range of complex national problems has increased the importance of the White House as an administrative force. Policies dealing with health care, the environment, energy, civil rights, trade, and the economy, among many others, came to rest with the federal bureaucracy, which was held responsible for implementing far-reaching programs conceived by the president and Congress.

The authority to administer this explosion of new national programs was located on a piecemeal basis in the Executive Branch. But the president's capacity to coordinate or to manage was not improved because congressional delegations of authority were often ambiguous, raising confusion and doubt as to where the real power to implement programs rested. The Executive Branch grew in size and complexity and had greater responsibility for program management, but its authority was highly dispersed and fragmented.

BUREAUCRATIC GROWTH: MYTH AND REALITY

Candidates have so deeply implanted in the public mind the image of swarms of bureaucrats multiplying like locusts in the nation's capital that it may be impossible to convince anyone that the federal work force has actually grown very little since 1952 and has actually *declined* since 1968. Table 4–1 reveals that federal employment has

TABLE 4-1 Government Employment and Population, 1952–1982

	GOVERNMENT EMPLOYMENT				POPULATION
FISCAL YEAR	Federal Executive Branch (thousands)	State and Local Governments (thousands)	All Governmental Units (thousands)	Federal as Percent of All Governmental Units	Federal Employment Per 1,000 Population
1952	2,574	4,134	6,708	38.4	16.3
1953	2,532	4,282	6,814	37.2	15.8
1954	2,382	4,552	6,934	34.4	14.6
1955	2,371	4,728	7,099	33.4	14.3
1956	2,372	5,064	7,436	31.9	14.0
1957	2,391	5,380	7,771	30.8	13.9
1958	2,355	5,630	7,985	29.5	13.5
1959	2,355	5,806	8,161	28.8	13.2
1960	2,371	6,073	8,444	28.1	13.1
1961	2,407	6,295	8,702	27.7	13.1
1962	2,485	6,533	9,018	27.6	13.0
1963	2,490	6,834	9,324	26.7	13.2
1964	2,469	7,236	9,705	25.4	12.9
1965	2,496	7,683	10,179	24.5	12.8
1966	2,664	8,259	10,923	24.4	13.6
1967	2,877	8,730	11,607	24.8	14.5
1968	2,951	9,141	12,092	24.4	14.7
1969	2,980	9,496	12,476	23.9	14.7
1970	2,944	9,869	12,813	23.0	14.4
1971	2,883	10,372	13,255	21.8	13.9
1972	2,823	10,896	13,719	20.6	13.5
1973	2,775	11,286	14,061	19.7	13.2
1974	2,847	11,713	14,560	19.6	13.4
1975	2,848	12,114	14,962	19.0	13.3
1976	2,832	12,282	15,114	18.7	13.2
1977	2,789	12,704	15,493	18.0	12.8
1978	2,820	13,050	15,870	17.8	12.9
1979	2,823	13,308	16,131	17.5	12.8
1980	2,821	13,445	16,266	17.3	12.7
1981 (est.)	2,800	—	—	17.1	12.6
1982 (est.)	2,811	—	—	17.0	12.4

SOURCE: *Special Analyses Budget of the United States Government Fiscal Year, 1982* (Washington, D.C.: Government Printing Office, 1981), p. 288.

remained almost stable for thirty years while the number of state and local bureaucrats has tripled. As a percentage of all governmental employees at all levels, the federal government's share has declined by more than half. During this same period federal expenditures increased from $42.6 billion in 1950 to $659 billion in 1980 (200 percent in terms of inflation-adjusted dollars). The number of federal governmental regulations meanwhile sextupled. Figure 4-1 depicts the significantly widening gap between federal employment, government spending, and regulations for the period 1950-1975.[24]

FIGURE 4–1 Federal Government Growth: Money, Rules, and People (1949 = 100)

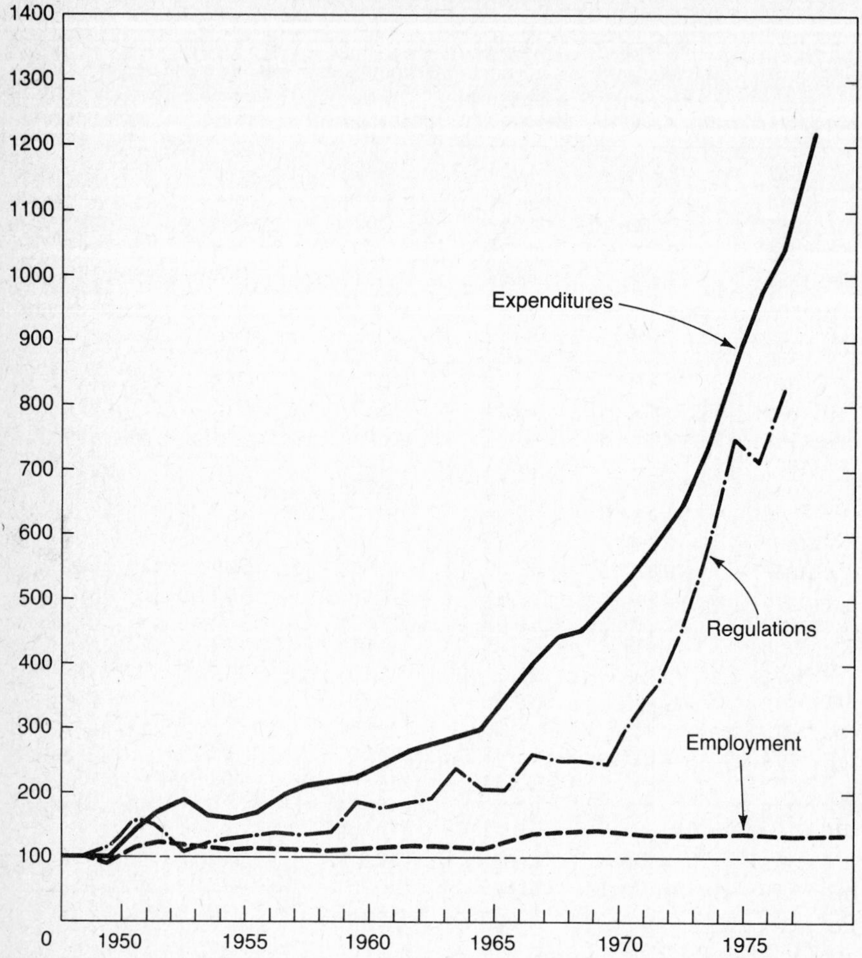

Note: Federal spending on income and product account. Figures are on an accrual basis and include trust account transactions with the public as well as grants-in-aid to state and local governments. Employment covers total end-of-year civilian employees in full-time, permanent, temporary, part-time, and intermittent employment in the executive branch, including the Postal Service. Regulations are indicated by numbers of pages in *The Federal Register.*

Source: The Tax Foundation, *Facts and Figures on Government Finance, 1977,* table 20, p. 33; U.S. Office of Management and Budget, *Special Analyses Budget of the U.S. Government, 1979,* p. 210. Figures are taken from an unpublished table compiled by the Executive Agencies Division, Office of the Federal Register, Washington, D.C. I wish to express my gratitude to this division for their cooperation in supplying information.

Figure is taken from Hugh Heclo's "The Executive Establishment," in A. King, ed., *The New American Political System* (Washington, D.C.: American Enterprise Institute, 1978), 90.

This does not mean that federal bureaucrats are working twice as hard or are much more proficient at spending the taxpayer's money. Much of the increase in federal spending was due to sharply rising costs of existing programs. It does not take more bureaucrats to write larger checks.[25] At least 80 percent of the federal budget is chronically "locked in" by already mandated programs or commitments that can only be reversed by Congress.

Another myth holds that almost all the federal government's bureaucrats are clustered along the Potomac River when in truth 87 percent of those employed by the federal government work outside Washington, D.C., in cities and towns across the country or in posts overseas.[26] Washington has not tried to administer many programs directly to the national population through federal agents, but rather through a growing army of intermediaries—administrative go-betweens such as state and local governments, third-party payers, consultants, contractors, or quasi-public corporations. Narrow, issue-oriented interest groups are more successful working through such third-party payers in dominating the policy process and in thwarting the goals of an administration. These intermediaries or third parties are committed to specific programs but less concerned with the development of broad national policies or the administration's policy agenda. Federal regulatory activities have flourished, because, instead of building and policing its own delivery systems, Washington discovered it could rest content with telling other third-party public and private bureaucracies what to do.[27] This enabled federal policymakers to distribute not only the ever growing federal funds but also the blame when things went wrong. Between 1970 and 1980 social regulatory bodies increased in number from twelve to eighteen and their budgets increased 500 percent from $1.5 to $7.5 billion.[28]

People may want the federal government to "get off their backs," but they also want the government to solve their needs or problems. Policy goals frequently are piled up on top of one another without attention to national goals or administrative procedures to achieve them. The president is held responsible by the public for poor program execution, but he is besieged with bills from intermediaries over whom he has little or no control.[29]

ADMINISTRATIVE COMPLEXITY AND FRAGMENTATION

The dispersion of administrative authority outward is reflected by fragmented power within the Executive Branch. The federal executive establishment is so complex and its authority so scattered among a multitude of agencies, programs, and jurisdictions that only those intimately concerned or connected with programs or policies know where responsibility lies. It is said that Gerald R. Ford was amazed by the complexity and number of units included on an organizational chart of the Department of Health, Education, and Welfare unfurled in front of him at a cabinet department briefing. John P. Roche, a political scientist who served on Johnson's White House staff, recalls LBJ exploding one day when he discovered someone in the Department of Health, Education, and Welfare had nipped a Great Society program in the bud. Roche told Johnson that he ought to "fire the s.o.b."

"Fire him!" Johnson roared. "I can't even *find* him!"[30]

If one major cabinet department can seem like a fathomless pit to the president, the overall organizational arrangement of the Executive Branch must resemble an impenetrable jungle filled with mysteries and strangers. Figure 4–2 depicts the formal organization of the Executive Branch, and Figure 4–3 displays the present arrangement of major units in the Department of Health and Human Services, the cabinet department that succeeded HEW after education was given separate cabinet status by Congress.

A formal organizational chart of the Executive Branch distinguishes units according to whether they are cabinet departments, independent regulatory agencies, or independent federal agencies or government corporations. These distinctions highlight important differences in structures and functions, but they do not really mean a great deal as far as the president's authority is concerned. Numerous agencies have overlapping and even contradictory jurisdictions. As a result, there is often duplication of efforts, policy goals at cross-purposes, and fuzzy lines of responsibility or accountability.

Cabinet Departments

The thirteen cabinet departments are supposed to be the most accountable of all the federal agencies to presidential control because the secretaries who head these departments as well as the undersecretaries, deputy undersecretaries, and assistant secretaries are all appointed by the president, subject to Senate confirmation. The myth of cabinet government, however, is one of the most common but misleading of all the myths surrounding the presidency. For as we will see later in this chapter, a cabinet department is actually a collection of agencies, bureaus, and programs, each of which functions with a momentum of its own—often against the policy goals of the cabinet chief and in defiance of White House efforts to coordinate its activities.

FIGURE 4-2 The Executive Branch

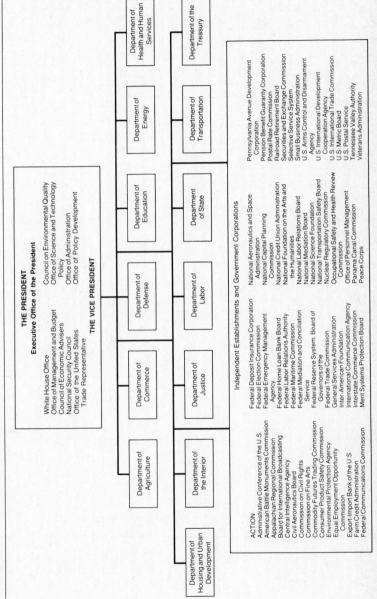

THE PRESIDENT
Executive Office of the President

White House Office	Council on Environmental Quality
Office of Management and Budget	Office of Science and Technology
Council of Economic Advisers	Policy
National Security Council	Office of Administration
Office of the United States	Office of Policy Development
Trade Representative	

THE VICE PRESIDENT

Department of Housing and Urban Development

Department of the Interior

Department of Agriculture

Department of Commerce

Department of Defense

Department of Education

Department of Health and Human Services

Department of Justice

Department of Labor

Department of State

Department of Energy

Department of Transportation

Department of the Treasury

Independent Establishments and Government Corporations

ACTION
Administrative Conference of the U.S.
American Battle Monuments Commission
Appalachian Regional Commission
Board for International Broadcasting
Central Intelligence Agency
Civil Aeronautics Board
Commission on Civil Rights
Commission on Fine Arts
Commodity Futures Trading Commission
Consumer Product Safety Commission
Environmental Protection Agency
Equal Employment Opportunity Commission
Export-Import Bank of the U.S.
Farm Credit Administration
Federal Communications Commission

Federal Deposit Insurance Corporation
Federal Election Commission
Federal Emergency Management Agency
Federal Home Loan Bank Board
Federal Labor Relations Authority
Federal Maritime Commission
Federal Mediation and Conciliation Service
Federal Reserve System, Board of Governors of the
Federal Trade Commission
General Services Administration
Inter-American Foundation
International Communication Agency
Interstate Commerce Commission
Merit Systems Protection Board

National Aeronautics and Space Administration
National Capital Planning Commission
National Credit Union Administration
National Foundation on the Arts and the Humanities
National Labor Relations Board
National Mediation Board
National Science Foundation
National Transportation Safety Board
Nuclear Regulatory Commission
Occupational Safety and Health Review Commission
Office of Personnel Management
Panama Canal Commission
Peace Corps

Pennsylvania Avenue Development Corporation
Pension Benefit Guaranty Corporation
Postal Rate Commission
Railroad Retirement Board
Securities and Exchange Commission
Selective Service System
Small Business Administration
U.S. Arms Control and Disarmament Agency
U.S. International Development Cooperation Agency
U.S. International Trade Commission
U.S. Metric Board
U.S. Postal Service
Tennessee Valley Authority
Veterans Administration

SOURCE: *The United States Government Manual, 1982–83, 792.*

FIGURE 4-3   Department of Health and Human Services

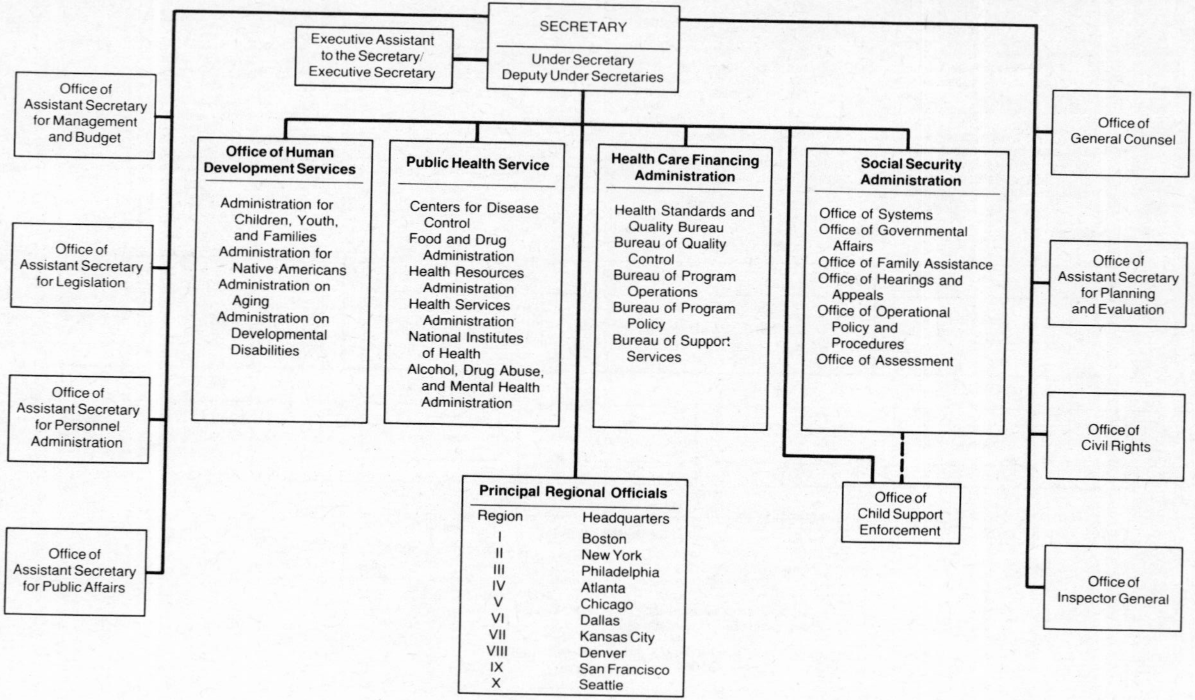

SECRETARY
Under Secretary
Deputy Under Secretaries

Executive Assistant
to the Secretary/
Executive Secretary

Office of
General Counsel

Office of
Assistant Secretary
for Planning
and Evaluation

Office of
Civil Rights

Office of
Inspector General

Office of
Assistant Secretary
for Management
and Budget

Office of
Assistant Secretary
for Legislation

Office of
Assistant Secretary
for Personnel
Administration

Office of
Assistant Secretary
for Public Affairs

**Office of Human
Development Services**

Administration for
Children, Youth,
and Families
Administration for
Native Americans
Administration on
Aging
Administration on
Developmental
Disabilities

Public Health Service

Centers for Disease
Control
Food and Drug
Administration
Health Resources
Administration
Health Services
Administration
National Institutes
of Health
Alcohol, Drug Abuse,
and Mental Health
Administration

**Health Care Financing
Administration**

Health Standards and
Quality Bureau
Bureau of Quality
Control
Bureau of Program
Operations
Bureau of Program
Policy
Bureau of Support
Services

**Social Security
Administration**

Office of Systems
Office of Governmental
Affairs
Office of Family Assistance
Office of Hearings and
Appeals
Office of Operational
Policy and
Procedures
Office of Assessment

Office of
Child Support
Enforcement

Principal Regional Officials

Region	Headquarters
I	Boston
II	New York
III	Philadelphia
IV	Atlanta
V	Chicago
VI	Dallas
VII	Kansas City
VIII	Denver
IX	San Francisco
X	Seattle

SOURCE: *The United States Government Manual, 1981–82,* 830.

Independent Executive Agencies

Approximately sixty agencies, bureaus, commissions, and government corporations exist outside the cabinet departments and the Executive Office of the President. The president is not completely devoid of influence over these agencies, for he has the authority to appoint heads of independent agencies and his budgetary power occasionally enables him to reward or punish in accord with how well the agencies follow the administration's line.

The biggest of these agencies in terms of budget are the Veterans Administration, which spends billions in benefits to veterans each year; the National Aeronautics and Space Administration (NASA), which directed the moon landings and the nation's space exploration programs; and the General Services Administration (GSA), which is responsible for federal buildings, supplies and purchasing (but not for rodent control on the White House grounds!). Government corporations such as the U.S. Postal Service, or the Tennessee Valley Authority, which provides electricity, irrigation, and flood control, are public corporations owned by the government. Thus they are less vulnerable to administrative or budgetary control by either the president or Congress.

Independent Regulatory Commissions

Agencies like the Interstate Commerce Commission (ICC), the Federal Communications Commission (FCC), and the Federal Trade Commission (FTC) are responsible for regulating the marketplace, the work place, and other sectors of the economy involving the public interest. Usually granted broad discretionary rule-making powers by Congress, each regulatory commission is governed by a board of between three and ten members appointed to fixed but staggered terms by the president, subject to Senate confirmation. In some cases the president is required to appoint individuals from the opposition party to insure bipartisanship on the commission. The president cannot fire regulatory appointees the way he can cabinet-level executives.

Some regulatory agencies, nonetheless, have become linked to the White House because of presidential appointments of chairpersons or members who are clearly identified with the president's policies or with powerful interests instrumental in the president's winning office. A congressional investigation from 1975 to 1976 concluded that nine regulatory agencies held a commitment to "special interests of regulated industry and [a] lack of sufficient concern for underrepresented interests" of the public.[31]

Administrative Confusion

The great growth in federal programs during the past twenty years created considerable interdependence among many Executive Branch units, but it also muddied the bureaucratic waters. Agencies have evolved under one jurisdiction but with policy responsibilities or interests in another. Why, for example, should the Forest Service be located in the Department of Agriculture when its interests are more with other agencies in Interior? The Office of Environmental Quality in Agriculture shares as many concerns with the Environmental Protection Agency (EPA) as with farmers. The Mine Safety and Health Bureau is under the Labor Department, but the Bureau of Mines is in Interior. The president of the Solar Energy and Energy Conservation Bank is in Housing and Urban Development rather than the Department of Energy.

Programs involving the development of energy resources invariably entail trade-offs in environmental policies; this results in conflict between agencies in the Department of Energy and various agencies in the Department of Interior as well as with the EPA. The Forest Service and Interior's Bureau of Land Management often clash over policies for federal lands and resources. Bad blood is also common between the Department of Defense and the State Department over foreign and national security policies.

This dispersion of authority and confusion of responsibilities not only makes it difficult for the president to achieve coordinated national programs but it also contributes to contradictory policies that are costly to taxpayers as well as counterproductive. For example, the Carter administration promoted a national program of preventive health care to reduce the risk of cancer, cardiovascular diseases, and other major health problems. Medical experts were unanimous in urging the government to attack cigarette smoking because numerous studies had confirmed it as the leading controllable factor in increasing the risk of killer diseases. Congress established an Office of Smoking and Health and funded an antismoking campaign with $52 million. The U.S. Surgeon General issued a new report implicating cigarettes more directly than ever before to cancer, heart disease, strokes and other major health problems. Meanwhile, tobacco growers received millions of dollars in price supports from the Department of Agriculture, and the Commodity Credit Corporation used an unusual credit procedure to save the tobacco industry some $2 million in interest owed to the federal corporation.[32]

THE FEDERAL WORK FORCE

Coordinated, systematic authority over federal agencies is stymied not only by fragmentation and contradictory jurisdictions but also by the lack of accountability built into the career federal service. Almost all federal employees obtain their jobs through merit examinations or professional qualifications. Responsibility for personnel lies with the Office of Personnel Management, whose members are appointed by the president and confirmed by the Senate. The OPM operates under strict rules concerning hiring, firing, promotion and employment conditions, much as did its predecessor—the U.S. Civil Service Commission. In actual practice, however, the OPM is a paper tiger, for it rarely is able to use its authority to impose real standards of performance. From its beginning with the Pendleton Act of 1883, the civil service system was aimed at protecting government employees from dismissal because of political reasons. But over the years these protections have become iron-clad guarantees of job security preserving and protecting virtually *all* federal employees from dismissal or rigorous evaluations of performance on the job.

The rate of dismissal because of improper job performance or inefficiency is less than one seventh of 1 percent. A person who cannot be removed from duty obviously cannot be held accountable by superiors, especially by presidential appointees who are only temporary members of an agency, and who lack the experience and expertise of permanent personnel. Rarely are federal civil servants given anything but positive job evaluations, and merit pay increases are virtually automatic. One study showed that during the 1970s, 99 percent of all federal employees were given merit pay increases.[33]

Managerial accountability is not much better. Two classes of officials serve in the Executive Branch: presidential appointees and career executives. Approximately seven hundred top-ranking executives are named by the president to head the cabinet departments and various agencies, or to serve as assistant secretaries or in other high-level positions in which they theoretically represent the president's interests. Another seven thousand upper-level civil servants are career executives who typically have spent most of their government service in one or two agencies or in a narrow field of governmental activity.

If a president is to gain administrative influence over the federal bureaucracy, it must come through his top-ranking political executives. Unless these people share his major political goals and aspirations, the permanent bureaucratic establishment will overwhelm his administration and work against even the mere suggestion of managerial cohesion. Thus, the choice of the hundreds of executives who provide linkage with the permanent career executives is critical. Heclo has suggested that in their effect on the everyday work of the government, " . . . these hundreds of personnel selections add up to a cumulative act of choice that may be at least as important as the electorate's single act of choice for president every four years."[34] No other democratic government in the world turns out such a large percentage of competent high-level decision makers when there is a change of regimes as occurs in Washington, D.C., with the change in administrations.

In one of his first cabinet meetings Nixon set forth his guidelines for staffing these ranks as he delegated to his cabinet heads the primary responsibility for filling noncareer political executive positions. He asked only that the jobs be filled on the basis of, first, ability, and second, loyalty to the White House. As he left the cabinet room, the new president turned to an aide and said softly, "I just made a big mistake."[35] His mistake—one repeated by almost every president—is to assume that through his cabinet heads he will have the loyalty of these appointees. Unless he has chosen individuals of unquestioning dedication to him personally or to his political ideology, the president quickly finds political appointees converted to the agencies' values rather than the White House's. Carter also was inattentive in his subcabinet appointments. But Reagan and his personal staff selected subcabinet officials with the greatest of caution, making certain that they chose "Reaganites"—that is, proven conservatives or others sharing the president's views on foreign and domestic policies.

Presidential appointees coexist with career executives in a relationship marked initially by mutual distrust, hostility, organizational jealousies, and cross-purposes. If the political appointee is successful in gaining the trust and confidence of the agency, it is frequently at the risk of losing his ties to the White House.

The typical presidential appointee is often an amateur in government. He or she lacks the knowledge, skills, or expertise essential to successfully managing that department or agency. Political executives quickly become dependent on career administrators for help in managing the organization—often with the result that loyalty to the president's programs is submerged by a growing loyalty to the agency in its attempts to win support and funding from the White House and Congress.

Presidential appointees rarely serve long enough in government to develop the expertise or experience which would give them greater leverage over the permanent bureaucracy. The average cabinet chief holds office for about two years, while the typical undersecretary or assistant secretary remains for about twenty-two months.[36] This frequent turnover in the top ranks creates what Heclo has called a "government of strangers," for governmental executives have only a fleeting chance to learn how to work together, much less to know each other.

Presidential influence over departments and agencies is further diminished by the fact that they are established by Congress, which provides the money, permanent personnel, and authority for continued operations. Congress, in turn, provides broad delegations of authority to federal agencies because not only is it impossible to legislate detailed rules on every conceivable application of policies but it is also politically safer to place responsibility on the Executive Branch for implementation of rules and regulations which are frequently unpopular with one or more groups.

On the surface, broad grants of rule-making and regulatory authority to bureaucracies appear to enhance the powers of the president. In fact, they contribute to reducing the influence of the White House because federal agencies increasingly are dominated by a new breed of executive whose authority is based on expertise, knowledge, and specialization. Heclo has coined the term *technopols* to describe these new government executives.

TECHNOPOLS: BUREAUCRATS BEYOND THE PALE

The relative slowdown in the growth of federal bureaucrats described earlier is misleading, for it reflects a decline in blue-collar employment. But it does not reveal the significant increase over the past twenty years in the levels of management—especially in policy specialists or technical experts in mid- to high-level executive positions. These policy technicians or specialists are increasingly appointed to Executive Branch managerial positions from which they can exert considerable influence over the national agenda. They easily dominate political executives and, in fact, an increasing number of political appointees themselves become a part of this new class as their allegiance shifts from the White House to policy networks and their newly developed expertise eventually makes them indispensable to the career service.[37]

The requirements for managing a more specialized and complex policy bureaucracy forced political leaders who were normally generalists to ignore other politicians for what had once been explicitly political appointments and to seek out persons with specialized technical skills and knowledge. (Thus the shift of many political executives into the professional managerial ranks is not surprising.) Executive agencies grew more and more politicized as they became involved in programs and policies benefitting various groups.

Paradoxically, as the bureaucracy became politicized, the Executive Branch grew more bureaucratized. A rapid increase in the number of mid-level executive positions occurred during the 1960s when the expansion in domestic programs created the need for managerial expertise. From 1961 to 1974 federal civilian employment on the whole increased by only 15 percent, while the population of mid-level executives increased by 200 percent.[38] This growth in the top- and mid-ranges of the executive corps was marked by increased numbers of new positions, more specialized duties and responsibilities, and new layers of organization that pushed political appointees into higher levels of departmental organization.

No president any longer deludes himself, however, that growing numbers of political executives necessarily represent additional influence for the White House. This is because one more political appointee usually "means one more person with a potential for setting directions and subdividing responsibility for what is happening."[39] Under little pressure or inclination to recruit political party faithfuls, the president bends to the logic of expertise and professionalism and hires more qualified administrators. This means appointing someone with expertise in special policy areas, someone who has maintained ties to influentials in the policy areas with which he or she will work. It leads to layers of officials who become indistinguishable from career bureaucrats in the departments and agencies—both in their commitment to policies and their lack of loyalty to the administration. More important, it closes off policy options for the president because the bureaucracy becomes even more resistant to change.

EXECUTIVE BRANCH INERTIA AND MOMENTUM

Eight months after taking office, Carter confessed to a journalist, "I underestimated the inertia or the momentum of the federal bureaucracy. . . . It is difficult to change."[40]

Public administration scholar Francis Rourke notes that Executive Branch departments, bureaus, and independent agencies have their own agendas set by laws that long predated any president's arrival in office. "[The] president may view his election as a mandate for change, [but] there is a massive undertow throughout the bureaucracy that pulls not in the direction of change, but towards continuity."[41]

The growing strength of specialists and policy technicians among career federal executives makes it increasingly difficult for a president to eliminate costly or duplicative programs and services or to reverse the expansion of existing policies. Brought into government because of a specific program or policy development, such executives become dedicated to advancing their programs or at least to resisting any retrenchment by the government. Nowhere is this more clearly represented than in the area of entitlements—payments and benefits for which people automatically qualify by virtue of their age, income, occupation, or disability.

About 48 percent of the 1982 federal budget was consumed by entitlements, the largest being social security. Other costly entitlements include veterans' pensions and benefits, federal retirement pen-

Berry's World

'Think of it! Presidents come and go, but we go on forever!'

sions, Medicare and Medicaid, welfare payments to the poor, price supports for farmers, and unemployment compensation. In addition to these programs, the government is also committed to spending another 25¢ of every dollar for national defense and 10¢ for interest payments on the national debt. This left 17¢ on every dollar spent by the Executive Branch for everything else the federal government does: crime prevention, national parks upkeep, grants to state and local governments, diplomacy, and so on.[42]

Any attempt to make major changes within this distribution scheme—and the White House as well as Congress are constantly besieged with demands for changes—must run a gauntlet of bureaucratic agencies, members of Congress, and organized interest groups. All of them will fiercely resist any changes other than ones which benefit them and their constituencies. Usually increases gained from the federal government are incremental, but in time small additions add up to large and permanent gains, providing a form of momentum which is politically hazardous for any president to try to slow down or to reverse.

SUBGOVERNMENTS AND PRESIDENTIAL LEADERSHIP

Most major policies in American politics are the "unintended by-product of many separate decisions taken by interested parties comprising subgovernments."[43] The term *subgovernments* was invented by Douglas Cater, who suggested that combinations of power brokers outside normal political controls and procedures of government were able to shape policy with little regard for democratic institutions of authority.[44] Subgovernments are frequently successful in preventing collective or national policy leadership because their influence is felt at every step of the political process, and they are able to fragment executive leadership.

Often called *iron triangles* or *triple alliances*, subgovernments are clusters of individuals making most of the routine decisions for a substantive policy area. A typical subgovernment consists of federal agency officials, representatives of interest groups or organizations interested in a policy area, and members of Congress, especially members from committees or subcommittees with the primary or sole jurisdiction over the policy area which is the focus of the subgovernment's attention. Political scientists Randall Ripley and Grace Franklin suggest that subgovernments are created by the complexity of the national policy agenda, and that they help sustain that complexity. They also are most prevalent and influential in those policy areas that are the least visible to the average citizen.[45]

Such alliances are nothing new to American politics, of course. Eisenhower warned in his farewell address of the dangers in an emerging "military-industrial complex" of powerful and wealthy defense contractors working in tandem with Defense Department officials and key committees in Congress to sustain unnecessarily high levels of military spending. In his farewell speech twenty years later Carter echoed Eisenhower's concerns, declaring that the domination of interest groups over the federal government had become the most serious handicap in providing good government.

Where subgovernments are strong, expressions of a collective governmental will are rare. Major policies emerge gradually as the unintended by-product of many separate decisions taken by various elements of the subgovernment.[46] Subgovernments constitute clearly recognizable issue networks; groups of people sharing similar attitudes or knowledge about some narrow public-policy matter can be mobilized by interest groups, federal agencies, or members of Congress.

Subgovernments are increasing in scale, controversy and political significance at the same time as the new technological elite is gaining positions of power and influence in middle and upper levels of the Executive Branch bureaucracy. At the same time, both subgovernments and technopols who dominate the agencies that deal with such triangular policy networks are becoming more and more independent of direction by the one nationally elected politician who represents collective authority—the president. Subgovernments exist in every policy area involving the federal government, and new ones constantly attempt to break into the policy structure. No matter how important or worthy a new policy might be, however, it is difficult to overcome the existing subgovernment if the results of a new policy threaten its privileged relationship with the federal government.

The influence that an established subgovernment has over the president was revealed by the tobacco industry during Carter's administration. Carter's announced intention for a national program of preventive health care initially encouraged HEW Secretary Joseph Califano, Jr., a reformed smoker, to launch a campaign against cigarette smoking. But such a campaign clearly was an attack on the tobacco industry as well. The tobacco lobby first fought HEW's efforts to have tobacco subsidies cut by the Department of Agriculture. The tobacco interests also succeeded in getting Congress to deny the use of Office of Education funds to inform young people—the ones most vulnerable to advertising in favor of smoking—about the dangers of cigarettes. Moreover, members of Congress from tobacco-growing states prevailed on Carter to disassociate himself from the campaign at HEW and to order Califano to go slow. (The president could write off tobacco states in the 1980 election if the antismoking effort persisted, he was warned.) Carter visited a tobacco warehouse in North Carolina where he proclaimed that his family had grown tobacco in North Carolina before moving to Georgia to grow peanuts, and he promised to conduct research to "make the smoking of tobacco even more safe than it is today."[47]

What is the nature of a subgovernment so powerful that it can intimidate presidents and have its way with Congress despite studies confirming hazards to the public's health? Obviously the strength of the tobacco lobby rests with the millions of cigarette smokers who are addicted to a habit costing in excess of $20 billion a year. Two million jobs in twenty-two states are tied to tobacco, with a payroll of $30 billion. Twenty-two billion dollars in taxes are contributed to government coffers. And tobacco accounts for 2.5 percent of the gross national product.[48]

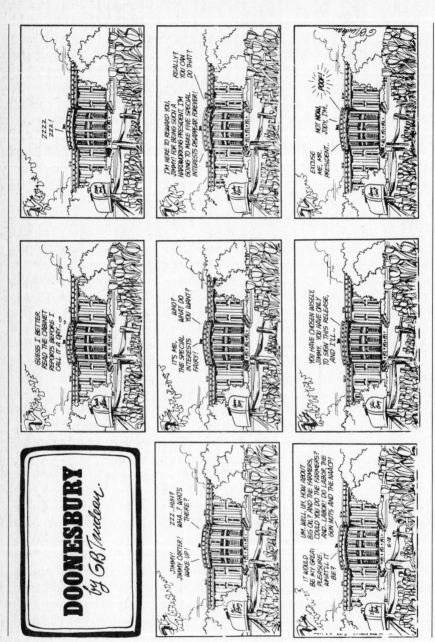

The iron triangle in tobacco includes paid representatives of tobacco growers, marketing organizations, and cigarette companies. Members of Congress from tobacco districts and leading members of four subcommittees in Congress—two appropriations subcommittees and two substantive legislative committees in each house—are part of the system. Also involved are certain officials and agencies in the Department of Agriculture, especially the Tobacco Division. The subgovernment involves small groups of people well known to one another and knowledgeable about most aspects of the tobacco industry and its governmental relationship.[49]

Similar subgovernments exist in virtually every policy area in the federal government. They distort the power of the president (as well as of Congress) because their power is substantial in relationship to collective authority. Most of the policymaking in which subgovernments engage involves routine matters—policies not embroiled in a high degree of controversy. The president's influence in most routine policy matters is less than that of Congress, whose interests dovetail with the narrow, parochial interests of various subgovernments. Subcommittees in Congress scrutinize particular recommendations according to what suits the subgovernments more than according to the national interest. This is because powerful, organized interests are able to apply constituency pressures selectively.[50] The president, meanwhile, is the only one responsible for the national constituency. The federal budget typically is less what the president wants than what Congress will enact in response to the demands and pressures of subgovernments. Even when there is a clear-cut need for a new national policy, a president treads on shaky political ground because new policies almost always present risks to one or more existing subgovernments.

THE MYTH OF CABINET GOVERNMENT

Presidents attempt to overcome the fragmentation caused by subgovernments by trying to form a cabinet-styled government. But this approach never works because the American cabinet is not and never has been a collective entity with clear-cut lines of responsibility leading to the president. It is, instead, a collection of highly individualistic appointees who come from varying political, professional, and ideological backgrounds. The exercise of administrative authority by the various departments that make up the cabinet is the result of a hodgepodge of congressional statutes, departmental rules and regulations, executive orders and directives, court rulings, and personal applications of bureaucratic policy. The cabinet evolved by practice rather than formal design, and from the very first it reflected divided loyalties and competition among various parts of the government vying for influence and resources.

The heads of the first governmental departments created by Congress in 1789—State, Treasury, and War—as well as the attorney general, who did not have a department, quickly assumed the function of informal advisers to President Washington. All owed their appointments and continued service in office to the president, but each was "so constituted that the members of each should have as little agency as possible in the appointment of the members of the others."[51] The term *cabinet* came into use before long, referring to an extralegal creation that would be institutionalized only by usage; its authority would depend totally on the individual president.

The president is not required by statute to form or keep a cabinet, nor to heed the advice of cabinet members. (Lincoln once called for a vote on an issue at a cabinet meeting. After all members voted against him, Lincoln announced the results as "seven nays and one aye, the ayes have it.")[52] Franklin D. Roosevelt seldom used his cabinet as an advisory body, but he encouraged cabinet members to take the major responsibilities for running their departments and to help develop legislation. Truman saw the cabinet at first as the principal medium through which the president controls his administration. During his early months in office he equated it with a board of directors, and frequently asked its members to vote on major issues confronting the White House.[53] Truman eventually retreated from his board-of-directors notion when he realized that he had to guard jealously his own powers and freedom of decision making if he were to make the tough decisions for which he was responsible. Gradually he relied more and more on advice from old political friends and allies or from his closest advisers on the White House staff, who pressed him to ignore much of the advice from the cabinet.

Eisenhower's conception of the cabinet differed considerably from Truman's in that he attempted to turn the cabinet into a genuine deliberative body, permitting cabinet secretaries to exercise personal authority without White House interference. Eisenhower's cabinet met regularly. He sought the views of all members even when their departments were not directly involved in a decision. And he was attentive to cabinet discussions, even though he retained the power to make the final decision. As a result, Eisenhower's cabinet members stayed in office longer than any others in modern times.

A chronic decline in the influence of the cabinet was set in motion by John F. Kennedy, and has persisted to the present. This development was directly related to the emergence of a strong White House staff. The proximity and close personal ties that key White House assistants enjoyed with Kennedy, along with their positions astride action-forcing processes, enabled them and not the cabinet chiefs to have "the eyes of the king." (The following chapter contains additional information on this point.) "Cabinet meetings are simply useless," Kennedy lamented. "Why should the Postmaster General [then a member of the cabinet] sit there and listen to a discussion of the problems of Laos?"[54] Kennedy, like FDR and most presidents ever since, preferred the counsel of small groups of friends and trusted advisers—informal meetings with individuals with whom he was comfortable and in whom he had confidence. His dealings with the cabinet typically involved one-on-one briefing sessions.

This trend was even more pronounced during the next two administrations. First Johnson, and then Nixon, built up the informal advisory capability of the White House while relegating most cabinet department chiefs to second-class status. Occasionally a secretary of state, or defense, or treasury, or an attorney general might be included in the charmed circle of important presidential advisers, but as Neustadt suggests, compared with cabinet members under Eisenhower or earlier, most cabinet secretaries from the 1960s on have been far more dependent on the president's support than he on theirs.[55]

Johnson made a half-hearted attempt early in his administration to elevate his cabinet but the results were short-lived. George Reedy, LBJ's press secretary, recalls that cabinet meetings were held regularly—at first with fully predetermined agendas and prewritten statements, but they were "regarded by all participants except the president as a painful experience, somewhat akin to sitting with the preacher in the parlor on Sunday."[56] Whatever influence the cabinet had on Johnson reflected the influence of individuals rather than that of a group. Johnson was far too suspicious and distrustful to give *anyone* independent authority.

Nixon introduced his cabinet at a televised ceremony in 1969, declaring that he did not want "a cabinet of 'Yes' men." Every member of his cabinet would be urged to speak out both in the cabinet and the administration "so that the decisions we make will be the best decisions we can possibly reach."[57] Before the year was over, most of his cabinet had about as much access to the president as a butcher from Dubuque and about as much autonomy as a member of the Supreme Soviet. When Secretary of the Interior Walter Hickel made public a letter criticizing the president for losing touch with his cabinet and with the American people, he was summarily fired. Others in Nixon's cabinet complained privately that they never saw the president, and they could seldom get past the Gestapo-like White House aides who hermetically sealed Nixon off as if he were in danger of being contaminated by political microorganisms. John Ehrlichman, Nixon's chief domestic adviser, saw the problem from another perspective: he claimed that after Nixon appointed key officials to high posts and they had their pictures taken with the president, "We only see them at the annual White House Christmas party; they go off and marry the natives."[58]

Carter appeared intent on creating a strong cabinet at the start of his administration, partly in reaction to the excesses of the White House staff during Nixon's administration and partly because of Carter's inclination toward a strong managerial organization in which responsibility was delegated to subordinates. He declared:

> *I believe in cabinet government. . . . There will never be an instance while I am president where members of the White House staff dominate or act in a superior position to the members of our cabinet.*[59]

Carter conducted some sixty cabinet meetings during his first two years in office. But before long, his senior White House staff began to complain that most of the cabinet secretaries were disloyal to the president and were undermining him by building up their own fiefdoms. By the spring of 1979, Carter himself had grown so disenchanted with his experiment in cabinet government that he finally gave in to his staff's wishes for a cabinet shake-up. He asked all members of the cabinet to tender their resignations, and he accepted four of them. At the same time Carter announced that Hamilton Jordan, his closest White House aide, would become chief of staff. Thus Carter's administration ended up with a chain of command identical to Nixon's.

Reagan also began office promising to make cabinet government work. Hoping to succeed where all recent presidents had failed, Reagan and his staff devised a new organizational structure linking cabinet heads to the executive office through five cabinet councils. Each council was to be formally chaired by the president and was to include cabinet secretaries whose area of responsibility concerned the council. The most senior cabinet chief on a council was to serve as its chair pro tem. The five councils were concerned with commerce and trade, economic affairs, food and agriculture, human resources, and natural resources and the environment. Each council had as its executive secretary a senior member of the president's own policy development staff located in the EOP—a linkage that insured more dialogue between cabinet officers and policy staff from the Executive Office of the President. Ten members of the policy development staff assigned a significant block of their time to cabinet council matters.

To further bind policymaking units from the EOP with the cabinet, Reagan made the director of the Office of Management and Budget a member of the cabinet; the OMB deputy director was a member of the White House senior staff. Reagan's decision to include the OMB director as an informal member of the Cabinet reflected his emphasis on using the budget to shape a coherent program. By making the deputy director of OMB a member of Reagan's White House staff, he hoped that greater coordination could be achieved among the White House staff, cabinet departments, and the OMB.

Less than a year into his administration, Reagan also began to retreat from cabinet government. He grew less and less dependent on department heads as his personal staff increasingly dominated decision making. As a result, one top White House assistant suggested, "Cabinet government is a myth. I'm not sure it has dawned on the members yet that they have been cut out of the decision-making process."[60] Eventually it did dawn on them, however, as major new policy initiatives were increasingly forged by the White House with little or no cabinet involvement. Cabinet meetings grew less frequent and more ceremonial. Friction between White House officials and cabinet secretaries increased, and one cabinet secretary complained that he was being bullied by "know-it-alls" at the White House. New advisory groups proliferated in the White House as responsibilities shifted from the departments to the domestic and foreign policy units closest to the president.[61] The cabinet councils, meanwhile, appeared to have become caricatures of the cabinet itself as Reagan increasingly leaned on his four closest aides, Edwin Meese, James A. Baker III, Michael Deaver, and National Security Adviser William Clark.

TIES THAT CHAFE: CABINET RELATIONS WITH THE WHITE HOUSE

The American cabinet "does not fall together, but neither does it stand together."[62] Just as the president has the nation as his constituency, the cabinet officer increasingly becomes enmeshed in the tangled needs and concerns of his or her own constituencies, which include the department, its various agencies and bureaus, and the public and interest groups affected by departmental programs and policies. The pressures for the cabinet secretary to respond to his or her constituents are every bit as strong as the pressures on the president to provide national leadership. Theodore Sorensen, who was President Kennedy's principal domestic adviser, explained:

> [E]ach department has its own clientele and point of view, its own experts and bureaucratic interest, its own relations with the Congress and certain subcommittees, its own statutory authority, objectives, and standards of success. No cabinet member is free to ignore all this without impairing the morale and efficiency of his department, his standing therein, and his relations with the powerful interest groups and congressmen who consider it partly their own.[63]

Inevitably, for most cabinet secretaries constituency pressures come to outweigh loyalty to the White House. Or the cabinet chief may leave government, exasperated at having tried to master his department and at having failed. Departmentalism thus begins to separate every cabinet chief from the president.

In spite of all the evidence that genuine cabinet government is a chimera, it is proclaimed at the start of every new administration as the president introduces with lavish praise the "highly qualified, independent" new cabinet heads who will enjoy "unlimited access to the president," who will provide a collective decision-making capability, and who will be valued for their "openness, candor, and free-spirited thinking." As political realities begin to intrude and the president's honeymoon with Congress, the press, and the public wanes, vows of faithfulness and collegiality between the president and his cabinet are soon forgotten or violated. Before long, loyal White House advisers begin to restrict the access of cabinet heads considered poor team players and to lobby against departmental heads they see as dangerous to the president. Soon the advisers succeed in erecting a protective barrier between the chief executive and many of his cabinet officials, and life goes on as usual in the White House.

Political scientist Thomas E. Cronin has charted a predictable pattern in the deterioration in White House–cabinet relations over the course of an administration. During the early months the newly staffed Executive Branch seethes with new policies, new ideas, and potential breakthroughs as the administration ambitiously tries to recast the national political agenda:

> But all too soon, domestic crises and international developments begin to monopolize the presidential schedule. He has less time for personal contacts with cabinet officers, and they in turn become wary of being rebuffed and inclined to save their calls for critical issues only. . . . It becomes the task of the White House staff to "handle" the cabinet.[64]

At that point the cabinet has reached the condition it will hold for the rest of the administration. Meetings will grow less frequent; the few that are held will be more for symbolic value than for a substantive collegial discussion of pressing issues. Eventually cabinet meetings become nothing more than "show-and-tell" sessions, tedious gatherings filled with banal reports. A cabinet member during Nixon's presidency recalls how Vice-President Agnew was often called on to provide a rambling "travelogue" during cabinet meetings. And President Johnson supposedly told friends that his major concern during most cabinet meetings was whether the members could stay awake. Clearly the American cabinet lacks both influence and purpose.

A real cabinet system can invoke the powers of government when the need to make a collective or unified decision is required, but the American government was never designed to act in such a way, nor was the Executive Branch ever intended to be managed or administered by a single person. The president's cabinet consequently is a myth if one means cabinet on the order of the British system. For ours does not function as a true cabinet nor can it overcome the essentially pluralistic nature of our national political system. It is unrealistic to hope that any president can unify for long the diverse forces pressing on his cabinet departments and appointees. The Constitution, Congress, and our federal system institutionalize access to political officials to a degree unimaginable in any other national government. Interest groups can press their claims through one or more of any 535 Representatives and Senators, through a welter of agencies, bureaus, committees, commissions, or offices, through the courts, in the press, at the level of state, local, regional governments, or in the private marketplace. To hope that a president assisted by thirteen top-level departmental executives and several hundred ranking deputies and assistants can evolve and impose a collective administrative will is fantasy.

The counterpressures weighing on cabinet members surface during cabinet meetings which ideally are supposed to be occasions for various cabinet department heads to come together to work as a team, to cooperate, to coordinate, and to help the president with government-wide problems. Departmentalism, however, works against all such assumptions about teamwork or administrative unity. Richard J. Fenno notes:

> The cabinet meeting tends to become a diplomatic assembly in which the departmentalism of the ambassadors replaces nationalism as the psychological bar to unity and cooperation. There is too often a lack of any sustaining desire within the group to function as a group, and a lack of will to carry on serious business at the cabinet meeting.[65]

The cabinet concept virtually disintegrates in the course of the members' activities *outside* cabinet meetings. Ties binding cabinet officers to the president have always proven weaker than the chains forged by outside interest groups with Congress and government departments. In the daily grind of running a massive department, each cabinet secretary must fend for himself or herself without much concern for cabinet unity which "has only a symbolic value [that] readily disappears when the need for action supersedes the need for a show window."[66]

The first stumbling block in the path of a new cabinet secretary is the existence of an organization which already has extensive and deeply rooted personal and power relationships forged over a long period of time. Intense personal commitment and involvement in the department's way of doing things and in its policy networks, many of which were developed over many administrations, is common. Because these existing relationships, procedures, and values have developed through accommodation and adjustment, most bureaucratic organizations are resistant to change.

Cabinet chiefs have some opportunity to restructure the top hierarchy of the departmental organization through appointment of undersecretaries, assistants, or deputy secretaries. But in recent administrations less than half of these political appointees have had much of a record in political party activities. Increasingly, political appointees in the second echelon of cabinet leadership—the group most in contact with federal bureaucrats—have been program-oriented rather than president- or party-oriented. They quickly become more comfortable with the technopols described earlier, and in fact many become part of the specialist network dominating federal agencies. Most are assistant secretaries "for something"; consequently they are easily identified with specific government activities or programs.[67] Top-ranking presidential appointees frequently are hopelessly dependent on such subordinates, and this inevitably influences loyalty to the president.

The temporary nature of cabinet service keeps secretaries and their top assistants or deputies from establishing authority or credibility. The loyalty of the cabinet secretary and top political appointees is weakened by the fact that the president's influence takes second place to that of Congress after appointment. The official-designate is dependent on Senate confirmation. Departments and cabinet secretaries are created by congressional statute, as are the powers of cabinet officers and departmental responsibilities, which are subject in most cases to various forms of congressional oversight. The only clout over his appointees remaining to a president is the power to fire them, a not uncommon solution but one that is fraught with problems for the chief executive. The dismissal of a cabinet head or other important federal official is national news, and it often focuses the attention of certain groups on the possibility that their interests may be jeopardized by the firing. It also may be embarrassing to the president because it suggests he made a poor choice to begin with.

Generally the problem of departmentalism, with cabinet leaders going off "to join the natives," is greatest in what is popularly called the "outer cabinet." This consists of departments where interest groups are politically active in developing and maintaining exceptionally strong and close ties—Agriculture, Education, Energy, Transportation, Labor, Commerce, and Housing and Urban Development. The "inner cabinet"—the Departments of Justice, Defense, Treasury, and State—are less vulnerable because these departments are traditionally involved in more direct and closer policy planning with the White House. Their programs and policies tend to be of a broader national or international nature, and thus less amenable to lobbying tactics or influence.[68]

Republican presidents find it particularly difficult to make inroads via their cabinet appointees into outer-cabinet departments. This is because many of the programs and personnel of these departments were nurtured and rewarded by Democratic administrations and legislative initiatives. The new cabinet chief is seen as a hostile intruder unless or until he or she is proven otherwise by supporting existing procedures or programs. Departments like Housing and Urban Development and Health and Human Services are particularly hostile to Republican leadership because they are essentially fiefdoms of career employees and mid-level executives sympathetic to liberal Democratic party politicians. In contrast, Democratic presidents like Kennedy, Johnson, and Carter frequently complained of problems with the Department of Defense because of its strongly conservative and Republican bias. This bias is the result of generally more favorable defense budgets and more expansive programs under Republican administrations.

The authority exercised by Congress over the departments constitutes an even greater problem than the transience of presidential appointees. Congress is able to control and direct executive departments and agencies through its control of the purse strings. Without congressional compliance in his administration of the federal government, a president finds he can achieve little. The White House and cabinet chiefs are limited in their capacity to reorganize units, to transfer duties and responsibilities, or to alter budgets. Congressional oversight has grown even more rigorous in the aftermath of Nixon's attempt to use impoundments to sidetrack legislative programs, to eliminate agencies such as the Office of Economic Opportunity, and to reorganize cabinet departments under four White House supercabinet heads. Reagan's attempt to eliminate agencies or programs, to restructure or shift responsibilities, and to trim departmental budgets was sharply limited by Congress, which responded to pleas and complaints from interest groups whose benefits were threatened.

Some bureau or agency chiefs are virtually beyond presidential or cabinet control because of their considerable influence with Congress and widespread popular support, or because of their highly specialized activities that provide considerable autonomy. One of the best examples for many years was J. Edgar Hoover and the Federal Bureau of Investigation. Hoover's name became indistinguishable from the FBI; his careful exploitation of his name in conjunction with the agency in movies and the mass media built him a massive popular following and made him invulnerable to presidential control or removal. Chief executives from FDR on found they had little choice but to reappoint Hoover even though he began to use questionable tactics to spy on American groups and celebrities he disliked. Hoover frequently refused to obey directives or requests from the White House or from his superior, the attorney general of the United States.

Another agency unto itself is the Corps of Engineers of the U.S. Army, which is responsible for a wide range of flood control and navigational activities. Although a part of the Army it is organizationally within the Department of Defense. But the corps sees itself as a congressional agency and Congress pampers the corps as if it were an only child. The Corps of Engineers oversees the planning and development of a great number of pork-barrel projects dear to the hearts of every member of Congress; as a result, it enjoys the kind of independence other agencies can only envy or try to emulate. No other large federal agency is as well protected by powerful external interest groups—farmers, recreational sports enthusiasts, real estate developers, local and state politicians—anyone benefitting from one or another of the countless projects carrying the corps's castle symbol. Congressional subcommittees are especially solicitous of the corps since it directly benefits constituents of committee members, and the corps is generously cared for in budget requests. Congress has consistently refused to allow the president to include the corps in any reorganization plan, the most recent of which would have shifted its civil functions to the Department of Interior.[69]

Every president finds that about the best he can hope for from his cabinet is that a few secretaries with whom he has good personal rapport or close ties may be extraordinarily gifted in managing their departments. In that case the president's goals will enjoy a moderate rate of success. Beyond this, there is not much hope for advances in executive leadership because the goal of utilizing the cabinet more effectively remains unattainable. What most presidents have in mind is a collective authority resembling the parliamentary-cabinet systems found in Europe. But as we have seen, this model is totally inappropriate in our system of checks and balances and separation of powers.

"The people whom the president can command in the White House do not have their hands on the operating agencies of government," Rose has written. "Even those whom the president appoints to direct the major departments of government are only overseers of the bureaus that collectively constitute the principal operating agencies of the executive branch."[70] Presidents are unable to control their administration through their cabinets because they do not actually *have* a cabinet. The European cabinet provides collective authority sufficiently strong to reconcile differences among subgovernments, but the American system is lopsided in favor of subgovernments, whose power is much more substantial than the collective authority of the president.

REORGANIZING THE EXECUTIVE BRANCH

A number of political theorists have warned that the concentration of power in organizations of technical expertise which are not subject to democratic political control is as threatening to civil society as authority which is too centralized and too strong.[71] There is support for the idea that governmental bureaucracies ought to be politicized if they are to be responsible to the wishes of the electorate, and this political power must rest with the president.

A more realistic view suggests that the best a president can hope for as chief executive is to use his persuasive talents, his personality, and his electoral mandate to influence people in government to do what they are supposed to be doing. Organizing the presidency in this view is akin to reinventing the wheel. Each president—by using his symbolic status, his drama, and the wide range of political resources available to him—can establish the White House as the core of governmental operations; force would then extend outward like spokes of a wheel, causing the government to move along at his direction. This conception parallels the Rooseveltian model for managing the Executive Branch. It relies on ad hoc, personalized efforts to prod the existing bureaucracy into action.

All efforts to make the presidency more effective administratively are variations on these two basic conceptions. The first approach was the one that evolved during the earlier years of the presidency in response to our system's fragmentation of authority. The second is a byproduct of civil service reforms and the removal of much of the executive bureaucracy from the president's political control. FDR's major reorganization attempted to restore the political model but ended up refining the personalized managerial approach. Two reorganization efforts headed by former President Herbert H. Hoover did little to reverse this trend toward White House–centered management techniques, interspersed with an increasingly independent and professional government service. Not until the 1970s was a renewed assault on the independence of the federal bureaucracy mounted, this time by President Nixon, who was determined to use administrative authority instead of legislative tactics to achieve his policy goals.

Nixon's Plan

Nixon decided even before the end of his first term that the only way he would ever achieve his policy agenda of reducing the federal government's role in social programs and of enhancing his global powers would be by taking over the bureaucracy and taking on Congress. Hopelessly disadvantaged by substantial Democratic majorities in both houses of Congress, Nixon believed that he could use his authority as chief administrative officer to downgrade the legislative process. What he was unable to accomplish through Congress he would achieve through directives to his agencies.[72]

Presidents increasingly had come to rely on White House staffs and EOP staffs to overcome the subgovernmental tendencies of departments and agencies. But Nixon discovered early on that this had the negative effect of creating a growing counterbureaucracy in the White House, which resulted in major stumbling blocks. The deeper the White House staff dug into agency affairs, the more serious the problems became. According to political scientist Richard Nathan, " . . . as the White House became more and more involved in routine administrative matters, the time and energy it had to devote to truly important policy issues was correspondingly reduced."[73] The result more often than not was confusion because the White House people were trying to do too much. Usually inexperienced in substantive policy matters, the people surrounding the president spent too much time reviewing programs while taking on more and more new decisions. Responsibilities became blurred, decisions had to be reviewed over and over again, and operational delays became chronic (see the following chapter for a further discussion of this point).

The alternative to working through a White House bureaucracy was to rely on strong, presidentially appointed program managers assigned to executive agencies with clear lines of authority to the president. Since Nixon and his top aides believed that most of his initial cabinet secretaries had "gone off to marry the natives," this arrangement required major changes in personnel as well as new lines of authority and new procedures.

The day after his landslide reelection victory in 1972, Nixon held a cabinet meeting. He thanked each of his cabinet secretaries for their assistance in the campaign, and then asked all of them to submit their resignations at once so that he could completely reorganize his administration. The same day the president briefly thanked hundreds of other top administration officials for their help. Afterward, White House Chief of Staff H. R. Haldeman asked all these people to submit their resignations; it was made clear that many of the resignations would be accepted.

In addition to appointing loyal Nixon people to high-level posts, a major element in this reorganization scheme—which Nixon believed could be accomplished *without* Congressional approval—involved putting some agencies and programs out of business and shaking up the lines of responsibilities in others. He hoped to accomplish these changes through his budgetary powers, especially the president's infrequently used authority to impound funds. Nixon attempted, for example, to abolish the Office of Economic Opportunity (OEO) by eliminating from his budget its requests for funds.

Another key element in Nixon's reorganization plan was the regrouping of domestic responsibilities held by cabinet secretaries under a "supercabinet." This supercabinet was to consist of four special counsellors to the president—each of whom then headed a major cabinet department; the loyalty of these officials to Nixon was more established than that of their colleagues. The four supercabinet secretaries would be paired with four members of the White House staff—Haldeman, Ehrlichman, National Security Adviser Henry A. Kissinger, and Roy Ash, the new director of the OMB. The personnel in the executive office would be cut in half since the new supersecretaries would have plenty of room to function in their assigned areas of policy; they would be in frequent contact with the president and his four top White House advisers.

Since no plan to improve the accountability of the bureaucracy could succeed without gaining control over the senior levels of the career civil service, the Nixon administration had special plans for difficult members of this privileged group. A fascinating array of tactics—many of them in direct violation of civil service statutes—were developed to bring careerists into line or to push them out of Nixon's way. A sampling of some of the more unusual tactics appeared in a *Federal Political Personnel Manual*, which circulated privately among White House staff members. The manual contained the following suggestions:

1. *The frontal assault.* The individual is called in by the superior, and told that he or she is no longer wanted; assistance will be provided in finding another job. The employee is kept on until other employment is found, but most duties are relinquished and the employee is given makeshift, boring work pending departure. The bureaucrat leaves "with honor and with the finest recommendation, a farewell luncheon, and perhaps even a departmental award."[74] If the employee will not accept this offer and has to be forced out, a not-too-subtle warning is issued: his or her personnel record will not be as good as it would have been if the original offer had been taken. (The manual warned against using this tactic against a strong-willed employee who is superconscious of civil service rights and duties. It should be reserved for the "timid at heart.")

2. *The transfer technique.* This entails careful research into the background of an employee to find the geographical area and/or governmental agency to which the employee would rather resign than be transferred. For example:

    . . . if there was an employee who was born and raised in New England and was currently serving in a Boston Regional Office, and his record shows reluctance to move far . . . a transfer accom-

panied by a promotion to an existing or newly created position in Dallas, Texas, would fill the bill. . . .

3. *The traveling salesman.* Aimed at the family man who does not enjoy traveling, this approach involves assigning the employee to a special research and evaluation project that would take him away from home and send him to the most unappealing sites imaginable. As an illustration, the manual suggested a hypothetical program analyst with the Department of Transportation who might be sent on an inspection of transportation systems in all U.S. cities and towns of 20,000 or less:

Along with his promotion and assignment [the] expert was given extensive travel orders criss-crossing . . . the country to towns (hopefully with the worst accommodations possible) . . . until his wife threatened him with divorce unless he quit. . . . When he finally asked for relief, they tearfully reiterated the importance of the project and stated he must continue to obey travel orders or resign. Failure to obey travel orders is grounds for immediate separation.

Other sections suggested the following tactics: "layering" over insubordinate managers with new loyal managers by creating additional slots and supergrade positions; bypassing recalcitrant executives by "promoting" them to other positions and filling key jobs with administration supporters; or shifting responsibilities so that an executive or entire agency might be isolated or bypassed.

Nixon's reorganization scheme was derailed by Watergate in the spring of 1973 before he could begin to implement it. After the Senate Watergate Committee hearings and the resignations of many top White House aides who would have overseen the plan, there was little steam left in Nixon's plan. Meanwhile, an investigation by the U.S. Civil Service Commission tipped off Congress to numerous violations by the White House.

Efforts of Carter and Reagan

The most sweeping changes in the Executive Branch since FDR's time were achieved by Carter in the Civil Service Reform Act of 1978, which replaced the Civil Service Commission with the Office of Personnel Management (OPM). It also created a Merit Systems Protection Board to hear appeals or complaints from federal employees and applicants for federal jobs.

Carter's complex reorganization sought to improve management by making it easier to fire incompetent civil servants. Special counsel was provided to protect whistle blowers who risked their jobs by reporting wrongdoing. Procedures for hearing complaints of unfair labor practices were included. Federal workers were guaranteed the right to unionize and to collective bargaining. To improve the quality and responsiveness of high-ranking federal executives, a Senior Executive Service was created as an elite corps of managers whose compensation, tenure, and retention would be based on performance. Nonpolitical career managers, supervisors, and program directors were encouraged to give up civil service protection in exchange for joining the SES and thereby qualifying for cash awards and annual bonuses for outstanding service. Nearly all the 6000 senior executives joined, giving up their job security for what Carter described as "the risks and rewards of competitive life."[75]

Whether these reforms will make the bureaucracy more responsible or accountable to the president and his political appointees remains to be seen. Morale was shaken among members of the SES when it appeared that many were not paid the bonuses promised by Congress.[76] As for punishing incompetence, in 1976 (prior to the reform) only 3500 tenured civil servants were fired for poor job performance—a discharge rate of one seventh of 1 percent. In 1980 (two years after the reform) the number of civil servants fired for poor performance totalled 2632—about one tenth of 1 percent. During the first three years of the SES, only one senior executive was dropped.[77]

The 1978 reforms did not reduce the paperwork or laborious procedures required to dismiss an employee and to handle appeals. Unionization created new roadblocks for officials in the form of quarrels over a wide range of activities that federal employees now try to avoid through detailed bargaining agreements. The reorganization provided that presidential appointees could reassign career executives to other agencies or programs after a waiting period of 120 days so long as such moves were not made for political or personal favoritism or racial discrimination.[78]

Reagan used the 1978 Civil Service Reform Act to try to pack the upper levels of the career bureaucracy with Reaganites and conservatives. First of all, great care was taken at the beginning of his administration to choose cabinet and subcabinet political appointees who shared Reagan's conservative political philosophy. A condition made clear to everyone offered a cabinet secretaryship was that the president-elect and his transition team would have the major voice in choosing subcabinet officials since this was the level at which control over the professional bureaucrats would be attempted.[79] Once in office, Reagan's operatives attempted to use RIFs—"reductions in force"—to weed out careerists who were seen as hostile to Reagan's objectives. Although employees were notified that their positions had been terminated, under civil service regulations it is seniority that determines who actually loses a job. As a result, each RIF could initiate a series of "bumps" from one job to another, much like a row of dominoes falling; eventually persons with the least amount of service in the bureaucracy would be laid off. Many senior career executives, however, ended up in routine jobs with little substantive power, usually at the same pay.[80]

Reagan's appointee to head the Office of Personnel Management—theoretically an independent government agency replacing the Civil Service Commission—admitted that 11,000 federal employees had been separated during the first two years of the administration, and that three people were affected by job changes for each separation. This meant that as many as 30,000 persons were shifted in their jobs although not all to lower grade positions.[81]

Charges were levelled that the OPM was politicizing the civil service in violation of the 1978 reorganization's intent. The number of political appointees to agencies increased even as the OPM reduced overall federal employment. The Federal Managers Association, which represents many top career executives, declared that the productivity of the federal work force declined by 20 to 30 percent as a result of the RIFs. One official at the Merit Systems Protection Board resigned his $44,000 a year job because he protested that under the director Reagan appointed to that appeals board no studies were being initiated to look into the many charges of abuses of the federal personnel practices.[82]

A study of Reagan's staffing procedures by Richard Nathan, however, argues that Reagan was simply using the 1978 reforms effectively as an administrative tool to gain accountability. "It can be argued that the new law is working exactly the way it should, despite the pain involved for the persons removed from office."[83]

It is not axiomatic, however, that Reagan's aggressive use of Carter's reforms have led to greater presidential control over the bureaucracy. Several of Reagan's appointees gained national attention by overzealously pushing administration policies in the face of agency resistance. The image projected to the public was of presidential appointees who had little regard for the environment or public interest. Reagan's top political appointees to the Environmental Protection Agency (EPA) were forced to resign in a showdown with EPA career officials who were able to prove attempts to block cleanups of a number of dangerous toxic waste sites, as well as improper use of agency cleanup funds. The episode proved that there were hazards awaiting any political executive who ignored or went against the collective advice and expertise of career executives or who tried to bend the bureaucracy's will too much in the direction of administration policy. The political fallout from presidential appointees who clearly try to circumvent the intent of Congress or the public interest may be more than any president can tolerate in order to gain the upper hand over the bureaucracy.

Even if Reagan succeeds in politicizing the bureaucracy—a goal many public administration theorists would support as logical if presidents are to ever manage successfully—there is nothing to stop the next administration from employing similar tactics to shift the bureaucracy in the reverse direction politically. Eventually, the federal bureaucracy would lose considerable expertise and professionalism as it became nothing more nor less than a political football to be tossed back and forth between succeeding administrations. Congress and public opinion would not tolerate such a trend for long, however, since the tradition of an independent, nonpartisan civil service is deeply ingrained in our system.

CONCLUSION

The bureaucracy or administrative arm of government is assuming more and more power at the expense of the legislative and judicial branches of government in all modern industrial societies, according to Peter Woll, an expert on public administration. Since the increasing power of the bureaucracy has reduced in many cases the influence of the main political executives in these countries, it is misleading to regard the bureaucracy as a *part* of the Executive Branch and as controlled by the president or his cabinet.[84]

The only occasions when the president appears capable of managing the government is when there is a planned or lucky conjunction of his own goals with those of particular groups within or outside the government. This is not frequent enough, however, to enable a president to perform the chief executive's role in the manner expected of him. As a result, presidents increasingly appear not only incapable of achieving policy agenda that they promise to the public but they also seem incompetent at managing the existing policies.

The illusion that presidents can succeed as chief executives is primarily an outgrowth of the presidency of Franklin D. Roosevelt. It is a misconception that presidents can make the American "cabinet" system into a hybrid of the British ministerial-cabinet government. Roosevelt's success was due to the fact that many federal agencies were new; he also used a personal, ad hoc–styled managerial system to achieve results. But Roosevelt's approach encouraged the evolution of a far less professional and more fragmented government bureaucracy whose functioning depended on the creative capacities of White House staffers to implement the president's programs.

The British model is inappropriate for the presidency because British prime ministers collectively share executive power with the legislature. The British civil service—a permanent, highly professionalized and nonpartisan force—owes complete loyalty to the cabinet because it shares responsibility with the democratically elected parliament. The American executive lacks this collective focus in policymaking and implementation. In the absence of a formal linkage between these two major functions, the presidency ends up exceptionally vulnerable to all kinds of external and internal pressures.

Even presidential political appointees end up with divided loyalties because the pressures from subgovernments provide substantial counterbalances to presidential direction. Ironically, the president is faulted by the opposition party, by the news media, and by the electorate for failing to control the bureaucracy, but if he attempts to exert political authority—as Nixon and Reagan did—he is accused of corrupting the civil service and of "politicizing" the bureaucracy.

Americans do not have a single institution capable of asserting collective authority on major issues. The president finds it impossible to get a handle on government because there is no handle there.

NOTES

1. Hedrick Smith, "Problems of a Problem Solver," *New York Times Magazine*, January 8, 1978, 31-2.
2. Robert Sherrill, *Why They Call It Politics* (New York: Harcourt Brace Jovanovich, 1974), 8.
3. Richard E. Neustadt, *Presidential Power* (New York: John Wiley & Sons, 1960), 9.
4. Richard Rose, "Governments Against Sub-governments," in Richard Rose and Ezra Suleiman, eds., *Presidents and Prime Ministers* (Washington, D.C.: American Enterprise Institute, 1980), 297.
5. Harold Seidman, *Politics, Position and Power* (New York: Oxford University Press, 1980), 14.
6. Clinton Rossiter, *The American Presidency* (New York: Harvest Books, 1960), 59.
7. Quoted in Seidman, 121.
8. Hugh Heclo, *A Government of Strangers* (Washington, D.C.: Brookings Institution, 1977), 86.
9. Rose, 293.
10. Ibid., 292.
11. Ibid.
12. Richard E. Neustadt, "White House and Whitehall," in Francis E. Rourke, ed., *Bureaucratic Power in National Politics* (Boston: Little, Brown and Company, 1972), 166-67.
13. Ibid.
14. Richard Rose, *Managing Presidential Objectives* (New York: Free Press, 1976), 145.
15. Stephen T. Early, Jr., and Barbara Knight, *Responsible Government: American and British* (Chicago: Nelson-Hall Publishers, 1981), 207-8.
16. Seidman, 101.
17. Godfrey Hodgson, *All Things to All Men* (New York: Simon & Schuster, 1980), 57.
18. Richard Polenberg, *Reorganizing Roosevelt's Government, 1936-1939* (Cambridge, Mass.: Harvard University Press, 1966), 193.

19. Hodgson, 58.

20. Ibid.

21. Bruce Miroff, "Monopolizing the Public Space: The President as a Problem Solver for Democratic Politics," in Thomas E. Cronin, ed., *Rethinking the Presidency* (Boston: Little, Brown and Company, 1982), 219.

22. Ibid., 225.

23. Heclo (1977), 86.

24. James T. Bennett, "How Big is the Federal Government?" *Economic Review*, December 1981, 44.

25. Hugh Heclo, "Issue Networks and the Executive Establishment," in Anthony King, ed., *The New American Political System* (Washington, D.C.: American Enterprise Institute, 1978), 91.

26. U.S. Civil Service Commission, *Federal Civil Work Force Statistics (1978.)*

27. Heclo, 93.

28. Theodore H. White, *American In Search of Itself* (New York: Harper & Row, Publishers, 1982), 128.

29. Heclo (1978), 93.

30. *Newsweek*, January 26, 1981, 42.

31. *Congressional Quarterly Almanac, 1976*, 513.

32. Joseph A. Califano, Jr., *Governing America* (New York: Simon & Schuster, 1981), 181-99.

33. Charles Peters, *How Washington Really Works* (Reading, Mass: Addison-Wesley Publishing Co., 1980), 37.

34. Heclo (1977), 88.

35. Richard P. Nathan, *The Plot That Failed: Nixon and the Administrative Presidency* (New York: John Wiley & Sons, 1975), 49-50.

36. Heclo (1977), 103-4.

37. Ibid., 110-12.

38. Ibid., 63

39. Ibid., 65.

40. *New York Times*, October 23, 1977.

41. Francis Rourke, "Grappling with Bureaucracy," in Arnold Meltsner, ed., *Politics and the Oval Office* (San Francisco: Institute for Contemporary Studies, 1981), 125.

42. William Greider, "The Education of David Stockman," *Atlantic*, December 1981, 33.

43. Rose, 294.

44. Douglas Cater, *Power in Washington* (New York: Vintage Books, 1964).

45. Randall Ripley and Grace Franklin, *Congress, the Bureaucracy, and Public Policy*, rev. ed. (Homewood, Ill.: Dorsey Press, 1980), 8-11.

46. Rose, 294.

47. Califano, 193.

48. A. Lee Fritschler, *Smoking and Politics*, 3d ed. (Englewood Cliffs, N.J.: Prentice-Hall, 1983), 128.

49. Ibid., 6-7.

50. Rose, 295.

51. *The Federalist* (New York: Random House, Modern Library, 1937)

52. Thomas E. Cronin, *The State of the Presidency* (Boston: Little, Brown and Company, 1980), 254.

53. Stephen Hess, *Organizing the White House* (Washington, D.C.: Brookings Institution, 1976), 44–58.

54. Arthur Schlesinger, Jr., *A Thousand Days* (Boston: Houghton Mifflin Company, 1965), 688.

55. Richard E. Neustadt, *Presidential Power: the Politics of Leadership* (New York: John Wiley & Sons, 1976), 15.

56. George E. Reedy, *The Twilight of the Presidency* (New York: Mentor Books, 1970), 78.

57. Nathan, 37.

58. Ibid., 40.

59. Dom Bonafede, "Carter's White House: Heavy on Function, Light on Frills," *National Journal*, February 12, 1977, 234.

60. U.S. News & World Report, March 29, 1982, 28.

61. Ibid.

62. Richard F. Fenno, *The President's Cabinet* (Cambridge, Mass.: Harvard University Press, 1959), 133.

63. Theodore Sorensen, *Decision-Making in the White House* (New York: Columbia University Press, 1963), 68.

64. Thomas E. Cronin, "Conflict over the Cabinet," *New York Times Magazine*, August 12, 1979.

65. Fenno, 134.

66. Ibid., 247.

67. Heclo (1977), 103.

68. Cronin, 276–78.

69. A.A. Maass, "Congress and Water Resources," *American Political Science Review* 44 (1950), 576–93.

70. Rose, 295.

71. See Theodore J. Lowi, *The End of Liberalism* (New York: W.W. Norton & Company, 1979); and Grant McConnell, *Private Power and American Democracy* (New York: Alfred A. Knopf, 1966).

72. Nathan, 80–91.

73. Ibid., 51.

74. "Federal Political Personnel Manual," included in *Hearings, Select Committee on Presidential Campaign Activities*, 93rd Congress, 2d Sess, vol. 19 (1974).

75. Leonard Reed, "Bureaucrats 2, Presidents 0," *Harper's Magazine*, November 1982, reprinted in *Annual Editions: American Government*, 1983–84 (Guilford, Conn.: Dushkin Publishing Group, 1983), 128.

76. *National Journal*, November 29, 1980, 2028.

77. Reed, 126.

78. *National Journal*, April 9, 1983, 735.

79. G. Calvin Mackenzie, "Cabinet and Subcabinet Personnel Selection in Reagan's First Year: New Variations on Some Not-So-Old-Themes," paper delivered at the

Annual Meeting, American Political Science Association, New York City, September 2-5, 1981.

80. *National Journal*, April 19, 1983, 735.

81. Ibid.

82. *San Antonio Express*, Ápril 20, 1983, 8-A.

83. *National Journal*, April 9, 1983, 732.

84. Peter Woll, *American Bureaucracy* (New York: W.W. Norton & Company, 1963), 3.

Chapter 5

The **Mirror-Image Machine**
The Presidential Establishment

*The first impression that one gets of a ruler and
of his brains is from seeing the men that he has
around him. When they are competent and faithful one can always consider him wise, as he has
been able to recognize their ability and to keep
them faithful. But when they are the reverse, one
can always form an unfavorable opinion of him,
because the first mistake that he makes is in
making this choice.*

    Niccolò Machiavelli, *The Prince*

*The White House is small, but if you're not at the
center it seems enormous. You get the feeling
there are all sorts of meetings going on without
you, all sorts of people clustered in small groups,
whispering, always whispering.*

    Lyndon B. Johnson

When attempts at cabinet government fail, when a president's legislative agenda bogs down in the congressional swamp and the mass media
begin to pick apart his administration, the president instinctively
retreats into the White House. Then his closest aides and advisers
"circle the wagons," mounting counteroffensives against those who
threaten the administration.

Each new president may genuinely believe early in his administration that he will succeed with cabinet government, that he will be able to conduct an open administration. But after opposition begins to jell against his policies and decisions, and after his personal electoral coalition begins to weaken or fall apart in the face of powerful pressures from subgovernments or triple alliances, the president begins to reduce his contacts with others in the political environment. Every president sooner or later comes to depend on the counsel and company of his own loyalists in the Executive Office of the President (EOP), especially members of the White House staff.

The allegiance of some 1700 people in ten EOP units and of another 500 or so in the White House office extends first and foremost to the president. But the president's own bureaucracy has grown so complex and is so propelled by its own internal dynamics that it has become an additional bureaucratic hurdle for every president to surmount. The EOP has grown into a "bloated and disorderly grabbag of separate and mutually suspicious staffs, units, councils, boards, and groups with strikingly different histories, purposes and problems," according to two assistant cabinet secretaries who served in the Carter administration.[1] The president now needs help in dealing with his helpers!

Presidents depend on EOP units, especially White House personal staffs, because of the vast number of unavoidable responsibilities that have been grafted onto the White House. Heclo counted forty-three separate statutory requirements for annual presidential reports on subjects as diverse as the environment, foreign arms sales, and the like. Such reports, along with all the other administrative and policy responsibilities now weighing on the White House, require more staff work, specialization, and bureaucratic routine within the presidency. Each new process that becomes "institutionalized" in the White House gives someone else a proprietary interest in what is done in the name of the president.[2]

An expanded presidential establishment has become essential to the president's staying on top of the action-forcing processes that confront him. Eisenhower once warned Kennedy, "There are no easy matters that will come to you as president. If they are easy, they will be settled at a lower level."[3] Problems that come to the attention of the White House usually require fast, decisive responses or coordinated action. Many are crises which impose hard deadlines with immediate priorities on the president. Key members of the presidential establishment almost always find themselves astride such processes; their proximity and access to the president enable them to handle crises or action-forced problems far more expeditiously and in line with the president's wishes than if the decisions were left to the regular bureaucracy.

As more and more units and persons assist the president in dealing with action-forcing policy matters, he increasingly becomes dependent on a smaller and smaller clique of individuals whose loyalty is beyond question. While these presidential assistants zealously try to serve the president's best interests, they frequently end up serving as his mirror-image—telling him what he *wants* to hear and advising him in directions the president already wants to move. Joseph A. Califano, Jr., who served both Johnson and Carter, has noted:

> *Thwarted by the Congress in attempts at executive reorganization, frustrated by the fragmentation of authority and responsibility among the inefficiently organized departments and agencies, harassed by crises they are expected to resolve, tempted by the potential of effectively exercising the increasing powers laid at the White House door and by their personal ability to focus attention on pet programs, it was inevitable that presidents would take the only action solely within their control: they would enlarge their own staffs. . . .*[4]

The expanded White House staff has made the presidency virtually a collegial office—a corps of "shadow presidents."[5] The president's capacity to respond to the demands of his office is significantly increased by such assistance, but his political power is also seriously dispersed. White House assistants extend the president's reach at the same time as they seal him off from other politicians. As political scientist Robert Wood comments, operational matters flow to the top as central staffs become preoccupied with subduing outlying bureaucracies, but policymaking emerges at the bottom. "At the top, minor problems squeeze out major ones, and individuals lower down the echelons who have the time for reflection and mischief-making take up issues of fundamental philosophical and political significance."[6]

This chapter examines the illusion that a president can use his personal establishment to govern effectively. We begin by considering the problems inherent in a presidential bureaucracy superimposed on the executive bureaucracy. Then we will see how various presidents have tried to organize their staffs to maximize their personal powers. The chapter will conclude by considering how and why presidential establishments frequently function contrary to the president's interests.

EXECUTIVE OFFICE OF THE PRESIDENT

As Congress moved to establish a number of specialized agencies and new departments to deal with a broad range of domestic and world problems, presidents over the years were given additional responsibilities and authority for overseeing their operations. The president's duties as administrator came to rival if not surpass the responsibility for enforcing federal laws and statutes by the time Franklin D. Roosevelt was sworn into office for his second term. It was increasingly clear to many, however, that the presidency was overburdened and understaffed. FDR noted that President William McKinley had been able to deal with the entire Executive Branch through eight cabinet secretaries and the heads of two commissions. "Now . . . it has become physically impossible for one man to see so many persons, to receive reports directly from them, and to attempt to advise them on their problems."[7]

The Committee on Administrative Management headed by Louis Brownlow declared in 1937 that "the president needs help." After Congress granted FDR authority to reorganize the Executive Branch, Roosevelt issued an executive order creating the Executive Office of the President to coordinate and assist the president's management of federal agencies. Since Roosevelt, there has been a succession of new advisory units, new layers of staff, and new roles and responsibilities grafted onto the EOP in an attempt to coordinate administrative leadership in the White House. A study by John Helmer and Louis Maisel, for example, reveals that personnel in the EOP increased by 50 percent between 1950 and 1980 while the budget increased eightfold.[8]

The evolution of a high-level presidential bureaucracy contributes to the illusion that the presidency is institutionalized. In fact, the EOP's institutionalization of authority is as much a myth as any of the illusions which suggest the president enjoys systematic or regular powers. Henry Fairlie insists that there is no high political office which is less institutionalized since an institution presupposes a corporate existence independent of a supreme but temporary officeholder.[9] The British cabinet and government service are institutionalized, but the EOP has none of the structural or functional predictability of these systems.

The organizational chart in Figure 5-1 deceptively shows a form of administrative order in the presidential establishment; in truth, there is no overall structure or systematic order. Instead, there is considerable confusion and intermingling of economic, social, budgetary, defense, foreign policy, political, and personal staffs, all of which are engaged in palace intrigues and court politics.[10]

The reason EOP units exist in a freewheeling relationship to one another is that the presidential establishment evolved out of a series of responses by successive presidents to problems of domestic and foreign policy. As noted in Chapter 3, for example, the Office of Management and Budget (OMB) and a domestic policy unit, the Domestic Council, emerged under President Nixon as part of an attempt to improve White

Figure 5-1 Executive Office of the President

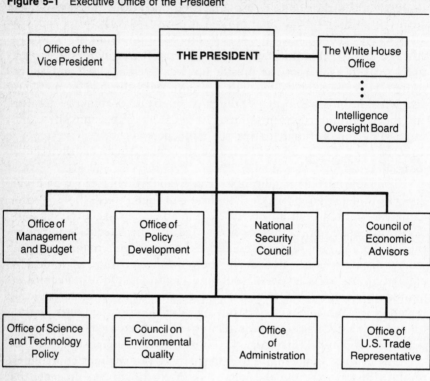

SOURCE: White House Office of Administration.

House control over the domestic policy agenda. Both agencies remain in the forefront of the president's policy system, although the status of each has varied from one administration to the next. From 1972 to 1974 the OMB frequently clashed with the Domestic Council as each attempted to gain dominance over the president's domestic agenda. The Domestic Council was tarnished by its role in the Watergate scandal, but it recovered during the Carter administration. The OMB, in contrast, was less influential during Carter's presidency, partly because of the early departure of its first director, Bert Lance, one of Carter's closest confidants, and partly because of the emergence of the skillful and persuasive Stuart Eizenstat as Carter's domestic policy chief. The OMB regained its influence in the Reagan administration because Reagan was determined to use the federal budget process to reduce the government's involvement in domestic programs. Reagan's OMB director, David Stockman, became the administration's number two man and "OMB was running the show as never before," according to a former Carter budget official.[11]

Typically the influence and power of EOP units depend on how well the chiefs get along with the president, for personal contact in the upper echelons of the presidential establishment is the name of the game. Nowhere is this more apparent than in the foreign policy-national defense structure in the EOP, where the organization created by Congress to assist the president—the National Security Council—is of far less importance than the national security assistant, who is the president's personal assistant.

The National Security Council

Comprised of the president, vice-president, secretaries of state and defense, plus other top foreign- and military-policy advisers, the NSC was created by the National Defense Act of 1947 to help the president coordinate foreign and military policies with domestic policy during international crises or threats to the nation's security. The influence of the NSC, however, is not so much due to its existence as a formal unit but rather to the capability its permanent staff provides the president. The NSC provides the president with a full range of intelligence, data, and policy recommendations because it is privy to all such communications received by the Departments of State and Defense as well as by the Central Intelligence Agency. Meetings of the full NSC thus have little meaning other than as ceremonial functions; the expertise of the NSC permanent staff is channeled through the national security adviser.

The national security adviser emerged as the president's leading global adviser during the Kennedy administration. While Kennedy was openly frustrated with the bureaucratic inertia and unresponsiveness of the State Department, McGeorge Bundy, his NSC adviser, was able to provide the direct, no-holds-barred advice and data Kennedy needed. Power continued to flow into the hands of the presidential adviser throughout the Vietnam War, reaching its zenith under Nixon's national security assistant, Henry A. Kissinger.

The emergence of what was essentially a one-man foreign-policy apparatus in the EOP generated hostility in other Executive Branch agencies traditionally responsible for foreign affairs, especially the Department of State. Conflict pitting the secretary of state and the Foreign Service against the national security adviser has become almost a chronic feature of decision making in the Executive Branch. (This problem will be examined in more detail in the next chapter.)

The Council of Economic Advisers

Another key EOP unit, especially in the development of the president's fiscal policy and legislative agenda, is the Council of Economic Advisers. The CEA, which was established by the Employment Act of 1946, consists of a chief economist and two other members supported by another eighteen professional economists. The CEA was important in developing the Great Society legislation during the Johnson administration and in recommending fiscal policies to Reagan as he dismantled some of the same social-welfare programs begun under Johnson. CEA advisers were also involved in decisions during the Carter administration to deregulate airlines, railroads, and trucking, as well as in shaping Carter's energy program. The CEA enjoyed virtually a monopoly over economic policy until the 1970s. Gradually its influence has declined as economic planning has become important throughout the government. The increased capability of Congress through its budget office has diminished the CEA's influence; the agency has also been overshadowed in recent years by the OMB.

Other EOP units have come into being or disappeared as various presidents attempted to respond to specific policy crises or needs requiring long-range coordination or direction. The Council on Environmental Quality was created by Congress during Nixon's administration to help the president deal with the growing threat of environmental pollution. The Special Trade Representative was created in 1974 to advise and coordinate national policies on foreign trade. President Ford established an Economic Policy Board, the Council on Wage-Price Stability, and the Labor Management Committee to deal with the economic stagflation wracking the nation during the mid-1970s. The Energy Resources Council—whose duties were later absorbed by the new Energy Department—was a response to the energy crises of the 1970s. In general, just how important these units were to the president depended on the president, who could make as much or as little of them as he wished. This was especially true of what traditionally has been the most underutilized unit of all in the EOP: the Office of the Vice-President.

The Vice-Presidency

Although Jimmy Carter has been faulted by critics for a number of shortcomings, he will be remembered for at least one major accomplishment: discovering a purpose for the vice-presidency and encouraging Walter F. Mondale to become the first full-fledged working vice-president in our history.

Jokes about vice-presidents abound. Prior to Mondale, the vice-presidency had seldom amounted to much more than a "pitcher of warm spit," in former Vice-President John Nance Garner's memorable assessment of the office. The Founding Fathers created the vice-presidency as an afterthought—a way of appeasing the individual who came in second in electoral college balloting. By making him the legitimate successor to the president, they hoped there would be less temptation for any runner-up to mount a coup d' état. The vice president was given the privilege of presiding over the U.S. Senate—a most unlikely hybrid duty since his office was not really a part of the legislature, and the legislature would consider anyone from the Executive Branch an interloper if he tried to involve himself in the legislative process. The vice-president was given the authority to cast a vote in case of ties in the Senate, a power rarely used.

Even rarer, however, was the inclusion of the vice-president in the president's decision making. Every president must feel uncomfortable around his vice-president because the VP is a constant reminder of what the journalists call the "death watch"—the ever present possibility that the president's life might be snatched away at any time. The vice-president is always at hand, ready to step in and assume the presidency. Not liking to be reminded of his own mortality, every president has kept his vice-president out of sight as well as out of mind. When Truman took over after the death of Roosevelt, he had had few briefings on the conduct of the war and knew nothing about the Manhattan Project to develop the atomic bomb. Although Nixon was vice-president for eight years under Eisenhower, he had never set foot in the living quarters of the White House until 1969 when President and Mrs. Johnson entertained him prior to Nixon's own inauguration.

Four times in this century, the vice-president has succeeded to the White House on the sudden death of a president, and on one occasion as a result of resignation. In addition, two presidents—Wilson and Eisenhower—were incapacitated for long periods by illness. Although Reagan was only briefly disabled by wounds suffered during the attempt on his life in 1981, attention focused once again on the Twenty-fifth Amendment to the Constitution, which provides for the orderly but temporary transfer of the president's authority to the vice-president in case of the chief executive's inability to discharge the powers and duties of his office. The president may inform Congress of his incapacity, or the vice-president may if the president is unwilling or unable to do so. If a majority of the president's cabinet or any other body provided for by Congress agrees and the president accepts their judgment, the vice-president becomes acting president until the disability is removed. If the president continues to dispute the finding that he is unable to carry on, Congress may have to resolve the issue.

The extent to which a president uses his vice-president depends on the president's personal relationship to the vice-president. Johnson was always an outsider as far as Kennedy's White House intimates were concerned. Although Kennedy tried to assign Johnson important diplomatic tasks and to include him on several councils and task forces, there never was any doubt that Johnson might just as well have been lounging along the Pedernales River in Texas for all the influence he carried in the administration. LBJ as president used Hubert H. Humphrey to maintain contacts with liberal Democrats and Congress. But Humphrey was never really a part of Johnson's inner circle of advisers and was often treated patronizingly by the president.

Nixon and his staff considered Agnew a buffoon, but valuable as a hatchet man for the president. Ford gave his vice-president, Nelson Rockefeller, more responsibilities than most vice-presidents. But Ford was always aware that Rockefeller enjoyed more celebrity status than the president, and that Rockefeller was a formidable politician who could easily overshadow the less charismatic and less known Ford.

Mondale was given unprecedented access to Carter and a wide range of responsibilities that previously were parcelled out only to close presidential aides. Mondale was well suited to help the president since Carter—more than any chief executive in recent memory—lacked political ties and experience. The vice-president became a general adviser and troubleshooter on a broad range of domestic and foreign policy issues. He assisted with congressional relations, and immersed himself in party activities in support of administration policies. Carter gave Mondale an office in the West Wing of the White House, just down the hall from the Oval Office, and the two met frequently. Mondale was privy to the morning presidential briefings and to classified information that flowed into the Oval Office but to which no previous vice-president had ever been granted access on a regular basis. Mondale also was a member of virtually every established and ad hoc group in the EOP, and he and the president lunched privately once a week to exchange views.

Vice-President George Bush was also given a major role in the Reagan administration, despite earlier predictions that he would be relegated to the closet because of his vigorous battle for the nomination against Reagan. Bush's broad experience in government, however, helped make him a White House insider during the early months of the administration. Bush won the admiration and trust of both the president and his personal staff for the way he assumed many of the president's duties after an assassination attempt on the president. Bush was careful not to appear to be filling the president's shoes; he projected the image of a steady, faithful, and highly responsible subordinate who helped command the ship while the captain was momentarily incapacitated.

The logic for utilizing the vice-president perhaps has become clearer as a result of the assassination of Kennedy, the near miss on Reagan, and the sudden elevation of an appointed vice-president (Ford) to the presidency. Carter particularly indicated a concern that the vice-president should be more involved in the day-to-day activities of the White House so that—should something happen to the president—he would be well prepared to take over. Another factor also is at work: vice-presidents in recent years have been more representative of the kind of politicians who once won the presidency. As noted in Chapter 2, national politicians who are in the middle of the political mainstream are disadvantaged in running and winning today's campaigns while celebrities or individuals from the fringes are increasingly more successful. But the kinds of candidates who now win the nomination must seek the political support of the party, and vice-presidents typically are chosen because they frequently represent the party regulars and because of the political contacts they can provide for the president.

The fact that the vice-president owes his position to the president provides the kind of personal loyalty well-suited to an adviser at the highest level of the EOP. So long as the vice-president does not try to upstage his mentor and is willing to be supportive, the vice-president may provide advice and help far more valuable to the president than almost any other appointed political executive. For the vice-president's position is constitutionally mandated and his potential for accession to the office cannot be ignored.

Aside from the vice-presidency and other more visible and influential EOP units, the presidential establishment generally has evolved haphazardly and in a jumbled fashion because Congress wills it so and because the presidency itself is so highly personalized. The EOP's links to the rest of the government are tenuous and amorphous because there is little or no organizational or constitutional basis for accountability or for responsibilities. Consequently, the expectation that a bigger or better EOP will somehow succeed in converting presidential commands into results invariably ends in disappointment and frustration for the president and his closest advisers.

Organizational Confusion in the EOP

The EOP obviously would be a real asset to the president if its units were able to mobilize the government into responding to the president's goals or directives. But this rarely happens because the EOP itself is too big and too fragmented to discern the president's will, much less respond to it.

The expansion of staffs, the creation of additional new EOP units, and the delegation of decision-making authority to ever increasing numbers of assistants results in exaggerating the amount of upward and sideway reporting in the presidential establishment. This proliferation of staffs and responsibilities widens the networks of contacts involved in presidential staff work, making worse problems in role definition. Too many chief cooks clearly spoil the White House broth, preventing coordination of advice and administration. According to former EOP administrators Ben W. Heineman, Jr., and Curtis A. Hessler, "EOP's many chiefs and Indians spend most of their time and energy maneuvering with, around, and against each other rather than providing coherence and strategy to the rest of government."[11] (One of the most common examples of such rivalry pits the vice-president and his staff against the White House assistants of the president. Tensions are particularly high among these staffs because the president's assistants know they would automatically be purged by the vice-president's people should anything happen to the president.)

Bureaucratic expansion increases the complexity of decision making for the president while dispersing the authority he needs to make decisions. Staff coordination becomes increasingly more difficult as additional levels of staff are created to deal with special problems. But an increase in staffing an issue in one section of the EOP usually is not balanced by a decline in staff dealing with the same issue elsewhere in the Executive Branch. A good example of this is the president's economic powers. The OMB and Council of Economic Advisers—both key units in planning budgetary policies—are separate from the Department of Treasury, and all three of these organizations function outside the Federal Reserve Board, which determines monetary policy. In typical cabinet governments all of these functions would be combined in a finance ministry. But in the United States, the "finance ministry" is so fragmented that achieving any coordinated economic policy is difficult if not impossible (see Chapter 8).

As new issues or programs gain presidential attention and priority, all EOP units fight to gain new resources or to throw more staff into the policy fray. Staff output correspondingly increases as more staff time is consumed in processing and coordinating the flow of paper and in committee meetings. As one observer has noted, "All staff like to be where the action is, even if only on the margins, and once there they prove difficult to silence or remove."[12]

Whenever Congress or an agency invents a program that fits awkwardly in the existing framework of the Executive Branch, the favorite solution is to put it into the EOP. The EOP consequently becomes a full-fledged bureaucratic agency, with all the disadvantages of duplicating the activities of other agencies, providing alternative opportunities to interest groups, and adding additional strength to forces within government lobbying the president. The EOP was not designed to *operate* programs but to facilitate the president's management of them.[13] If anything, the president needs fewer pleaders of special programs or causes rather than an additional layer of such advocates within his own establishment.

The expansion of the EOP also adds to the problem of policy coordination on a much more basic level: as more and more senior staff are added, policy papers have to clear increasing numbers of signatures on their way up to the president. This reduces the likelihood that the president will receive a wider range of views or options on a policy while complicating or even sanitizing issues or options by the time they reach the Oval Office. Important options or information often can be ignored or never even considered by the president because of the views of those with privileged access to the president.

The EOP is almost constantly paralyzed by internal conflicts, especially conflicts that pit advisers and units on the fringes against the president's closest aides. The lack of established organizational jurisdictions among units means that "everyone has ample excuse to nose into everyone else's business."[14] Seldom is it clear who is in charge, who is managing, or who is responsible for decisions because of this organizational confusion. Issues move through EOP structures at a snail's pace, with meetings and draft papers piling up on top of each other as issues or problems move from one office to another.

Such administrative chaos means that ordered relations are seldom found in the presidential establishment. Each policy area has its own networks and routines, but none are ever linked in a broad, collective way so that national goals can be articulated or achieved. Issues are studied on a piecemeal basis rather than systematically or comprehensively, and there is no strategic center—although the president is the logical person to be one.

The end result is that too many issues or problems are pushed into the Oval Office for the president's decision that should have been settled at a much lower level. This, in turn, has served to make a much enlarged White House staff the central element in presidential decision making with immense ramifications for the nature of presidential power.

EVOLUTION OF THE WHITE HOUSE STAFF

The most remarkable development in the structure of the modern presidency has been the evolution of a sizeable White House bureaucracy—a "palace guard" of assistants, public-relations experts, advisers, valets, servants, clerical workers, and sycophants, all of whom supposedly are devoted to the needs and will of the president.

Until the twentieth century presidents generally depended on a few unemployed relatives or friends for assistance. Washington's personal business adviser, Tobias Lear, became the first presidential assistant when he assumed the pretentious but unofficial title of "Personal Secretary to His Excellency the President of the United States."[15] Congress did not appropriate funds for White House assistance until the administration of James Buchanan, when the grand sum of $2500 a year was made available for a staff secretary.[16] Throughout most of the nineteenth century serving as a presidential assistant held little of the glamour, prestige, or power it does today. One man offered the post as secretary to President William McKinley turned it down because he thought the recognition value of the job was too low.[17]

The White House staff numbered only seven as late as Wilson's second term. By the time Franklin D. Roosevelt became president, the staff had swollen to thirty-seven, the most important of whom were assigned to handling appointments, press relations, and presidential correspondence.[18] The expansion of the president's personal staff, however, had not kept pace with the increased burdens on the office. As a result, Roosevelt borrowed assistant secretaries and top-ranking executives from various departments and agencies to help with the increased flow of White House business. This caused confusion since many staffers continued to be carried as personnel of their parent agencies which paid their salaries.[19] The need for a larger and more permanent staff for the presidency was obvious.

The modern White House staff was born with Roosevelt's 1939 reorganization of the Executive Branch. The Brownlow Committee in its recommendations for reform argued:

> *Where can there be found an executive in any way comparable upon whom so much petty work is thrown? Or who is forced to see so many people on related matters and to make so many decisions on . . . incomplete information? How is it humanly possible to know fully the affairs and problems of over 100 separate major agencies, to say nothing of being responsible for their general direction and coordination?*[20]

The president needed assistants who could serve as direct emissaries to the burgeoning federal agencies and departments. But these aides were never to be allowed to constitute a bureaucracy unto itself. The White House staff was to be limited to a "small number" of professionals experienced in government and management who would not try to become surrogate presidents with authority to make decisions or issue instructions on their own. Their primary responsibility would be to assist the president in obtaining quickly information from departments and agencies and to keep administrators informed about the president's actions. The staff would *not* be interposed between the president and his cabinet:

> *Their effectiveness in assisting the president will . . . be directly proportional to their ability to discharge their functions with restraint. They would remain in the background, issue no orders, make no decisions, emit no public statements.*[21]

Such a staff would equip the president with the same kind of assistance enjoyed by executives of any large organization, the Brownlow Committee proposed. Those chosen for the White House staff normally were to come from within and outside the government. The most important criterion was that they should be individuals in whom the president could have complete confidence and who were not bent on building their own independent bases of personal political power.

A White House staff reflects the organizational preferences and personality of the president it serves. Some White House offices have been highly unstructured, with presidential assistants functioning virtually as personal extensions of the president. Others, however, have been structured as tightly as a military command post, with rigid lines of authority linking the president to assistants through clearly designated staff delegations of responsibility, access to the president, and privilege. Several staffs fell in between these two extremes, with a mix of both structured and freewheeling relationships between the president and his assistants. There are obvious strengths and weaknesses to any staffing arrangement. We will examine them by first considering the unstructured form—a highly personalized approach some times referred to as the *wheel*.

At least three modern presidents depended on freewheeling White House staffs, in which every assistant was expected to be a generalist at the personal beck and call of the president. The model for such a White House operation was FDR's.

THE PRESIDENT AT THE CENTER OF DECISION MAKING

Roosevelt ran his office personally, informally, and with great flexibility, using his aides as extensions of his own personality. Confined to a wheelchair by paralysis, FDR never allowed his dependence on others to cut him off from outside political influences. He used his personal assistants virtually as roving ambassadors collecting intelligence throughout the Executive Branch. Roosevelt's antennae were always out, receiving signals from countless lieutenants and supporters. He had an insatiable appetite for information, and his assistants always recognized their responsibilities and limitations.[22] Aware of how jealously individuals compete for status and influence with a president, Roosevelt frequently assigned the same task to different aides, hoping to light a fire as well as to test loyalty. He elicited the fierce rivalry of his assistants, which was not without cost in staff tensions and rivalries.

Although FDR did not have a chief of staff, one man stood out from all the rest because of his unique personal relationship to the president. Harry Lloyd Hopkins had no official title nor did he even possess a desk in the White House, but he was perhaps the most powerful presidential adviser of all time. Hopkins enjoyed the privilege of being a permanent house guest in Roosevelt's White House, and became Roosevelt's constant companion and closest confidant. He once told a friend, "I don't give a damn who sees Roosevelt during the day. I see him at night, the last half-hour before he goes to bed. . . . [A] half-hour then is worth two hours any other time."[23]

Roosevelt dispatched Hopkins on numerous important special missions during World War II, and in the course of his trips Hopkins won the friendship and trust of both Winston Churchill and Joseph Stalin, America's two most powerful allies. As a result, Hopkins's influence far outweighed even that of the secretary of state or other important foreign- or military-policy advisers.

But not even Hopkins monopolized Roosevelt's attention. FDR utilized so many different sources and played so many assistants and advisers off against one another that he avoided narrowing his field of vision. His staff was filled with individuals of such rare ability and dedication that they served for years as the benchmarks against which future White House assistants would be measured.

John F. Kennedy's White House staff was largely modeled after Roosevelt's. Kennedy was influenced by Richard E. Neustadt's 1960 book *Presidential Power*, which praised Roosevelt's managerial approach and suggested that organizing the White House staff by putting people of clashing temperament, outlooks, and ideas in key positions would result in subordinates pushing up to the president choices they could not make themselves. Decision making would be consolidated in the president's own hands because he held all the strings of influence and status. The president who wanted to control others had to be constantly at the center of a band of competitive loyalists who were "calling signals to each other in the thick of action, like basketball players developing plays as the game moved on."[24]

Kennedy's organization thus resembled a wheel; its spokes radiated outward in every direction, but the president was always the axis—his own chief of staff. Kennedy wanted staff members to be fully involved in the substance of decisions at every level because he himself was a generalist. He expected creativity no matter what the person's expertise or position. Arthur M. Schlesinger, Jr., noted that Kennedy had a "distressing tendency to take up whatever happened to be on his desk and hand it over to whoever happened to be in the room."[25] JFK insisted he did not want his staff to interfere with the daily operations of the cabinet departments and agencies, but this was inevitably the result as special teams of assistants assumed adversarial roles or oversight functions toward the rest of the Executive Branch.[26]

Kennedy was confident that he could delegate authority to his assistants without fear they would act against his interests. He believed that if "a task was important enough, it was necessary to have someone at the White House with responsibility for prodding the bureaucracy."[27] Such an attitude reflected suspicions about the competence and loyalty not only of cabinet appointees but also of the federal civil service. Roosevelt had created new agencies to break bottlenecks. Kennedy turned to his personal aides, who understood they had carte blanche to prod and to push.

The media portrayed Kennedy's assistants as an Ivy League brain trust—the "best and the brightest" that Harvard or Massachusetts Institute of Technology (MIT) had to offer. Assistants like Press Secretary Pierre Salinger and Arthur Schlesinger, Jr., the White House "intellectual-in-resident," became household names through their identification with Kennedy. This development ran counter to what had been envisioned in creating an office of presidential assistants with a "passion for anonymity."

Kennedy's White House operation grew because there was little resistance to its expansion, and creating another White House office settled all kinds of personnel or constituency problems. A new staff position or unit could be used to appeal to certain groups in the electorate important to the president's personal electoral coalition. Campaign loyalists could be rewarded, the vice-president given special assignments, and even a pet project of the president's wife (in the case of Jacqueline Kennedy—the arts) could be advanced by the creation of special offices or ad hoc positions in the White House. At the top was a privileged handful of the president's most trusted and intimate loyalists. Scattered throughout the rest of the White House's West Wing was a growing number of aides and special assistants with vested interests in bringing policy problems into the vortex of the presidential establishment. Authority once vested exclusively in the president was gradually bestowed on numerous subordinates almost like grants of knighthood, creating temporary classes of nobles empowered to speak in the king's name.

While Kennedy ran the White House with his "happy band of brothers," LBJ bullied, cajoled, harassed, and otherwise made life uncertain if not frequently miserable for his personal assistants, who likewise were expected to be generalists. Johnson too disliked formal structures and meetings, preferring instead to deal directly, one-on-one with people. LBJ expected his aides to be capable of responding to any and all assignments. Unlike Kennedy, Johnson kept his staff on a short leash. He would not tolerate anyone becoming too popular with the press or more visible than himself, and he required more personal loyalty than Kennedy did from his staff. LBJ could be a tyrant. George

Christian, his press secretary, recalls that Johnson might lash out at whoever was near him for some trivial reason, but would later present the chastened aide with a wristwatch bearing the initials LBJ. According to Christian, Johnson had a closet full of watches because he was always trying to make amends with someone whose feelings he had hurt.[28]

Because of his harsh temper and frenetic pace, Johnson was constantly losing staff members, including some of his most talented assistants. He seemed always on top of the smallest detail because he made two workdays out of every twenty-four hours. He would work from 7 A.M. until noon; then after lunch and a nap, he would begin late in the afternoon another day that ran until late at night. LBJ expected everyone else to keep the same schedule.

Johnson believed he could get his "action" from younger assistants and his "advice from the older men."[29] Like Kennedy, he was more inclined toward action than deliberation. As a result, his White House staff was constantly out in front of the cabinet secretaries and agency officials in policy and decision-making matters. Johnson used his staff to reverse the traditional path of legislative planning, which proceeded from departments and agencies via the president's budgetary unit to the president. For example, his chief domestic adviser was in charge of initiatives for the administration's domestic agenda, overseeing task forces of leaders from business, labor, education, and science. Other White House–centered units blended presidential staffs with outside advisers or with departments and agencies to the point that the dividing line between the Executive Branch and the rest of government was blurred.

Both Kennedy and Johnson favored special task forces for foreign-policy decision making. Typically these units included key White House advisers as well as selected departmental chiefs and military leaders. As we shall see in the next chapter, the major foreign-policy crises of the 1960s were deliberated and plans for action developed by such ad hoc groups within the White House.

The weakness in such arrangements is they are more likely to provide a sense of euphoria that leads to carelessness, overconfidence, and a lack of orderliness. General Maxwell Taylor, who served as Kennedy's military representative, perhaps best summed up the problems with such informal decision making:

> As an old military type, I was accustomed to the support of a highly professional staff trained to prepare careful analyses of issues in advance of decisions and to take meticulous care of classified information. . . . I found that I could walk into almost any [White House] office, request and receive a sheaf of top secret papers, and depart without signing a receipt. . . . There was little

perceptible method in the assignment of duties within the staff. . . . When important new problems arose, they were usually assigned to ad hoc task forces with members drawn from the White House staff and other departments. These task forces did their work, filed their reports, and then dissolved into the bureaucratic limbo without leaving a trace or contributing to the permanent base of governmental experience.[30]

The personalized style in which the president was the hub of a wheel of loyal assistants worked well for Roosevelt because the White House operation was much smaller and far less specialized than it had become by the 1960s. An unstructured staff presents a great risk that those closest to the president will be generalists. Because of their deep commitment to him, they may be sycophants rather than seers, and they may try to shelter the president rather than to serve as his eyes and ears in the government. The alternative—a rigidly structured White House organization—unfortunately may have the same results, however.

THE PYRAMID WHITE HOUSE: EISENHOWER AND NIXON

Eisenhower understandably favored a military-styled chain of command for his White House, with clearly designated staff responsibilities as well as detailed and precise procedures. He wanted to be kept free of petty administrative details, and he wanted problems not requiring his personal involvement or decision to be filtered out. But Washington reporter Richard Rovere described the staff as "a conspiracy to perpetuate [the President's] unawareness."[31]

The key to making a hierarchical staff system work was to have a chief of staff who could excel at being the president's "son of a bitch." Eisenhower found the perfect candidate in Sherman Adams, the taciturn former governor of New Hampshire. Adams dealt with Senators, members of Congress, department and agency heads, and everyone else with a brusqueness and rudeness that earned him considerable enmity. But he provided Eisenhower with the privacy and orderliness the president prized, and Adams was a perfect lightning rod for a president who remained too popular to criticize.[32]

Nothing went to Eisenhower if it could be dealt with at a lower level. But if a matter had to go to him, it had to be reduced to a single-page memorandum with specific recommendations, and it had to be initialled by Sherman Adams. While this system was autocratic, authority was widely distributed, particularly to individual cabinet secretaries, who enjoyed greater power and independence under Eisenhower than under any president before or since. Still, never before had a White House assistant been given so much power and control over access to a president. In complete charge of the president's daily schedule (even though Eisenhower had an appointments secretary), Adams monopolized the president's sources of contact, and had considerable influence over the priorities brought before the president. Eisenhower's heart attack in September 1955 was a major factor in enhancing Adam's control because almost all access to the president was cut off for months, and cabinet secretaries and congressional leaders who previously had been able to have an occasional fifteen minutes with Eisenhower now found it virtually impossible to see him.

Adams's position was eroded during Eisenhower's second term, however, after a House subcommittee disclosed that the seemingly incorruptible New Englander had received expensive gifts and payments of personal expenses from a textile millionaire, Bernard Goldfine. Adams had made inquiries on Goldfine's behalf to the Securities and Exchange Commission and Federal Trade Commission as both agencies were preparing to charge Goldfine with violation of federal regulations. The scandal was joyfully seized on not only by Democrats who had not forgotten the Republican attacks on Truman's staff but also by Republicans resentful of Adams's privileged position with the president. Adams was eventually forced to resign.

Eisenhower's SOB was only the tip of an elaborate chain of command in the White House. The staff reflected considerable experience in the federal government. Several of its members had served as congressional aides, another had served in Congress, and seven others had had experience in the Executive Branch.[33] While critics saw such dependence as indicative of a weak or disengaged executive, others saw it as a skillful exercise and delegation of authority. Rexford G. Tugwell, who had been a member of FDR's White House staff, observed, "No president had ever known so well [as Eisenhower] how to use a staff."[34]

Nixon resurrected Eisenhower's model, for he too prized order and solitude. But Nixon intended to reduce the size and trim the cost of the White House staff because he believed that it had grown unwieldy under Kennedy and Johnson. The *New York Times* reported prior to Nixon's inauguration:

Nixon intends . . . not to allow his personal White House staff to dominate the functions or control the direction of the major agencies and bureaus of government. Sensitive to the possibility of empire building within his own small cadre of assistants, he plans instead to organize the White House staff [to] encourage not inhibit direct communication between his cabinet officers and the president.[35]

It did not take long, however, before it dawned on Nixon that his cabinet chiefs did not share his policy goals and that many of his cabinet appointments were unable to discuss politically sensitive issues or programs involving large expenditures with him.[36] The White House staff gradually assumed a larger and larger role. (Nixon's national security assistant, Henry A. Kissinger, already had cornered the agenda on foreign policymaking.)

As noted in the preceding chapter, a major factor in the growing influence of the White House staff was Nixon's shift from a legislative to a managerial strategy. White House "working groups" chaired and staffed by presidential assistants or various EOP staff members began to dominate policy and issue areas concerned with welfare, labor, education, model cities and urban growth, social services, and transportation. Cabinet secretaries and other key departmental officials found themselves slowly squeezed out of important policy deliberations.

In addition to the working groups, the White House staff became involved in policy matters in the lower reaches of the federal bureaucracy in an attempt to rally support for the administration's goals. White House clearance was required for a growing number of issues, and such clearance was harder to obtain. Cabinet secretaries increasingly complained about being left out of policy deliberations until programs were fully developed; some openly criticized the White House for running their departments. Interior Secretary Walter Hickel wrote the president that he was "isolated and just sitting around listening to his staff."[37] Hickel complained of receiving letters opposing his programs from people in the White House he had never heard of. Shortly after Hickel made his letter available to the news media, he was fired by Nixon.

Richard Nathan's study of Nixon's attempt to improve the managerial efficiency of the White House suggested that the results of trying to center control in the White House were quite predictable. "When a junior White House staffer calls a career expert in an agency, the relationship that they develop offers wide latitude for agency personnel to develop their own lines into the White House." This only further isolated the cabinet secretary and reinforced the tendency for the secretary and his or her close associates to draw up ranks and act on the basis of we versus they, "they" being the president's own staff.[38] Paradoxically, this development *increased* the power of career bureaucrats to influence the White House instead of diminishing it, which was just the opposite of what Nixon intended. According to Robert C. Wood:

Confusion is created when men try to do too much at the top. In order to know what decisions are being made elsewhere in gov-

ernment, the White House tends either to spend time reviewing programs or to take more and more decisions on itself. The separate responsibilities of the White House, the Executive Office, and the agencies are fudged, and the demarcations of who does what become uncertain. The result is a blurring of the distinction between staff and line, between program and policy. Decisions tend to be reviewed and reviewed; and operational delays increase accordingly.[39]

By the end of his first term, Nixon had rejected the idea of White House–centered control, as we saw in Chapter 5. Thus was born his notion of supercabinet secretaries. His White House staff by this time, however, had become firmly entrenched as a presidential privy council. The men who were closest to the president learned that what Nixon wanted was not only unquestioned loyalty but almost total isolation. Few people could reach the president without first penetrating the wall of assistants hermetically sealing him off from the rest of the government. A loner who was ill at ease with all but a few intimate friends, Nixon believed he functioned better as problem solver and decision maker when he had solitude. His closest aides knew that Nixon found it difficult to be tough or demanding of subordinates he did not know well. But when alone, he was capable of strengthening his resolve and acting much more forcefully—especially if his will could be carried out by tough-minded assistants.

The most influential of all in Nixon's White House was H. R. (Bob) Haldeman, the White House chief of staff. Next in line were Ehrlichman and Kissinger. These three men together held more power than any clique in the history of the Oval Office. Not even Sherman Adams controlled the president's contact with the outside world as thoroughly as Haldeman did Nixon's. No one—not even members of the president's own family—entered Nixon's presence without going past Haldeman. He set the president's daily schedule, was the exclusive conduit for carrying out Nixon's personal orders, and ran the White House as if it were a Prussian army regiment. Aides joked they could hear the click of a subordinate's heels whenever Haldeman dismissed him after issuing an order. Rigid, ruthlessly efficient, and fiercely protective of Nixon, Haldeman served as the president's SOB with an efficiency even Adams would have admired.

Haldeman was an advertising executive in Los Angeles prior to his association with Nixon. Many of the younger men he recruited to work in the White House were likewise from the world of commercials and public-relations pitches. (Ehrlichman was a Seattle zoning lawyer and a classmate of Haldeman's at UCLA.) Theodore H. White wrote of them and the people they brought into the White House that they came into government "with no greater knowledge of how power works than the political intrigues of the political antechamber and the folklore of advance men . . ."[40] They were media-wise only in their knowledge of how to package a person or product to sell to a market-researched audience. They did not understand nor were they comfortable with the messy world of politics. Unable to understand the hard news dimension of the mass media, they believed the same tactics used in their advertising experience would be successful in dealing with reporters and the public. That Nixon was profoundly influenced by such men is suggested by private conversations taped in the Oval Office between him and his staff. Time and again, Nixon appears fascinated with what he called "PR" and "scenarios." "How will it play?" was a favorite question the president and his assistants raised with each other.

It is not surprising that such a staff, suspicious of an environment it could neither understand nor manipulate would soon find irresistible the use of the power and influence at their command to neutralize anyone standing in the president's way. "Nobody is a friend of ours, let's face it," Nixon warned his aides prior to his 1972 reelection. After the election Nixon instructed his chief counsel, John Dean, that "I want the most comprehensive notes on all those who tried to do us in. They didn't have to do it . . . they are asking for it and they're going to get it!"[41]

Such an attitude prompted the break-in at the Democratic Party National Committee headquarters in the Watergate by a group recruited by the Committee to Reelect the President in June 1972. This bungled burglary ultimately proved the undoing of Nixon's presidency. It was only one of the crimes and questionable practices stemming from decisions made by Nixon's White House staff. Some of these "dirty tricks" and illegal operations were sanctioned directly by the president while others occurred without his overt knowledge but with the tacit understanding that they were part of the standard operating procedure in the Nixon White House.

Many—including Nixon himself—blamed his downfall on the White House staff. But Nixon had chosen to surround himself with such men and to keep at a distance individuals of greater political wisdom, experience, and morality. Watergate revealed how easily a president's weaknesses and shortcomings carry over to his staff and are magnified. Previously law-abiding people, many of them young men just beginning their careers, were tempted to consider themselves and their responsibilities as above the law simply because they acted in the name of the president of the United States. The Nixon episode reveals the enormous risks awaiting any chief executive who permits an excessively loyal staff to program his every move and to hermetically seal him off from other countervailing political forces. A hierarchical, tightly controlled White House staff worked for Eisenhower because he never cut himself off from contacts with cabinet secretaries or key leaders of Congress. The same kind of system contributed to Nixon's downfall because he allowed too much control to his chief lieutenants and encouraged them to seal him off from his cabinet and Congress.

THE GEORGIA MAFIA

Nixon's palace guard mode of White House staffing was openly repudiated by Jimmy Carter. Soon after taking office, Carter announced a reorganization of the Executive Office that called for a 28 percent reduction in the size of the White House staff, from 485 to 351. But the reduction was more symbolic than real for it mostly involved moving certain housekeeping functions, payroll, and postal services to a new central administrative unit.[42] At the same time as he was making a show of trimming the staff, Carter placed a number of assistants who continued to serve him personally on departmental payrolls.

Carter made the pro forma declaration that he would be his own chief of staff, and that no one would come between him and his cabinet chiefs. At first his staff was structured in keeping with this promise. Lacking a formal chain of command, it included nine top assistants close to the president. Substantive staff functions were distributed among these key aides, although three were more influential than their amorphous titles or duties suggested. They were Hamilton Jordan, who had been chief architect of Carter's long campaign and election victory; Jody Powell, who also played an important role in Carter's candidacy; and Stuart Eizenstat, an Atlanta lawyer and strategist on important issues. Three other top assistants were from Georgia, and had been with Carter in one capacity or another from his days as governor or from the beginning of his campaign.

Although Jordan and Powell lacked the formal titles or status of chief of staff and presidential assistant, they emerged as Carter's closest confidants and advisers. Neither had had experience in national politics other than their involvement in Carter's campaign, but their commitment to Carter was total. Jordan, who served as Carter's chief political aide during the early months, had a substantial impact on policy matters. Press Secretary Powell's influence also ranged far beyond the official duties of the White House press operation. Both appeared more interested in the campaign aspects of the presidency than its substantive operations. Journalist James Fallows, for example, recalls hearing one Carter staff member voice what was perhaps the prevailing feeling among the staff: "You know, there ought to be a place for people like us between elections, someplace we could rest up and get ready for the next one."[43]

Others equally inexperienced in the ways of Washington were

responsible for handling the president's congressional relations, scheduling, political contacts, and public relations. Unstructured and loosely run, the staff seemed always more preoccupied with the image of power than its substance. While the president paid lip service to cabinet government, he was increasingly centralizing authority in his staff, where it lay dormant or became diffused because of a lack of direction or focus. Carter's staff problems stemmed from his inability to articulate a grand strategy for his administration. Without strong leadership, his White House floundered from one political miscalculation and policy crisis to the next.

An engineer by training and in the way he approached problems, Carter was uncomfortable making decisions without a thorough knowledge and understanding of all the details involved. He was unable to see the forest because he was so overwhelmed with the task of counting and examining the leaves. Early in his administration he would leave for Camp David, the presidential retreat in the Maryland mountains, lugging thick briefing books over which he would spend hours studying budget tables and checking arithmetic. He wasted his time by personally reviewing requests to use the White House tennis courts and correcting grammar and spelling mistakes on staff members' memos.

Unwilling to delegate ultimate authority, Carter ended up bogged down in his own. Concerned about finding the *right* decision, he often was unable to come up with one at all. One staff member confided to a reporter that "every night is amateur night at the White House."[44] Another suggested that Carter's staff was "like a movie set for a Marx Brothers' picture, only instead of four brothers, there were about a dozen."[45] Carter wanted to avoid the kind of authoritarian, closed staff system that had gotten Nixon into much trouble, but his own amateurish operation achieved the same results. Fallows described Carter's White House staff as an entrenched hierarchy in which everyone had a fixed place "from God and the Angels, through kings, noblemen, and serfs, down to animals, plants and stones."[46] Such a system created morale problems among many staff members, making the Carter White House truly a collection of "sad young men."

Disagreements between the White House and cabinet secretaries grew more frequent and open, heightened by the disarray in administration from the top. The most publicized break came between Secretary of State Cyrus Vance and National Security Adviser Zbigniew Brzezinski over foreign policy, but Carter faced similar quarrels between other departments and his staff. Before long, the Carter White House was the object of disenchantment if not scorn from many officials in the Executive Branch and from Congress as it became obvious that the president had lost control of his administration.

The president and his closest aides began to circle the wagons as early as the spring of 1978 when a staff meeting concluded that the White House needed to begin monitoring the performance and policy views of assistant cabinet secretaries to weed out disloyal appointees. White House aides attributed doubts about the president's leadership abilities to these dissidents within the departments. A White House aide declared, "If an assistant secretary is fighting the president's budget or the president's policies, we're not going to tolerate that. We're putting everybody on notice that we expect them to work with the president in a positive way."[47] To confirm his full retreat from cabinet government, Carter added a number of new staff members to the White House staff. Their functions ranged from imposing more rigorous control over political appointments and patronage to improving the president's faltering image with the public.

A year later Carter and his aides were still pondering what went wrong, as polls showed a widespread lack of confidence or enthusiasm in the administration. This time, the president took a twelve-day sabbatical at Camp David to analyze his administration and to seek explanations from a wide range of people as to what had gone wrong. The gist of the recommendations Carter heard suggested that he must personally take charge of his own administration and vigorously wield the powers available to him and him alone. The president needed to seize the initiative rather than to let events overwhelm him.

When Carter descended from the mountain, he formally made Jordan his chief of staff—a role the young Georgian was already exercising in practice if not in name. He fired four cabinet secretaries and accepted the resignation of a fifth. Then he reorganized his personal staff, leaving virtually intact his inner circle of Georgians and giving them greater authority over the cabinet than they had held before. Carter clearly was closing ranks behind an inexperienced White House staff which had been a major factor in contributing to his indecisive leadership to begin with.

Nixon's staff had been instrumental in bringing him down by reinforcing his worst political instincts. Carter's staff reflected the president's inexperience, thereby reinforcing his political isolation from those who might have helped him through his critical on-the-job training. Unfortunately, once Carter decided to let his aides worry about details and to act on their advice, he neglected the corollary need: to make his aides responsible for the *quality* of their judgments.[48]

"CHAIRMAN OF THE BOARD": REAGAN AND HIS STAFF

No president since Eisenhower had greater promise of gaining control over his staff and of making cabinet government work than Ronald

Reagan. Reagan, the media observed, knew how to delegate authority. As governor of California, he had surrounded himself with competent and experienced people, but had reserved the ultimate power of decision for himself. No personal staff would ever come between Reagan and his political appointees, for Reagan would depend on the expertise of those he selected to run his departments. He preferred to let others fuss over the details of policy development and administration while he presided at the apex of the system, conceiving the broad outlines of programs and selling them to others.

From the outset Reagan pledged to establish an Eisenhower-like chain of command with the cabinet serving as his "inner circle of advisers—almost like a 'board of directors.'"[49] Indeed, if one image of Reagan stood out among all the others to predict his style of leadership, it was that of Reagan as chairman of the board. His staff would mostly serve as facilitators, coordinating the actions of departmental chiefs with the president's goals. But such exchanges would take place through extensive interactions between his personal aides and the cabinet. Reagan preferred to conduct business directly and personally rather than through written reports. He tolerated memoranda if they were concise and provided clear-cut options, but was most comfortable and confident in one-on-one exchanges with government officials, heads of state, and staff members. Reagan would be responsible for guiding his policies along, using his formidable talents as the great communicator, but it would be the responsibility of his staff to make certain he did not overburden himself.

Even before the inauguration, the media had begun to question whether Reagan or his transition staff was really in charge. Stories proliferated about the president-elect's detachment from important decisions. Edwin Meese III, who headed the transition team, served as Reagan's surrogate policy planner, chief recruiting agent, and chief spokesperson. Appearing on TV talk shows and holding press conferences regularly, Meese quickly earned the nickname "President Meese." Meanwhile, Reagan was shown chopping wood, riding his horse, and relaxing at his California ranch, seemingly undisturbed and uninvolved in the decisions shaping his forthcoming administration.

The press quickly picked up on the theme that this president, unlike his predecessor, was a "9 to 5" executive. His staff, it was said, arrived early and stayed late, but the president rarely put in longer than an eight-hour day. Reagan defended his approach by asserting, "Show me an executive who works long, overtime hours, and I'll show you a bad executive."[50]

Reagan's near brush with death by assassination contributed to the impression that he was surrounded by more than a few shadow presidents. Anxious to reassure the public that the president was still in complete control of the government following his surgery and month-long recovery, the White House staff arranged meetings twice a day at his hospital bedside. An assistant, however, was quoted in the *New York Times* as saying:

> *. . . despite an impression held by the public that presidents pass the day making difficult decisions, most presidents in fact spend most of their time attending ceremonies, attempting to win support for their programs, and generally seeking to put into effect decisions that have already been made.*[51]

Not too many months into the Reagan administration, stories began to surface in the media that the president's three leading assistants in the White House—Edwin Meese III, James A. Baker III, and Michael K. Deaver—were the most powerful troika in the White House since Nixon's days. The impression that these three men were exercising the real executive power became a major problem of public relations. While the president was on vacation at his California ranch, U.S. Navy jets shot down two Libyan fighter planes attacking American naval vessels near the Libyan coast. Meese, who was at the Reagan ranch, refused to awaken the president until six hours after reports of the incident were received at 4:30 A.M. Pacific Coast time. The reason was that Meese did not consider the incident serious enough to disturb the president's sleep.

At the same time news reports described a lengthy visit by a Texas bootmaker with the president during which a gift of four pairs of hand-tooled cowboy boots bearing the presidential seal was presented to Reagan. After forty-five minutes of conversation with the president, the bootmaker suggested that he might be disrupting a busy schedule.

"I know you have a lot more important things to do than stand around and fool with us," he told the president.

"No," Reagan responded. "You know four pairs of boots in forty-five minutes—that's pretty good."

The bootmaker confided to reporters as he left the president that Reagan had acted as if there was nothing else in the world he had to do, nothing else on his mind.[52]

David Gergen, director of the White House communications office, admitted that when the president returned to Washington from his vacation, his staff quickly prevailed on him to be more guarded about his laid-back style and to reemphasize that *he* was the only one making really important decisions. Top White House assistants, meanwhile, attempted to fade into the woodwork as Reagan began to act more like a chief executive on top of everything.[53]

The image that Reagan was not much involved in decision making persisted nonetheless, as Reagan frequently seemed unfamilar with issues or with details of important policies. (Aides described him as a president who would plow through every briefing book they provided, but he never demanded information beyond what his advisers provided.[54])

Reagan's staff illustrated the risks involved in not designating a single top assistant to run the White House office, as well as the dangers of having individuals with strong ideological political views in key positions. Staff members seemed to be engaged in a perpetual war among themselves, with conservatives facing off against moderate-pragmatists. OMB Director Stockman was often lined up against Treasury Secretary Donald T. Regan on the question of raising taxes to ward off huge federal deficits. Reagan's first secretary of state, Alexander M. Haig, Jr., was forever pitted against everyone, fighting at various times with Defense Secretary Caspar W. Weinberger, UN Ambassador Jeane J. Kirkpatrick, and Richard Allen, the first national security adviser. Haig's relations with the White House staff were particularly bad after he appeared on nationwide television minutes after Reagan was shot in an assassination attempt to nervously proclaim that "I am in control" of the government. (Haig claimed erroneously the constitutional authority to take charge, an oversight quickly rectified by Reagan's White House assistants.)

The internal fighting eventually engulfed even the president's top assistants. The "Big Three"—Baker, Meese, and Deaver—eventually became the "Big Four" after William Clark, an old California friend of the president, replaced Allen as national security adviser. As a dedicated conservative and hard-liner on foreign policy, Clark insisted on

Reagan's holding to a proposed 10 percent increase in defense spending despite fierce congressional opposition. Baker, who emerged as the leading moderate-pragmatist, urged Reagan to settle for only a 7.5 percent hike. He also urged Reagan to compromise on several major policies, including accepting a tax increase in 1982 to help reduce the budget deficit and a jobs bill to alleviate unemployment during the recession. Conservatives on the staff viewed Baker as a loyalist of Vice-President Bush, whose campaign Baker had directed prior to joining Reagan's side. Deaver usually sided with Baker on major issues while Meese was in Clark's camp. Details of the feuding between the two camps of advisers frequently surfaced in the media, and the impression grew that Reagan's personal staff was so badly split that it was difficult to get any sustained cooperation on major problems facing the administration.[55]

PRESIDENTIAL SALESMEN: THE NEW WHITE HOUSE ELITES

A president is supposed to be able to indulge his personal tastes in setting up his White House staff. In fact, he is free only in the choice of personalities since his selection is limited not only by the need to appease special interests but also by commitments to the loyal supporters and professionals who helped him to win the election. No presidential aspirant can mount a credible run for the White House today without a team of highly skilled campaign technicians and marketing experts. But when he wins the race, the president-elect feels both obligated and willing to choose his campaign leaders as his top White House aides. These campaign and mass-marketing professionals have become the new presidential elite.

No matter what title or rank they possess, individuals in frequent and close contact with a president enjoy a privileged position and influence that few others in the Executive Branch know. They have considerable control over whom the president sees, where he goes, what information gains his attention, who is hired or fired, and what kinds of images about him are projected to the world beyond the White House. White House staffs from Roosevelt to Eisenhower have almost always been headed by men whose eyeteeth were cut in party political wars. Roosevelt's inner circle, for example, included James Farley, Louis Howe, and Thomas Corcoran, individuals who were involved in Democratic party politics most of their lives. Truman's staff could rival any American county courthouse gang for time and energy spent in politics. Eisenhower's chief aides also had considerable experience in national and state politics. If a common thread ran through the backgrounds of most chief presidential aides prior to the 1960s, it was the political party tie.

Kennedy was the first president to discover that a well-organized, skilled campaign organization could count for more than a national party in winning both nomination and election to the White House. His triumph in 1960 was a victory of the new technologist over the old party strategist. JFK believed, as political commentator James Mac-Gregor Burns wrote, that the "Democratic party was something to win through, not to govern through."[56] Kennedy's White House staff came to exemplify the widening gulf between old-line party professionals and the presidency, for as historian W. G. Carleton pointed out, Kennedy was mostly responsible for the shift toward personal staffs and direct mass-media presentation of the presidency, a development that "dwarfed politicians, party, and Congress . . . and contributed to the personalized and plebiscitary presidency."[57]

White House staffs ever since Kennedy have reflected the impact of campaign technology on the president's choice of his key assistants. Increasingly a new breed emerged that was markedly younger and more talented at selling the president to the electorate but less experienced in the practice of politics in government. They were marvelously talented in knowing what it took to win elections, but many had not the vaguest notion about how to exercise power once it was won. Most lacked a sense of party attachment since the importance of political parties had been declining in their generation and their political involvement was almost exclusively candidate-centered and campaign-directed.

Because such types helped win the prize, and because they were committed to the president rather than to an abstract set of ideologies or to a party, they constituted a safe and logical place from which to begin to recruit a personal staff. The president would rarely have any doubts about where their loyalties lay because his candidacy had constituted the solitary motivating force of their experience with the presidency.

This new breed of presidential aide, however, possessed certain characteristics that would significantly affect the decision-making environment of the White House. They tended to be overreachers—highly ambitious, hard-driving men for whom the ends frequently justified the means. (No woman has ever been a member of the president's inner circle.) The White House was no place for the timid of heart, for the inner life at the top was essentially the life of the barnyard—the pecking order among chickens. Former White House Press Secretary George Reedy has suggested:

It is a question of who has the right to peck whom and who must submit to being pecked. There are only two important differences. The first is that the pecking order is determined by the individual strength and forcefulness of each chicken, whereas in the White House it depends upon the relationship to the barnyard keeper.

The second is that no one outside the barnyard glorifies the chickens and expects them to order the affairs of mankind.[58]

The White House is an up-tight place because every presidential aide has one overwhelming goal: to gain and maintain access to and influence with the president. An assistant who is critical of the president, who bears too many bad tidings or who happens to be in the wrong place at the wrong time will never make it into the charmed circle. Or he may lose his place in the pecking order to others more crafty and fortunate. Reedy stretches his analogy of the environment of the White House to suggest it is also like a royal court, designed for one purpose and one purpose only—to serve the material needs and desires of a single man.[59]

A study by Stephen Wayne of the Nixon, Ford, and Carter staffs found fierce competition for recognition, status, and power among presidential aides.[60] The "can do" spirit of the Marine Corps permeates recruits to the White House corps, particularly among younger staff members anxious to prove their mettle and gain the recognition of their important superiors—perhaps even to gain the president's attention. The accepted demeanor is "White House cool," the appearance that one is coldly efficient. One assistant in the Ford White House admitted to Wayne that there was a tendency always to act in a substantive manner, but "when you do that, you really do lose touch with reality [for] a lot of life is inefficiency."[61] Haldeman, who had a notorious reputation for efficiency, once returned a memo to a junior aide with the cryptic inscription "TL^2." When the confused aide had the nerve to ask what TL^2 meant, Nixon's chief of staff snapped back, "Too little, too late."[62]

The White House aide most admired is quick, calm, tough, and extremely hard-working. Without question, he is a "team player" loyal to the president. He does not waste his time in idle conversation even if, as the Watergate tapes showed of Nixon, the president himself may. Such traits encourage an assistant to posture and role-play while trying to prove himself and improve his status in the pecking order. The problem with such behavior is that as the president turns increasingly inward to his staff because of a growing opposition to his policies and leadership, he requires honesty, candor, and straightforward advice. Unfortunately, loyalty assumes an even greater importance at such a time; as a result, aides are encouraged to become sycophants instead of sage advisers. Reedy suggests that invariably in any "battle between courtiers and advisers, the courtiers will win out" because as the president becomes more and more isolated by his own people, he begins no longer to feel subject to the normal checks and balances faced by other politicians.

Loyalty is almost always returned by the president, at times with unfortunate consequences. A strong personal bond appears to develop between every president and his topmost assistants, even to the extent that those who violate his trust or the public's confidence are rarely reprimanded or dismissed. Incompetence or poor judgment is seldom punished. Nixon accepted the resignations of Haldeman and Ehrlichman only because his own job was at stake, but he was visibly shaken at having to let them go. Haldeman once suggested that the bond between a president and his closest aides is not unlike that shared by men who face combat together. In both cases a comradely feeling of "we" versus "they" develops. Whatever its basis, in virtually every case in which a White House aide has been embroiled in scandal or caught in a situation embarrassing to the president, the president has staunchly defended his man.

It is a waste of time to try to drive a wedge between a president and his aides, no matter how much damage they may be doing his administration. Clark Clifford tried to tell Carter in 1979 that an incompetent personal staff was one of his biggest problems, but Carter ended up increasing the authority of the very men Clifford had in mind. As Reedy argues, one might just as well try to inform a father of the shortcomings of his son:

> *A president can go through an entire term without knowing that some of his most trusted assistants have created resentments that have undermined his political position. He will . . . read occasional articles in the newspapers describing the activities. These he is bound to regard as merely attacks by a jealous opposition and the effect upon his thinking will be the reverse of what was intended.*[63]

In "giving the president what he wants," loyal aides seemingly make life more comfortable for him, but they reinforce illusions about his power and popularity that cannot stand up to the facts. A president may begin his administration fresh from the political wars with a considerable dash of realism in his thinking, but before long he is hermetically sealed off by his palace guard. "Since they are the only people the president sees on a day-to-day basis, they become to him the voice of the people. They represent the closest approximation that he has of outside contacts, and it is inevitable that he comes to regard them as humanity itself."[64]

WHITE HOUSE PR

Not only does the president's staff provide a sanitized environment within the White House but it also attempts to recreate that environment for the outside world through a massive White House public-relations effort. The selling of the president engaged in during the campaign is continued, usually by the same people, once the office is won.

Given the backgrounds of many White House aides, it is not surprising that a considerable amount of time and attention is devoted to protecting the president's image and trying to put the best of all possible slants on information coming out of the White House. Management of the mass media is an obsession not only with the staff but also with the president himself because his media success largely determines his success with Congress, the public, and other political leaders. As a result, all White House staff members, particularly key assistants at the top of the hierarchy, are continually engaged in one form or another of public relations.

Like any public-relations operation, the White House mirror-image machine attempts to create the best possible image of its product. But unlike more typical PR efforts, it must merchandize to a market that is perpetually cynical, questioning, and probing for weak spots. Furthermore, the White House PR efforts present serious risks to the president because they threaten to isolate him even more from reality with their handouts. The temptation for a president to believe the glowing releases and assessments of his in-house press agents outweighs his tolerance for the constant criticism and sniping of the real world's press. His relations with the various media invariably deteriorate over the duration of his term as his dependence on White House flacks grows. We will examine this trend in greater detail in Chapter 9.

Nixon's fascination with whether or not something would "play in Peoria" was a blunt admission of just how much the president is caught up in his own White House public-relations fix. During the Nixon administration at least one hundred aides were involved full-time in various aspects of packaging and selling the president. More than fifty of them were employed in an "editorial department" that included speechwriters and units for news summaries, correspondence, messages, and research.[65] (Nixon was perhaps the first president to send himself congratulatory telegrams and letters after a major speech.)

Despite all the publicity about Ford's "de-imperializing" the presidency after Nixon, Ford's White House was equally caught up in PR. Michael Grossman and Martha Joynt Kumar, who studied the mass media–presidential relationship, were told by a former Ford aide that almost everyone on the staff was either a megaphone or a support mechanism for a megaphone:

[M]ore than 60 percent of the political staff in the White House were used in promoting and publicizing the president. A congres-

*sional staff assistant who has evaluated White House organiza-
tions in the postwar period estimates that 85 percent of those
working in the White House, including those in policy-making
and service roles, are involved directly in public relations activities.*[66]

An accounting of high-ranking Carter aides revealed that of forty-
nine assistants, fifteen or about one third were assigned jobs that
clearly involved media relations or public-relations policy. Carter created several additional top-level jobs during his first year, including a
director and a deputy to the Office of the Assistant to the President for
Communications; other positions involved with press relations were
upgraded. Grossman and Kumar found White House officials generally
reluctant to discuss the full extent of the resources devoted to PR and
the mass media. But many admitted that such functions claimed an
increasingly greater proportion of staff time, money, and energy during
the 1970s.

Cronin has noted of this trend:

*[P]residential press agentry has not only expanded public expec-
tations of the presidency, but has also distorted the self-percep-
tions of persons within the presidential establishment; it's a kind
of press-agentry that feeds on itself . . . . [N]o president wants to
look uncertain or weak. The much publicized flexing of presidential muscles, the continuous stream of messages to Congress, and
the impressive presidential travels abroad seem occasioned in
part because the public expects such displays of boldness and
leadership. Soon a president can find himself having to pedal
faster in the same place—needing yet more speechwriters, joke-
smiths, communications directors, and public information directors. . . .*[67]

THE LONE RANGER PRESIDENT:
REESTABLISHING AN ILLUSION

A popular myth about the president holds that he is a solitary figure
holding "the loneliest job in the world," struggling against all odds to
master the awesome and overwhelming duties and challenges of the
White House. A television commercial during the 1980 campaign
showed a single light burning late at night at an upstairs window of the
White House. Nearby sat an intent President Carter pondering all by
himself the great problems besetting the nation. A somber voice in-
toned that only one man could know what it meant to be president.

Such an image is compelling but profoundly misleading. A more
accurate representation would portray the presidency as a freewheeling

collection of people and offices acting and making decisions on behalf of the president, but with the chief executive often detached from much of what is done in his name. According to Heclo:

> *What that familiar face ponders in the Oval Office is likely to be a series of conversations with advisers or a few pages of paper containing several options. These represent the last distillates produced by immense rivers of information flowing from sources—and condensed in ways—about which the president knows little.*[68]

The notion that a president is overwhelmed by the immensity and complexity of his job ignores the fact that the White House staff now diverts most of the details and trivia from the president's desk unless he wishes to become involved. Reedy has noted that in spite of the widespread maxim that every president is terribly overworked, there is in fact far less activity than meets the eye:

> *[I]n terms of actual administrative work the presidency is pretty much what the president wants to make of it. He can delegate "work" to subordinates and reserve for himself only the powers of decision . . . or he can insist upon maintaining tight control over every minor detail.*[69]

Brad Patterson, who served on both Eisenhower's and Nixon's staffs, once admitted that presidents are not nearly as overwhelmed by daily schedules as the popular perception holds. "There is a great deal of time available to a president to ponder the great questions of state because most of his administrative duties are assumed for him by the White House staff," according to Patterson.[70]

The impression of the presidency as a one-man operation persists because it is important for the president to continue this illusion. Lacking the party majority of a prime minister, much less the ministerial accountability, a president is dependent on his personal relationship to the electorate to win his office and to govern. He cannot afford to share this power or to even give the impression that anyone other than himself is in charge. Thus it is unacceptable for any White House assistant to upstage or to embarrass the president or to detract from his accomplishments. Aides are dispensable, for they are handy targets on which to pin presidential failures, as Nixon tried to do when he fired his top assistants in the Watergate scandal.

THE ILLUSION OF WHITE HOUSE CONTROL

Every president may find it difficult if not impossible to get the Executive Branch or Congress to do his bidding. But there is scant evidence to support the inevitable inward turn to the White House staff as a remedy for powerlessness. While the White House office has steadily been increasing in numbers, responsibilities, and influence, the authority of a succession of presidents has if anything been deteriorating. The White House office obviously is not the major or only cause for this long-range decline in presidential fortunes, but it is an important contributing factor. As presidents grew more and more dependent on their personal staffs, they became increasingly isolated from other institutions and individuals vital to collectively governing.

In at least two cases—the Nixon and Carter administrations—the president permitted inexperienced assistants virtually to sever political ties with the rest of Washington. Kennedy and Johnson had more seasoned political staffs, but both men preferred to create ad hoc units within their staffs to deal with policy problems that might have been better handled through the cabinets and agencies. Both, however, received the kind of advice *they* wanted, and each stumbled into foreign-policy crises as a result of their in-house policymaking structures. Eisenhower, who had the most successfully organized staff, was constantly criticized for delegating so many of his responsibilities to subordinates. And Reagan appeared so dependent on his personal staff that he was portrayed as the casual, part-time president—a chief executive managed by his staff rather than vice versa.

Why, then, do presidents continue to retreat into White House government when the record has been less than smashingly successful? Perhaps the most obvious explanation is that the White House staff constitutes the *only* organization in the federal government on which the president can put his personal imprint, and from which he can expect accountability and loyalty.

Aides who enjoy close daily contact with the president usually have dedicated considerable time and effort to his political advancement. A mutual attachment develops which is important both to the president and the assistant. There is something about the White House—its "splendid isolation," its pressure-cooker atmosphere, its goldfish bowl visibility—that compels a president to turn to those he has known from prepresidential times for assistance, friendship, advice, and social company. Some of these people cast their fates with him long before he became president; their efforts and skills were partly responsible for his occupying the White House. Their fortunes become inextricably intertwined, not just during the term of office but often for long afterward. FDR defended his much criticized friendship and dependence on Harry Hopkins by explaining that practically everyone who came through the Oval Office door wanted something of the president. "You learn what a lonely job this is, and you discover the need for somebody like Harry Hopkins, who asks nothing except to serve you."[71]

The needs of White House staff members, however, are not necessarily always the same as those of a president. The president shapes his staff to fit his personal whims, his style, and his political goals by choosing subordinates he knows well and with whom he feels comfortable. But no president can ever be certain that their interests and his coincide. Those who have identified with him and helped him to win office are invariably individuals who are themselves motivated by the drive for power and self-enhancement. Once they make it into the White House, the overriding preoccupation of their lives is to gain and maintain access and influence with the president.

Heclo suggests that the Executive Office of the President is largely a given that the president can only change slowly, if at all, because of the complex motivations that underlie service in the White House. The White House office is a web of other people's expectations and needs, he notes. "On the surface, the new president seems to inherit an empty house. In fact, he enters an office already shaped and crowded by other people's desires."[72] Nonetheless, each new incumbent suffers from an illusion that there *is* a magical formula for setting up a White House organization that can gain control over the federal establishment, and that the president can control its design, personnel, and procedures.

Such a perception runs up against the fact that the White House staff today is a highly institutionalized bureaucracy, despite the presidential individuality it theoretically reflects. Congress has imposed a number of statutory requirements on the White House staff that limit what a chief executive can do. Heclo found forty-three separate requirements for annual presidential reports, ranging from environmental impact statements to accounting for foreign arms sales. Rarely does a president become personally involved in the preparation of such reports. But the White House staff does, with the result that more work, more specialists, and more details crowd in on the presidential office. Each statutory requirement gives someone other than the president a proprietary interest in what is being done in the president's name.[73] Over the years these statutory requirements have become an accepted part of the presidency. Although individual chief executives have disregarded whatever suited their purpose, expectations are built into the office that cannot be totally ignored or eliminated. For example, although the president is provided with a National Security Council located within the EOP, it is up to the president to determine how he will use it. Most have included the national security adviser in their inner circle, but the council itself is almost a rubber-stamp body. Other units in the EOP fare less well, invariably losing ground to the White House staff in policymaking. The Council of Economic Advisers offers a good example. Although it is supposed to be the president's chief economic policymaking unit, the CEA almost always is subordinate to the OMB and to in-house presidential advisers. When Murray L. Weidenbaum quit as Reagan's chair, the press reported that he was frustrated by having little voice in setting economic policy, and that presidential aides ignored his warnings about White House business forecasts that were overly optimistic.[74]

The president's efforts to utilize his White House staff for greater efficiency thus are not unlike his attempts to gain control over the cabinet and federal agencies in early stages of his administration. In both cases, good intentions inevitably run up against bureaucratic patterns and personal interests resistant to systematic, centralized control. The major difference between the two approaches, however, is that the president deludes himself into believing the White House way is better. There are, unfortunately for presidents, a number of factors in the internal dynamics of White House staffs that make such units less loyal, efficient, and responsive than meets the eye. Broadly, these factors include the considerable expansion that has marked recent White House staffs along with a growing specialization in new personnel and offices; changes in the experience and qualifications of staff; and problems in both internal organization as well as external relations of the staff.

BIGGER—NOT NECESSARILY BETTER—WHITE HOUSE STAFFS

Roosevelt's White House office numbered forty-eight at the peak of World War II. Because of congressional delegation of broad foreign and domestic powers to the presidency during the Truman years, the total personnel jumped to more than 250. Staff size remained relatively stable through the next three presidencies until Nixon's, when it doubled. Despite public assertions by every president since, the staff size has remained at that level or may even be larger because presidents continue to "borrow" additional staff assistants from other departments. If "temporary" White House personnel are included, the White House staff in recent years would probably total slightly in excess of 600.[75]

Stephen Hess, of the Brookings Institution, has argued that the lesson of recent administrations shows that "a president's reach cannot be extended beyond a certain point through White House surrogates."[76] White House aides become counterproductive when they are so numerous that a president cannot monitor their behavior, much less even know who they are. (John Dean, Nixon's personal lawyer, was surprised to find that the president even knew his name—two years after hiring him as special counsel!) The chance that a presidential directive will be distorted increases with each pair of hands through

FIGURE 5–2   The White House Office

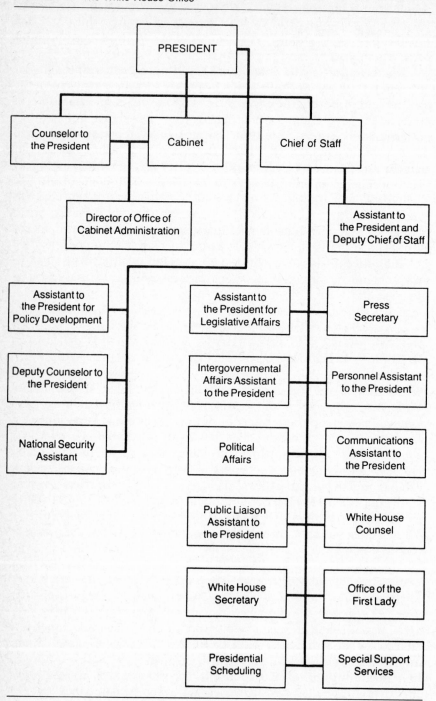

which it must pass. Consequently, each new office added to the White House staff and every additional new recruit pose new risks to the president's chain of command. As orders pass down the line, they become increasingly blurred or interpreted through different perspectives.

Ironically, it is usually the president himself who is responsible for staff inflation. Every president quickly becomes frustrated with trying to overcome through existing bureaucratic channels the dispersion of political responsibility that makes his job impossible. Eventually he decides he needs a new office or position, or he seeks a new face who can be trusted and held accountable for achieving specific goals. "Get someone in the White House to handle it" has become the standard reaction of presidents to many if not most of their problems. For it has become evident that the White House is the only place where national priorities can be established and coordinated, if at all. Only the president commands the resources to force cooperation between departments.

Presidents before Nixon usually employed existing White House personnel to light a fire under the departments. Truman was the first to appoint an aide to deal with a special-interest group when he assigned someone to minority problems. But Nixon established a number of special new units with broad powers and large staffs to deal with problems generated by special interests or problems that defied solution by any one department. Under Nixon, units dealing with intergovernmental relations, drug abuse, international trade, environmental protection, and fuel shortages were established, among others. Before long the presidency became entangled in a web of special-interest networks advancing their own narrow views. Representative offices dedicated to women, blacks, Mexican-Americans, youth, big cities, business, Jews, and labor were located in the White House. The effect was to discredit and even demoralize the regular departments and agencies while overloading the presidency. As Heclo has noted of this trend, "Each president has felt compelled to mobilize the White House to build the equivalent of a presidential party for governing."[77]

Increasing the staff sets in motion a snowball effect, according to Hess. Each new presidential assistant, in keeping with bureaucratic imperatives, measures his own importance by the size of his staff, and each additional staff member added to his office finds ways to justify the position.[78] The president ends up with no more accountability or success in terms of his performance among the special groups, but rarely is such a unit dislodged once established. Typically a special office or new position becomes a symbol of the administration's "concern," but seldom does it carry much real weight in the deliberations of the White House inner circle. Reagan promoted his top-ranking black aide to the rank of special assistant and appointed another black to the staff to handle trade policy as part of a broader effort to improve his administration's poor image with black Americans and the needy. The White House declared that the staff changes were part of an attempt to place a "key black White House staff member in the mainstream of administration policy development," and to give this member responsibility for monitoring the impact of administration policies on minorities and the disadvantaged.[79] There was little evidence that the appointment led to any real involvement in inner-staff deliberations or that it had much influence on administration policies affecting minorities.

Although special pleaders have constituted a major aspect of the expansion of the White House office, they have rarely equalled the president's inner staff in influence. The specialists are often regarded as nuisances to be tolerated in the interest of the president's personal political coalition, for in more ways than one they are carbon copies of the specialists in the iron triangles existing among federal agencies, Congress, and the special-interest groups.

The addition of units and new personnel causes many problems to be vacuumed into the White House that properly belong to the departments or agencies. It reduces the time a president and his key advisers can spend on major policy problems and deliberations. As the president spends time in the care and feeding of his staff, policy problems and details fall on his lap that should have been handled at a much lower level of administration.[80] Most White House assistants are constantly engaged in empire building much like everyone else in official Washington. Reinforcement of one's political base of support and strength through a special constituency is the name of the game. For top staff assistants chosen because of their loyalty or previous service to the president, the chief executive is their only constituency; advancement results from gaining his trust and confidence. But for staff assistants selected because of their affiliation with special interests, the tendency is to become an advocate rather than an adviser. Outside groups are tempted to ignore the departments and to take their demands directly to such advocates, knowing they have someone in the White House who is sympathetic to their goals.

As the staff increases and the number of assistants authorized to speak and act on behalf of the president multiplies, he finds his privacy, confidentiality, and flexibility increasingly jeopardized. Ambitious aides are frequently tempted to leak to the press embarrassing information and gossip about one another or about a cabinet head who is considered guilty of disloyalty or lack of cooperation. Such a practice can be debilitating to the president because it makes him appear to have made poor choices in his subordinates or incompetent in his ability to manage his staff. Nonetheless, staff leaks occasionally are sanctioned by a president anxious to relieve himself of an administrative albatross. More than one cabinet chief has been consigned to the wastebasket by media accounts of his incompetence or indiscretions that have been leaked by "White House sources." Such practices contribute, however, to the impression of disarray and incompetence that has become almost a standard in media coverage of the presidency during the past decade.

CONCLUSION

The White House office, which was created to provide much-needed assistance for the presidency, has grown so large and cumbersome that every president now needs help in controlling his own helpers. The White House staff now suffers from many of the same bureaucratic problems it was designed to eliminate. People chosen to be assistants are increasingly image merchants—campaign technicians who lack the kind of experience needed to help the chief executive deal with a complex national government. Staff personnel with self-serving motivations assume that the president's authority is transferable, and confuse the president's interest with their own. Aides isolate the president, assuming that their excessive loyalty requires them to ward off anyone who disagrees or might challenge the president's views. Information is distorted as it passes along the chain of command.

There does not appear to be a perfect staff arrangement to overcome these problems. If the president runs roughshod over the staff, bullying them through intimidation and fear, he runs the risk of losing his most independent-minded and skilled aides. If he encourages them to be generalists, he ends up with a staff of dilettantes dabbling in areas and departments in which they are usually over their heads. When he tries to centralize all power in his own hands, he becomes overloaded and consequently even more dependent on those nearest to him. If he tries to develop a well-structured hierarchy through which vast amounts of lower-level decision making can be relegated, he runs the risk of letting his staff run him. And if he gives virtually full powers to his key aides, then their weaknesses, failures, and problems become his. In truth, there may be no easy solution to the staffing needs of the presidency, for these needs are tied to inherent weaknesses in the office itself. The White House staff is highly unstructured and ad hoc because the president's own authority tends to be that way. Recruitment of staff personnel eerily resembles the recruitment of presidential candidates themselves. And the inner-staff dynamics reflects the same uncertain political environment in which the president operates.

The dangers inherent in today's White House staff are reinforced by the fact that presidents rely for advice more and more on courtiers rather than on seasoned politicians or party coalitions. As the number and scope of problems brought into the White House continue to grow, the risks multiply correspondingly that no staffing arrangement can work. The White House office itself has become one of the central agencies that perpetuate unrealistic images and illusions about the presidency, both for the incumbent as well as for the public.

NOTES

1. Ben W. Heineman, Jr., and Curtis A. Hessler, *Memorandum for the President: A Strategic Approach to Domestic Affairs in the 1980s* (New York: Random House, 1980), 177.

2. Hugh Heclo, "The Changing Office," in Arnold Meltsner, ed., *Politics and the Oval Office* (San Francisco: Institute for Contemporary Studies, 1981), 166.

3. Theodore Sorensen, *Decision-Making in the White House* (New York: Columbia University Press, 1963), 13.

4. Joseph A. Califano, Jr., *A Presidential Nation* (New York: W. W. Norton & Company, 1975), 37.

5. Michael Medved, *The Shadow Presidents* (New York: New York Times Books, 1979).

6. Robert C. Wood, "When Government Works," in A. Wildavsky, ed., *Perspectives on the Presidency* (Boston: Little, Brown and Company, 1975), 396-97.

7. President's Committee on Administrative Management, *Administrative Management in the Government of the United States* (Washington, D.C.: U.S. Government Printing Office, 1937), 4.

8. John Helmer and Louis Maisel, "Analytical Problems in the Study of Presidential Advice: The Domestic Council in Flux," unpublished paper presented at the 1977 Annual Meeting of the American Political Science Association, Washington, D.C., 2.

9. Henry Fairlie, "Thoughts on the Presidency," in Lewis Lipsitz, ed., *The Confused Eagle* (Boston: Allyn & Bacon, 1973), 219.

10. Heineman and Hessler, 177.

11. *National Journal*, April 3, 1982, 588.

12. Helmer and Maisel, 5.

13. Heineman and Hessler, 176-98.

14. Ibid., 192.

15. Medved, 6.

16. Ibid.

17. Alex B. Lacy, Jr., "The White House Staff Bureaucracy," *Trans-action*, January 1969, 50.

18. Stephen Hess, *Organizing the Presidency* (Washington, D.C.: Brookings Institution, 1976), 27.

19. Ibid., 27-43.

20. President's Committee on Administrative Management, 5.

21. Ibid.

22. Richard E. Neustadt, *Presidential Power* (New York: John Wiley & Sons, 1980), 115.

23. Patrick Anderson, *The President's Men* (Garden City, N.Y.: Doubleday and Company, 1968), 8.

24. Gary Wills, *The Kennedy Imprisonment* (Boston: Little, Brown and Company, 1981), 167.

25. Arthur M. Schlesinger, Jr., *A Thousand Days* (Boston: Houghton Mifflin Company, 1965), 687.

26. Wills, 165.

27. Hess, 88 and 110.

28. Personal communication from George Christian, July 27, 1975.

29. Hugh Sidey, "The White House Staff Versus the Cabinet," in Charles Peters and John Rothchild, eds., *Inside the System* (New York: Praeger Publishers, 1973), 48.

30. Wills, 245.

31. Richard Rovere, *Affairs of State: The Eisenhower Years* (New York: Farrar, Straus and Cudahy, 1956), 356.

32. Herbert S. Parmet, *Eisenhower and the American Crusades* (New York: Macmillan, 1972), 177-81.

33. Hess, 67.

34. Rexford G. Tugwell, *The Enlargement of the Presidency* (New York: Doubleday and Company, 1960), 458.

35. *New York Times*, November 21, 1968, 13.

36. Richard Nathan, *The Plot That Failed: Nixon and the Administrative Presidency* (New York: John Wiley & Sons, 1975), 43.

37. Ibid., 46.

38. Ibid., 48.

39. Wood, 396.

40. Theodore H. White, *Breach of Faith* (New York: Atheneum Publishers–Readers Digest Books, 1975), 325.

41. *The White House Transcripts* (New York: Bantam Books, 1974), 5 and 61.

42. Richard M. Pious, *The American Presidency* (New York: Basic Books, 1979), 248.

43. James Fallows, "The Passionless Presidency," pt. 2, *Atlantic*, June 1979, 77.

44. *New York Times*, October 23, 1977, 36.

45. *National Journal*, November 10, 1979, 1894.

46. Fallows, 79.

47. *National Journal*, November 18, 1978, 1852.

48. Fallows, "The Passionless Presidency," pt. 2, *Atlantic*, May 1979, 33–48.

49. *U.S. News & World Report*, March 29, 1982, 28.

50. Ibid., March 23, 1981, 27.

51. *New York Times*, April 19, 1981, 1.

52. Ibid., September 2, 1981, 4.

53. Personal communication from David Gergen, September 3, 1981.

54. *U.S. News & World Report*, May 23, 1983, 21.

55. Ibid., 20–21.

56. James MacGregor Burns, *The Deadlock of Democracy* (Englewood Cliffs, N.J.: Prentice-Hall, 1963), 308.

57. William G. Carleton, "Kennedy in History: An Early Appraisal," *Antioch Review*, 24 (1964), 277-99.

58. George E. Reedy, *The Twilight of the Presidency* (New York: New American Library, 1970), xi.

59. Ibid., 18.

60. Stephen Wayne, "Working in the White House: Psychological Dimensions of the Job," unpublished paper presented at the 1977 Annual Meeting of the Southern Political Science Association, New Orleans, November 3-5, 1977.

61. Ibid., 18.

62. Medved, 311.

63. Reedy, 99.

64. Ibid., 96

65. Michael Grossman and Martha Joynt Kumar, *Portraying the President* (Baltimore: Johns Hopkins University Press, 1981), 107.

66. Ibid., 83.

67. Thomas E. Cronin, *The State of the Presidency* (Boston: Little, Brown and Company, 1975), 137.

68. Heclo (1981), 162.

69. Reedy, 31.

70. Personal communication from Brad Patterson, July 12, 1977.

71. Medved, 198.

72. Heclo, 165.

73. Ibid., 166.

74. *U.S. News & World Report*, August 2, 1982, 16.

75. Cronin, 119.

76. Hess, 159.

77. Heclo, 169.

78. Hess, 159.

79. *Today*, April 30, 1982, 13.

80. Hess, 159.

Chapter 6

Leader of the Free World
Imperial or Imperiled President?

Power? The only power I've got is nuclear
. . . and I can't use that.

Lyndon B. Johnson

I can walk into my office, pick up the telephone,
and in 20 minutes 70 million people will be dead.

Richard M. Nixon

If there is an arena in which presidents have some chance of measuring up to extraordinary expectations, it is in the conduct of foreign policy and as the nation's military commander in chief. Former Secretary of State Henry A. Kissinger has suggested that every new president enters office "not only with plans to change the world, but acting as if he created it."[1] Certainly most recent presidents have admitted to a preference for global policymaking because they believed they had greater control over the decision-making process, or because the opportunities for accomplishment seemed substantially improved over domestic policymaking.[2]

The notion of the president single-handedly setting the U.S. course in world affairs does have some basis in fact. His ability to involve American armed forces throughout the world has been demonstrated time and again. And it is no exaggeration to claim that the president has the power to destroy millions of people within minutes should he unleash a nuclear attack or counterattack.

The U.S. Constitution may grant authority to both president and Congress to conduct foreign policy and to oversee military operations, but from World War II on presidents have increasingly dominated Congress. Power flowed to the White House because diplomacy in the twentieth century became entwined with military power and strategy. The president's authority as commander in chief gave him an extraordinary advantage over Congress since he was capable of acting more quickly and decisively to deal with foreign crises or threats to national security.

World leadership became a key element in substantially enhancing the image of presidents and in increasing expectations for their performance. The awareness that one man held the fate not only of Americans but of the entire world in his hands added an awesome dimension to his political image. It was hard to accept that the man whose finger was poised over the nuclear button, and who was capable of sending American troops to fight throughout the world on his personal command, could not resolve domestic problems of a far lesser magnitude.

The gap between what the president is expected to accomplish in foreign and military policymaking and what is realistically possible is, however, as great as any of the other gaps existing between the image or illusion of the presidency and its actual capacity to function. The image of the president as a twentieth-century global Paul Bunyan, the towering protector of the free world, is a major component in the illusion of the modern presidency. It is primarily based on a twenty-five-year period that began with World War II and ended with American military power becoming mired in Vietnam.

Vietnam was a "presidential war," for it was initiated, prosecuted, and continued by three presidents far beyond the patience of the American people. More important, it revealed the extent to which presidents could use American military power to achieve foreign-policy goals. Vietnam confirmed that the credibility of the president's global powers was considerably dependent on the support of the American public and favorable mass-media coverage. Since the illusion of power is power, an American president must rally public opinion behind his policies and must enjoy relatively positive press coverage, or his power will appear to be only illusory to other nations.

Global leadership has always been dependent on symbolic posturing—proving to others the strength of will and determination of a leader and his people to resist force and to protect their national interests. In today's global mass-communications village, where the potential for catastrophic destruction is quite real, the need to be convincing is critical.

Since Vietnam, the image of presidential leadership now widely projected holds that each president "has lost control over American foreign policy," or that "no one is in charge" of the foreign-policy establishment. From an imperial presidency we have moved toward what former President Ford called an "imperiled presidency."[3] The image of a president imperiled in global leadership contains enough substance to make it plausible, but it may be as much an over-simplification as the imperial image once was. The ability of presidents to influence foreign affairs has always depended on domestic and international conditions. Only rarely is this environment conducive to the kind of raw exercises of power expected or feared of presidents. If the United States today seems to stumble from one global crisis to the next, making up foreign policy as it goes, it may be because every other nation does likewise and always has.

Global trends since World War II have diminished the capacity of any single leader or nation to dominate international politics for long. Superpowers in fact increasingly have found themselves handicapped by their awesome resources. The international arena has been marked by considerable diversity and confusion as one country after another gained independence and began to chip away at the economic, political, and military monopolies once enjoyed by the major powers. The development of the economies of western Europe and Japan challenged the United States as competition for raw products, resources, and markets increased. Challenges to the status quo by newly independent, underdeveloped countries added to this competition, causing world-wide inflation and economic upheaval along with increasingly unstable alliances among nations as each attempted to improve its economic and political position vis-à-vis the other.

Presidential power and prestige in world affairs had peaked during a period when the United States was virtually unchallenged in its productive capacity or military superiority. Bipolarity marked the balance of power from World War II until about the mid-1960s; only the Soviet Union was able to challenge American military power, and no other nation was able to equal our economic position. Gradually from the mid-1960s on, the United States began to lose its dominant ranking in technology, nuclear power, productivity, and military weaponry.

U.S. economic and military superiority might be waning, but the nation continued to serve not only as the symbol of greatness but also of the old order to developing countries. Americans increasingly became the target of envy, fear, and sometimes hatred as peoples world-wide held the United States responsible for all kinds of social and political inequalities, for international tensions, or for problems within their own nations. The president was the personification of these inequities and injustices. Both the United States and its president came to symbolize reactionary forces bent on resisting change in the world, and presidents found themselves the victims of images and illusions based on an omnipotence they no longer enjoyed.

One could almost draw an analogy between the persistent demands placed on the presidency by fragmented and frustrated groups in the American public and the rising tide of expectations and frustrations of people globally, which frequently focused on the White House. In either case the president became the target of dissatisfaction in spite of the perception being badly out of joint with the times and with reality. Perceptions are meaningful in a world in which less powerful nations have acquired influence and in which the number of actors has increased. Stanley Hoffman has suggested that "when the skills of persuasion have to be spread over so many players, the uncertainty of the game . . . escalates."[4] The multipolar environment of today forces a president to campaign for support among other nations almost as vigorously as he does to win election and support at home. He must perform credibly for a vast global audience, convincing allies of his leadership and loyalty and adversaries of his toughness and resolve.

It may be difficult to separate reality from illusions in foreign and defense policymaking, so dependent is power on the *impression* of power. This chapter explores this dilemma, beginning with an assessment of the period during which presidents were believed to hold imperial control over foreign affairs. We will then consider the constraints operating against presidents as global leaders, concluding with an examination of the influence of images and illusions on the exercise of the role of "leader of the free world."

ORIGINS OF AN IMPERIAL PRESIDENCY

During the late 1930s and early 1940s President Roosevelt viewed Nazi Germany and Japan as threatening not only to the existence of our allies but also to the existence of the United States. Roosevelt was especially concerned with strengthening the British after the surrender of France to the Nazis in 1940, for it was widely believed that an invasion of England would be next. Congress, however, remained mostly isolationist in its mood, forcing the president to shortcut the legislative process in his attempts to aid Britain. FDR steered the United States along a course of undeclared war, primarily using his authority as commander in chief and his ability to make executive agreements without congressional approval. His famous destroyers-for-bases deal with the British was Roosevelt's first executive agreement in foreign policy; it was done secretly and without congressional assent.

What was unique about Roosevelt's command over diplomacy and war was its intensely personal nature. FDR was supremely confident of his personal powers of persuasion, believing that he could deal with leaders like Churchill or Stalin by establishing a personal relationship and by direct negotiations. The State Department had never played much of a role prior to the war in influencing Roosevelt's foreign policy, but after Pearl Harbor its influence diminished even more. Roosevelt never had much use for formal organizations anyway, preferring to rely almost exclusively on his own network of trusted friends like Harry Hopkins to serve as diplomatic envoys or as policy advisers, regardless of their official rank or lack of it. Such individuals appeared far more responsive to the president's needs and sympathetic to his plans than the traditional bureaucrats from State. Consequently, foreign policymaking was almost totally centralized in the White House.

FDR's position as commander in chief provided him with immense authority and influence over diplomacy because it was impossible during wartime to separate military from diplomatic concerns. Political scientist Thomas E. Etzold has noted that during the war, as the luster of the State Department dimmed, the status of the military services grew brighter. "Diplomacy and strategy often become one and the same during a war and require the intrusion of military officers into discussions and decisions that in peacetime might not be any of their concern."[5] The importance assumed by military advisers in the White House inner circles was reflected in the central importance attached to the planning and preparation for administering occupied enemy countries once the war ended. As early as 1942, when the war was not going well for the Allies, the U.S. Army was establishing schools to train military and civilian personnel to administer areas seized from the Axis powers.[6] Many of the military officials who played key roles in planning the occupation remained after the war to serve President Truman, and their influence over foreign policy was incalculable.

INSTITUTIONALIZING FOREIGN POLICY: THE TRUMAN YEARS

"I make foreign policy," Truman once declared, and so he did, as much or more than any president before or since. The monopoly over diplomacy and military power that had begun with Roosevelt in World War II culminated in the postwar era with what appeared to be the institutionalization of both responsibilities in the White House.

The American public expected rapid demobilization after the war, but worsening relations between the Soviet Union and the United States and its allies over the political shape and future of Europe soon dashed such hopes. The Soviets appeared determined to install communist satellite regimes in the eastern European countries occupied by Soviet forces at the end of the war. Soviet-backed guerillas threatened the Western-backed government in Greece. The Soviet Union had military units poised along the border of Turkey, and Moscow armed a communist separatist movement in northern Iran which posed the threat of annexing to the Soviet Union the province of Azerbaidzhan. Concern was growing that further appeasement of Soviet aggression pointed to another "Munich"—a sellout by the West to force. A general consensus emerged in Congress and among much of the public that the United States would have to assume the leading role in stopping the expansion of the Soviets or World War III would soon occur.

Since diplomacy had already been submerged with military strategy in the White House, the president was the logical choice to lead the struggle against the communist menace. Truman's use of the atomic bomb to hasten the end of the war in Asia added a frightening but convincing dimension to the president's authority, while the Cold War provided an urgency to systematize and coordinate national defense strategy in the president's hands.

Truman issued an ultimatum to Moscow to remove its forces from Iran, and the Soviets eventually complied. The president unveiled his grand strategy for dealing with the Soviet threat in a special session of Congress when he asked for emergency aid for Greece and Turkey. Declaring it must be the policy of the United States to support free peoples who were resisting subjugation by armed minorities or outside pressures, Truman asserted that American foreign policy would create the conditions under which nations could work out their own way of life free from coercion, for "totalitarian regimes imposed on free peoples by direct or indirect aggression undermine the foundations of international peace and hence the security of the United States."[7]

The Truman Doctrine, as the president's speech soon became known, cast the United States as the world's chief protector, assuming responsibilities for the presidency which it previously had held only during wartime or when national security was directly threatened. Many Republicans in Congress were unenthusiastic about reinforcing the president's foreign- and military-policy authority, but enough supported him to provide bipartisan support for the new activist American policy. Congress enacted a Greek-Turkish Aid Program to prevent the fall of those two nations to communist force. Shortly afterward the Marshall Plan, the most ambitious and generous foreign-aid program in the history of the world, was enacted; it targeted more than $15 billion in grants and loans to help rebuild the war-torn economies of Europe.

Subsequent delegations of authority to the White House by Congress continued the expansion of the president's capacity to plan and execute foreign and military policies. The Selective Service Act provided the president with the authority to draft men during peacetime.

A series of defense treaties created a network of alliances which committed the United States to protect the security of nations throughout the world, and which enhanced the president's military and diplomatic prerogatives. The National Security Act of 1947 resulted in the reorganization of the armed services into a single Department of Defense directly responsible to the president; the creation of the Central Intelligence Agency (CIA) to assist the president in gathering and analyzing intelligence from the Departments of State and Defense as well as from foreign countries; and the creation of the National Security Council to advise the president on national security matters and to assist him in coordinating diplomatic, military, and intelligence decision making.

All the new agencies reinforced the influence of the military because they were much more weighted toward national defense than diplomacy. Etzold argues that "communist intransigence decrease[d] the area within which American diplomats worked and increased the province of the military."[8] The newly created Defense Department quickly overshadowed the State Department not only because the president's decision-making system was overloaded with military people but also because Defense's budget dwarfed that of State; the military also had far more funds for intelligence. In addition, Defense had a natural ally in Congress because many Representatives and Senators were dependent on spending for military bases or defense plants located in their districts and states. Ironically, although every president would voice misgivings about the dangers of too much military advice, each ended up depending as much if not more on military responses and Defense's perception of global problems than on his diplomatic corps.

Events during the rest of Truman's administration only served to reaffirm the importance of a strong military component in American foreign policymaking. Czechoslovakia's shaky postwar government fell to a Soviet-engineered coup in 1948. The Soviet Union attempted to squeeze off access to the Western-held sector of Berlin, which was a hundred miles inside the East German border. Communist forces triumphed over the forces of Chiang Kai-shek* in China, forcing Chiang to flee with hundreds of thousands of his troops to Taiwan, a large island just off the coast of China. But the most serious threat to Truman's doctrine of containment came with the invasion of South Korea by communist North Korea in June 1950.

The Korean War was a watershed in the president's capacity to formulate foreign policy and to engage troops in an undeclared war. It

---

*Throughout this text Chinese names of persons and places appear in pinyin, which is now the preferred way of transliterating Chinese words. An exception is made here for Chiang Kai-shek, whose name is shown in the earlier Wade-Giles system because he is best known under this form. In pinyin his name is Jiang Gai-shek.

signalled an ominous expansion of the authority of the commander in chief. The war also tested the willingness of the American people to uphold the president's containment policy, for without such support the policy would soon prove to our adversaries to be merely rhetoric. Not even the subsequent approval by the United Nations Security Council authorizing joint military resistance to the invasion, nor Truman's own insistence that Korea was a "police action" and not a war, could obscure the fact that an American president, acting almost totally on his own authority, had committed the nation to a major conflict on another continent without a formal declaration of war by Congress.

In spite of the president's bold action, conservatives mounted a campaign of invective against Truman, accusing him of being "soft on communism." The charge stemmed from the fall of China to the communists and from a wave of anticommunist hysteria generated by Senator Joseph McCarthy of Wisconsin. Truman became a scapegoat because he had refused to prop up the corrupt and inept Chiang Kai-shek. After the communists' rout of Chiang's forces and his exodus to Taiwan with hundreds of thousands of Nationalist Chinese troops, American conservatives joined in a chorus with the so-called China Lobby to insist that the United States should help Chiang retake the mainland. Truman was understandably reluctant to apply the containment policy so broadly as to involve American troops in a land war in Asia.

This pressure forced a reversal of past American policy of disengagement from the Asian continent, and forced Truman into a more aggressive military position in Korea, which ultimately provoked Chinese intervention. U.S. General Douglas MacArthur, commander of the United Nations forces in Korea, talked Truman into approving an invasion of North Korea following early military victories. The UN was treated as little more than an instrument of American policy because MacArthur was determined to destroy China. China's entrance into the conflict in November 1950 prolonged the war by another two and a half years, and made Korea one of the bloodiest conflicts in recent history.[9]

MacArthur insisted that Truman should permit him to expand the war by bombing China and by moving across the Yalu River into China. Truman refused because he believed such actions might bring the Soviet Union into the war and result in World War III. Because MacArthur made his case in public, Truman was forced to fire him for insubordination in April 1951. A massive groundswell of sympathy for the general swept the United States and public opinion turned sharply against Truman's conduct of the war. The president's reluctance to prosecute the war with the conventional goal of winning caused public opinion to turn against him as the war dragged on. He grew increasingly vulnerable to the charge that he was soft on communists.

EISENHOWER'S "BIG STICK" POLICY: MASSIVE RETALIATION

Dwight D. Eisenhower's first obligation on entering the White House was to end the war in Korea. Diplomacy with the communists was suspect because it was vulnerable to charges of appeasement, sellout, or recklessness; even the word *negotiation* seemed an obscenity to conservatives.[10] Eisenhower had promised he would go to Korea if elected and find a way out of the conflict, and he did precisely that, giving the impression that foreign policy was now in the hands of a decisive and forceful president. Eisenhower's basic policies, however, were primarily a continuation of Truman's but with an important new twist: our nuclear superiority would now be used as a diplomatic weapon to prevent aggression. The United States would use nuclear force to prevent aggression. Such a threat was successful when used against China to force a truce and negotiations in Korea. It convinced Eisenhower and Secretary of State John Foster Dulles that the *threat* of massive nuclear retaliation could serve American national security better than conventional military force.

Eisenhower saw the Truman Doctrine as posing the risk of spreading American strength "nowhere and bankruptcy everywhere."[11] The cost of maintaining a conventional military strength capable of responding to communist aggression would be unbearable to the federal budget as well as to a country whose citizens were clearly not militarily inclined. Eisenhower believed there was one solution and one only:

> *[and] that is for the free world to develop the will and organize the means to retaliate instantly against open aggression by Red armies, so that, if it occurred anywhere, we could and would strike back where it hurts, by the means of our own choosing.*[12]

Such a policy transformed the "awesome nuclear capability from an instrument of last resort to one of first resort." It was appealing because it removed the responsibility for fighting drawn-out wars of containment from the shoulders of American troops and placed it squarely on superior military technology.[13]

The strategy lost its credibility before long because the Soviet Union developed its own nuclear capability, and other nations were soon entering the nuclear club. Eisenhower's two terms, nonetheless, were marked by a deceptive tranquillity as tensions between East and

West eased after the death of Stalin and economic relations gradually developed between the two blocs. The Soviet Union, meanwhile, turned its attention to the underdeveloped countries, offering formerly colonialized peoples Soviet military and economic aid as a means to improved living conditions. The communists gradually began to spread their influence into Africa, Southeast Asia, the Middle East, and Latin America, while the United States gradually discovered that its nuclear superiority offered no advantage to containing communist subversion or influence. Eisenhower refused to introduce American military forces into Indochina in 1954 after the defeat of the French by Vietminh communist forces. In 1956 the United States was forced to turn a deaf ear to pleas for help by Hungarians as Soviet forces put down an attempt to oust the Moscow-backed regime in Budapest. Closer to home, the administration was unable to prevent the establishment of a communist regime in Cuba.

Eisenhower's stature as a world leader and man of peace was seriously tarnished during his final months in office by incidents that revealed the inadequacies of an all-or-nothing defense strategy. The Soviets captured an American pilot, Francis Gary Powers, who was taking photographs of operational intercontinental ballistic missile (ICBM) installations in the Soviet Union from a U-2 spy plane that was shot down. At first the president assured Soviet Premier Nikita Khrushchev that he had no knowledge of the flight, but Eisenhower soon reversed himself and admitted that he had been aware of the mission, which was part of our ongoing national security operations. Khrushchev cancelled a forthcoming Paris summit meeting and rescinded an invitation to Eisenhower to be the first American president to visit the Soviet Union. A few weeks later the Japanese government withdrew its invitation to the president for a visit to Japan after violent opposition erupted against a new mutual security pact between the United States and Japan because of Japanese fears that their country might be used as a base for future U-2 flights.

EXPANDING COMMITMENTS:
KENNEDY'S GLOBAL FRONTIER

The main issue in the 1960 presidential election campaign was whether or not American power and prestige had declined worldwide during the Eisenhower years. Kennedy insisted that a widening missile gap and a deterioration in conventional military power seriously threatened U.S. security; the United States was said to be unable to respond to brushfire wars in countries facing internal or external communist aggression. Our former monopoly over nuclear weapons had disappeared, Kennedy asserted, leaving our commitment to resist communist expansion in shreds. Kennedy made the following vow in his inaugural address:

> *Let every nation know, whether it wishes us well or ill, that we shall pay any price, bear any burden, meet any hardship, support any friend, oppose any foe to assure the survival and the success of liberty. This much we pledge—and more.*[14]

Such rhetoric was inspiring, but it cast responsibilities for global leadership on the presidency that would prove to be unrealistic and impractical. Kennedy was promising responsibility for virtually the totality of global events, a task of heroic dimensions but of dubious logic, given the changing configurations of world power by the early 1960s. His strategic doctrine was linked to the idea of "flexible response," which required a buildup in American military capabilities at all levels: conventional military force, special units to fight guerilla wars, as well as continued development of nuclear weapons. Kennedy envisioned an American military presence capable of engaging the communist threat anywhere and at any level, a policy that was highly vulnerable on several counts.

For one thing, it assumed that Americans would be willing to pay the costs—in lives and long-range military and financial commitments—to sustain U.S. military power. Kennedy's first test of will, however, provided to be a humiliation for American credibility. He approved a CIA plan for an invasion of Cuba by Cuban refugees trained and equipped in the United States. The CIA predicted that 1400 men would be sufficient to touch off a popular uprising against Fidel Castro if they were provided tactical air cover as soon as they hit the beaches at the Bay of Pigs. Kennedy approved the broad outlines of the plan but he refused to permit the use of U.S. air cover because he did not want the invasion to be clearly linked to Washington. The force was quickly defeated, many Cuban refugees were killed or captured, and Kennedy's half-hearted and clumsy attempt to make it appear that the United States was not involved proved a failure.

The bungling of the Cuban invasion convinced Khrushchev that the young president's declaration of resolve to resist aggression was mostly rhetoric. At a Vienna summit meeting a few months later, Khrushchev warned Kennedy that the Soviets would not be able to "restrain" much longer East Germany from reasserting its "rights" over all of Berlin. Kennedy responded to this threat over access to Berlin by calling up army reservists and by strengthening allied forces in West Germany. The communists reacted by building a wall between East and West Germany to stem the tide of people attempting to flee East Germany.

Khrushchev remained unconvinced of Kennedy's toughness, and in the autumn of 1962 the Soviets began to secretly construct medium-range missile sites equipped with nuclear warheads in Cuba. Kennedy demanded that the Soviets dismantle the bases because it was feared that, if the sites were made operational, the United States would be increasingly vulnerable to nuclear attack. The Soviets offered to dismantle and remove the missiles if Kennedy would remove American missiles from Turkey. Kennedy earlier had ordered the removal of these missiles, which were no longer militarily vital, but his order had never been carried out. The Soviet insistence on a quid pro quo amounted to blackmail, and Kennedy had no alternative but to refuse to consider the offer. He responded with another ultimatum to the Soviets to either dismantle and remove their missiles or the United States would.

Kennedy's first step in a series of planned, measured responses was to blockade Cuba to prevent the Soviets from supplying additional supplies or warheads to the missile sites. With the world seemingly poised on the brink of nuclear confrontation, Khrushchev agreed to remove the missiles in exchange for a pledge by the president never to invade Cuba or to interfere in its internal affairs.

The Cuban missile crisis was a turning point for Soviet military power. Moscow's leaders decided that the USSR must achieve nuclear parity—if not supremacy over the United States—so that the Russians would never again be humiliated in a showdown. Even as Soviet leaders cooperated with the Kennedy administration in developing a test-ban treaty in 1963, they embarked on a long-range buildup of nuclear weapons which ultimately would enable Moscow to equal if not surpass in some weapons the United States and its North Atlantic Treaty Organization (NATO) allies.

The missile crisis may have forced a new determination on the Soviet hierarchy, but it also strengthened the confidence of the Kennedy administration in its ability to stand up to communists in other parts of the world. The most important test of this new determination would come in Vietnam.

VIETNAM: THE WAR BETWEEN IMAGE AND REALITY

In 1954 the French suffered at Dienbienphu a disastrous military defeat at the hands of Vietnamese revolutionary forces. Shortly afterward, the Geneva conference established what was to be a temporary partition of Vietnam between its southern provinces, which were ruled by anti-communists, and the communist-held North. Free elections were to be conducted to determine whether the two parts of Vietnam would be unified under one government. The United States refused to participate in the Geneva accords, preferring instead to support a pro-Western puppet government in Saigon that was committed to maintaining its independence from the communists in Hanoi. The elections were never held, and communist rebels in the South eventually reopened hostilities in an attempt to topple the Saigon regime, which by the early 1960s was controlled by an unpopular president, Ngo Dinh Diem.

Eisenhower had refused to use American force in Vietnam even though there was reason to be concerned that Hanoi's military victory might result in attempts by the militarily aggressive North Vietnamese to topple other governments in the region. Kennedy, however, decided in November 1961 to increase military aid and to send as "advisers" the first American counterinsurgency units—the Green Berets—to South Vietnam. The size of the American military contingent in Vietnam increased without fanfare because Kennedy and his advisers anticipated a lukewarm response from the American public to the idea of again involving Americans in an Asian conflict.

Kennedy faced the possibility that a massive infusion of American military force would eventually be required in Vietnam. In November 1963 Diem was assassinated during a coup some believe may have been supported by the CIA. Kennedy then ordered U.S. Ambassador Henry Cabot Lodge, Jr., to reassess the situation in Saigon. Kennedy was assassinated two days before Lodge was due to make his report. President Johnson received Lodge's warning that unless the United States stepped up its military assistance, Saigon would soon fall to the communists.

"JOHNSON'S NASTY LITTLE WAR"

Kennedy loyalists insist that if he had lived, the United States would not have become mired in a protracted war in Vietnam. A popular thesis holds that at the time of his death, Kennedy was considering curtailing American involvement because Vietnam appeared unwinnable. Nonetheless, the initial policy deliberations leading to U.S. military involvement in Vietnam began with Kennedy's foreign-policy brain trust: National Security Assistant McGeorge Bundy; Secretary of Defense Robert McNamara; Secretary of State Dean Rusk; and Roger Hillsman, JFK's adviser on Far Eastern policy. These men later encouraged Johnson to declare, "I am not going to lose Vietnam. I am not going to be the president who saw Southeast Asia go the way China went."[15]

Johnson campaigned for the presidency in 1964 as a dove on Vietnam, suggesting that his opponent, Senator Barry M. Goldwater, would involve the United States in a land war. But secretly Johnson was planning to widen American involvement in Vietnam. Through the Gulf of Tonkin resolution after an alleged North Vietnamese attack on two U.S. destroyers, he secured authority from Congress to increase our military presence in South Vietnam. Johnson used this authority for the next four years to justify air strikes against targets in both North and South Vietnam, and an eventual buildup in troop strength to more than a half-million Americans by 1968.

The Vietnam War dragged on throughout Johnson's administration with little evidence of progress while Johnson attempted to push negotiations with the North Vietnamese. He was rebuffed because Hanoi was convinced that time and American public opinion were ultimately on their side. The administration, meanwhile, painted a continually optimistic picture of the war, predicting "the light at the end of the tunnel." This view, however, contrasted sharply with what the news media were reporting, and it resulted in a massive credibility gap for Johnson. By 1967 an increasing number of Americans, particularly younger men eligible to be drafted to fight in Vietnam, were taking to the streets to protest "Johnson's war."

In his 1968 State of the Union address, LBJ once again predicted that the war was almost won. But a few days later the enemy unleashed a desperate and furious assault—the Tet offensive—on civilian centers of authority and military command posts throughout South Vietnam, including the American Embassy in Saigon. This offensive was, in fact, an act of desperation by a faltering enemy, but TV coverage suggested that the Viet Cong were far from vanquished. What remaining credibility LBJ had was virtually erased at that time. Johnson decided shortly thereafter not to seek his party's renomination.

THE PRESIDENTIAL DILEMMA: THE WAR AT HOME

The heir to Johnson's war, Richard M. Nixon, once observed that the most important battle in Vietnam had to be fought for the "hearts and minds of the American people."[16] A series of presidents offered the American public explanations of why we were in Vietnam. The earliest and most persistent claim was the domino theory, which posited that the United States was fighting to prevent the spread of global communism by proving that aggression does not pay. If the United States "permitted" the Vietnamese rebels backed by North Vietnam and supplied by the USSR and China to overthrow the Saigon government, a chain reaction was predicted in which one country after another would topple like a row of falling dominoes. Another explanation held that the United States was fighting to preserve democracy and freedom—an untenable claim in view of reporting by the news media that the Saigon regime was anything but democratic or free.

The most candid rationale offered was that the United States was fighting to protect our credibility—a euphemism for images of national power and the willingness of presidents to use power to shape global events. Evidence that this was the dominant goal appeared in the Pentagon Papers. These were classified government memoranda and documents published in 1971 which revealed how the Kennedy and Johnson administrations had deceived the American public as they led the nation deeper into the Vietnam conflict.

Long before the Nixon administration assumed responsibility for Vietnam in 1969, justification for the massive American buildup had begun to shift from the domino theory to the credibility thesis. Assistant Secretary of Defense John T. McNaughton wrote a memo in 1966 to President Johnson arguing that the original reasons the United States had gone into Vietnam were by then largely academic. The United States could *not* withdraw, according to McNaughton, because the "present U.S. objective in Vietnam is to avoid humiliation."[17] The psychological goal of emerging from the war with "as good an image as possible in U.S., allied, and enemy eyes" was paramount. The war thus had become a performance aimed at relevant audiences, including "the communists (who must feel strong pressures), the South Vietnamese (whose morale must be buoyed), our allies (who must trust us as "underwriters"), and the U.S. public (which must support our risk-taking with lives and prestige.)"[18]

Henry A. Kissinger, who as secretary of state later presided over the American disengagement from Vietnam, argued that the need to prove credibility was rooted firmly in the doctrine of nuclear deterrence. The dilemma of nuclear power lies in the fact that "the enormity of modern weapons makes the thought of war repugnant, but the refusal to run any risks would amount to giving the Soviet rulers a blank check."[19] This results in a paradox, however. In order to sustain peace, the United States must prove its willingness to go to war. Yet the massiveness of our military power paralyzes the president from acting except in limited, measured ways. A strategy of a limited war is fought for political objectives and not for military solutions. Such a war is aimed at affecting an opponent's will, not crushing it, and it is directed primarily at inflicting losses or posing risks for the enemy that are "out of proportion to the objectives under dispute."[20] Limited war would prevent the Soviet bloc from overrunning nations, and would permit a wider range of military capabilities. It could prove American strength and resolve without running the risk of an all-out nuclear confrontation.

The willingness to become involved in limited wars, however, poses intolerable burdens on the president, for he becomes linked in military actions in which battles are fought "not to achieve concrete ends but to create appearances," a world of images and illusions.[21] Such conflicts invariably become unpopular with the public because of their imprecise goals and hidden agenda. They demand human and economic sacrifices from a nation which is decidedly nonmilitaristic and not bent on sacrifices for hazy, symbolic goals. Journalist Jonathan Schell, who briefly covered the war, noted that such an "image world" is:

> . . . not the world of borders defended, of strategic positions won or lost, of foes defeated in great and bloody battles; it was the world of "reputations," of "psychological impacts," of "audiences."[22]

A setting of this kind gives rise to illusions of presidential omnipotence, for the president must cultivate the impression that he can and will act decisively whenever American interests or influence are tested. The president symbolized American will. If he could be convincing, American foreign policy would also be convincing. If he were able to keep other nations off balance, the United States would appear steady. Nixon, in particular, understood the value of appearing unpredictable—even dangerous—to one's foe. His administration executed several risky military moves during the Vietnam War: the mining of Haiphong Harbor in 1972 just prior to Nixon's visit to Moscow, and the unleashing of a murderous wave of bombing assaults on Hanoi at Christmas in the face of worldwide and American moral condemnation. Soviet and North Vietnamese leaders were caught off guard by what seemed to be Nixon's "irrational" behavior. But the fact that the president appeared capable of almost any kind of action strengthened his hand.

The world of credibility, on the other hand, gave rise to the illusion of presidential impotence whenever the United States appeared to have lost its resolve or when the president lost the support of Congress, public opinion, or the media. The McCarthyites' charge that Truman "lost" China naively suggested that it was his to begin with. Roosevelt was charged with selling out Poland to Stalin at Yalta even though the Soviet army's occupation of Poland was already an established fact and there was little the allies could do about it.*

The fear of presidential impotence in global politics—a symbol of what political scientist Cecil V. Crabb, Jr., calls "the illusion of American impotence"—requires every president (with the assistance of his White House publicity machine) to make himself the unchallenged scenarist of American political life.[23] This requires the presentation of

---

*Roosevelt loved to recount how Churchill had warned Stalin that the pope would be displeased if the Soviets imposed their rule on Poland by establishing a communistic puppet regime. "And how many divisions does the pope have?" Stalin is said to have asked.

much if not most of the country's foreign-policy and defense strategy in misleading terms. Rhetoric and explanations acceptable to the vast majority of public opinion have to be used, for to explain a policy truthfully would undermine it. As a result, White House strategists and the public the president is supposed to represent and to lead "live in two different worlds," each of which ceases to understand the other.[24]

To succeed, the president must undermine any opposition—whether it be the press pointing up incongruities or distortions in his policies; the opposition political party bent on discrediting the president's decisions; or segments of the public openly criticizing and protesting his actions. Internal dissent must be treated as a threat to national security, since the image of a great country is said to be vulnerable to assault from every side on the home front. According to Schell:

> *In a democracy, where anyone can say whatever he wants to say, and frequently can get on television saying it, the national image is the composite impression made by countless voices and countless deeds, all of them open to inspection by the whole world. It is not only the president and his men who form the image but anyone who wants to get out on the street with a sign. . . . If the standing of the United States as the greatest power in the world was conditional upon its behaving like the greatest power in the world, then the way the public . . . behave[d] at home was far more important to the national defense than the way a few hundred thousand soldiers were seen to behave nine thousand miles away.*[25]

THE END OF THE IMPERIAL PRESIDENCY IN GLOBAL AFFAIRS

From this perspective, Watergate—with its spying, wiretaps, sabotage, and dirty tricks—was inevitable, in fact imperative, if the White House was to control the political environment at home sufficiently to conduct a convincing foreign policy. The president had to undermine the democratic system and its safeguards of checks and balances and limited authority. Having placed on the president's shoulders the awesome responsibility for global policies designed to prevent nuclear war while preserving American security, the White House could not afford the opposition of Congress or journalists, much less of teenagers marching in the streets to disrupt those policies.[26]

Charged with carrying out a foreign policy based not on tangible results such as land won, armies crushed, or principles of freedom upheld, Nixon reacted by employing the same tactics of clandestine warfare and secretive manipulation practiced by Moscow and Hanoi.

Many of the abuses of power associated with Watergate could be traced to Nixon's secrecy and deception in trying to unilaterally direct the Vietnam War. He ordered the bombing of Cambodia for fourteen months from March 1969 until May 1970 when he ordered American troops into Cambodia. He secretly bombed Laos. He used the White House "plumbers" unit to break into the office of a psychiatrist treating Daniel Ellsberg, the man who had leaked the Pentagon Papers, in order to obtain evidence that would smear Ellsberg.

So long as he could hide these activities from the mass media, public, Congress, and the opposition party, Nixon's global strategies worked. The North Vietnamese and Viet Cong agreed to end hostilities in early 1973 after it appeared that Nixon, fresh from his landslide reelection, would continue to batter Vietnam for four more years. Public opinion was muted because the administration had "Viet-namized" the war, removing the bulk of our fighting men from Vietnam. American casualties declined sharply as Nixon conducted a punitive war, using American air power to maintain the fiction that he had extricated the nation from Vietnam and that South Vietnamese forces were "winning the peace." The end of the draft in the United States eliminated much of the youthful opposition to the war.

Nixon and Kissinger had no illusions about the ultimate goal of Hanoi to subjugate all of Indochina—a concern openly voiced by the leaders of Thailand and Laos prior to the signing of the Paris peace accords that ended the Vietnam War.

Both Nixon and Kissinger were convinced the American people would not sustain the war much longer; it was evident by early 1973 that Congress was about to cut off funds for Vietnam.[27] Subsequent events proved the domino theory to be partially correct as Hanoi—encouraged by Nixon's political demise during Watergate and by American weariness with further involvement in Vietnam—resumed the conflict against the South in 1974. Less than a year later the North Vietnamese conquered Saigon; they then proceeded to occupy Cambodia, to invade Laos, and even later to threaten China.

The failure of American policy in Vietnam demonstrated the constraints facing any president who uses conventional military power to achieve foreign-policy goals which do not have an immediate or direct impact on national security. Containment might have been accepted in spirit and theory by the American people, but they were never willing to support interminable sacrifices of men, matériel, and money in a protracted and seemingly pointless war.

The Nixon-Kissinger policy was embedded in the principle of realpolitik, which suggested judicious applications of the carrot and stick (based on strength and self-interest) to achieve a relaxation of tensions between the superpowers. Deeply distrustful of the Soviets, Nixon and his foreign-policy architect nonetheless believed successful negotiations to reduce tensions could begin from a clear demonstration of military strength and a willingness to use it. But this policy also meant sharing our technical expertise, agricultural and economic productivity, and cultural advancements to encourage cooperation and détente with the Soviets if they were willing to stabilize relationships.

The flaw in détente was that the president's margin for maneuverability was slimmer than that allowed his Soviet counterparts.[28] Détente requires the nation to keep up its military guard at the same time it is negotiating away the likelihood of using that power. The idea that containment must be maintained while pursuing coexistence is not a concept easily assimilated by the more pragmatic and nonmilitary-minded American populace. The expectation that a relaxation of tensions should lead to reductions in military spending or preparedness was easily assumed by both the public and Congress. The failure of our military strategy in Vietnam produced a form of national soul-searching which damaged the nation's commitment to containment. Presidents after Nixon confronted a political environment in which realistic demonstrations of American strength lacked credibility.

AN IMPERILED PRESIDENT: GLOBAL
LEADERSHIP AFTER VIETNAM

As we noted in Chapter 3, Congress has moved on a number of fronts to reduce presidential control over foreign policy. In the process it has undermined our commitment to a strong military position in the global order. Vietnam and Watergate were the primary factors in de-imperializing the presidency, but the relaxation of tensions through détente has encouraged the process. The president's authority to make executive agreements was limited by the Case Act. The War Powers Act challenged his authority to commit military forces abroad without congressional approval, and a measure establishing a congressional veto on arms sales exceeding $25 million placed additional restrictions on his foreign policy maneuverability.

To some extent these reassertions of congressional authority over foreign policymaking were as much cosmetic as substantive. Presidents have been able to get around them when it suited their purposes. President Ford, for example, violated the War Powers Act when he sent the Marines into Cambodia without prior notification of Congress. The purpose of this action was to rescue U.S. sailors seized by Cambodian patrols from the U.S. merchant ship *Mayaguez*. Presidents have not been severely cramped in their ability to make executive agreements since Congress usually is not anxious to negate presidential accords with another government. It is in the broader context of foreign-policy power, however, that the president's authority has been eroded and the credibility of American power undermined. Beginning with President Ford, presidents have suffered as a result of more congressional and public questioning of their foreign-policy leadership. The monopoly enjoyed by presidents from FDR to Nixon has been considerably diminished.

Ford's most immediate problem involved a growing resistance by Congress to appropriate funds sought by the Executive Branch to conduct foreign policy. Congress refused to approve funds requested by Ford to help resist a Soviet-backed guerilla war in Angola in 1975. It refused pleas from the White House to restore cuts in aid to Turkey made by Congress to punish that nation's continued involvement in drug trafficking in the United States, and it turned down in 1975 Ford's request for $700 million for aid to South Vietnam in the dying days of the Saigon regime.

Ford's troubles were broader than mere funding rejections, however. Liberals in Congress who opposed Kissinger's Vietnam policies under Nixon sought to dump Kissinger as national security assistant. Conservatives were angry with Kissinger for his role in détente and for opening up relations with the People's Republic of China. The national media, meanwhile, suggested that Ford lacked the personal knowledge, experience, and ability to conduct foreign policy, and that he was the dupe of Kissinger.

Ford did not help his cause with his performance in a presidential campaign debate on foreign policy with Jimmy Carter, whose experience and knowledge about foreign affairs was less substantial than Ford's. Ford declared that he did not think the Polish people considered themselves dominated by the Soviet Union, a lapse of thinking that Carter pounced on and that later resulted in Ford's having to make a public retraction of his "misstatement."

Carter benefitted in 1976 from the fact that a sizeable number of voters wanted to excise the last vestiges of Vietnam and Watergate from their memories. He promised a departure from the imperial foreign-policy style of the past by conducting an open, honest foreign policy, one that would reflect the values that had made America great instead of the secretive, aggressive practices that had marked recent administrations.

Carter believed that his predecessors had overemphasized U.S. relations with the Soviet Union and China at the expense of our European allies and Japan. He was particularly critical of what he saw as Kissinger's disregard for human rights. Regimes which regularly and systematically tortured their people, arbitrarily arrested and imprisoned individuals, and withheld basic human freedoms as well as the necessities of life were often supported by the United States for no other reason than that they opposed communism. Promising to make Americans "feel proud again," Carter issued a directive declaring a major objective of American foreign policy would be to promote human rights throughout the world.

Carter's human rights campaign risked alienating several allies by pointing out their obvious shortcomings. It faced its biggest risk with the Soviet Union and China, where the impracticalities of such a strategy were overwhelming. The administration tried to link Soviet noncompliance with human rights with American economic and diplomatic sanctions, a move which substantially departed from détente. Pressures on Moscow to ease up on human rights violations only caused the Soviet government to crack down even harder on dissidents because the policy was seen as interference in internal Soviet affairs. China was exempted from pressures on the human rights issue although its record was hardly any better than the Soviet Union's, but establishment of formal diplomatic relations between Washington and Beijing was more important to Carter's foreign policy than pushing the Chinese on the rights question.

Carter's open foreign policy was so porous that dirty linen from conflicts within his administration was laundered almost daily in public and in the press. Zbigniew Brzezinski, his national security assistant and a hard-liner on Soviet relations, squared off against Secretary of State Cyrus Vance, who was more the conciliator and diplomat on East-West relations. United Nations Ambassador Andrew Young was quoted by the media as suggesting that "there are hundreds, perhaps even thousands of people whom I would call political prisoners in the United States," at the very moment the administration was criticizing the Soviet government's sentencing of two prominent dissidents to prison.

Carter was too quick to concede that American power was not what it had once been, and many actions which telegraphed American weakness were explained realistically and logically but with telling effect. Carter abandoned the B-1 bomber, stretched out development of the MX missile, and retarded development of the Trident missile, all the while supporting reduced defense expenditures. Republicans criticized him for not coming to the aid of the shah of Iran, who was forced into exile by Muslim radicals. Carter was also blamed for allowing our defense force to decline in the face of a Soviet buildup. Democrats, concerned over his irresolution, spoke of the need "to stiffen the president's spine" in his dealing with China on Taiwan, or in his devising a new Middle East policy which would combat Soviet influence in that oil-rich region.[29]

A series of incidents indicated that Carter was incapable of identifying, much less protecting, American interests. The assassination of American Ambassador Adolph Dubs in Afghanistan was followed by the seizure of the American embassy in Iran. American embassies in Libya and Pakistan were attacked and burned to the ground. Carter delivered a strongly worded warning to the Soviet Union in 1979 after a sizeable contingent of Soviet troops was discovered to be in Cuba, but a few weeks later he dismissed the force as inconsequential. He characterized the Soviet Union's 1979 invasion of Afghanistan as the most dangerous crisis since World War II. But his response was limited to cutting off grain sales to the Soviets and to ordering the United States to boycott the 1980 Olympic games in Moscow, measures which failed to gain the support of farmers or Olympic athletes.

Almost lost in these setbacks to America's global prestige and credibility were Carter's important foreign-policy accomplishments: ratification of the Panama Canal treaties, restoration of aid to Turkey, establishment of diplomatic relations with the People's Republic of China, and negotiation of a new Strategic Arms Limitation Agreement (SALT II) with the Soviets. (SALT II was never presented to the Senate for ratification.) The crowning achievement of Carter's foreign policy was the signing of the Camp David accords, which he personally engineered between Israel and Egypt in 1978. But not even this achievement silenced critics who charged that Carter had no long-range policy for dealing with the Middle East, a region whose oil resources made it vital to American national security.

Carter eventually agreed to significant increases in the defense budget in the aftermath of the incidents in Iran and Afghanistan. But he never eradicated the impression that he was incapable of acting forcefully to protect American interests, or that he understood how to exercise power in a rapidly changing global arena. Senator Howard H. Baker, Jr., a candidate for the Republican presidential nomination in 1980, asserted that people wanted their president to be "firmer, more consistent, a little less smiling and Mr. Nice Guy."[30] The most devastating indictment of Carter's global leadership came from the Republicans' 1980 campaign resolution, which declared that he was "presiding over the decay of American influence and decline of American military power worldwide."[31]

REAGAN: COLD WAR RHETORIC
VERSUS GLOBAL REALITIES

President Reagan repudiated not only Carter's open, human rights policy but he also rejected détente. Reagan wanted improved relations with Taiwan at the expense of the People's Republic of China. He planned to scrap SALT II, to apply economic sanctions against the Soviet Union, to support Israel's claims to annexation of occupied territories, to deepen American involvement in a Marxist-backed brushfire war in El Salvador, and to undermine a leftist regime in Nicaragua. Reagan pushed for the deployment of new nuclear missiles in western Europe, and supported funding of major military-weapons systems which had been rejected or put into cold storage during the Carter administration. Reagan was adamant about a massive increase in defense spending, even in the face of extraordinarily high budget deficits.

Foreign policy from Truman to Carter had been directed at preserving a tenuous balance of power through military actions as well as diplomacy. But the Reagan administration held the view that negotiations with the Soviets were of little use since Moscow was committed to an expansionist policy, and could not be trusted to keep any agreement. Reagan's strategy thus was to commit the United States and its allies to an aggressive foreign policy targeted at undermining Soviet strength militarily, economically, and technologically.

Such a policy required the United States and its allies not only to beef up their military capabilities but also to tighten the screws on trade with the Soviet Union and its puppet regimes. Reagan's approach required agreement among our major allies as to the nature of the Soviet threat; it also required massive new commitments to defense spending as well as willingness to renounce economic trade with the communist bloc, which had become substantial.

European governments shared Reagan's concerns about the Soviet Union, but wanted to continue to trade with the Soviets. Reagan attempted to block construction of a Soviet pipeline that would supply a steady source of natural gas to western Europe and earn Moscow as much as $10 billion a year in western currency—money that could help fuel the Soviet arms buildup. The Europeans considered the pipeline to be critical to their future energy needs. Since it provided jobs at a time of high unemployment, they refused to support Reagan. Disappointed, Reagan banned the delivery of American-made equipment needed for the pipeline, and threatened to bar European-based companies contributing to the project from importing equipment or technology from the United States. When angry European leaders threatened to retaliate with economic sanctions against the United States, the administration was forced to relax its ban. Reagan's position was weakened considerably by his approval of a year's extension on sales of American grain to the Soviet Union. The administration rationalized its action by insisting there was a difference between selling grain, which *cost* the Soviets hard currency, and extending credits, technology, and currency, which might benefit the Soviet Union in the arms race.

A major weakness in Reagan's foreign policy was his exaggerated rhetoric in describing the Soviet threat. He sent shivers down the spines of Europeans with a casual comment that the West could sustain a limited nuclear war with the Soviet Union and still survive. Secretary of State Alexander M. Haig, Jr., made matters worse by speaking about a "demonstration nuclear warning shot" as part of NATO doctrine in Europe, and Defense Secretary Caspar W. Weinberger tried to explain how it was possible to fight a "limited nuclear war." Such concepts had always been part of strategic planning, but the way they were publicly mentioned by the Reagan administration made it seem trigger-happy with nuclear weapons; by comparison, the Soviet Union appeared more restrained. An antinuclear movement swept western Europe and the United States with mass public demonstrations directed at the Reagan administration. Eventually the president had to restate his views in a televised speech targeted primarily at European audiences. He sounded more conciliatory by calling for sharp reductions in nuclear arms and for new talks with the Soviet Union. The House of Representatives, meanwhile, rebuked Reagan by approving a resolution favoring a nuclear arms freeze for both the United States and the USSR.

Reagan's foreign policy was not helped by having too many divergent voices and insufficient coordination at the top. One aide was quoted as suggesting that Reagan's main source of information on global events was Dan Rather, the anchor of the CBS Evening News.[32] A critic described Reagan's foreign-policy decision making as having "almost none of the strengths and most of the weaknesses of everything that's gone before."[33] Reagan held strong ideological views about foreign policy, which he frequently imposed over the opposition of his advisers. Such an approach encouraged the airing of divergent views in public as conflicting advisers attempted to build bases of consensus to influence the president. The president contributed to the chaos and conflict by making frequent off-the-cuff remarks which advisers later had to clarify or deny. Foreign-policy initiatives were occasionally undertaken without the usual advance consultation with our allies. All of this produced an impression of confusion and dissension in the ranks, and led to an endless series of poorly interrelated decisions.

William P. Clark, an old California friend of the president, became Reagan's national security adviser in 1982. Soon Clark had more influence on foreign policy than any of Reagan's top aides. Clark's hardline views on the Soviet Union paralleled Reagan's, raising concern that moderate voices were being shut out and that the president was sealing himself off in an ideological chamber. Reagan faced trouble from the Republican-controlled Senate, where the Senate Budget Committee cut in half his proposed increase in defense spending for fiscal 1984. Congress also balked at fully funding the MX missile, voting only to allow minimal research and development on this controversial new weapon.

Another challenge to Reagan's foreign-policy leadership arose in Central America, where American advisers were attempting to help the conservative military regime of El Salvador put down Marxist revolutionary forces. The United States was involved in arming and training guerillas in Honduras who were waging a war against the Marxist (Sandinista) regime of Nicaragua. The Sandinistas, along with Cuba and the Soviet Union, were arming and training Marxist factions in El Salvador. Thus a major aim of Reagan's policy in Central America was to harass the Sandinistas. Congress, however, voted to cut off aid to the guerillas because such covert activities evoked memories of past CIA ventures in Cuba as well as of U.S. involvement in Vietnam.

Reagan attempted to rally public support for his foreign policy by reviving the domino theory and claiming that the stakes were as big in Central America as they had been in Europe after World War II. Yet he repeatedly stated that he had no intention of sending U.S. combat troops into the region. Although the president declared U.S. credibility to be at stake, most of our allies viewed the Central American conflicts as local civil struggles; they urged the United States to try negotiations rather than a military response. Unfortunately, the true aim of our policy in the region was not clear. Reagan's insistence on preventing a communist victory required the administration to support unpopular military regimes and to oppose political and social changes. This left the door wide open to Soviet-Cuban influence, which claimed to be aligned to the needs of the oppressed.

Paradoxically, the administration denied any analogy between its deepening role in Central America and what had happened twenty years earlier in Vietnam. Yet the administration's motivation, rhetoric, and tactics bore an eerie resemblance to the events in Vietnam. Part of Reagan's problem could be attributed to the fact that it was difficult for any president to shape a consensus for a foreign policy involving "compromise, subtlety, patience, restrained gestures, prior consultation with allies, and the deft geopolitical maneuvering that is required when one is no longer the world's preeminent locus of military and economic power."[34]

CONSTRAINTS ON PRESIDENTS AS GLOBAL LEADERS

The difficulties in achieving a coherent foreign policy go far beyond the strengths or weaknesses of any president or the personalities advising him—even beyond shifts in the world's balance of power. The major problem confronting presidents as global leaders is that our foreign-policy system was neither designed for nor is it capable of making coherent policy.[35] Like many other aspects of presidential power, the Executive Branch's foreign policymaking apparatus has developed in a piecemeal fashion with ad hoc units. Authority is fragmented, frequently more responsive to countervailing centers of power and influence than to the president's centralized control, and increasingly dependent on a shifting, unpredictable, and volatile public opinion. A president's ability to build a consensus behind his global policies no longer can be taken for granted. Numerous constraints have developed that are as difficult to overcome as the hurdles created by iron triangles or triple alliances in domestic politics.

Foremost among the constraints on the president as global leader is Congress. The British ambassador to the United States during the Carter years was asked what surprised him most about American diplomacy. "The extraordinary power of your Congress over foreign policy . . . ," he responded.[36] The illusion prevails that Congress was basically passive and inactive before the Vietnam War, but political scientist Edward A. Kolodziej argues that just the opposite was the case. The post–World War II era has been "fraught with congressional-presidential conflict over the methods and objectives of American foreign policy and the scope of authority of the legislative and executive branches in making and conducting foreign affairs."[37] This conflict has become endemic to the entire foreign-policy process since at least the early 1970s. Each president has had to try to fashion a stable, reliable foreign policy from a fluid set of ad hoc congressional coalitions crystallized around narrow policy issues. In effect, the White House today has to deal with 536 secretaries of state instead of one.[38]

The policymaking system that evolved in the Executive Branch over the past forty years constitutes another formidable hurdle to presidential control. Although expertise is concentrated in the White House, every president finds it as difficult to inspire a consensus or to expect accountability from subordinates for his foreign-policy initiatives as for his domestic programs. It would be more accurate to speak of foreign-policy establishments instead of the presidential foreign-policy establishment because national-defense and foreign-affairs policies are now influenced if not shaped by a number of diverse agencies, commissions, and departments, each of which has its own institutional imperatives and hidden agenda.

Public opinion, once considered a reasonably predictable and stable source of support for a president's global leadership, has become a third element in making global leadership more difficult. Americans traditionally have been willing to leave major questions of foreign policy to their president, believing he "knows best." Television, however, has brought global events and foreign affairs into the living room. As a result, while there may still be a low level of substantive knowledge in the public about world affairs, there is a much higher *involvement*. The American public has grown more cynical, negative, and critical of foreign-policy leadership and less willing to accept the president's assessment of what is in the nation's best interests.[39]

Economic, military, and political changes in the world over the past several decades, in tandem with the emergence of a global mass-media technology, have significantly changed the nature and form of power. The nuclear age ushered in a new period of superpower diplomacy in which images and illusions became as important as armies, weapons, or missiles in winning goals and influencing nations. American presidents are at a distinct disadvantage in such an environment because the porous nature of our political system makes it almost impossible for them to control the images projected to other nations and their leaders.

CONGRESS VERSUS THE PRESIDENT

During the peak of U.S. involvement in Vietnam in the late 1960s, one of our best-known political commentators wrote that he could not think of "a single major foreign policy move any president wanted to make since the Second World War that he was unable to carry through because of the opposition of the press or of Congress."[40] The prevalent concern among political observers at the beginning of the 1970s was that Congress seemed perilously close to extinction as a counterweight to an imperial presidency. By the end of the 1970s, however, instead of an imperial presidency running roughshod over a confused and impotent Congress, the tables were turned and foreign policy seemed a free-for-all in which a resurgent Congress challenged the White House at virtually every step of the decision-making process. More than any other issue, the presidential election of 1980 turned on the impression that the presidency under Carter had been reduced to a pitiful shadow of its once great image as a position of world leadership.

It is a myth that foreign policy was once conducted *without* a test of wills between Congress and the Executive Branch, or that there once existed an era of bipartisan consensus in which presidents were given a free hand to shape foreign policy unilaterally. The record of administrations from Truman to Reagan suggests that conflict is more likely than consensus. Congress has rarely been as subservient to White House direction as our memories seem to describe. It is an illusion that presidential authority in foreign affairs was ever as extensive as the image of the imperial presidency implied. The evidence is that all postwar presidents have acted from a base of weakness or uncertainty as much as from genuine strength.

Conflicts between Congress and the White House have arisen repeatedly over defense spending, over programs of foreign economic aid, and especially over unilateral exercises by presidents of their military power. In recent years, however, members of Congress have become involved in other broad policy areas affecting our foreign relations, such as trade, energy, natural resources, markets, as well as monetary and fiscal policies. Congress now requires the Executive Branch to prepare a massive and ever increasing number of reports on every conceivable aspect of international relations. In addition to requiring the White House to submit for congressional clearance every arms sale of any consequence to foreign nations, Congress now prepares its own list of countries that are specifically eligible or ineligible (depending on the whim of Congress at the moment) for military and economic assistance. More than 150 statutory limitations on the conduct of U.S. foreign relations were identified by an Executive Branch analysis at the end of the 1970s.[41] The Supreme Court's 1983 decision overturning the legislative veto may serve to once again strengthen the president's hand in foreign policymaking, although it is still too early to tell.

Many forces of change affecting Congress and the Executive Branch that were described in Chapters 3 and 4 also contribute to the growing involvement of individual legislators in foreign policy. The decline in political party unity in Congress paralleled the weakening of congressional leadership. This has led to a breakdown not only in bipartisan support of presidential initiatives on major policies but also to a tendency for individual members to shape their global positions and strategies on the basis of their own self-interest. The expansion of congressional staffs provided legislators with information needed to form more autonomous perspectives or positions. The proliferation of single-issue and ethnic pressure groups targeting their foreign-policy interests at Congress encouraged further fragmentation of any global-policy consensus. Finally, the New Politics in which capturing headlines or gaining exposure on network television looms more important than supporting a party or a president's program has contributed to an "every-member-is-a-statesman" outlook in many legislators.[42]

Some members of Congress have taken on unauthorized diplomatic missions which undermined presidential efforts at negotiations. Representative Elizabeth Holtzman of New York headed a women's caucus from Congress which attempted to negotiate with the Vietnamese-backed regime in Cambodia in 1979 for American food shipments to starving Cambodian peasants. In 1980 Representative George Hansen of Idaho tried to negotiate the release of the American hostages in Iran by promising to investigate the "crimes of the Shah of Iran."[43]

The responsiveness of Congress to ethnic or special-interest groups constitutes another hazard to executive direction of foreign policy. The Greek-American lobby, for example, was instrumental in getting Congress to cut off military aid to Turkey because of the dispute between Greece and Turkey over Cyprus. (The Turkish-American lobby, by contrast, is neither large nor influential in American politics.) Members of the black caucus in the House were aligned with the Greek lobby because Turkey's involvement in the drug trade posed a particular problem in black ghettoes.

No ethnic minority interest group is more potent with Congress, however, than the pro-Israeli lobby. Congress traditionally has been Israel's strongest supporter in the foreign-policy process, partly in response to the large, well-organized, and effective Jewish minority in the United States and partly as a result of strong convictions by members of Congress and the American public that Israel is a strategic ally in the troubled Middle East. Since the early 1970s the Executive Branch has attempted to add greater balance to American policy in the region, paying more attention to the interests of such Arab states as Egypt, Jordan, and Saudi Arabia. When the Reagan administration tried to stop the Israeli shelling and bombing of Beirut in 1982 and prevent Israel's occupation of the city, Prime Minister Menachem Begin virtually ignored White House entreaties. He felt confident that U.S. aid would not be lifted or American sanctions placed on Israel because of support in Congress for Israel.

The commitment of members of Congress to foreign policies benefitting particular interests may reflect personal assessments that such policies are in the best interest of the United States. It also suggests that legislators are less resistant to political pressures than the White House. There is a temptation for members of Congress to play politics with issues that require a strong national consensus. In addition, an inclination not to accept the president's claim to represent the nation's interests is growing.

Other governments are both aware and wary of the involvement of members of Congress in the foreign-policy process. This is particularly so for heads of committees or subcommittees and members whose decisions have an impact on American aid or support. Nicaraguan General Anastasio Somoza's personal friendship with Representative John M. Murphy, chair of the House Merchant Marine and Fisheries Committee, was a factor influencing hearings by the Panama Canal subcommittee of Murphy's standing committee on charges of Panamanian gunrunning to Somoza's enemies. The hearings, which occurred just two weeks before the House was to consider the implementing legislation for the Panama Canal treaties, were dominated by testimony from the vice-president of Nicaragua's Chamber of Deputies. This was perhaps the first time a foreign government has used a congressional hearing to denounce a neighboring country.*

Senator Jesse Helms (Republican of North Carolina) dispatched two staff members to London to observe the British government's negotiations to settle the civil war in Rhodesia (which is known as

---

*Rarely does Congress formally hear testimony from foreign officials since this might be considered an infringement on the authority of the Executive Branch as well as poor diplomatic practice. Only the executive theoretically is empowered to have formal communications with foreign governments. Murphy's actions opened Congress to the risk that conflicting foreign factions might seek to be heard in the future. Nicaragua clearly was attempting to ask Congress to pass judgment on whether or not Panama had violated international law.

Zimbabwe). The British government protested to the Carter administration that Helms's aides had interfered in the negotiations. But the Senator denied any interference, saying his aides were sent because "I don't trust the State Department on this issue."[44]

Congress may not be capable of initiating foreign policy, but it has numerous opportunities to veto, upset, or sidetrack presidential initiatives through legislation or by withholding appropriations. Congress has also been known to weaken a president's hand in foreign affairs by divulging or leaking secrets. Members often are unwilling or unable to keep confidential information to which they are privy. Yet the White House runs the risk of alienating Congress if it does not consult with Congress on important policy matters. Congress is also quick to reflect shifts in public opinion in spite of the fact that public opinion on foreign policy is usually based on insubstantial information or inadequate understanding.

A leading student of the presidency wrote during the Vietnam War that "no important policy, domestic or foreign, can be pursued for long by even the most forceful president unless Congress comes to his support with laws and money."[45] That observation is even more accurate today as the boundaries between foreign and domestic policymaking become more and more indistinguishable, and the political system increasingly fragmented. A significant change in the U.S. position in the world and in our ability to direct or control political forces and conflict means that issues are no longer easily resolvable by unilateral decision making. Congress's reassertion of its prerogatives in foreign policy reflects not only the failure of successive presidents to master the global environment but also the increasingly complex interrelationships of the world in the 1980s.

PRESIDENTIAL FOREIGN-POLICY ESTABLISHMENTS

The illusion is that every president is heir to a powerful foreign-policy machine which is much more responsive to his touch than anything in the domestic realm. According to this myth, a truly experienced and skillful chief executive has only himself to blame if he does not master this establishment, which can provide him with a monopoly of information and resources unmatched by any other decision-making system in the national government.

The problem with this view is that the national security decision-making system—like Congress, the cabinet, and the entire federal bureaucracy—is fragmented and marked by bureaucratic politics and infighting. There is, in fact, as political scientist James Oliver has suggested, no *single* foreign-policy establishment but rather *several*, each of which serves as both a source of and a major constraint on the president's exercise of global leadership.[46] Diplomacy is supposed to be the main province of the Department of State; national defense strategy resides with the Defense Department, the National Security Agency, the intelligence bureaucracies of Defense and State, and the Central Intelligence Agency. The blending of military policy with diplomacy since World War II has, however, blurred distinctions among these major agencies so that responsibility for control or for shaping policies is frequently difficult to pinpoint.

The growing economic and social interdependence of nations, moreover, has led to a growing involvement of such domestic bureaucracies as the Departments of Agriculture, Treasury, and Commerce in the foreign-policy process. Administration policies result from a complex and often prolonged process of interaction among these agencies. Who provides input to the president and who has jurisdiction over foreign-policy decision making depends on a number of factors. The most obvious consideration is whether the matter is a crisis, a high-level policy matter involving big stakes, a particular personal concern of the president's, a policy involving both domestic- and foreign-policy concerns, or a routine matter.

THE NATURE AND OPERATION OF THE FOREIGN-POLICY MACHINERY

A crisis decision is forced on the president whenever the United States is caught by surprise and the nation's security, economy, or credibility is threatened by a foreign nation or by events. Kennedy's Cuban missile confrontation is an ideal example of a crisis decision. Such situations invariably involve ad hoc structures consisting of a small number of the high-ranking, trusted advisers in the presidential establishment. Typically the national security assistant, defense secretary, joint chiefs of staff, secretary of state, and UN ambassador play key roles. In addition, White House assistants or cabinet leaders outside the foreign-policy establishment may also be involved if their advice is valued by the president. In the Cuban missile decision, no one equalled the influence of Kennedy's brother Bobby, the U.S. attorney general, who was the president's most trusted confidant and who reflected JFK's own predilections.

Crisis decision-making groups are especially vulnerable to groupthink—a psychological drive for consensus at any cost that suppresses dissent and prevents a more reasoned consideration of alternative strategies.[47] Although a president may encourage his advisers to be candid, constraints work against anyone fully expressing views or options when the president's preferences are obvious or when a consensus has emerged behind the president.

Decisions involving important stakes, such as major economic relations with allies and trading partners or high-level decisions affecting relations between the United States and the Soviet Union, usually involve a small elite group of officials. They may include the chief of the Office of the U.S. Trade Representative, the secretary of state, or perhaps the secretaries of agriculture, treasury, or commerce, as well as other top-ranking assistants, deputies, or agency chiefs. Such groups are likewise ad hoc, including high-ranking officials or skilled executives whose input is needed for policies replete with technical or professional details.

Most noncrisis foreign-policy matters are settled outside the White House by bureaucrats below the level of cabinet rank. The president and his chief lieutenants rarely become involved in routine policy decisions because normally such matters can be resolved through lower-level negotiations. (Routine matters constitute the bulk of the government's foreign-policy activities.) The White House invariably is preoccupied with the few problems that are far more visible and significant. Of course, these problems are more difficult to settle or resolve.

Some less visible, routine decisions which are settled at lower levels in the bureaucracy can influence relations at a higher level or even create conditions that later ripen into crises or threats to national security. Oil-import policies did not become an almost constant matter of concern to the White House until the Arab oil embargo of 1973 and the emergence of the Organization of Petroleum Exporting Countries (OPEC) proved how vulnerable the United States was to an oil shutoff. Since then, energy policies have become a major aspect of foreign policymaking. Bureaucratic power thus is a function of presidential (and even congressional and public) inattention. Federal bureaucracies play their most prominent roles in routine matters and their smallest role in crises or in decisions in which the stakes are high.

Presidential influence is limited by the fact there are so many potential units and actors in the foreign-policy process, as well as because those responsible for policies are motivated by organizational enhancement and self-interest. We earlier alluded to the competition between military and diplomatic interests, but disagreements and disputes arise also because of other forms of internal conflict in the Executive Branch. One source of conflict pits policymakers who are ideologues or "moralists"—individuals dogmatic in their views of the world—against those who are pragmatic or realistic. Friction also arises, as we noted earlier, over which regimes or political interests should be extended or denied American backing. There also is frequent conflict between White House advisers concerned primarily with protecting the president's political flanks and foreign-policy professionals whose concerns are with broader global questions.

HARD-LINERS VERSUS DIPLOMATS

Ideologists are usually hard-liners—individuals who view foreign policy mostly as conflicts between the forces of good and evil, right and wrong. Hard-liners see the communist countries, for example, as implacable if not monolithic threats which should be dealt with by economic or military sanctions plus a strong threat of deterrence. Hard-liners often are associated with the Department of Defense or the National Security Council where their perspectives may be more congenial, but they can be found throughout the foreign-policy apparatus.

Pragmatists tend to be found more often in the ranks of the State Department or with an agency such as the United Nations in which diplomacy and negotiations are the main activities. Pragmatists generally are more inclined toward compromise than confrontation; they are less prone to see every move by our adversaries as a threat to national security or as part of a monolithic threat.

Most foreign-policy practitioners are mixtures of these two types, some leaning more toward the ideological side, others to the so-called realistic end. Each group coexists with the other in a state of constant tension in every administration, regardless of where they are located or which one is dominant. They constitute a challenge to the president to define precisely what his policy is toward the world. In the Carter and Reagan presidencies, the national security adviser was always chief among the administration hard-liners; each tended to be an ideologue on the key questions of American policy toward the Soviets while the secretaries of state generally were pragmatists. As a result, both Carter and Reagan frequently appeared unable to present a unified foreign policy. Carter's attempt to project a human rights policy was so flexibly applied it confused both allies and adversaries. National Security Assistant Brzezinski presented a tough front to the Soviet Union while Secretary of State Cyrus R. Vance and his successor, Edmund S. Muskie, offered a more diplomatic perspective. Reagan's strong anti-Soviet rhetoric was shared by his national security assistants while his State Department typically sounded more conciliatory.

ETHNIC AND POLICY FACTIONS

Sharp differences surface also over which regimes or ethnic groups should benefit from American policies. These differences frequently crosscut the ideologist-realist, militarist-diplomat spectra. One such division pits supporters of Israel against those who would tilt American policy toward a more moderate course in the Middle East and Arab world. American-Chinese relations likewise constituted a source of conflict over whether Beijing or Taipei ought to be favored. The pro-Taiwan faction in the State Department was still dominant in the early 1970s when Kissinger secretly was laying the groundwork for President Nixon's historic trip to China and the establishment of American diplomatic ties with the People's Republic of China. Had State gotten wind of Kissinger's plans, it undoubtedly would have done everything within its power to sabotage the visit.

One scholar suggests conceptions of the national interest are so colored by the institutional perspectives and needs of bureaucratic actors involved in foreign policymaking that struggles are inevitable over which image of reality will prevail, whose policy prescriptions will win out, and which agency will get the lion's share of budgetary resources. A president may occupy the central position in this struggle, but he becomes as much the object of bureaucratic political processes as their controller. Every president depends nonetheless on such bureaucracies and personalities for the information and policy options from which he must choose.[48]

WHITE HOUSE INSIDERS VERSUS PROFESSIONALS

As responsibility for foreign and military policy shifted to the Executive Office of the President after World War II, the inner circle of White House assistants and presidential confidants gradually became involved with professional foreign policymakers and national security advisers. (Woodrow Wilson's friend, Colonel Edward M. House, was the prototype and Roosevelt's Harry Hopkins, the best-known model of a presidential intimate who enjoyed immense influence over foreign and military policy.) Presidents increasingly grew dependent on ad hoc arrangements as diplomacy and military strategy became one and the same. Inevitably the influence of close associates and advisers who enjoyed frequent and direct contact with the president became greater than that of foreign-policy bureaucrats.

The lack of a centralized, coordinated structure of decision making responsible to presidential control encouraged the White House to become a "mini" State and Defense Department. A succession of presidents complained of being unable to manage either the State or Defense establishment. The national security unit located directly in the EOP after 1947 was much more responsive to the president's needs and perspectives. State as well as Defense officials invariably were pressured by demands from various entrenched interests, and were charged with the difficult task of representing the president before Congress. The national security adviser, however, had no such constituency or departmental imperatives. Since loyalty to the president was personal, he inevitably became a part of the inner White House circle.[49]

Crisis decisions particularly enhanced the influence of the national security adviser, who along with other top diplomatic and military leaders and White House aides constituted the decision-making structure that emerged in the White House. According to one authoritative definition, a foreign policy crisis is any situation that threatens the high-priority goals of the national decision-making unit, limits the time available to make the decision, and surprises the decision makers.[50] Political scientist Charles F. Hermann suggests that crisis decisions monopolize the highest level of government because of the threat they seem to pose to our national security and other national interests. Normal bureaucratic procedures are sidestepped since the high rank of the decision makers enables them to act without deference to other bureaucrats. Information is at a premium because there is insufficient time to obtain new data. Decision makers make inferences and act on the basis of previous situations. Personal antagonisms between decision makers are subdued because of the obvious need for consensus, and extreme responses may be encouraged because of the limited data and the enhanced importance of the decision makers. Finally, because there is a great deal of uncertainty surrounding such decisions, considerable effort is expended to gain the support of allies and others.[51]

Because many important foreign-policy decisions today contain elements of crisis, formal organizations play less of a role than presidential insiders in shaping responses. The actual decision-making process in the higher echelons of the foreign and defense establishments tends to flow downward from the White House to the bureaucracies rather than vice versa, as in much of the domestic-policy agenda. As a consequence, the president is tempted to rely on people he knows and trusts best and with whom he is comfortable. White House staff members—usually inexperienced in global affairs—often end up playing crucial roles in such decisions simply because of their usual inside track in most aspects of presidential decision making. Washington journalist John Osborne noted of Carter's White House staff that he "thrusts all of them [Jody Powell, press secretary; Hamilton Jordan, chief of staff; Robert Strauss, political adviser; and Vice-President Walter Mondale] into domestic, foreign policy, and foreign intelligence matters."[52]

Formal bureaucracies tend to be more involved in programmatic decisions involving long-term goals with drawn-out negotiations and planning. Most foreign-policy decisions are of this type; they include such matters as trade agreements, defense treaties, foreign or military aid, and disarmament negotiations. The involvement of the president or his chief advisers in the details of programmatic decisions may be minimal or even nonexistent. In fact, it has been argued that bureaucratic power in foreign affairs is directly proportional to presidential inattention![53]

Programmatic decisions may originate in the White House or at the top of the policy structure. But they require congressional funding and approval; they demand the efforts of departmental or agency personnel to implement; and they frequently enlist the support or opposition of interest groups concerned with the impact or outcomes. The general public and mass media usually pay little attention to such decisions because they lack the dramatic appeal that crisis decisions have. (Few Americans, for example, get wrought up over negotiations on fishing rights in coastal waters.)

The president has much less at stake in image or credibility with programmatic decisions, even though the results frequently are vital to economic prosperity, national security, or the well-being of many Americans. Indeed, many decisions made in the routine day-to-day conduct of foreign policy profoundly influence domestic policies, a development that will be more fully explored in the next two chapters.

Because the public's perception of global events and expectations for presidential leadership are geared to the resolution of crises, and because these are the kinds of decisions that lend themselves to centralized authority, the White House monopolizes the process. If the national security adviser is himself a powerful personality—a Henry Kissinger, for example—he will dominate the foreign-policy process, and policies may bear at least some measure of cohesiveness. But the presidential foreign-policy establishment is porous, and opportunities for other decision makers to assert themselves is seldom foreclosed. Those involved in diplomatic solutions invariably run up against those opting for a military response or at least a more aggressive response. The impulse to manage foreign and national security policies with an eye on the electoral calendar or the president's standing in public-opinion polls leads the White House staff to become more involved than their collective experience would otherwise dictate.

Conflict is unavoidable in such a loosely formed, personality-centered system. Much of this conflict stems from the inherent tensions between the military and diplomatic perspectives, as well as from ethnic and ideological differences. But the main problem is organizational. The State Department will always be concerned with maintaining ties with allies and negotiating differences with adversaries. The Pentagon and national security experts will inevitably worry about sustaining the credibility of the nation's military superiority and the capability of its armed forces. White House aides will logically fret over the fallout from foreign-policy decisions on the president's popularity at home.

Since Kennedy, winners of the conflict for control over foreign policy have been the security and military units along with the White House staff. Only one secretary of state since the Eisenhower administration has dominated foreign policy—Kissinger, whose appointment to that position was an attempt to prevent the unraveling of the Nixon administration because of Watergate. As noted earlier, Kissinger retained also the title of national security adviser until late in Ford's administration, and only gave it up after Congress brought pressure to bear on the president for having one man occupy the two key foreign-policy positions in the government.

A long line of secretaries of state have found their influence and authority over foreign affairs checked by the national security adviser and the White House "mini" State Department. Secretary of State Dean Rusk under Kennedy and Johnson consistently acquiesced in the policies of both administrations, but was usually upstaged first by Kennedy's national security adviser, McGeorge Bundy, and later by Johnson's, Walt Rostow. Prior to his appointment to be secretary of state, Kissinger might have held the title of national security adviser under Nixon, but in reality he was a White House secretary of state with a staff of some fifty people. William Rogers, Nixon's *real* secretary of state, was nothing more nor less than a figurehead. Cyrus R. Vance, Carter's secretary of state, was a diplomat's diplomat—calm, low-key, a superb negotiator with broad experience in foreign affairs. His influence with Carter quickly waned, however, as the stock of Zbigniew Brzezinski climbed. Their differences over a number of major issues frequently spilled over into the national news media. Vance resigned after disagreeing with both the president and Brzezinski over an ill-fated attempt to rescue the American hostages in Iran in 1980. Vance's successor, Senator Edmund S. Muskie, was promised that he would be the number one foreign policy adviser, but Brzezinski clearly remained the most influential decision maker in the Carter administration.

Secretary of State Alexander M. Haig, Jr.'s, attempt to become the "vicar" of Reagan's foreign-policy establishment ended up predictably with his forced resignation and the ultimate triumph of the White House staff. Haig's disputes with Reagan's first national security adviser, Richard Allen, resulted in Haig coming out on top, partly because Allen was incompetent and largely because Allen was never seen as a good team player by other White House aides. When Haig began to feud with Allen's successor, William P. Clark, an old friend of Reagan's, Haig reached the point of no return as far as the White House staff was concerned. Haig's public claim that the White House staff was out to "get" him were confirmed in June 1982, as the president and his inner circle decided they could no longer tolerate a secretary of state who challenged virtually every other key decision maker in the administration on strategic policies toward the Soviets, the Middle East, and other problem areas.

Reagan's foreign-policy procedures gave every indication that the trend toward White House ad hoc decision making would continue, if not even become more pronounced. Clark, for example, lacked experience in both diplomatic and military policymaking, but he quickly emerged as the strong man in the administration, largely because of his ability to work well with Reagan and his staff. Clark's main responsibility was to oversee the refinement of issues and options before they were presented to the president. The goal became not to use the National Security Council as a decision-making unit, according to a White House aide, but to "get Reagan to reflect upon what he has heard and to hold further discussions with White House aides before he makes up his mind."[54]

The outer limits to which a president depends on loyal but unseasoned White House advisers in addition to his national security assistant may have been reached during Carter's attempt to resolve the Iranian crisis. Hamilton Jordan played a secret role in having the shah of Iran moved from a military hospital in Texas, where he was undergoing treatment for cancer, to a hospital in Panama. Then Jordan negotiated with French intermediaries in various European capitals for the release of the hostages. Traveling under an alias—"Mr. Thompson"—and wearing a wig and fake beard provided by the CIA, Jordan met in Paris a top Iranian government official who suggested that the hostage crisis could be resolved if the United States would kill the shah. When Jordan responded this was impossible, the Iranian suggested that the CIA could do it and make it appear as if it were a natural death. This cloak-and-dagger episode, which was revealed by Jordan after leaving the White House, raised serious questions as to whether *this* was how a superpower ought to conduct diplomatic negotiations.[55]

AN IMPERIAL PUBLIC?

Americans have long given their president the benefit of the doubt because he was presumed to possess information and expertise unavailable to anyone else. It was generally held to be in the national interest to support him. Since 1974, however, presidents have found themselves having to justify their initiatives to an increasingly critical and reluctant public. Public frustration over Vietnam, the nation's seeming helplessness in the oil-rich Middle East, the alleged decline of American power vis-à-vis the Soviet Union, and renewed fears of a loss of control and of the possibility of a nuclear holocaust—all these factors have tended to focus the attention of the mass media and public on foreign policy. According to pollster Daniel Yankelovich, public opinion has grown much more "skeptical, opinionated, critical, impatient, giving careful scrutiny to all initiatives, and quick to conclude that while the president may mean well he may not know what he is doing."[56] The major source of this new aggressiveness is television, which has expanded the audience for foreign-policy news and created opinions where there formerly were none.[57]

Before television, the public was insulated from a great deal of information about foreign affairs; they ignored it, or edited it out of their lives. Most Americans chose not to read about what went on globally because traditionally the United States was isolated from the rest of the world. Television, however, created a vast new audience of persons who, although not much *interested* in foreign affairs, were nonetheless *involved* in them, holding opinions which were strongly felt but anchored to insubstantial information or knowledge.[58]

About 60 percent, or as much as two thirds of the American public, are not particularly interested in or informed about foreign affairs. Mass-media scholar William Schneider calls them the "noninternationalist public"—a group which is mostly against foreign aid, against troop involvement in other countries, and against anything suggesting foreign entanglements. This substantial element of the electorate believes that much of what the United States does for the rest of the world is senseless, wasteful, and unappreciated. As a result, they are against U.S. involvement in other countries unless a clear-cut issue of national interest or national security is involved. If U.S. security or other interests are threatened, they want quick, decisive action but no long-term commitment.

The attentive public, by contrast, is better educated and follows foreign policy regularly. In the past it supported presidential initiatives more than the noninternationalist public, but today the attentive public is divided between those who reduce foreign policy to a struggle between East and West and favor an aggressive response, and those who disagree with interventionist policies. The emergence of television with the split in the attentive public creates a far less stable foreign-policy environment, Schneider argues:

> The public has become less patient with foreign policy initiatives. The attentive elites compete for allies in the noninternationalist public, each on its own grounds. The net impact is a good deal more cynicism and distrust among the public which finds it leaders increasingly critical and deeply divided.[59]

This new public involvement may foreshadow the movement from an imperial presidency to an "imperial public." Theodore Sorensen has suggested that because the public is ill informed and mercurial in its attention to global politics, as foreign policy begins to resemble the more vulnerable, politically sensitive realm of domestic policy, the United States will hover "precariously on the brink of degenerating into a 'messenger-boy' presidency."[60]

CONCLUSION

The illusion that the president possesses imperial powers in global affairs has been replaced by the widespread impression that no president is really very good at protecting American interests, preserving the peace, or controlling his own foreign-policy establishment. The abuse of power seems to have given way to the atrophy of power. Covert activities and secrecy now constitute less of a risk to American global leadership. Far more dangerous is the president's inability to keep foreign-policy decision making from spilling out in newspapers and on television the conflicts, failures, and weaknesses within the top levels of government.

In reality, presidents never enjoyed as much authority as they were reputed to have, even at the peak of the imperial age of American power. Their global power rested on American economic and military dominance during a brief period that began with World War II and lasted until the 1960s. Much of the foreign-policy activity of the past twenty-five years has involved, in fact, a series of presidents attempting to confirm their authority over global affairs. Foreign-policy failures have been a source of embarrassment if not political defeat for many presidents since Roosevelt (and even FDR is faulted for "selling out" to Stalin at Yalta).

Instead of being a source of satisfaction, global policymaking has frustrated or defeated most modern presidents. Truman's "loss of China" and his inability to win the Korean War contributed to his political demise. Eisenhower was criticized for allowing American military power to decline during the 1950s. Kennedy suffered a humiliating defeat at the Bay of Pigs, only redeemed by risking a nuclear confrontation in the Cuban missile crisis. Johnson became mired in Vietnam, losing his presidency. Nixon resorted to massive violations of the Constitution's system of checks and balances to achieve a fleeting peace in Vietnam. Even his monumental achievements in opening relations with the People's Republic of China and gaining détente with the Soviet Union were rejected by many segments of the American electorate. Ford appeared naive and uninformed, a captive to the Nixon-Kissinger foreign policies of the Vietnam era. Carter lost the presidency because he appeared to have permitted the United States to suffer humiliation in Iran. His accomplishments—the Camp David accords, the Panama Canal treaties, and the restoration of diplomatic ties with China—were largely forgotten. Reagan was criticized for not resurrecting a "two Chinas" policy as much as for letting relations with Beijing turn sour. He was fiercely challenged on his attempts to increase defense spending, to develop a new nuclear policy, and to exert American power in Central America.

Presidents seldom have had the kind of imperial power in the world affairs widely attributed to them. As U.S. military, economic, and diplomatic superiority declined relative to the rest of the world, political forces and trends both within the United States and globally were changing the political relationships established at the end of World War II. The United States—once the model of hope to have-nots throughout the world—gradually emerged as a leading political force preventing change. The president symbolized on the one hand the hopes and on the other the frustrations of many peoples, just as he represented for Americans the expectation that he would keep the United States number one. Before long, it became difficult to distinguish between the president's shortcomings and limitations at home and his failure as a global leader. In either case the credibility of both the president and the American system was undermined.

A president is seriously handicapped in trying to deal with other foreign policymakers. Not only is he under pressure to confirm American power and credibility, but he must do so with all his cards faceup on the table. Few national leaders have to operate in a decision-making environment as porous or as unstable as that of the United States. All leaders obviously suffer from handicaps and weaknesses in their decision-making powers, but it is easier to project an image of resolute strength and toughness in a closed system than in Washington, D.C.

One prominent theory of international relations suggests that politics today involves less a struggle for genuine power or dominance than a contest for shaping perceptions nations and leaders form of one another.[61] If that is the case, the American people and their presidents are as poorly served by images of presidential impotence as they once were by illusions of the president's imperial greatness. In either case the representation is a distortion of reality.

The ultimate weakness—and perhaps the greatest flaw in American foreign policy—is its lack of continuity. As we dispose of one president after another, frequently making dramatic changes in personalities and political perspectives, our foreign policy shifts back and forth, confusing both allies and foes. Not only does American policy become less predictable, but the possibility also increases that mixed signals about American intentions or capacities will be sent out every time a new president assumes office and tries to rebuild credibility in his own leadership as well as in the nation's power and resolve.

NOTES

1. Personal communication from Henry A. Kissinger, September 15, 1982.
2. Aaron Wildavsky, "The Two Presidencies," in A. Wildavsky's *Perspectives on the Presidency* (Boston: Little, Brown and Company, 1975).

3. For a good discussion of the "imperiled" presidency, see Thomas E. Cronin, "An Imperiled Presidency?," *Society*, November-December 1978.

4. Stanley Hoffman, "Perceptions, Reality, and the Franco-American Conflict," in John C. Farrell and A. Smith, eds., *Image and Reality in World Politics* (New York: Columbia University Press, 1968), 59.

5. Thomas E. Etzold, *The Conduct of American Foreign Relations* (New York: New Viewpoints, 1977), 67–78.

6. Ibid.

7. Harry S. Truman, *Memoirs* (New York: Signet Books, 1957), 2: 129.

8. Etzold, 67–81.

9. Lewis McCarroll Purifoy, *Harry Truman's China Policy* (New York: New Viewpoints, 1976).

10. Ibid.

11. Townsend Hoopes, *The Devil and John Foster Dulles* (Boston: Atlantic-Little, Brown 1973), 127.

12. Ibid.

13. Ibid., 127–28.

14. John F. Kennedy, "Inaugural Address, January 20, 1961," *Public Papers*, 1961, 5.

15. Quoted in Tom Wicker, *JFK and LBJ: The Influence of Personality on Politics* (Baltimore: Pelican Books, 1968), 205.

16. Jonathan Schell, *The Time of Illusion* (New York: Vintage Books, 1975), 368.

17. Neil Sheehan, *The Pentagon Papers* (New York: Signet Books, 1971), 492.

18. Ibid., 372.

19. Henry A. Kissinger, *Nuclear Weapons and Foreign Policy* (New York: W. W. Norton & Company, 1969), 4.

20. Ibid., 123–24.

21. Schell, 367.

22. Ibid.

23. See Cecil V. Crabb, Jr., and Pat Holt, *Invitation to Struggle: Congress, President and Foreign Policy* (Washington, D.C.: Congressional Quarterly Press, 1980).

24. Schell, 376.

25. Ibid., 368.

26. Ibid., 382.

27. Henry A. Kissinger, *Years of Upheaval* (Boston: Little, Brown and Company, 1982), 11.

28. Ibid., 235–46.

29. *New York Times*, February 17, 1979, L–3.

30. Ibid.

31. Ibid.

32. *San Antonio Express*, July 27, 1982, 17.

33. *San Antonio Express*, October 17, 1981, 18.

34. Daniel Yankelovich and Larry Kaagan, "Assertive America," *Foreign Affairs* 49 (1980): 697.

35. *Time*, July 5, 1982, 14.

36. Ambassador Peter Jay, quoted in William D. Rogers, "Who's in Charge of Foreign Policy?," *New York Times Magazine*, September 9, 1979, 49.

37. Edward A. Kolodziej, "Formulating Foreign Policy," in Richard M. Pious, ed., *The Power to Govern* (Proceedings of the Academy of Political Science) 34, no. 2 (1981): 176.

38. Ibid., 188.

39. William Schneider, "Bang-Bang Television: The New Super-Power," *Public Opinion*, April-May 1982, 15.

40. James B. Reston, "The Press, the President, and Foreign Policy," *Foreign Affairs* 44 (July 1966): 560.

41. Kolodziej, 176.

42. Rogers, 47.

43. Frank Kessler, *The Dilemmas of Presidential Leadership* (Englewood Cliffs, N.J.: Prentice-Hall, 1982), 179.

44. *New York Times*, September 21, 1979.

45. Clinton Rossiter, "Presidents and Congress in the 1960s," in Cyril Roseman et al., *Dimensions of Political Analysis* (Englewood Cliffs, N.J.: Prentice-Hall, 1966), 34.

46. James K. Oliver, "Presidents as National Security Policymakers," in Thomas Cronin, ed., *Rethinking the Presidency* (Boston: Little, Brown and Company, 1982), 391-92.

47. See Irving L. Janis, *Victims of Groupthink* (Boston: Houghton Mifflin Company, 1972).

48. Oliver, 392.

49. Ibid., 393.

50. Charles F. Hermann, "Some Issues in the Study of International Crises," in Charles F. Hermann, ed., *International Crises: Insights From Behavioral Research* (New York: Free Press, 1972), 3-17.

51. _____, "International Crises as a Situational Variable," in James N. Rosenau, ed., *International Politics and Foreign Policy* (New York: Free Press, 1969), 416-17.

52. John Osborne, "White House Watch: Choosing Symbols," *The New Republic*, January 21, 1978, 9.

53. John Spanier and Eric Uslaner, *How American Foreign Policy Is Made*, 2d ed. (New York: Praeger Publishers, 1978), 10.

54. *National Journal*, July 17, 1982, 1245.

55. Hamilton Jordan, *Crisis: The Last Year of the Carter Presidency* (New York: G. P. Putnam's Sons, 1982); see also comments by Dom Bonafede, "The Jordan View," *National Journal*, September 25, 1982, 1645.

56. Daniel Yankelovich, "Farewell to 'President Knows Best,'" *Foreign Affairs–America and the World 1978*, 57 (1979): 670.

57. Schneider, 13.

58. Ibid.

59. Ibid., 15.

60. Yankelovich, 672-73.

61. Ivo Duchacek, *Nations and Man*, 3d ed. (Hinsdale, Ill.: Dryden Press, 1975), 211.

Chapter 7

Unattainable Expectations
Presidents as Domestic Problem Solvers

It's difficult to develop national policies when the public attitude tends to be "every man for himself."

Jimmy Carter

Moses would have had difficulty getting the Ten Commandments through Congress today.

Stuart Eizenstat, Chief Domestic-Policy Adviser to President Jimmy Carter

For the past half century the image of the president as the nation's domestic-policy leader has paralleled the expansion of the federal government's power and influence. First came the New Deal with its radical restructuring of the relationship between the national government and the people, followed by a steady but inexorable mushrooming of governmental agencies, programs, and regulations. Then the Great Society of the Kennedy-Johnson years pushed the government's reach into every household, office, school, financial institution, medical facility, factory, and neighborhood in the land. The federal government became the target and hope of every conceivable interest group with needs to be fulfilled or grievances to be redressed.

This enlargement of the federal government to every nook and cranny in American life might have been inspired initially by virtue, but inevitably it assumed political motives as well. Legislators insured their seats in Congress on the basis of how well they obtained for their constituents a fair share—or more than an equitable distribution—of the federal giveaway, often at great cost to the federal treasury or to broader national interests. Each president became dependent on an electoral base built of numerous narrow issue or interest groups which, like a member of Congress's constituents, expected specific rewards from the White House in exchange for their votes and financial support.

The wholesale distribution of federal largesse and protection was accompanied in the late 1960s and 1970s by attempts to achieve not only equality of access to the great cornucopia of Washington goodies and benefits but also by legislation to overcompensate those previously denied or shortchanged by the system. First the civil rights movement stirred the conscience of the nation. Eventually it moved the White House and members of Congress, resulting in a spate of new laws and regulations to guarantee not only social equality but also economic opportunity to all Americans. Then followed demands by women, the handicapped, Spanish-speaking or Spanish-surnamed Americans—by every group with a legitimate and sometimes not so legitimate claim to federal help or protection.

In every case popular expectation for federal assistance—whatever the need or wrong—inevitably came to rest on the White House. Network television reduced many if not most of the major domestic policy problems to the dimensions of the presidency, suggesting with some logic and truth that if there were to be national solutions, they would have to come through the Oval Office. If there had been a grudging acceptance in the past that a president might be "interested" in domestic legislation, after Roosevelt and the New Deal it was taken for granted that he would be *the* force, not only for initiating programs but also for making certain they worked.[1] The White House gradually assumed responsibility for the nation's domestic agenda, including all the visibility and influence as well as all the risks this entailed.

As long as the American economy expanded and national productivity remained high, the domestic policy agenda was mostly a plus for the president. Yet there were always political pressures from a growing number of groups attempting to maximize their political returns. Beginning with the 1970s, however, the policy agenda began to change as government found it more and more difficult to sustain the high cost of existing programs, much less to develop new ones. Paradoxically, demands and expectations on the federal government increased as the capacity to create new or keep pace with existing programs declined in the face of chronic economic problems.

By the beginning of the 1980s, public frustration and disappointment with presidential direction of domestic policies had become chronic and widespread. It seemed that no matter who occupied the

White House, the president was unable to solve our nation's problems. Each president—cut adrift from his political party and dependent on a personally built electoral coalition—unsuccessfully wrestled with the dilemma of trying to achieve vital national policy goals without alienating the many groups to which he owed his political base of support. At times the choice appeared almost to be between good national policies and enhancement of reelection chances. But no matter how judiciously each president tried to balance the goal of national policies against the demands of countless interest groups, his public-opinion polls declined with predictable regularity as programs or decisions angered or disappointed one group after another of his shaky electoral coalition.

The main reason presidents inevitably fail in the domestic arena is that they no longer have the luxury of winning over voters or influencing large numbers of groups with generous federal programs. From FDR to LBJ, most presidents were in the business of promoting policies which expanded opportunities or increased federal assistance. But since Nixon, presidents have become Scrooges, restraining a kindhearted Congress from spending the nation into further debt or commitments. The presidency of the 1980s is quite different from that of preceding decades because as Paul C. Light, an expert on presidential domestic-policy leadership, has suggested, political and economic costs have escalated, while the president's ability to absorb the "inflation" has not kept pace. The result is a "no-win" presidency in domestic affairs.[2]

Every president begins office with the same set of formal powers in domestic policymaking, but these formal powers are limited and less important than a number of resources that vary considerably and unpredictably, depending on the personality of the president, the times, and the economic and political environment.

This chapter will explore the changing role of the president as our domestic policy leader. We begin by considering the more important social, economic and political changes that have occurred in the United States in recent years. Then we will examine how these changes have served to exaggerate the president's leadership over domestic policy even as major trends and forces were undermining his ability to fulfill public expectations.

THE DOMESTIC POLICY MAZE OF THE 1980S

Several years ago Saudi Arabian officials were quoted in the American press as ready to give up hope that President Carter would ever achieve a national energy policy for the United States, the Saudis' leading oil customer. Anxious to stabilize world oil prices, the Saudis urged the adoption of conservation measures because Americans consumed more oil than any other nation in the world. The Carter administraion appeared incapable of achieving such a policy because—in Saudi eyes—no one was in control.

Many Americans have themselves come to share the Saudi frustration over the inability of the United States government to act. Much of the electorate has grown cynical about politicians because while social and economic problems seem to multiply and spread like a plague of locusts, no one is capable of solving them. Presidents, in particular, have appeared inadequate to the challenges.

Domestic policymaking frustrates every president because most of our problems are so complex and divisive. Rarely can a president rally a majority of Americans around the flag to help him solve domestic problems, as he can occasionally during major foreign-policy crises. Invariably one group's gain is another's loss in domestic politics. As the United States fragments into narrower and narrower issue or policy constituencies, the ability of any president to achieve a national consensus on important policy needs or problems grows ever more remote. Normally a domestic crisis must reach the boiling point before the president can marshal sufficient resources in Congress and the bureaucracy to achieve policy change. Even then, there is still much uncertainty that the policy will be carried out to the president's satisfaction by those responsible for administration.

Often a president leaves office before his domestic policies can be fully implemented, and his successor may dismantle key provisions or undermine the original intent of the programs. Nixon, for example, set out to eliminate or substantially weaken certain Great Society programs. When he was unable to trim their budgets in the face of congressional opposition, he resorted to impoundments. Reagan attempted to kill off the Departments of Education and Energy—both created during Carter's administration. Although Reagan did not succeed, he was able to substantially cut funds for a number of programs begun under Carter in the areas of developing synthetic fuels and funding for educational projects.

Political scientist Everett Carll Ladd, Jr., suggests that as new issues rush across the national stage, it is to the president more than any other political officeholder that the citizenry looks for cues and direction.[3] But while the American people as a whole may look to him for national answers, powerful interest groups and single-issue groups attempt to use the presidency to advance narrow, particularistic policies, values, or goals. As a result, the president confronts an increasingly impossible dilemma: he is held accountable for broad, national policies since his election victory and support are based on a national mass electorate. But he is virtually hamstrung by interest groups exerting their demands and influence on the Executive Branch and Congress through the nominating and election system.

The irreconcilable tension between the need for national policies and the pressure for particularistic programs lies at the very heart of the impossible presidency. Members of Congress and government officials who are far more responsive to the particularistic and pluralistic demands of groups escape the responsibility for their actions that prevents presidents from achieving national goals. As we noted in earlier chapters, a majority of Representatives and Senators are re-elected year after year. Bureaucrats are seldom dismissed for favoritism or incompetence. But the president always pays the price of failures or shortcomings in national policy. Dependent on his own personal "coalition of minorities" to win the nomination, every president is later destroyed by elements of this coalition because he has failed to live up to their expectations. Or he may be faulted for being unable to lead Congress or to administer the nation's programs adequately.

The president's task is made impossible by the ambivalence of the American electorate. While people generally distrust big government and centralized authority, many nonetheless hold a strong faith that rational administrative leadership ought to be able to transform society. There is, however, a lack of public consensus on precisely how society should be changed, or on what the government should do. Carter tried unsuccessfully throughout his administration to convince the public that strong energy conservation measures were vital, but a majority of Americans refused to believe that a genuine energy shortage existed. It is difficult if not impossible for any president to generate a public consensus when people are confused or divided in loyalties by socioeconomic, ethnic, or regional differences, or when they are cynical about the motivation behind proposed new policies.

When there is a lack of widespread popular consensus for presidential leadership in domestic policy, interest groups are far more influential because of their close ties to members of Congress, congressional committees, and entrenched bureaucrats. This triple alliance invariably triumphs over the president when he attempts to formulate national policies or strategies. Paradoxically, even when the president achieves national goals, the end result is much the same as if the triple alliance had been behind them to begin with. Most national programs lead eventually to greater centralization of the policy process in the Executive Branch. As the number of programs proliferated from the New Deal on into the 1960s, and as federal spending grew to include an ever expanding number of groups and people, the number of groups vying for influence in the policy process likewise increased. Ultimately their influence over the administrative process prevailed.

Specialized federal programs inevitably result in the evolution of new issue networks which, along with the older, more established interest groups, only serve to enhance the influence of narrow, particularistic, and pluralistic elements in Congress and federal agencies. Ben W. Heinemann and Curtis A. Hessler, two Carter administration officials, note that "small, well-organized, intensely committed special interests have always been able to overcome diffuse, poorly-organized efforts undertaken in the name of the national (or majority) interest." A president can declare an energy crisis or a crisis in federal deficit spending and vow to provide solutions, but "the grandeur of the goal and the drama of the problem can get lost, often forever, in the trenches, where technical details and obscurely worded amendments can distort or destroy [the president's] intentions." Presidents can always be certain that "special interests will be in those trenches with their bayonets fixed."[4]

The president has the reputation of being the nation's great domestic-policy innovator. But the public itself is not unified on what it wants him to do, and the president's control over what ultimately makes it out of Congress is dispersed because of a lack of national purpose in Congress and the Executive Branch. It may be a small consolation to recognize that this situation reflects our nation's political culture: a loosely aggregated number of constituencies, each of which jealously watches out for its own interests and well-being. Federal Judge Abner Mikva, a former congressman from Illinois, has asserted:

> There really isn't a strong sense of national identity and unity in America. There is no sense of nationhood. And whatever else [Congress] does or does not do, it is very good at reflecting the national attitude.[5]

THE MYTH OF THE "CAN-DO" PRESIDENT

The dominant popular myth holds that a president ought to preside over domestic policymaking with reasonable success—meaning he should be able to meet both national needs as well as the particularistic interests of various groups. This perception is tied to the illusion that the president enjoys a kind of parliamentary power. As a result, if he does not deal successfully with Congress or the bureaucracy, he is seen as revealing flaws in his political skills or personality. The modern source for this myth, as with so many other presidential myths, was Franklin D. Roosevelt, who convinced people they should believe in him, and consequently in themselves, as they accepted a vastly expanded role for the presidency and the national government in their lives. Kennedy revived the myth after what was held to be eight lackluster years of domestic leadership by Eisenhower. Kennedy's rhetoric inspired many into believing that there was little the national government could not do if Americans had the will. Kennedy told Walter Heller, chairman of his Council of Economic Advisers, "I want to go beyond the things that have already been accomplished. Give me facts and figures on the things we still have to do. . . ."[6]

Lyndon B. Johnson added force to the myth with his supreme self-confidence that he could eradicate poverty and racism, heal the sick, educate the masses, retrain the unemployable—and at the same time, deploy massive American military power in Southeast Asia. (LBJ frequently suggested he would like to do for the people of Vietnam all that he had accomplished for Americans. *That* would eliminate all the nonsense about a communist revolution!) When a cabinet member once suggested in Johnson's presence that a proposal was impossible, LBJ leaped out of his chair and jabbed a finger at him, shouting, "Don't say that! There is *nothing* this country can't do. Remember that!"[7]

Certainly by the middle of the 1960s, it appeared as if the legislative powers of the presidency had "extended beyond the mere suggestion of policy to the declaration of it," as political scientist Stephen Wayne has written.[8] For the first half of the sixties, there was almost a public euphoria about what presidents could accomplish through federal governmental programs. It seemed as if there were few problems that the government could not solve if it really wanted to because the resources of the nation appeared unlimited and the source of this optimism almost exclusively emanated from the White House, if not in deed, at least in rhetoric.

"INTERMESTIC" POLICYMAKING

Another important component of the optimism of the 1960s stemmed from the imperial presidency myth. If the president were all-powerful in global policymaking—as the Cuban missile crisis and our decision to become involved in Southeast Asia seemed to indicate—then he ought to be at the very least the prince of domestic policy.

Ironically, the linkage between the president's leadership in foreign affairs and his importance in domestic policy was growing ever more obvious during the 1960s as international and domestic problems, issues, and forces became increasingly intermixed. The nations of the world had grown enormously interdependent between the end of World War II and the 1960s. Sometimes even though the origin of a problem was external, it spilled over into the domestic arena, as when the Arab oil-producing nations raised oil prices and slapped an embargo on shipments to the United States in retaliation for American support for Israel in the Six-Day War of 1973. At other times a problem's origin might be internal, but it spilled over into the foreign-policy realm, as when Carter ordered an embargo on American grain sales to the Soviet Union because of its invasion of Afghanistan in 1979. No matter what their origins might be, most major public policies today are "intermestic"—that is, combinations of international and domestic policies.[9] The disruption of supplies of raw materials or manufactured products or parts can hurt the economies and military security of entire nations or regions. So too can cartels formed by groups of nations using resources as political blackmail or fixing prices at artificially high levels. The United States, which has 6 percent of the world's population, for a long time used a third of its resources. Thus our country is particularly vulnerable to such pressures, and American foreign policy is frequently inseparable from policy in such domestic areas as agriculture, commerce, labor, and treasury.

The use of domestic resources as a tool of diplomacy is widespread today. The Arabs have demonstrated how oil could be used as a potent trump card. Many observers credit the oil embargo of 1973 with helping to make American foreign policy in the Middle East more flexible, that is, more sympathetic to the Arabs. However, whenever the president attempts to use a similar strategy, he runs into a wall of opposition from groups whose economic interests may be jeopardized. Carter's embargo on grain sales to the Soviets infuriated our farmers, who believed they were being singled out unfairly to bear the brunt of the administration's get-tough policy with Moscow. Reagan promised to end the embargo if elected, and he did. But he ran into the same opposition when he threatened to reinstitute the embargo to punish the Soviets for the Polish government's crackdown on the trade union Solidarity in 1981. Reagan was forced to reverse course and to announce a few weeks before the 1982 congressional elections that grain sales to the Soviet Union would be expanded rather than halted.

The intertwining of foreign and domestic policies has occurred primarily because of the emergence of a global economy. Trade between nations is now as important a tool of diplomacy as military force, and increased competition for raw products, resources, and markets for finished goods is more common today than disputes over borders or terrain. The most serious conflicts between the more advanced, industrialized nations of the world now turn more on disputes over the exports of automobiles, television sets, electronic equipment, and textiles than on the exportation of ideologies or war matériel.

The president's role in economic policy is also tied to intermestic policymaking. While this subject will be dealt with more extensively in the next chapter, it is important to note here the impact of economics on domestic policies. The United States may have emerged from World War II as the world's greatest military, political, and economic power, but that position was held only because of our monopoly on nuclear power and our self-sufficiency in such raw materials as oil, coal, natural gas, minerals, and food. By the 1950s, nations whose economies had been devastated by war enjoyed a renewal and an expansion of their productive capacity. At the same time many new emerging nations began to exert economic and political demands on the world's resources. The United States—gradually at first, and then rather quickly by the 1960s—began to lose its dominant position. Our rapidly expanding consumer-oriented economy, however, placed more and more demands on our resources. While the United States once was self-sufficient in important raw materials, it grew increasingly dependent on imports from other nations.

At the same time countries like West Germany and Japan, whose industrial plants had been almost totally destroyed during the war, arose from the ashes with new plants, modern technology, and highly skilled work forces. They, along with other advanced industrial nations, began to play a more prominent role in world trade. Soon they became major competitors to the United States in the production of steel, electronics, and automobiles. Countries previously considered underdeveloped—such as South Korea, Singapore, Taiwan, Hong Kong, Brazil, and Mexico—became major manufacturers. Because of low labor costs they could produce goods that were highly competitive with American products. The single most damaging blow to American economic dominance was the Arab oil embargo of 1973 and the resulting growth of power of the Organization of Petroleum Exporting Countries (OPEC) to set world oil prices. Prior to the embargo crude oil had sold at between two and three dollars a barrel, but by 1980 it reached a price as high as forty dollars or more. The United States, which depended on foreign crude oil for more than half of its petroleum needs, suffered an enormous shock to its economic system. The nation's balance-of-payments—the net balance between total income and expenditures of a country in its business and trade relations with the rest of the world—turned highly unfavorable. Not only were Americans paying more for the vast quantities of petroleum imported from abroad but the value of manufactured goods imported into the United States exceeded the value of American goods sold to foreign countries. Multinational corporations (often American-owned) spread American capital, technology, and management techniques worldwide. This development was frequently at the cost of jobs for American workers and of reduced levels of production at home.

These events inevitably led to a decline in American leadership over world trade. There were enormous ramifications for domestic policies in the United States as Americans had to adjust to persistent inflation, increased unemployment, higher interest rates, and a generally lower standard of living for many. The impact on the president's domestic policy leadership also has been immense. The era of dynamic, innovative domestic policymaking in the White House was brief, lasting only during the first two thirds of the 1960s. It paralleled prosperous times when governmental revenues seemd to rise inexorably, permitting the federal government to provide more and better services to increasing numbers of people. The age of scarcity—which began in the early 1970s—saw most of the industrial nations of the world slide into a prolonged recession. Inflation, unemployment, declining productivity, and fierce international competition for global markets ended the golden era. After 1968, in fact, presidents became increasingly committed to putting the brake on expanding federal services or programs, as a cycle of consolidation in domestic policymaking set in. Paradoxically, recent presidents have suffered as much from domestic leadership not because they have done so little, but because they have tried to prevent Congress from doing too much. The White House—once the center of innovative planning of new domestic legislation—has become the graveyard for federal programs. Presidents increasingly find themselves saying no to congressional attempts to continue or expand costly federal activities already on the books.

At the same time, scarcity has forced presidents to take the lead in seeking domestic legislation that requires sacrifices instead of providing federal largesse. Robert S. Weaver, former secretary of housing and urban development, believes that Carter's failure to convince Americans that scarcity was now a part of our national way of life, and his inability to obtain an effective energy program, raise the following serious question: can any president deal effectively and realistically with the unpleasant fact of scarcity? Weaver thinks that only the president can deal with a national crisis. This is because he can best make the electorate understand the nature and seriousness of an issue, particularly if the president is skilled in public relations and the use of the media. But he must also persuade Congress through skilled legislative liaison efforts as well as a judicious application of public opinion. And this grows increasingly more difficult in today's social and political environment.[10]

FROM THE BABY BOOM TO THE GRAYING OF AMERICA

The age of scarcity both paralleled and was a factor in changes occurring between 1960 and the beginning of the 1980s in the American population and its life-style. The post–World War II baby boom resulted in a rapidly expanding population of young people during the 1960s. The federal government was called on to help fund new schools and to expand opportunities for education. In addition, it was expected to provide a variety of new programs that would help an enormous wave of citizens seeking employment and a share in the "good life." Many outside the mainstream of American life sought federal help in overcoming both economic and social barriers. The government responded to these demands with a vast range of programs benefitting Americans from the cradle to the grave. The 1960s would, in fact, represent a unique era of remarkable growth, characterized by widespread prosperity, low inflation, and high levels of employment. Economic activity remained high as the federal government depended on an ever expanding source of revenue to fuel the growth of new programs and to increase existing ones.

By the 1970s, however, a starkly different landscape took shape. The baby boom ended as birth control pills led to dramatic new changes in attitudes toward marriage and sexual behavior. Young adults opted for later and later marriages or for no marriage at all; childbearing declined. Medical advances, meanwhile, added years to the lives of older people. The baby-boom generation, which had earlier overwhelmed the nation's educational system, matured into young adults seeking jobs, housing, and the material wealth they had been brought up to expect as their share in the American dream. The sheer size of this generation resulted in an intensely competitive job market. Opportunities were not improved by a stagnating economy; there seemed to never be enough jobs to match the demands or qualifications of applicants. "Stagflation"—a no-growth economy with inflation—became the normal condition of the nation as the gross national product was reduced or remained stationary while inflation became endemic. More Americans were chasing after more goods despite a decline in their own productivity and a rise in foreign competition.

Nowhere were changes in American society more noticeable by the beginning of the 1980s than in the aging of our population. If the 1960s were a time of youth, the eighties promised to shape up as the decade of the grey-haired and middle-aged. Americans aged sixty-five and over as a percentage of the total U.S. population rose from 4 percent in 1900 to 11 percent in 1980. Even more remarkable, U.S. Census Bureau projections indicated that by the year 2030 those aged sixty-five or over would amount to 20 percent.

According to the 1980 census, roughly 80 million Americans between seventeen and thirty-six years of age were members of the baby-boom generation. They constituted about 35 percent of the nation's population. Almost all had reached voting age by 1980, although less than half actually voted in the 1980 presidential election. Many had begun households and were raising families. Patrick H. Caddell, Carter's pollster for the 1980 election, called them "the largest block of people in history that are sitting outside the political system."[11] They could turn the political system upside down if all of them were to enter it tomorrow and to make demands on politicians.

Past voting behavior research shows that turnout is poorest in the group aged eighteen to twenty-four, but it rises sharply as people reach age thirty-five. The huge baby-boom generation could soon become the dominant voting force in national politics. Along with the aging of the rest of the electorate, the maturing of the United States presents immense challenges to the presidency because older Americans increasingly look to the White House for policies aimed at improving their health care, provisions for their income maintenance, and their rights as full-fledged members of society. As their proportion in the population increases, the political influence of older Americans will grow. The most likely target for their political pressure will be the presidency.

REGIONAL SHIFTS: FROSTBELT VERSUS SUNBELT POLITICS

Not only is America aging but it is also shifting from east to west and from north to south, a trend that complicates even more the domestic policy maze. California, Florida, and Texas accounted for almost half the nation's population increase between 1970 and 1980; the fastest growing states were Nevada, 63.5 percent; Arizona, 53.1 percent; Florida, 43.4; Wyoming, 41.6; and Utah, 37.9.[12] Climate was one factor but only one among many in this shift. States in which the population boom was most pronounced were generally the richest in energy and natural resources, particularly oil and natural gas. In a time of mounting concern over the availability of oil and the reliability of oil-producing nations, industries and corporations began to migrate to states where energy sources were most abundant. Left behind were the states and urban areas of the New England, Midwest, and Middle Atlantic region, where aging heavy industries were dependent on imported fuels. Many of these industries had been severely hurt by foreign competition in such products as steel, automobiles, and textiles.

The population shift has generated problems and hostilities among states and regions the dimensions of which are only beginning to be understood. States like Texas, Louisiana, and Oklahoma, which are rich in petroleum reserves, grew even more prosperous from massive hikes in the cost of oil. Meanwhile, energy-poor states made an effort in Congress to place a cap on state severance taxes, a move not favored by the conservative Reagan administration. The transfer of wealth from states lacking energy resources, such as Massachusetts, Rhode Island, and New York, means that those states suffer not only from higher energy costs but also from the loss of jobs and population to the energy-rich states. At the same time interstate and interregional conflicts of another kind have surfaced in rapidly growing areas of the

Southwest and West, where major battles broke out over scarce water resources needed to support population growth and industrial development. Other conflicts have developed over federal policies on environmental protection versus proposals to develop energy resources and real estate. A major issue in the 1980 presidential election, in fact, revolved around the Carter administration's resistance to unleashing developers in the West to find new energy resources. Reagan vowed to relax stringent environmental regulations and to expand the search for energy even if it meant arousing the opposition of environmentalist groups and the Environmental Protection Agency.

The president has been caught squarely in the middle of regional and interstate political conflicts because he is the only politician who can provide a national perspective. Invariably, Representatives and Senators respond to state, local, or regional pressures on policies deeply affecting their constituents. But conflicts involving the president's policy leadership go beyond environment and energy. They include conflicts over the use of federal moneys for national defense, agriculture, and military bases as well as for transfer payments to veterans, the aged, the unemployed, the poor, and other beneficiaries of federal aid. Military expenditures disproportionally benefit the West and South because of the heavy concentration of defense industries and military bases in those regions. Agricultural policies clearly are vital for the Middle West and Great Plains states, while aid to minorities, unemployed, and the poor have become important to the Frostbelt, particularly the Northeast. The increased population of the Sunbelt also translates into more political strength—in Congress and in the selection process for the president and electoral college. As a result of the 1980 census, southern and western states gained seventeen new representatives in the House while such states as New York, Pennsylvania, Illinois, and Ohio lost a total of eleven. Presidential elections increasingly shape up as contests among regions. The New Politics, which emphasizes candidate rather than party efforts to capture primaries or caucuses, encourages presidential hopefuls to appeal to the distinctive needs of states and regions, often at the cost of having to backtrack during the general election by trying to present a national appeal rather than a regional or local appeal.

The 1976 election divided the nation almost perfectly on an east-west basis; Carter won most of the states east of the Mississippi, while Ford won all the states but Texas west of a line extending southward from the eastern border of North Dakota to the eastern boundary of Texas. In 1980 the only states Carter won, save for Hawaii and Minnesota, were in the east. This division is beginning to reflect perhaps the differences between the "haves" and "have-nots"; the more prosperous states and regions support more conservative, Republican presidential nominees, and the older states and regions with higher rates of unemployment, more older residents, declining populations and industrial bases, and increased tax burdens support liberal or Democratic candidates. Whether this trend will continue in the future remains to be seen, although it appears to be related to long-range economic and population shifts.

MEDIA IMPACT ON DOMESTIC POLICYMAKING

The mass media's growing influence on the presidency and the presidential recruitment process, which came at the expense of the two-party system, has also had a major impact on domestic-policy leadership. Parties traditionally organized into relatively simple, clear-cut political alternatives the widely divergent and incoherent preferences of the mass electorate. Even as late as the 1960s, a president could still count on a party-based coalition of groups to support most of his policy goals because generally *his* goals were congruent with the party's. Democrats usually could count on the support of labor, ethnic minority groups, Jews, Catholics, intellectuals, and the poor. As a result, a Democratic presidential candidate's position on a range of domestic issues would be well known and predictable. The Republican nominee would typically be the candidate of upper-middle class, white, Protestant, conservative voters in small towns and the suburbs. This kind of stable coalition was not only critical to winning elections but it also directly influenced the party's platform and the president's domestic policy agenda.

The emergence of television as the major source of voter information about presidential candidates, however, has converted elections into entertainment and theater. The candidate's personality and his position on specific issues became more important than his political party. As a result, single-issue coalitions became the core of the president's governing coalition. These new presidential "parties of one" were much less stable than the old-fashioned party coalitions, and the base they provided the president for leadership over domestic policy was about as solid as quicksand. For virtually every single presidential initiative or departmental policy today, a president must now develop from scratch a coalition of groups and interests to bring pressure to bear on a fragmented Congress. As was noted in Chapter 3, rarely can he depend on party loyalty in Congress to help pull his domestic agenda through because every member of Congress now has his or her own policy agenda.

The national media—particularly network and cable television news—spotlight the president's role in the domestic-policy conflict even though the process is far more complicated and difficult than the image of one-man leadership implies. At the same time, the importance of individual members of Congress, as well as of key subcommittees in the policy process, is ignored or downplayed. This gives the impression that the rare successes and frequent failures belong exclusively to the White House. Not only did television cut the president loose from party in the electoral connection but it also greatly magnified the office's symbolic importance in the domestic-policy arena, making the president responsible for all things to all people. His popularity and public-opinion ratings invariably begin to suffer when he disappoints or alienates one group after another because his policies or promises are not achieved. Members of Congress and federal bureaucrats clearly share the responsibility for public policy, but they easily duck the controversy that swirls around new domestic issues because they are invisible to the national press. The president is left to take the blame or receive the occasional plaudits because he is at center stage on television. When times were good and the president could play the great benefactor, such miscasting was usually a political plus for the White House. But with the advent of a new kind of politics— the politics of scarcity and limitations—the president becomes the prime target for all kinds of dissatisfactions.

THE POLITICS OF SCARCITY
AND DEPRIVATION

In less than a decade the United States has changed from a nation with unlimited optimism about its economic and military power to a country filled with self-doubts and insecurity about the future. Whether it was the failure of American power and will in Southeast Asia, the Arab oil embargo, or any number of lesser events and unnoticed trends, by the mid-1970s we had become a people trying to adjust to a new and uncomfortable proposition about ourselves: we might have lived through our finest hour and now be facing a future of scarcity and perhaps even of deprivation. In an age of scarcity and program retrenchment, even a Democratic president like Jimmy Carter was hard pressed to offer the kinds of promises or inducements given by presidential candidates or chief executives prior to the 1970s.

Carter offered a "Book of Promises" during his 1976 campaign, vowing to clean up the environment, halt inflation, reform the tax system, balance the federal budget, free the nation from dependence on foreign oil, shape a new energy program, and insure affirmative action and civil rights for all Americans. On the eve of his departure from office, with most of his wish list unfulfilled, Carter suggested that he had never had any idea of just how strong entrenched interests could be in resisting change. Carter assumed the presidency at a point in history when the American and world economies were in decline and conflict over scarce resources was significantly increasing. Achieving consensus on national goals, never a simple task, became impossible.

The disadvantaged are especially affected by domestic policies shaped by scarcity. Not only does the federal government, often a court of last resort for the underprivileged, cut back on programs of essential support but the economy also offers little hope for advancement. The energy crisis only worsens a bad situation. Long-standing inequalities in income distribution are accentuated in the process. According to Weaver:

> [H]igh rates of unemployment and underemployment are the scourge of the large black underclass, especially for its youth. But this problem cannot be separated from nonfunctional elementary and secondary education, the need for job training, and opening the suburbs to the disadvantaged. The decline of mass transportation accentuates the difficulties of gaining access to the expanding job market beyond the central city, rendering the group more vulnerable to the adverse impact of gasoline shortages and higher prices. Maintaining nutrition and health programs is also related.[13]

The problem of what to do about the disadvantaged is also peculiarly the president's—if anyone in the federal government is going to deal with it—because the normal bargaining and negotiating engaged in by organized interest groups with Congress and the bureaucracy is either absent or muted in influence. Organizations like the National Association for the Advancement of Colored People (NAACP) or the Mexican-American Unity Council may speak on behalf of ethnics who remain outside the social and economic mainstream, but they lack the political capital or resources held by more potent groups like those serving labor, the elderly, veterans, and business leaders.

Complicating prospects for new presidential initiatives in domestic policies for the dispossessed are the sharply rising numbers of both legal immigrants and illegal aliens flooding the United States. The Census Bureau allows for a constant net immigration increase in its forecasts for the rest of this century of about 400,000 persons a year. At that rate by the year 2000 there will be more than 8 million new American residents. The privately financed Population Reference Bureau claims, however, that 800,000 legal immigrants were added to the U.S. population in 1980 alone, with an additional 450,000 illegal aliens crossing the nation's relatively open borders.[14]

Nearly half these immigrants came from Latin America, 40 percent from Asia, and the rest from Europe and elsewhere. They are generally younger, and have a higher fertility rate than the present American population. While the newcomers exert an immense pressure on civil authorities at all levels of government, the problems they pose the federal government have just begun. Texas, for example, challenged federal laws requiring the education of illegal aliens by adopting a state statute forbidding state funds for their education in public schools. But the courts overruled this statute and left standing the requirement that Texas must educate aliens as well as resident citizens. Whether these immigrants and illegal aliens constitute a new wave of aggressive, ambitious people capable of eventually contributing to the nation's economic productivity or whether they constitute a permanent mass of disadvantaged unemployables remains to be seen.

If the past is any guide, this rapidly growing immigrant population will look to the White House for solutions to their problems. But presidential options will be much more limited than in the past. Not only has the politics of scarcity made large numbers of Americans exceptionally resistant to expanding coverage of politically entrenched federal programs but there is no longer money available in the federal budget if a president wanted to try to help these people. Fully 83 percent of the fiscal year 1982 budget was earmarked for what has come to be widely known as the *uncontrollables*—expenditures for programs structured into the budget by legislation that commits spending *in advance*, no matter what is happening to the nation's economy or society.

The massive outpouring of social programs and federal assistance during the 1960s and early 1970s led to widespread dependence on federal subsidies, including housing loans, food stamps, and aid to health, education, and welfare. Social security benefits alone rose much faster than the real income of working Americans. Such expenditures now consume about 48¢ of every dollar spent by the federal government. Another 25¢ goes to the Pentagon for national defense, a share that is expected to rise appreciably over the next several years. Another 10¢ is absorbed as interest on the national debt—now near the trillion-dollar level.[15]

Federal taxes as a percentage of personal income and a percentage of our gross national product reached a point in 1980 that equalled the record highs registered during World War II because of income "creep"—the rise of personal and corporate incomes as a result of inflation. The result was that increasing numbers of Americans were pushed into ever higher tax brackets. Sharp increases in the social security payroll taxes add to this growing burden to such an extent that Heineman and Hessler predict political pressures will prevent federal taxes from exceeding for any length of time or by very much the high levels reached in 1980.[16] Such pressures underlay the election of Reagan in 1980 and his subsequent success in pushing through Congress in 1981 the biggest tax cut in history (see Chapter 8, pages 351 to 352). At the same time the stagnation of the American economy held down the long-term real income growth from which increased federal revenues were expected to come to pay for the new programs and expanded benefits that grew even faster with bad times and social distress.

All these factors make it highly unlikely that presidents in the foreseeable future will be able to provide the kind of domestic leadership on which historical reputations are built. There is little reason to believe that the kind of economic environment that encouraged federal intervention in most areas of American life during the 1960s will be experienced again soon. The main challenge to presidents now is to successfully manage the funds and programs already mandated, and to rally disparate elements of American society sufficiently to deal with the problems of scarcity and change. This is no small challenge. Public popularity undoubtedly is easier to obtain when the White House is in the business of giving instead of restricting or withdrawing federal rewards.

President Eisenhower's brother, Milton Eisenhower, who spent many years in government and the study of politics, once remarked, "If a candidate for president will tell the people the unvarnished truth about the four, five, or six problems that threaten us, I do not only think they will believe him, but if he will then go on to propose a tough program to deal with these problems. I think they'd be so goddamn grateful they'd sweep him into office."[17] Whether such a president would be successful in achieving policies to deal with the problems is questionable, however. Every presidential election involves the American people making judgments between candidates based on the promises each makes, the likelihood these promises will be carried out, and the relevance of the candidates' policies to the current needs of the nation. Once a candidate wins the White House, he finds the public will to be amorphous; in fact, it does not exist. Americans as a whole hold him responsible for the national good, but the national electorate disintegrates into countless interest groups and narrowly focused special-issue populations, each of which is attentive to a narrow range of policies and generally oblivious to or disinterested in those of a national nature that lie outside their concerns.

The development of national public policies on the surface would appear to be a relatively straightforward matter. Only a simple majority of both the House and Senate is required to adopt a president's programs. Because the president is elected in part on the basis of his policy promises, he ought to be able to convince a majority of each house of Congress to support him, particularly if his own political party controls a majority of Congress and if the program is needed and meritorious. A majority is not easy to achieve, however, because individual legislators are not accountable either to the president or their political party; thus each legislator is free to accept or reject any part or all of a president's policy agenda. Parts of a president's legislative program may be defeated or amended into an entirely different proposal with the result that his policy accomplishments end up bearing little resemblance to his original program. The more pressing the problem and the more at stake in the form of who is to be rewarded, assisted, or made to pay, the greater will the fragmentation of Congress be, and the more difficult will it be to achieve a majority behind the administration's goals.

Our system, in fact, encourages opposition to the president and national policy goals because it makes legislators more responsible for parts than the whole. The opponents of each element of a president's overall program usually differ from one element to another, according to Lloyd Cutler, who served as chief counsel to President Carter. These opponents are unable to get together on any overall program of their own or to obtain the congressional votes to carry it out. As a result, stalemate continues and the government achieves no program at all. "We cannot fairly hold the president accountable for the success or failure of his overall program, because he lacks the constitutional power to put that program into effect," Cutler argues.[18]

The need for national leadership never disappears, however, and the electorate eventually will hold the president accountable for the success or failure of programs the country needs but which the White House lacks the Constitutional or political power to develop or administer. The countervailing force of the triple alliance, combined with an increasingly fragmented, partyless electorate and an economy of scarcity, almost guarantees that a president will find it more and more difficult to achieve important domestic policies. This is particularly the case for any policies that would change the status quo and perhaps threaten an already established situation. His inability to solve pressing national problems nonetheless will continue to cause voters to seek—perhaps with decreasing optimism—another president when the incumbent's term is up.

Americans expect their government to function as efficiently and speedily as if it were a parliamentary system. The prime minister in a parliamentary government is chosen by the majority party in Parliament, and he or she appoints other key members of the majority as cabinet members. The majority is responsible for the executive, and the executive is responsible *to* the majority. If the majority rejects major parts of the cabinet's program, or if it votes "no confidence" in the government, the cabinet has to resign. A new government will be formed from within the ranks of the existing majority or from a coalition of parties able to constitute a new majority. If this is not possible, a new parliamentary election must be held. When the government is successful in legislating its program, the electorate is able to hold it accountable for the results.

The chief executive in a parliamentary system can, indeed, achieve new domestic policies rapidly and with few alterations, even when they represent a radical departure from present policies. The Labour government in Britain, for example, was able in 1946 to establish a National Health Service in less than a month of parliamentary debate, while it took nearly fifteen years for Congress to enact a form of health insurance originally proposed by President Truman. Prime Minister Margaret Thatcher succeeded in reducing income tax rates at the top of the income scale and in doubling the national value-added tax (VAT), a sales tax levied on almost all goods and services, within a month of her Conservative party victory in 1979. President Reagan too won a similar tax reform within six months, but his inability to fulfill the corollary to his tax cut—significant cuts across the board in all areas of domestic spending—proved that presidential dominance is episodic and restricted to the early months in office.

The extraordinary complexity and diversity of the issues and problems confronting the presidency today has only magnified the inherent weaknesses of the office. As Cutler writes, "The separation of powers between the legislative and executive branches, whatever its merits in 1793, has become a structure that almost guarantees stalemate today."[19] This deliberate fragmentation has been the main factor behind the rise of autonomous centers of authority within the Executive Branch. It also explains the growing influence and power of interest groups in the policy process.

THE RISING IMPACT OF TECHNOPOLS AND INTEREST GROUPS

Because the White House has become insolubly linked to domestic policies, control over the agenda becomes all-important—not only for the political survival of the incumbent but for his claim to posterity as well. Dominating the domestic policy process thus becomes a primary goal for every president hoping to extend his public visibility, his influence, and his image of exceptionalism.

It may be hard to believe today, but prior to 1933 almost all domestic public policy in the United States was developed and administered at the level of state, county, or local government. The role of the federal government in the daily lives of most people was minimal or nonexistent. The half century between Franklin D. Roosevelt and Ronald Reagan, however, changed all that. From the New Deal until the beginning of the 1980s, increasing numbers of Americans were to become as hooked on federal programs as addicts on their favorite drugs.

Most federal programs were designed to eliminate or at least ameliorate the rougher edges of a society and economy in which large
numbers of disadvantaged individuals were deprived of the necessities
of life or of essential rights of citizenship. Many other policies resulted
in a rapidly expanding universe of recipients. Their needs were less
obvious or pressing, but they were increasingly capable of exerting
their own demands for governmental support with success.

The New Deal, for example, had relatively modest goals: minimum wages, improved housing, public works, food assistance for the
needy, social security for the aged, regional economic development,
and the federal regulation of the banking and securities system. But
from the 1950s on, new policy groups anchored in "professional spe-
cialisms" emerged to make new kinds of demands on federal policymakers. Primarily coming from the natural or social sciences, these
new professionals "gave to technically and scientifically trained people
in government service a great and growing influence on the initiation
and formulation of public policy."[20]

The new professionals were highly influential in public policies
relating to defense and space. Similar forces also evolved in such fields
as health care, housing, urban renewal, crime prevention, highways
and transportation, welfare, education, poverty, the environment, and
energy and resource development. Drawing heavily on specialists and
technicians in and around the federal bureaucracy, these new professionals became important policy advocates as well as designers, helping to produce under the aegis of the White House a great range of
programs, including those of the Great Society.

Hugh Heclo described these new policy influentials as *jour-
neymen of issues* or *technopols* (see Chapter 4, pages 165 to 166).
Whatever their appellation, the process these technical policy professionals initiate follows a highly predictable course. Political scientist
Samuel H. Beer asserts that they first identify a problem, then promote
research into policy alternatives and solutions, attract a coalition
united behind the policy's goals, and lobby for its acceptance by the
White House and passage by Congress. Finally they administer the
resulting program, usually through federal-state cooperation.[21]

Political scientist Theodore J. Lowi has called the resulting politics *interest group liberalism*. Its most distinguishing characteristic is
that policymaking has changed from a Congress-centered function to
one centered in the presidency. The federal government has grown by
delegation, Lowi asserts. Although Congress formally continues to
possess the lawmaking authority:

> . . . it delegated that authority increasingly in statute after stat-
> ute to an agency in the Executive Branch or to the president, who
> had the power to subdelegate to an agency. At first this delegation

of power was rationalized as merely "filling in the details" of congressional intent and therefore consistent with even the most orthodox definition of the separation of powers. But ultimately, the delegation was recognized for what it really was—administrative legislation.[22]

Such a description implies considerable authority in the presidency. But this is far from the case, as we have repeatedly seen. What the expansion of policymaking responsibilities meant to the president, in terms of both breadth and performance, was that expectations were placed on his shoulders without a commensurate increase in real institutional power to carry out national policy programs. The president thus became more a broker among powers, even a hapless bystander, in the policy process rather than a genuine initiator. It has been up to each president to do the best he could in these circumstances to initiate, legislate, and administer a balanced national program. Yet all the while he has been swept this way and that way by all the other groups contending for programs beneficial to them.

In his classic study of the process, *The End of Liberalism*, Lowi writes that interest group liberalism has become institutionalized through a two-step model: first, the national government by formal action monopolizes a certain area of private activity, such as defense, space, hospitals, mass communications, or highways. Then policies are authorized and administrative agencies put into operation to work without legal guidelines through an elaborate, sponsored bargaining procedure in which the area monopolized by government edict is returned piece by piece as a privilege to individuals or groups on a case-by-case basis:[23]

Privileges in the form of money or license or underwriting are granted to established interests, largely in order to keep them established, and largely done in the name of maintaining public order and avoiding disequilibrium. The state grows, but the opportunities for sponsorship and privilege grow proportionately. Power goes up, but in the form of personal plunder rather than public choice. It would not be accurate to evaluate this model as "socialism for the rich and capitalism for the poor," because many thousands of low-income persons and groups have profited within the system. The more accurate characterization might be "socialism for the organized, capitalism for the unorganized."[24]

The domestic-policy agenda consequently has grown increasingly more complex and difficult for anyone to control or direct. The scope of the national government's involvement has broadened with responsibility and public accountability shifting to the White House, but in the meantime the capacity to profoundly affect the outcome of policy has remained with Congress and governmental agencies. For this reason powerful, well-organized interest groups invariably have a great influence over the final shape of much of the domestic policy agenda.

THE CHANGING DOMESTIC-POLICY AGENDA

Our nation's domestic agenda in recent years has undergone a "coinciding decline in the opportunities for presidential influence with a basic change in the pool of available ideas," according to Light.[25] Presidents are caught up in more cross-pressures than at any time in recent history, as the domestic policy agenda promises less and less, but at an ever increasing cost. Presidents must contend with a number of "constituentless" issues—huge welfare deficits, rising unemployment and inflation, social security financing reforms, changes in the welfare system, declining productivity, and energy conservation.

Lowi has categorized domestic policies as being distributive, redistributive, or regulatory, depending on their impact on clientele groups. The policy environment has changed in ways detrimental to the president for all three types of policy. The kinds of domestic policies within each category which increasingly are pushing to the forefront of our national agenda involve sacrifices and reduced expectations rather than increased benefits. Such policies are not conducive to any president's building a public consensus for his domestic agenda.

Distributive Policies

Often called *pork barrel*, distributive policies provide governmental benefits such as tax breaks, resources, or federal grants to specific individuals, interest groups, or localized communities. The national impact of such policies usually is not obvious unless the national media highlight the policies because they are such flagrant or colorful examples of pork barrel. Distributive policies invariably involve *logrolling*—the exchange of political favors—since legislators usually do not easily challenge one another's pet projects for fear their own may later be checked. Even a form of political patronage is involved because distributive policies reward localities, groups, or even states for their electoral support.[26]

A vast range of federal activities, including dams, rivers and harbors, public land resources, new federal installations, defense contracts, and agricultural policies, fall under this heading. They are characterized by the ease with which they can be broken down and dispensed unit by unit, each unit more or less separate from any other and from the general policy.

Lowi argues that distributive policies are not policies at all, but highly individualized decisions which can be called a "policy" only by accumulation. They are, in the best sense of the expression, "politics of every man for himself":

> Since there is no real basis for discriminating between those who should and those who should not be protected (or indulged), Congress seeks political support by giving limited protection (indulgence) to all interests strong enough to furnish formidable resistance.[27]

At first it would appear that the president is not as deeply involved in distributive policies as Congress since such policies are more relevant to the particularistic constituencies of the Representative or Senator. But this is not at all the case because the New Politics in presidential nominations and elections makes contemporary presidents very much dependent on the goodwill of the many different constituencies making up their "presidential party of one."

The president must deal with finite budget resources as well as with Congress in setting his policy goals. Invariably there are significantly different political pressures in terms of variety and magnitude which confront policymakers. Members of Congress are clearly more vulnerable to distributive policies because Senators and Representatives have powerful but more narrowly based constituencies pressing for governmental programs. But a president's base of political support includes a number of powerful and diverse constituencies whose electoral support was premised on the expectation that the White House would become a favorable source of policy support. At the same time, there is an unmistakable pressure from the national electorate as a whole for the president to act as a political leader who will seek holistic and collective policies needed by the country.

Nothing better illustrates the tension between the national perspective of the White House and the particularistic bent of Congress than the battles waged by Jimmy Carter against the perennial giant pork barrel of federal dams and water projects. Carter announced a national water policy in 1978 designed to tighten Executive Branch control over spending for these expensive public works projects, which by 1980 would affect 70 percent of the nation's congressional districts and cost at least $4.5 billion.[28] Carter proposed emphasizing water conservation, with more state participation in the planning and funding of water projects. Future authorizations would have to meet tough new conservation and environmental standards as well as to promise national economic benefits. A review panel would be established to provide an independent, uniform analysis of all such projects.

The new water policy got nowhere in Congress, however, and Carter was forced to veto the fiscal 1979 public works appropriation measure because it provided funds for numerous projects that did not meet the environmental or economic criteria of his policy. The White House had its own list of water projects it wanted funded to the point of completion, but Congress appropriated only enough funds for the first year of the projects—the method traditionally followed. Members of Congress were not about to give up their annual discretion over such choice pork-barrel projects. The stalemate over water funding continued throughout Carter's administration. In 1980 the House passed an appropriation measure that totally disregarded Carter's policy, both on environmental grounds and on cost. Carter was spared the need to veto the measure by the Senate, which refused to act on the House measure.

In contrast to Carter, Reagan favored water development, but he asked water users to put up at least 35 percent of the cost of projects compared to the 10 percent that had been part of Carter's original plan. Ironically, western members of Congress who earlier had resisted Carter's proposals appeared ready to accept Reagan's because he offered to accelerate project planning and to begin some new projects favored in their congressional districts.

Reagan proved politically sensitive to the importance of distributive policies when he personally overruled David A. Stockman, his director of the Office of Management and Budget. Stockman tried to trim price supports for tobacco during the administration's meat-ax attack on the federal budget in 1981. North Carolina Senator Jesse A. Helms, one of Reagan's chief political allies, rushed to the defense of his state's tobacco growers, and Reagan promised to continue the supports. The administration also caved in to resistance against cutting the Export-Import Bank, which provides trade subsidies for giant multinational corporations. Republican legislators led by Senator Nancy L. Kassebaum of Kansas argued that U.S. overseas sales and jobs at home would suffer without Ex-Im loans and guarantees. An aircraft corporation that was the major employer in Kansas depended heavily on such assistance. The House, however, raised the appropriation for Ex-In even higher with no resistance from the White House.[29]

Stockman conceded in a candid and controversial interview published by the *Atlantic* magazine toward the end of the Reagan administration's first year that many concessions had to be made to obtain the support of members of Congress for Reagan's massive federal budget cutbacks and reduced taxes. But it was the "weak clients"— black unemployed teenagers, welfare mothers, and the poor—who lost, not powerful groups accustomed to receiving pork-barrel projects or federal handouts. Federal subsidies for business and for well-organized interest groups were better protected against slashes in spending, and the trades, compromises, and giveaways were indistinguishable from any of the earlier interest group accommodations Reagan and his supporters had so self-righteously denounced prior to assuming power. All that had really changed was the socioeconomic status of the groups on the receiving end. Stockman admitted:

> *Power is contingent. . . . The power of these client groups [big business and well-organized interests] turned out to be stronger than I realized. The client groups know how to make themselves heard. The problem is, unorganized groups can't play this game.*[30]

Redistributive Policies

Unorganized groups began to depend on the federal government during the Great Depression for policies to relieve the plight of the aged, unemployed, disadvantaged, as well as of the owners of capital or property. Massive national programs to redistribute wealth and resources evolved, and for the first time in history Washington assumed responsibility for who would benefit and who would pay for sweeping policies affecting welfare, education, old-age assistance, unemployment, job retraining, and regulation of banking and securities activities.

Federal programs stemming from the New Deal and later from the Great Society of the 1960s constitute the best-known examples of what are termed redistributive policies. The national government sought to narrow the gap between rich and poor through a wide range of programs taxing the better-off and spending on behalf of the less fortunate. As the breadth and range of the federal government's activities expanded, redistributive policies eventually began to provide rewards and benefits to more than just the needy or disinherited. Coalitions of interest groups began to emerge to compete for the ever growing, immense payoffs at stake in the federal government's redistribution of resources.

Since such policies involve significant shifts of wealth or resources from one segment of the population to another, they are made at the highest level of the political system. A popular myth holds that it is the president who single-handedly shoulders the responsibility for both developing and successfully pushing such policies through Congress. Periods of great domestic policy movement and accomplishment, such as the New Deal or the Great Society, are widely credited to presidential initiatives. But as we noted in Chapter 3, with the exception of Roosevelt's first hundred days and Johnson's leadership in 1965, Congress played as important or even more critical a role in developing a majority of the programs of the 1930s and 1960s as did either president.

All the same, expectations for national redistributive policy leadership remain with the president. Not only does he symbolize collective responsibility but Congress is also frequently too fragmented to assume responsibility itself. In an era of economic instability and declining resources, the president is charged with an impossible task: he must contend with the usual demands for national policies to benefit large numbers of people who remain shortchanged by existing political, social, and economic arrangements. At the same time he must avoid alienating those who have already "made it" with the help of a variety of existing redistributive federal policies. These countervailing pressures came to a head during the Reagan administration in Reagan's economic policies and the crisis over social security.

Reagan viewed his decisive 1980 election triumph as a mandate to end the long era of what he called "tax and tax, spend and spend." Since the New Deal, the federal government's evolution into a gigantic machine for redistributing wealth had resulted by 1980 in the poorest fifth of the income spectrum relying on the government for more than a half of its income.[31] This led to an endless inflation and stagnant economic growth, Reagan insisted, because it meant the federal government favored consumption over investment. American investment capacity had withered so badly that it was difficult to generate new capital or to improve productivity. The result was the "supply side" of our economy had deteriorated. By cutting federal spending sharply and permitting those at the upper-income levels and corporations to keep more of their earnings, the government could increase investment and spur the economy. Inflation would be reduced and prosperity increased among all classes of American society.

What Reagan was proposing was nothing less than a major reversal of the domestic policies that had guided administrations since Roosevelt. The Reagan administration proposed budget cuts totalling in excess of $40 billion for the fiscal year 1982–83 budget submitted earlier by Carter, and an across-the-board tax cut of 30 percent over three years with indexing of future tax rates to compensate for inflation on taxpayers. Strong public support for Reagan—after all, *someone* was finally trying to do something about the nation's chronic economic woes—prompted Congress into approving budget cuts of $35 billion, and a tax cut totalling 25 percent with indexing after 1986. The tax cut would result in an extraordinary shortfall of some $750 billion to the federal treasury over the next five years.[32] In the following chapter we will examine the economic impact of these two major domestic policies, but for now we are concerned with their impact on the redistribution of domestic resources.

The administration claimed that the impact of the budget and tax cuts was equitably distributed, but critics charged that the rich would get richer and the poor poorer—a claim confirmed in a study published by the *National Journal,* a prestigious Washington political journal. Spending cuts were mostly targeted at programs benefitting the poor (as Stockman had admitted in his interview), while tax cuts overwhelmingly favored those in the upper-income levels. The *National Journal* calculated that if the cuts scheduled to begin in 1983 had been in effect in 1981, the latest year for which income data were available, the average family in the poorest fifth of the nation would have lost $70, while families in the top fifth would have gained $2040:[33]

> *Spending and tax cuts would have left families in the poorest fifth with only 4.2 percent of the national income after federal taxes, down from its actual share of 4.4 percent. The richest fifth would have received 43.4 percent, up from 42.5 percent. Such a shift would contribute to a reversal of a trend toward more even redistribution of the nation's income that began at least three decades ago.*
>
> *Any such shift seems certain to increase the number of persons living below the official poverty line. . . .*[34]

The 1982 elections turned on the issue of Reagan's economic policies, as the Democrats picked up 26 seats in the House while Republicans, in a series of close-call state races, just barely managed to hold onto control of the Senate. The outcome suggested, however, the immense political risks facing any incumbent president attempting to devise national policies involving significant shifts in redistributive programs. Members of Congress strongly supportive of the president's program fared particularly poorly, with fourteen freshmen elected on Reagan's coattails in 1980 losing.[35]

An equally dangerous redistributive policy pitting the White House against Congress was social security, by far the biggest and most inflationary of the cash-transfer programs in the federal budget. The social security system provides some 36 million people, about one in every six Americans, with a monthly check that prevents them from being impoverished as the result of old age, widowhood, or disability. When social security was first enacted in 1935, it was designed as a supplemental benefit, not the major source of retirement income since benefits were too small for total dependence on the program. Sixteen workers contributed social security taxes to support each retired recipient. By the late 1970s, however, the proportion of the elderly had grown so that it required three workers for every retired person.[36] Periodic changes in the Social Security Act provided for cost-of-living increases in benefits, plus an expanding range of other services, including Medicare, which provided hospital care, and Medicaid, which provided assistance for physicians and other medical service fees. These expansions, along with the growing proportion of the elderly, resulted in the system's teetering on the edge of bankruptcy by the late 1970s.

Projections by social security actuaries in 1981 revealed that by the year 2030, only two workers would have to support each retiree, although during the 1990s, when the relatively small depression generation reached old age, the system would enjoy a period of renewed financial strength. During the 1980s, however, as the proportion of retirees to workers increased, the amount of tax each worker had to contribute to keep the system solvent would increase correspondingly.

Congress approved a measure in 1977 designed to raise $227 billion in new taxes during the next ten years, and legislators believed they had guaranteed the solvency of social security for the next fifty years. But even with this tax hike, it quickly became clear that the system faced a short-term funding shortfall ranging from $10 billion to more than $100 billion, and that over the next seventy-five years the deficit could reach more than $1.5 trillion.[37]

The social security problem presented a particular threat to Reagan's economic program since it entailed huge deficits. Reagan proposed to confront the problem head-on with a series of changes, the most important of which would sharply reduce benefits paid to individuals retiring early at age sixty-two or prior to the normal retirement age of sixty-five. He also recommended elimination of minimum benefits for some 3 million Americans, a reduction in the annual cost-of-living increases pegged to the Consumer Price Index, and the elimination of college student survivor benefits which duplicated other forms of federal assistance.

Less than a week after Reagan unveiled his plan to rescue social security, the Republican-controlled Senate voted 96 to 0 against the president. Stung by this unanimous rebuke and by the groundswell of public opposition that followed his proposals, Reagan appeared on television to assure that under *no* circumstances would *he* permit the elderly to be cut off from or cut short of the benefits they so richly deserved. Reagan asked to delay cost-of-living benefits for a few months, however, to save the fund several billions of dollars, but this proposal too met with fierce opposition. Congress did enact minor changes in social security, including elimination of the minimum benefit provision, but even this was restored after strong constituent pressures on Congress.

Trustees of the social security system warned in late 1981 that without corrective legislation soon, the Old Age and Survivors Insurance Trust Fund would be unable to make benefit payments on time, even as early as the latter half of 1982. The administration and Congress agreed to a temporary but wholly inadequate stopgap solution in 1982 with a plan to borrow from the slightly more solvent Medicare and Medicaid funds. But this raised the specter of an eventual collapse of these funds within a few years.

The president's initial effort to restructure social security was put forth without adequate political consideration, White House aides later conceded. Since 64 percent of all those eligible for social security were taking *early* retirement, the proposal to sharply reduce benefits for this immense population clearly would generate an intense public reaction against the president's plan. Congressional Democrats could not resist the chance to accuse Reagan of having deliberately misled voters during the campaign by promising to exempt social security from budget cuts, and they charged the administration with attempting to balance the budget on the backs of the elderly and needy.

Economic reality required that something be done eventually. For if recipients did not accept a reduction in their benefits and expectations, taxes on workers would have to be increased once again. Younger workers as well as their employers grew more and more rebellious because they were being asked to pay for a system that was inflating benefits faster than workers' salaries. The insolvency of the system raised fears for many employees that there might not be anything in social security for *them* when it came time for their retirement. Reagan appointed a bipartisan commission to study changes, but its report was not completed until after the 1982 elections.

Social security remained a massive political football nonetheless. The Democrats tried to pillory the administration for trying to eliminate benefits for orphans, to cut back on early retirement benefits, and to repeal minimum benefits. The Republicans retaliated with an effective but deceptive television ad in which a genial, elderly "postman" delivering social security checks, including the most recent cost-of-living increase, gave *credit* to Reagan for the increase! Democrats howled that the increase had been mandated by Congress and Reagan had nothing to do with it—indeed, had even tried to prevent it. Public-opinion polls prior to the advertisement showed that 49 percent of the elderly believed Reagan had cut benefits while 17 percent thought he had raised them. After the commercial 41 percent believed he had cut them, but 37 percent thought he had raised them.[38]

The social security shortfall, meanwhile, was adding more than $10 billion to the largest federal deficit in history in 1983 because social security suffered far less from Reagan's budget cuts than any other domestic program. By the 1980s older Americans were claiming a bigger and bigger chunk of the federal budget, as reflected by the fact that only 15 percent of the nation's elderly were considered poor in 1982, compared to 35 percent in 1960.[39]

The political risks for the president and members of Congress in trying to stem or reverse the benefits of the social security program are impossible to exaggerate. As the proportion of elderly in the nation continues to grow, bitter intergenerational conflict could result if younger Americans were required to support with ever increasing payroll taxes what would eventually appear to be an evolving mandarin class of privileged elderly citizens. The tendency of Congress up to now has been to side with the elderly and to continually protect or to increase benefits, while in recent years the White House has had to assume the spoiler role because of the program's cost in terms of the broader national and foreign-policy agenda.

Regulatory Policy

In theory, presidents are supposed to be once removed from the regulatory process. In fact, they wield more influence with regulatory agencies than meets the public eye. Independent regulatory commissions are not really independent of presidential direction and control because the White House possesses numerous resources that can be brought to bear on regulatory agencies.

Foremost among these resources is the authority to appoint or remove heads of regulatory commissions, a power that is usually exercised with implicit or explicit policy goals or political values in mind. The president appoints other members of regulatory agencies, but this power is limited by the fact that their terms are fixed, staggered, and for periods of five years or longer. In addition, the chief executive cannot remove any member except for just cause. The president, in fact, must appoint members of the opposition party to maintain partisan balance on the various commissions. Most presidents, however, are able to appoint by the end of their four-year term in office a majority of members somewhat sympathetic to administration goals. A president may also refuse to reappoint incumbent members.

The White House also enjoys significant influence over regulatory agencies through the purse. Independent regulatory commissions are required to submit budget and policy proposals to the Office of Management and Budget, where they must be reconciled with administration priorities. The OMB also monitors all regulatory commission expenditures, providing the president with "a substantial capacity to influence the policy initiatives and performance of . . . agencies that in theory are independent of his control."[40]

Like redistributive policies, regulatory policies involve direct decisions as to who is to be rewarded or indulged and who is to be penalized or deprived. Regulatory policy is not supposed to be selective or particularistic, but selectivity invariably is an important by-product of regulation. The influence of special interests is particularly marked in regulatory decisions because regulatory agencies are highly vulnerable to interest group infiltration. Many members of the commissions, in fact, come from the industries or areas of interest which they must regulate.

Regulatory policymaking has become a major concern of recent presidents because so much of the domestic policy agenda is dependent on rules and regulations imposed on programs after congressional action. The decade of the 1970s in particular experienced a virtual explosion of regulatory policymaking as Congress confronted constant inflation, economic uncertainty, and social programs. Whereas in the past Congress legislated all kinds of expensive and expansive programs to meet problems, the recent response has been to throw regulations at problems rather than money.[41]

Political scientist Stephen Kelman distinguishes between two major types of governmental regulatory activity: vertical and horizontal. Most regulatory policy prior to the 1970s dealt with regulation of the marketplace and of industry. So-called vertical agencies, such as the Interstate Commerce Commission (ICC), Civil Aeronautics Board (CAB), Federal Communications Commission (FCC), and Securities and Exchange Commission (SEC), regulated rates, made rules, and set schedules for transportation, banking, stock market operations, and public airwaves. Many of these vertical agencies were either born or given new life during FDR's administration, but by World War II close ties between the president and regulatory commissions had loosened. It was replaced mainly by White House staff interaction only when policy matters seriously threatened the president.[42]

Newer regulatory agencies created during the past decade have been horizontal or "social" in that they were aimed at regulating nonmarket behavior by business firms whose actions might injure third parties. The Environmental Protection Agency (EPA), Occupational Safety and Health Administration (OSHA), National Transportation Safety Board, Consumer Product Safety Commission, and Equal Employment Opportunity Commission are examples of this type. Such agencies searching for evidence of discrimination or abuses of federal regulations could intrude into any school, hospital, factory, university, or countless other domains dependent on federal assistance or government contracts.

Regulatory policymaking began a century ago with the ICC as the federal government sought to ameliorate the harsh or cruel practices of emerging new industries and corporate giants. By the 1970s, however, regulation had become so extensive and widespread that few activities in American life were exempt from the watchful eye of a regulatory Big Brother. A cascade of new regulations threatened to drown businesses, private institutions, and even individual citizens under a tidal wave of bureaucratic forms, rules, and paperwork. The Code of Federal Regulations in 1970 totaled 54,482 pages, but by 1980 it had swollen to nearly

100,000 pages. Political observer Theodore H. White notes that all these regulations had the force of law, but only skilled lawyers and full-time lobbying firms heavily staffed by those who had helped with the regulations could understand them.[43]

Regulatory agencies involved in making rules on prices and competition or in rectifying social and human inequities inevitably cause problems for the economy as well as for politicians. Immense areas of domestic policymaking are removed effectively from the hands of elected officials and handed over to bureaucrats. Costly burdens are added to the production and distribution process, and inefficiency may be forced on management and labor. Monopolies and federally sanctioned fixing of prices often are by-products as well.

The Ninety-sixth Congress attempted to overhaul the entire regulatory system in 1979–80, but failed because of White House opposition to a provision for a legislative veto which would have enabled Congress to unilaterally eliminate proposed regulations. (The Carter administration saw this as posing a potential risk of even more fully politicizing the regulatory function and making it more vulnerable to interest group pressures.) President Carter nonetheless succeeded in deregulating airlines, railroads, and trucking industries—all leading priorities of his domestic agenda. Congress passed the Airline Deregulation Act in 1978, which relaxed controls of the CAB over passenger fares and airline routes. Carter's appointees to the ICC moved to deregulate the trucking industry, and Congress eventually mandated an end to regulations that had controlled routes truckers could drive and goods they could carry. Also ended were regulations that allowed truckers to fix prices through industry-dominated rate bureaus, stifling competition, wasting fuel, reducing service to small towns, and inflating prices. Congress completed Carter's deregulation agenda with legislation reducing the ICC's regulatory power over railroads. Railroads were given greater freedom to set their own competitive rates, but railroads lost their immunity from prosecution for rate-fixing violations of antitrust laws.

Both the airline and trucking industries fiercely opposed major elements of deregulation because of fears it would result in cutthroat competition, lower fares, and reduced profits. Regulations issued by social regulatory agencies generated another kind of opposition from business executives and industrial leaders, who argued that the regulations pushed up the cost of everything from automobiles and food to manufactured products. For example, regulations aimed at increasing the safety of the work place, reducing toxic chemicals in the environment and in factories, ending racial and sexual discrimination, and providing consumers with greater product information all came under fire.

As the national economy gradually confronted the problems of inflation, declining productivity, and increased competition, pressures on the president to reduce regulatory activity grew. Reagan's 1980 campaign call to disarm the regulatory monster fell on the receptive ears not only of corporate America but of the populace as well. Reagan succeeded, for example, in initiating important changes in OSHA rules governing inspections, citations, and penalties for industries. From the beginning OSHA had been one of the most severely criticized of the horizontal regulatory agencies because its rules were hard to understand, excessively rigid and detailed, and frequently antagonistic to business. The Occupational Safety and Health Act that created OSHA in 1970 attempted to guarantee every worker a safe and healthy work place, but Reagan's new appointee as director of OSHA announced in 1981 that work-place inspections would be conducted in the future only at companies with excessively high accident rates in the more hazardous industries.[44]

Reagan attempted to extend deregulation to broadcasting, automobile safety, environmental protection, and consumer rights among others. His strategy was to work within the regulatory bureaucracy to effect change rather than to seek legislation from Congress. A report showed that after increasing by nearly 240 percent during the 1970s, spending by the fifty-seven major federal regulatory agencies experienced only a 1 percent growth in 1981; in constant dollars, agency expenditures would decline by approximately one sixth by 1983.[45]

Whether Reagan's war on regulations would succeed or not remains to be seen. The administration claimed that the number of pages in the Federal Register decreased by one third during the first ten months of Reagan's presidency, and the number of new rules declined by 25 percent. But numerous groups of consumers, environmentalists, and others pressured Congress to prevent Reagan appointees from dismantling key elements of the regulatory structure, and opposition to further deregulation began to solidify.[46]

CONCLUSION

Regardless of the kind of domestic policy confronting a president, changes in the policy environment have significantly changed the domestic agenda, as well as the president's ability to manage it. Congress has become more fragmented, while competition among its members for policies favorable to their individual constituencies has increased. The decline of party influence and party leadership in Congress makes the policy process more complex and less certain than ever before. The weakness of parties is matched by a growing number and strength in interest groups. The increasing use of technopols or policy specialists further weakens the White House as well as Congress. As issues become more and more complex, and their provisions restrictive or less beneficial, it becomes increasingly difficult to build a national consensus behind the president. In the meantime the national media conceptualize major domestic-policy issues in terms of the president and the White House, raising his symbolic importance to a level in no way commensurate with his ability to deliver. Finally, each president complicates the problem by trying to master domestic policy through reorganizing his own domestic establishment, usually with the result that his administration is overorganized.

There is virtually no way out of the domestic policy maze for a president today. He may be the only nationally elected politician capable of providing the leadership necessary for collective policies and programs, but the political cost of such efforts has been more than any recent president could afford. The U.S. domestic-policy agenda has grown more complex, and the competition for a declining or more restrictive resource base has become fierce. Numerous competitors for shaping and implementing policy in Congress—the federal bureaucracy, the private sector, and even officials within the president's own inner circle—have made the policy process more fragmented and porous than ever before. Dramatic changes in the economic, social, and political environment have led to narcissistic politics—everyone-for-himself-or-herself policy goals. At the same time public expectations of presidential leadership have increased, largely because there is, in fact, no one else to whom the nation can look, and because of the mass media's overemphasis on his personal role in the policy process.

Whether the presidency becomes a chronic victim of a no-win domestic-policy agenda or whether this is only a temporary crisis depends, of course, on how deeply rooted are the changes in American life described in this chapter. If our economic, political, and social crises are only valleys in a historical cycle that is destined to turn upward at some future date, the White House may be able to once again regain some semblance of control and influence over the domestic agenda. Americans need, however, to divest themselves of the myth that presidents once enjoyed regular and systematic domination over policymaking, for such has rarely been the case.

The prognosis for more congenial working conditions for presidents is not good, however. So long as we elect our chief executives on the basis of personal coalitions rather than parties, we can expect presidents to fulfill the policy goals of countless diverse groups whose primary if not only commitment is anchored to narrow, selfish issues or ideologies. This creates immense pressures on the White House, for each candidate must promise a great many things to a great many groups in order to win the nation's highest office. Given the environ-

From *Herblock On All Fronts* (New American Library, 1980)

ment of the 1980s, each president inevitably finds he cannot deliver on many if not most of these promises—even if he really wants to. (This is true even for emotional issues that do not bear immense financial costs. Candidate Reagan promised Constitutional amendments banning abortions and permitting prayers in public schools, but both issues—deeply supported by the Moral Majority which helped elect Reagan—foundered in Congress.)

The future looks even bleaker when we contemplate domestic problems just now surfacing that will challenge the federal government. Among the more pressing are questions relating to the rebuilding of the nation's industrial capacity, repairing our vast infrastructure of public works and facilities, retraining and reemploying millions of workers made obsolete by changes in the economy, striking a balance between development and preservation of our national resources, tax reform, and improving public education. While the Reagan administration pushed for a retrenchment in federal spending and programs, these problems along with already existing domestic needs have created immense pressures on Congress for remedial legislation. (Rebuilding our infrastructure of roads, water and sewage systems, dams, urban transportation systems, and bridges, for example, will cost upwards of $2.5 to 3 trillion during the 1980s, the single most expensive government challenge for the rest of this century.[47])

If anything, the domestic policy environment is likely to become even more complex and resistant to centralized planning or control in coming years. Presidents nonetheless will be asked to lead the charge, and will be held accountable when forces are scattered and confusion reigns. For it is difficult to shake the notion that presidents are, after all, in command.

NOTES

1. Stephen J. Wayne, *The Legislative Presidency* (New York: Harper & Row Publishers, 1978).

2. Paul C. Light, *The President's Agenda* (Baltimore: Johns Hopkins University Press, 1982), 11–12.

3. Everett Carll Ladd, Jr., *Where Have All The Voters Gone?* (New York: W. W. Norton & Company, 1978), 36.

4. Ben W. Heineman, Jr., and Curtis Hessler, *Memorandum for the President: A Strategic Approach to Domestic Affairs in the 1980s* (New York: Random House, 1980), 105.

5. *Congressional Record*, 97th Cong., 1st sess., Senate, October 31, 1979, SI5596.

6. James L. Sundquist, *Politics and Policy: The Eisenhower, Kennedy, and Johnson Years* (Washington, D.C.: Brookings Institution, 1968), 112.

7. Merle Miller, *Lyndon: An Oral Biography* (New York: G. P. Putnam's Sons, 1980), 408.

8. Wayne, 20.

9. See John Spanier and Eric Uslaner, *How American Foreign Policy is Made*, 2d ed. (New York: Praeger Publishers, 1978).

10. Robert S. Weaver, "The Politics of Scarcity," in Richard Pious, ed., *The Power to Govern, Proceedings of the Academy of Political Science* (New York: Academy of Political Science, 1981), 245–46.

11. Dick Kirschten, "America on the Move," *National Journal*, November 14, 1981, 2016.

12. Ibid., 2020.

13. Weaver, 247.

14. Kirschten, 2017.

15. William Greider, "The Education of David Stockman," *Atlantic*, December 1981, 33.

16. Heineman and Hessler, 78.

17. *Congressional Record*, Senate, 1979, S15601.

18. Lloyd N. Cutler, "To Form a Government," *Foreign Affairs*, September 1980, 128.

19. Ibid.

20. Samuel H. Beer, "In Search of a New Public Philosophy," in Anthony King, ed., *The New American Political System* (Washington, D.C.: American Enterprise Institute for Public Policy Research, 1979), 18.

21. Ibid., 19.

22. Theodore J. Lowi, *The End of Liberalism*, 2d ed. (New York: W. W. Norton & Company, 1979), 274.

23. Ibid., 278.

24. Ibid., 278-79.

25. Light, 215-19.

26. Theodore J. Lowi, "The Functions of Government," in Randall Ripley, ed., *Public Policies and Their Politics* (New York: W. W. Norton & Company, 1966), 27-40.

27. Ibid., 29-30.

28. *Congressional Quarterly Almanac, 1978*, 759-66; and *Congressional Quarterly Almanac, 1980*, 596.

29. Greider, 40.

30. Ibid., 52.

31. Joel Haveman, "Sharing the Wealth," *National Journal*, October 23, 1982, 1788.

32. Greider, 47.

33. Haveman, 1791.

34. Ibid., 1789.

35. *Time*, November 15, 1982, 12.

36. Barry Crickman, "Social Security: Is a Patchup Enough?," *Nation's Business*, October 1981, 28-29.

37. *Congressional Quarterly*, November 28, 1981, 2333-34.

38. *San Antonio Express*, August 16, 1982, 17.

39. *U.S. News & World Report*, October 18, 1982, 55.

40. Terry M. Moe, "Regulatory Performance and Presidential Administration," *American Journal of Political Science* 26, no. 2 (May 1982): 197-224.

41. Theodore H. White, "Summing Up," *New York Times Magazine*, April 25, 1982, 44.

42. Steven Kelman, "Regulation That Works," *New Republic*, November 25, 1978, 13.

43. White, 44.

44. *Today, The Journal of Political News and Analysis*, October 30, 1981, 7.

45. John Helmer and Louis Maisel, "Analytical Problems in the Study of Presidential Advice: The Domestic Council in Flux," unpublished paper presented at the 1977 annual meeting, American Political Science Association, Washington, D.C., p. 2.

46. *National Journal*, September 26, 1981, 1735.

47. *U.S. News & World Report*, September 27, 1982, 57-61.

Chapter 8

Economic Master Mechanic

Optimism . . . is a mania for maintaining that all is well when things are going badly.

  Voltaire, *Candide*

An economist is a fellow who spends his life rearranging the deck chairs on the Titanic.

  Anonymous

The image of an all-powerful imperial president in foreign and domestic affairs coincided with the illusion that the president was capable of managing the American economy. Responsibility for sustaining high levels of employment and productivity and for controlling inflation shifted from the free marketplace to the White House during the administration of Franklin D. Roosevelt. After World War II presidents turned to economists in the belief that together—politicians and practitioners of the "dismal science"—they could fine-tune the world's most advanced and prosperous economy.

  For nearly a quarter century economic leadership was, if not a positive asset, at least not a political liability to presidential popularity and credibility. The U.S. economy between 1945 and 1970 generated the world's highest standard of living, and generations of Americans expected that their lives would be more prosperous and comfortable than their parents'. The American dream had always held out the promise of a better life, and by the 1950s and 1960s this dream seemed within reach of almost everyone. That all Americans were entitled to a home, at least one car, a television set, and countless other material goods seemed almost to be a natural law. In the past the prevailing belief was that it was up to the individual to achieve the good life through hard work—the Horatio Alger myth. But gradually during the postwar era Americans began to look to the federal government to help realize the dream.

America's burgeoning economy enabled the federal government not only to satisfy many of these aspirations, but also to create new demands. Returning veterans were provided federal help in going to college; minority groups were aided in their quest for equality of opportunity in the work place; the young were assisted in preparing for careers; and virtually everyone came to have a direct stake in policies made in Washington, D.C.

Economist Lester C. Thurow has argued that "when there are economic gains to be allocated, our political process can allocate them. When there are large economic losses to be allocated, our political process is paralyzed. And with political paralysis comes economic paralysis."[1] The U.S. economy found it more and more difficult to allocate gains in the early 1970s because our giant economy began to lose its productive edge in the emerging new global economy. The notion that life here could only get better, that there was an inevitability to our economic growth, began to diminish. The government—which had played a key role in encouraging optimism and expanding expectations—found itself in the untenable position of having to redistribute losses.

When the marketplace was the sole mechanism for economic readjustment, and economic losses had to be imposed, they fell on numerous powerless groups rather than on the population as a whole. The federal government, however, has created countless new groups in the population with direct interests in the government's economic policies. Few Americans are *not* organized, affiliated with, or in some way represented by groups with the resources and power to make themselves heard in Congress and the Executive Branch. The costs to any politician who must impose economic belt-tightening policies have become formidable. Members of Congress and federal bureaucrats are able to avoid political risks. As long as they watch out for their constituents or clients, members of Congress and bureaucrats can avoid direct, personal responsibility for economic problems even though their narrow concerns may contribute to these problems.

The president, on the other hand, cannot avoid the fallout from bad economic times because he bears responsibility for the nation's economy. Only he is in a position to take actions required in an increasingly uncertain and volatile economic environment. No one else has the status or visibility to educate the electorate, labor, business, and interest groups about economic conditions and what is needed to improve them. Nonetheless, whatever policies he urges in taxing and spending, he must make decisions that will result in some incomes declining and others going up. For every friend he makes, he

GOOSEMYER by Don Wilder and Brant Parker © 1983 Field Enterprises, Inc. Courtesy of Field Newspaper Syndicate.

creates a disappointed foe determined to defeat him in the next election.[2]

No president in truth enjoys economic power equal to the praise or blame heaped on him. The idea of "fine-tuning" the economy suggests that a highly skilled mechanic following the directions of economic engineers can somehow control or channel the activities and motivations of millions of consumers and investors, as well as business and corporation executives. A president's ability to manage or direct the immense, complex, fragmented, and free-wheeling American economy is about as likely as the ability of a captain on a foundering ship to hold back the waves.

Of all the illusions surrounding the presidency, the most frustrating for Americans is that their chief executive ought to be able to rekindle the economic prosperity and stability the nation enjoyed when it was unchallenged in the world's economy. Presidents encourage this illusion by overestimating the prospects for economic growth and underestimating the negative effects of stagflation—declining productivity, rising unemployment, and inflation. For years, every candidate for the presidency and every incumbent has encouraged false optimism about what could be accomplished with the economy.

THE ECONOMY AND PRESIDENTIAL POPULARITY

Since Herbert Hoover's name became associated with the Great Depression, no president has been able to avoid the fallout from leading economic indicators. Political scientists Richard A. Brody and Benjamin I. Page have suggested that the economy has provided strong incentives for every president since Hoover to keep the nation prosperous.[3]

Numerous studies document the impact of economic conditions on presidential popularity. One study found that long-term declines in presidential popularity between 1964 and 1980 paralleled downturns in the American economy. Inflation and unemployment constitute the primary concerns of voters about the economy, and the public critically watches a president's economic performance, punishing him if he is found wanting.[4] A study of administrations from Eisenhower to Nixon confirmed this conclusion, while another study discovered a positive relationship between low monthly unemployment rates and presidential popularity.[5] Research further suggests that changes in both the rate of unemployment and consumer prices may affect the public's perception and evaluation of economic conditions, and this assessment in turn affects presidential popularity.[6]

Other scholars have suggested that presidents resort to expediency at the expense of long-range economic policy to influence election outcomes. Political scientist Edward Tufte argues that an administration will manipulate short-run economic conditions with expansionary fiscal policies even when it means more inflation or increased rates of unemployment after the election.[7]

The double standard that charges the president with responsibility for domestic and foreign policy outcomes while excusing Congress exists also in economics. Members of Congress are not held accountable individually by the electorate for poor economic conditions, although Congress clearly shares a major responsibility for the economy. Congress as a body may be held responsible but rarely are individual members singled out by voters for punishment so long as they are perceived as watching out for their constituents' interests. Voters' perceptions of their economic well-being are tied to voting decisions in presidential elections, but less so in midterm congressional elections.[8]

When voters go to the polls, they have short memories, according to economist Alan S. Binder. The electorate cares most about the growth rate of real disposable income during the year before an election:

> [This] gives election-minded politicians the following temptation: By stimulating aggregate demand 18 months to a year before

an election, they are likely to face reelection during an exuberant economic boom . . . before the inflationary price tag shows up.[9]

Presidential attempts to bolster popularity by stimulating the economy may be a form of responsiveness to the electorate, but it is bad for the economy in the long run. Political expediency contributes to weaknesses in the economy because it results in policies benefitting or protecting special interests rather than long-range programs for resolving the economy's underlying shortcomings. Presidents and members of Congress invariably think in short-term, political time frames. As long as politicians believe voters reward incumbents for prosperity and punish them for recessions, they will attempt to spur growth before an election and short-term improvement will occur. But inevitably this will be followed by even more persistent inflation and stagnant growth afterward.

The deeper underlying problems with our economy are rarely addressed by electoral-economic cycles because politicians either do not understand the implications or consequences of their quick fixes, or they are unwilling or unable to address the real problems. Politicians are not especially capricious; they gradually learn that their capacity to manage the economy is unequal to the forces seeking short-term advantages. When the U.S. economy was able to expand without substantial inflation, presidents and members of Congress benefitted from the growing prosperity, and there were few reasons to limit government spending. Periodic stimulations of the economy could be absorbed without damage. Once the economy became mired in inflation along with stagnant growth, the politician's solution began to resemble the alcoholic's answer to personal problems: more drinks might ease the momentary distress, but with the dawn would come a massive hangover and the problems would still be there.

The linkage between economic policy and electoral outcomes is obvious to everyone, but the solution to our distress is less evident. The same forces contributing to the fragmentation of political institutions have weakened political parties and encouraged individualized candidacies for public office. But they have made collective economic policies difficult if not impossible to achieve. Economic leadership consequently has become even more a no-win proposition for presidents than domestic or foreign policy. To understand why, we must consider the extraordinary changes that have overtaken the economies not only of the United States but of nations worldwide. Then an examination of the expertise and tools available to the president for fine-tuning the economy will reveal why presidents rarely succeed as master mechanics. Finally, an analysis of the economic performance of recent presidents will show how shortsighted political goals seem to consistently triumph over long-range economic needs.

TABLE 8-1   **Per Capita Disposable Income, Unemployment, and Rate of Inflation**

YEAR	INCOME ($1972)	RATE OF UNEMPLOYMENT	RATE OF INFLATION
1952	2,434	3.0	1.5
1953	2,491	2.9	1.6
1954	2,476	5.5	1.2
1955	2,577	4.4	2.2
1956	2,645	4.1	3.2
1957	2,660	4.3	3.4
1958	2,645	6.8	1.7
1959	2,697	5.5	2.4
1960	2,709	5.5	1.6
1961	2,742	6.7	0.9
1962	2,813	5.5	1.8
1963	2,865	5.7	1.5
1964	3,026	5.2	1.5
1965	3,171	4.5	2.2
1966	3,290	3.8	3.2
1967	3,389	3.8	3.0
1968	3,493	3.6	4.4
1969	3,564	3.5	5.1
1970	3,663	4.9	5.4
1971	3,752	5.9	5.0
1972	3,860	5.6	4.2
1973	4,083	4.9	5.7
1974	4,013	5.6	8.7
1975	4,055	8.5	9.9
1976	4,161	7.7	5.2
1977	4,266	7.1	5.8
1978	4,409	6.1	7.3
1979	4,493	5.8	8.5
1980	4,473	7.1	9.0
1981	4,525	7.6	9.1

SOURCE: Walter Dean Burnham, *Democracy in the Making: American Government and Politics,* ©
1983, p. 486. Adapted by permission of Prentice-Hall, Inc., Englewood Cliffs, N.J.

AMERICAN ECONOMIC DOMINANCE

The American economy was a marvel to behold during the 1950s and
1960s. Table 8-1 shows that between 1952 and 1964, inflation averaged only 1.9 percent a year, per capita income rose steadily, and
unemployment exceeded 6 percent only twice. Between 1965 and 1969
the economy continued on a strong course with unemployment remaining low although inflation began to rise.

Then came the rude awakening of the 1970s. The cost of living
increased 5.4 percent in 1970, and by 1980 reached an annual rate of 9.1
percent. Unemployment also edged inexorably upward: 5.9 percent in

1971, 7.7 percent in 1976, and a post-depression high of nearly 11 percent in late 1982. The American economy, which once generated the highest per capita gross national product (GNP) in the industrialized world, began to grow more slowly than at least a half dozen other major industrial nations. Between the first quarters of 1981 and 1982, the American GNP declined in constant dollars by 1.6 percent.[10]

Economists were generally in agreement about the causes behind the persistent stagflation of the 1970s. The Great Society programs of the 1960s had ignited a sharp increase in public spending in the latter half of the 1960s that carried over into the 1970s, pushing domestic consumption to near capacity levels. President Johnson's decision not to raise taxes to pay for the Vietnam War between 1965 and 1967 created a classic case of excess-demand inflation.[11] Military spending for all kinds of goods competed with heavy domestic consumption, causing prices to rise as demand outpaced production.

The federal budget deficit assumed a built-in momentum in the 1970s. The deficit, which had averaged about $3.5 billion a year from 1965 to 1966, increased much faster after 1970. Figure 8–1 shows that the total aggregate debt jumped from $400 billion in 1971 to $1.079 trillion by 1982. The deficit for fiscal year 1982 alone was in excess of $200 billion.[12]

This explosion in the federal debt constituted the single greatest political risk to presidents because it had a ripple effect throughout the economy. Heavy government borrowing put pressure on interest rates, which in turn prevented the economy from sustaining a robust or long-term recovery. Interest rates vary but the most important—the prime rate charged by banks to their corporate borrowers—hovered around 5 to 6 percent throughout the late 1960s. Increasing federal deficits and an overheated economy forced the prime rate to rise during the Johnson administration. By the 1970s the prime zigzagged to ever higher levels, reaching a record high of 21.5 percent in late 1981. By late 1982 it had declined to a more moderate but still high 11.5 percent in the midst of the worst recession since the 1930s.[13]

High interest rates were generally conceded to be the key factor causing the United States to suffer through one recession after another, each deeper than the previous one. When money became too expensive to borrow, homebuilders, automobile manufacturers, major appliance and furniture businesses, and almost all other parts of the economy suffered from a lack of customers able to borrow for major purchases. Investment slowed down, stifling business because credit was not only too expensive but risky as well. State and local governments were hard-pressed to provide services. From 1970 on, restraining the growth of the federal debt and rising interest rates became the chief domestic challenge to presidents, and none seemed equal to that challenge.

FIGURE 8-1   The National Debt, 1973–1983 (in billions)

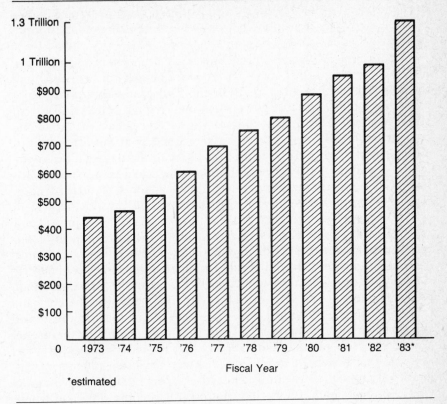

*estimated

SOURCE: Data from the Office of Management and Budget; Council of Economic Advisers; and the Congressional Budget Office.

THE ECONOMY OVER A BARREL

An out-of-control federal budget was one burden sapping the vitality of the American economy; the energy crisis that burst on the industrialized world in 1973 was another. Americans depend on gasoline and fossil fuels the way most living things depend on water. Indeed, for years it seemed that energy was almost as inexpensive as water in the United States. Suddenly in October 1973 Americans found themselves in long lines at service stations in gas-guzzling automobiles, waiting to buy gasoline which overnight had become scarce and expensive because of an Arab oil embargo against the United States. The Organization of Petroleum Exporting Countries (OPEC)—which had been formed years earlier but which had not significantly influenced the price or production of oil—woke up to the reality that it had immense political and economic power in the resource it sold on the free market. The cost of imported oil rose dramatically from $2.49 to $11.65 a barrel, and industrial economies worldwide were shaken to their foundations.

Prior to the 1970s, the United States had been a major oil exporter. But by 1973 it depended on imported oil for almost half its needs, and much of this petroleum came from the Arab states. A second major crisis erupted in 1979 after the Iranian revolution resulted in a virtual cutoff of exports from that nation—the second largest oil-producing country in OPEC. Once again Americans lined up at gasoline stations, and once again the shortfall in oil exports led to sharp price hikes in the cost of gasoline. A new wave of inflation wracked the industrial nations and economic activity slowed down in most of them. Underdeveloped nations dependent on oil for economic development were unable to generate the money to buy the energy they required, and most teetered on the edge of financial ruin. Americans looked to the president for solutions to the energy crisis, but there were no simple answers. President Carter in particular suffered from the nation's frustration with the energy problem, largely because of the impression that he had not acted to prevent the fall of America's ally, the shah of Iran.

Paradoxically, when oil prices began to fall in 1982 as a result of the worldwide recession with its corresponding decline in the use of petroleum, economists began to worry that too sharp a break in price might trigger a global depression. This was because a number of oil-producing countries had plunged heavily into debt to finance economic development in the expectation that oil prices could only go higher. Banks in the United States and Europe had lent hundreds of billions of dollars to nations like Mexico and Nigeria in the expectation that the sizeable oil reserves of these nations made them a safe bet for loans carrying extraordinarily high rates of interest. By 1983 the inability of these countries to even service their debt, much less to retire the principal, posed the risk of major banks collapsing with disastrous consequences for the world banking system and financial structure.[14]

MORE CONSUMPTION, LESS PRODUCTION

Carter blamed OPEC and the massive oil-price hikes for most of the nation's economic woes, especially for the chronic deterioration in the U.S. balance of trade with other countries. A country's exports of goods rarely balances with its imports, but the balance of payments deficit or surplus reveals a great deal about its economic vitality.[15] It signals whether a nation is a debtor or a creditor, and the nature of its economic productivity. It is also related to the value of its currency. Between 1890 and 1971 the United States exported more than it imported. Beginning in April 1971 the Department of Commerce posted the first of an unending series of deficits for the nation's trade balance.

Throughout the 1970s and into the 1980s, the nation's balance of payments ended up in the red, sometimes with extraordinarily high deficits. The deficit was expected to reach an all-time record high of $100 billion by the end of 1983.[16] Imported oil was one factor in these deficits, but by 1978 the United States had begun to reduce its dependence on imported oil to only 25 percent of our needs. (Japan and Germany, meanwhile, were importing 95 percent and 60 percent respectively, while recording sizeable trade surpluses.) The United States was importing two and a half times more manufactured goods than oil, suggesting that the real problem was that as a nation, we were "no longer efficient at converting materials and energy into manufactured goods."[17] Americans were proving to be far better consumers than producers.

The United States lost its edge to Japan and Germany in the manufacture of automobiles, electronics, steel, and a host of other products. It also lost markets to underdeveloped countries like South Korea, Singapore, Taiwan, and Brazil whose lower wages enabled them to undercut American businesses in a number of products, especially textiles and shoes. American industries and trade unions began to demand governmental restrictions on imports as a way of saving American jobs and preventing further deterioration in the economy. But such steps risked triggering a global round of protectionism similar to the one that occurred in the late 1920s and early 1930s and led to the worldwide depression. President Reagan confronted protectionist demands for steel, automobiles, and even motorcycles.

The problem of declining American exports ironically was brought on in part by American corporations themselves. U.S. business executives in effect helped to deindustrialize their own nation by moving production operations overseas to take advantage of cheaper labor. American management thus failed to sustain the nation's economy because business leaders preferred quick profits abroad instead of rebuilding American industries or retraining American workers.[18] Furthermore, in spite of widespread complaints about foreign competition, American consumers continued to buy imported products. In 1981, they purchased $253 billion in imports, ranging from caviar to Chinese beer, from toasters to television sets, and from pickup trucks to motor scooters, without much concern for the impact on American industries or workers.

Nowhere was evidence of America's economic decline more evident than in the slowdown of the nation's productivity, one of the major reasons behind our growing dependence on foreign imports.

Throughout most of the twentieth century, the United States had steadily increased its productivity—the relationship between the labor, material, and capital required to produce goods and services. Productivity increased an average of 3 percent a year from 1945 to 1965, but for the next decade the rate of growth declined to 2 percent. During the last half of the 1970s, productivity grew at only 1 percent a year; by the 1980s it was falling rather than rising. Meanwhile, Japan's rate of productivity was increasing four times faster than the United States'. Compensation for workers in the United States, however, was increasing by about 8 percent a year through the 1970s.[19]

DECLINE AND RESURRECTION OF THE DOLLAR

When a nation spends more abroad than it sells, the value of its currency usually declines. As the American appetite for imports increased and exports began to sag in the early 1970s, dollars flooded foreign banks and accounts. Nervous investors rushed to convert dollars into gold, which traditionally has served as backing for the dollar. The dollar had been pegged to gold at $35 per troy ounce from 1934 to 1968, which meant that the United States promised to buy or sell gold to other nations at roughly that rate. The dollar thus served as the world standard on which currencies were based.

The run on America's gold reserves prompted by foreign insecurity over the stability of the dollar caused our holdings to shrink from $25 billion to 10.5 billion by 1971.[20] President Nixon responded by declaring that the United States was going off the gold standard, thereby devaluing the dollar and permitting it to fluctuate freely against the currencies of other countries. Since the total supply of dollars available in foreign exchange markets was greater than the demand, the dollar eventually began to fall to levels dictated by supply and demand.

The move to a floating exchange rate resulted in the dollar dropping to post–World War II lows against a number of major currencies. American goods became cheaper abroad and imports more expensive at home. Still the downward trend in our trade gap was not reversed because demand for imports remained high in the United States. The nation's inflation rate continued to rise, moreover, because people now had to pay more dollars for foreign goods and American prices surged upward to match import prices.

The dollar began to reverse its decline in 1981 in spite of continuing high trade deficits because interest rates on short-term investments in the U.S. surged to record high levels, attracting foreign investors who first had to convert into dollars. The sharp decline in the rate of inflation during 1982 made the United States an attractive investment market, and the dollar continued to post gains against all major currencies. Paradoxically, the problem then became one of the dollar becoming too strong for its own good. This was because the strong dollar cut deeply into American exports since it represented a steep price hike for foreign consumers of American goods. American businesses suffered from declining overseas sales while our domestic economy was in a tailspin. A strong dollar likewise was an inducement for American consumers to buy even more imported goods, thereby increasing the balance-of-payments dilemma.

A SLOWDOWN OF YANKEE INGENUITY

Other more deeply rooted economic factors have come to plague presidents in addition to the obvious problems of inflation, declining productivity, and trade deficits. A major cause of our declining position in the industrial world has been a noticeable slowdown in technological advances in the United States. American corporations have fallen behind many of their foreign counterparts in supporting research and development. Indeed, scientific and mathematical education and skills have declined sharply in American schools in recent years, as fewer and fewer qualified teachers were available and fewer students entered math or science careers.[21] Some observers have suggested that the U.S. economy has become top-heavy with nonproductive jobs and skills, many of which pay exceptionally high salaries for little real productive input into the economy. Compared to Germany or Japan, for example, the United States has an extraordinary number of lawyers and accountants whose skills are directed more toward rearranging existing forms of wealth than creating new productive wealth.[22] Others argue that federal regulations as well as powerful pressures by environmental protection groups have increasingly hampered American industries in increasing productivity or developing domestic resources. A few critics insist that the American work ethic, the will and drive to work hard to succeed, has declined as successive generations began to expect more for less.[23]

As our economic problems multiplied and worsened, demands for the government to "do something" grew more urgent. People looked to the president for relief because for the past half century the White House has been the focal point for economic planning and policy leadership. The illusion evolved that presidents were capable of "fine-tuning" the economy, and in fact every candidate and incumbent promised the electorate he would make the American economy work the way it *should*.

If economists rarely succeed in predicting the course of the nation's economy or in coming up with nostrums to cure its maladies, there is not much likelihood politicians will either. A president faces special risks, however, for he is expected to come up with solutions. While he is elected for only four years, most of our economic difficulties would require years to resolve. But the electorate is impatient with economic distress. No president can indulge in realistic economic policies—even if he knows what they are—and hope to enhance his political popularity. Thurow has suggested all solutions to our economic problems require that:

> . . . someone *must suffer large economic losses. No one wants to volunteer for this role, and we have a political process that is incapable of forcing anyone to shoulder this burden. Everyone wants someone else to suffer the necessary economic losses, and as a consequence none of the possible solutions can be adopted.*[24]

Not only are the problems deeply rooted and complexly intertwined but the powers available to the president to attack them are insufficient.

THE PRESIDENT'S ECONOMIC POWERS

Government management of the economy to promote jobs, control inflation, and maximize productivity was a radical concept in American politics prior to the 1930s. Orthodox economics held that the natural forces of the free market would serve to moderate and control economic upheavals over the long run. When times were good, presidents ignored the economy, believing as Calvin Coolidge suggested that "the business of government is business." If unemployment increased and the economy went into a tailspin, presidents were supposed to reassure the public that patience, hard work, thrift, and time would eventually correct the situation. Meanwhile, the president was expected to maintain public order by helping to put down labor strikes, or he was held responsible for bailing out the banking system when it ran into difficulties.

ORTHODOX ECONOMIC THEORY

Orthodox economists maintain that the key to economic conditions always lies in interest rates. The greater the demand to borrow money, the higher the rate of interest that can be charged and the greater the willingness to save. Once there is a flood of savings, interest rates will fall, encouraging business executives and industries to borrow to invest in expansion, for expansion is easier when credit is less expensive. Expansion leads to increased employment, pushing the economy into a period of growth and prosperity because of the rising levels of investment, new capital development, and increased productivity. Government's only role should be to insure adequate resources for investment among the wealthier segment of the population, for they are the ones most likely to invest. The benefits of their investment ultimately will "trickle down" to the workers.

High employment and prosperity, however, ultimately begin to put pressure on prices since more and more people are chasing after a finite supply of money, goods, and services. When spending and the demand for credit exceed the supply of savings and the rate of investment increases, consumers and business executives find the cost of goods, capital equipment, and credit once again prohibitive. Eventually, interest rates reach a point where business expansion as well as consumer borrowing become prohibitive, production slows down, unemployment grows, and a recession or depression sets in. If nature is allowed to take its course, conditions will become ripe once again for a new surge of investment because the downturn relaxes pressure on credit, according to orthodox theory.

Orthodox economic theory went out the window, however, during the Great Depression. The collapse of the Wall Street stock market in October 1929 was followed by a disintegrating economy and widespread hardship. The downturn became so precipitous that conditions never improved for increased savings or new investment, despite a lowering of interest rates and deflation. An equilibrium was achieved between savings and investment, but at a level so low as to be useless to regenerate productivity. Massive unemployment, sharply reduced personal incomes, and dwindling production wracked not only the United States but also many other countries of the world. Trade restrictions broke out among nations as each tried to protect its own industries and workers against imports.

It was obvious that the private sector no longer was capable of providing sufficient demand to generate a revival of the nation's economy, much less to sustain growth. The Roosevelt administration consequently moved to augment the "hidden hand" of the free marketplace with the heavy hand of government in the belief that only the president could lead the economy toward recovery. The theoretical basis for this sea change in economic attitudes stemmed from the ideas of a British economist, John Maynard Keynes, who argued for a much greater role for government in stimulating demand.

THE KEYNESIAN REVOLUTION

John Maynard Keynes held that no economy could pull out of the Great Depression merely by cutting wages and prices or by reducing purchases of capital goods and stocks. What was needed was pump priming by the government—massive injections of governmental spending to stimulate the economy by increasing demand. Government could create new demand for the products of business and labor by increasing spending, cutting taxes, and, if necessary, by running up large budget deficits. Such intervention would push the economy onto higher levels of productivity, employment, and prosperity, and once the economy had regained its vigor, government could pull back and reduce its spending and pump priming until the next downturn.

Keynes believed that governmental taxing and spending policies should redistribute wealth, thus creating greater aggregate demand through a much increased public sector of the economy. This might mean an emphasis on borrowing over saving and consumption over investment, but it would enable the government to solve the age-old problem of how to maintain stability in the balance of supply and demand. Presidents since FDR have overseen these attempts to fine-tune the economy through the use of fiscal policies.

FISCAL POLICYMAKING

Fiscal policy—the use of taxing and spending to influence economic activity—is set out annually in the federal budget. Presidents invariably are associated with fiscal policy since federal budgets are prepared under their auspices. But presidents have about as much control over federal budgets and fiscal policies as they do over the weather. Federal budgets in recent years have grown out of control, with a momentum that is incompatible with the nation's economic performance.[25] Once widely held to be a major instrument of the powerful presidency, the federal budget now has become a ticking time bomb that no one has the courage or ability to defuse.

When the U.S. economy was growing at a fast clip and prosperity seemed irreversible, the federal budget and fiscal policy were matters of little interest and even less understanding to anyone other than U.S. government leaders, readers of the *Wall Street Journal*, economics teachers, and corporation executives. Stagflation and the decline in America's global economic position, however, have made the public more attentive to the problems of the federal budget and the nation's economy, and the president's central role in both.

Fiscal power *appears* to belong to the president, but the actual budget process is so porous that any coordinated effort at the top is doomed to failure. There is, first of all, a lack of consensus on economic goals. Congress has its own budgetary and fiscal powers, and seldom is it willing to cooperate with the White House for any length of time. The structure of the budget increasingly leads to less and less maneuverability by either the president or Congress because of the budget's complexity, its high stakes, the vast number of people with demands on the government, and the fact that much of the budget is already locked in by prior spending commitments. Finally, political expediency invariably wins out over long-term economic considerations.

BUDGET PREPARATION

In 1939 Congress delegated broad economic powers to the president by shifting the Bureau of the Budget from the Department of the Treasury to the new Executive Office of the President. In 1946 Congress passed the Employment Act, which made the president responsible for maintaining high levels of employment and production, and for stabilizing the purchasing power of the dollar. The Council of Economic Advisers (CEA) was created to assist the president in preparing an annual economic report to Congress. In 1971 President Nixon's reorganization of the BOB into the Office of Management and Budget (OMB) further enhanced the president's fiscal powers by adding new responsibilities for program evaluation, coordination of budgetary demands with needs, and fiscal planning.

The chairman of the CEA, the secretary of the Treasury, and the OMB director have formed what is essentially a Ministry of Finance. Treasury is primarily concerned with the soundness of the dollar and tax policies; OMB with spending policies and coordinating agency funding requests; and the CEA with overall coordination of the president's economic policies.

These key economic advisers and their staffs, along with virtually the entire range of other federal agency chiefs, departmental economists, program managers, budget examiners, congressional committees and subcommittees, and interested third parties, provide input into the budgetary process. Presidential involvement in details is limited, although the president's broad fiscal goals supposedly influence the actions of those working on his behalf. His budget priorities are advanced in messages to Congress, through the legislative liaison efforts of the White House staff, and by direct appeals to the public or interest groups.

Presidential scholar Frank Kessler details three stages in the executive budget process. The first involves developing policies a year before the State of the Union address, which is delivered in January. Assumptions about the state and direction of the economy guide planning and development at this point and set the stage for decisions about taxing and spending policies that will either balance the budget or result in a deficit or—what is most likely—a surplus. Agency estimates are compiled and submitted to the OMB during the second phase; the final stage involves OMB review and a decision by the president.[26]

The budget is sent to Congress in January, and this event results in months of debate over specific items as well as the overall budget projections. Usually Congress makes its decisions in September as to which parts of the president's budget it can support and which it will reject. The new budget is supposed to go into effect on October 1, when appropriations and spending are approved on the basis of projected tax revenues and expenditures.

While presidents typically are optimistic about their budgets, the record for misplaced fiscal optimism belongs to President Reagan. As a candidate in 1980, he predicted that revenues would increase by 60 percent during his four years while government spending would increase by only 35 percent, resulting in a budget surplus of $121 billion by fiscal 1985. By the time Reagan reached the White House, he had sobered up on his economic expectations, but still predicted a balanced budget by 1985 with a surplus of $7 billion.[27] Instead, budget deficits reached historic proportions, totaling more than $300 billion in just the first two years of Reagan's administration; the prospect was that they would total more than $700 billion by the end of his four-year term in 1985.

The road from presidential budgetary aspirations and projections to fiscal outcomes is lined with potholes and risks because the president exercises little control or discretion over his budgetary submissions and even less control over what happens once they reach Congress. Louis Fisher, a leading expert on the budgetary process, believes that "the United States has fiscal outcomes without a fiscal policy. The system operates largely on its own momentum, with little sense of accountability, responsibility, or control":

> *The president does not present a budget of his own making, representing in aggregate and in detail what he believes is best for the nation. He does not, and cannot, defend the contents. For the most part he submits estimates for programs over which he has no control. The president is not responsible for the budget in any meaningful sense.*[28]

THE UNCONTROLLABLES: FEDERAL TRANSFER PAYMENTS

A rich society can afford to be a compassionate and generous society. As a result, both Congress and the Executive Branch—motivated by a good conscience and social idealism—created one program after another guaranteeing that the world's greatest economic system would share its riches more equitably. Social security in the late 1930s was the first program to transfer through the auspices of the federal budget large sums of income to people. Between 1960 and 1980 an explosion of federal transfer payments in the form of new or expanded entitlements and income security programs, along with more narrowly targeted programs to relieve injustices or inequalities, gave to millions of Americans a direct stake in the federal budget. Medicare, Medicaid, school lunches, food stamps, student loans, federal aid to education, job retraining, and many other programs brought about federal transfers of income to more than a third of all American families. Monthly retirement checks went out to 36 million retired or disabled workers, their dependents, or survivors under social security; 28 million Medicare and 18 million Medicaid patients received assistance; 11 million Americans were recipients of Aid to Families with Dependent Children; 21 million received food stamps; and 25 million children participated in federally funded school lunch programs.[29]

By the beginning of the 1980s, federal payments to individuals had grown two and a half times faster than the GNP. In 1962 federal transfer payments totalled $29.5 billion—less than a third of the federal budget. By fiscal year 1983 such spending had reached $362 billion, accounting for nearly half the federal budget—an increase of more than 1100 percent in twenty years.[30]

Federal benefits for the needy, including such welfare programs as aid to dependent children or unemployment compensation, are entitlements. But all these programs accounted for only a sixth of the total federal transfer expenditures.[31] The remaining five-sixths were dispersed in social security, old-age retirement pensions and medical assistance, and federal retirement programs, all of which were pegged to the cost-of-living index. The federal budget crunch is mostly a retirement and pension fund crunch, making it a dangerous time bomb not only for an incumbent president but also for future chief executives.

When Congress establishes benefits for such programs, it does not set a limit on the total costs based on the federal government's ability to budget payments. Since the federal government is obligated to pay out benefits to anyone eligible, there is no way to predict how much money will ultimately flow out of the federal treasury.

Most of what remains in the federal budget after transfer payments is also locked in by equally binding commitments. Roughly 12.7 percent of the 1983 budget was consumed by interest on the national debt. Another 29.2 percent was targeted for national defense. Grants to states and localities for highways, crime prevention, environmental protection, education, and other programs absorbed another 5.8 percent, leaving only four cents of every federal dollar for all the remaining needs of the national government, including the Federal Bureau of Investigation, national parks, county agricultural services, federal museums and archives, federal institutional upkeep, and diplomatic services.[32] Table 8–2 shows how much the federal budget has grown beyond the president's control from 1970 to 1982.

Any president attempting to pursue a restrictive fiscal policy by cutting funds for existing programs faces immense resistance from Congress. President Reagan's efforts to arrest the growth in the federal budget's uncontrollable expenditures by cutting the budget by some $35 billion fell almost exclusively on the politically unorganized poor, while well-entrenched interest groups and the inflationary retirement benefits built into various entitlements went untouched. Reagan's inept attempt to cut back on social security benefits in 1981 convinced the White House that it would be suicidal to take on any of the sizeable or well-organized groups receiving benefits or payments from the federal government. Not even a bipartisan commission appointed in 1982 to study changes in the social security system was willing to urge Congress or the president to make significant cuts; consequently the pattern of cost-of-living increases continues.

For all of his promises to reduce government spending and cut back on the federal budget President Reagan was no more successful than any of his predecessors. The federal government's share of the GNP stood at 24.1 percent at the end of Reagan's first fiscal year in October, 1982, compared to 22 percent five years earlier. Reagan was unable to trim the federal government's spending totals in any significant way. He had merely changed the government's emphasis from nondefense spending to defense spending. This was without reversing the Great Society program, according to Rudolph Penner, a budget analyst with the American Enterprise Institute.[33]

OTHER CLAIMANTS ON THE BUDGET

Presidential control over budget policymaking has declined also as a result of increased competition for the ever growing funds and resources of the federal budget. The triple alliances and iron triangles discussed earlier in this study come into full play during the budgetary process, as virtually every group with a claim to federal support lobbies federal agencies, members of Congress, the mass media, and the White House. Agencies and bureaus within cabinet departments fight to protect their constituents and to maintain or increase their share of funding. Departments vie against one another, and everyone seeks to influence the president, the White House staff, and particularly the OMB, the chief guardian of the president's fiscal policy.

TABLE 8-2 **Executive Controllability of Federal Expenditures, 1970-1982**
(in billions of dollars and percentages)

OUTLAYS	1970	1976	1982 (est.)
Total outlays	$195.7	$364.5	$725.3
Relatively uncontrolled outlays	$123.2	$257.5	$544.7
(Percent of total outlays)	63	70	75
Relatively controlled outlays	$74.9	$111.2	$188.2
(Percent of total outlays)	37	30	25

SOURCE: *Statistical Abstract of the United States, 1982-83*, 248.

The OMB's authority to challenge ongoing programs and to reexamine spending levels each year makes it a source of frustration to all claimants on the federal purse. But even the OMB is usually helpless in restraining or redirecting spending on any substantial level. Rarely is it successful in coordinating presidential fiscal policies with budgetary revenues and outlays. Economic conditions can play havoc with a budget, and even the slightest deviations in the data in presidential economic forecasts can leave a budget in shambles. In fiscal 1981, for example, a 1 percent drop in the projected annual economic growth rate raised expenditures by $6 billion, reduced federal revenues by $13 billion, and increased the deficit by $19 billion. An increase of 1 percent in unemployment reduced receipts by $13 billion, increased outlays by $7 billion, and raised the deficit by $20 billion.[34] In fiscal 1982 the Reagan administration's rosy projection was for the GNP to grow 4.2 percent, adjusted for inflation at 8.3 percent. Instead, real, inflation-adjusted output of goods and services declined by 1.7 percent and inflation likewise slowed to near 6 percent, reducing expected revenues to the Treasury. The 1982 deficit consequently was more than double what the OMB had originally anticipated.[35]

Budget authority is also weakened by the practice of "backdoor spending"—the disbursement each fiscal year of billions of dollars which are not counted against the federal deficit, even though the U.S. Treasury must borrow to cover all budget deficits in the open market whether the debts are on or off the record. Backdoor spending results from a wide range of programs and activities not included in the federal budget because a program may have a status independent of government, or because Congress prefers to make the budget deficit look smaller. The U.S. Postal Service, for example, is left out of the budget, even though it depends on some federal funds. Other examples include the purchasing and storing of oil reserves, programs for small businesses or farmers, and low-rent housing development assistance. The Economic Unit of *U.S. News & World Report* calculated that backdoor spending between 1972 and 1982 totalled $103 billion. If the cumulative deficits of such spending during the period were figured into the federal deficit, it would increase it by 22 percent. In the fiscal year 1982 budget alone, the deficit for such spending amounted to $19 billion.[36]

THE CONGRESSIONAL BUDGET CHALLENGE

By the early 1970s it had become obvious to both president and Congress that neither could really control federal expenditures. But the perspectives on the nature of the problem and who was responsible differed from one vantage point to the other. The Nixon administration saw the developing economic malaise as stemming in large part from the recklessly extravagant Democratically controlled Congress. Many members of Congress, however, believed the White House was making a mockery of the policy process, and that fiscal authority had shifted too much to the president. Congress felt impotent to respond to budgetary programs because of the deteriorating economy, the growth in uncontrollables in the budget, and new tactics for spending which enabled executive agencies to bypass Congress. Nixon's use of impoundments to reduce programs already mandated by Congress added fuel to the fire.

From the president's side of the fiscal tangle, executive agencies and cabinet departments sought protection from the OMB by working on Congress, while congressional committees and their constituents sought shelter from annual appropriations challenges through building into legislation entitlements, backdoor spending, and third-party arrangements. The fragmentation of leadership and weakening party bonds made Congress more porous than ever before to narrow interests. Individual members were encouraged to tack riders onto bills to save all kinds of pork-barrel projects, and the budget continued to hemorrhage.

The Congressional Budget and Impoundment Act in 1974 was an attempt to restore to Congress greater control over the size and shape of the budget. But Congress has yet to master the authorization and appropriations procedures established by the act. The practice of adding irrelevant riders to appropriations measures increased after 1976, making it more and more difficult for Congress to meet budget deadlines for appropriation measures. Members of Congress improved their chances of obtaining fiscal data, but there was no parallel success in restraining spending. In fact, just the opposite occurred. Authorization and appropriation committees regularly exaggerated spending requests to protect against real budget cuts, much as departments and agencies in the Executive Branch had done for years.

The Congressional Budget Office frequently clashed with the White House over economic forecasts on which budget assumptions are based, and some congressional budget leaders saw the CBO as a major force enabling them to compete with the Executive Branch in economic leadership. The CBO angered the Carter administration by concluding that the president's energy program would fall far short of achieving energy savings. And the CBO earned the enmity of the Reagan White House by projecting budget deficits for 1983 and 1984 far in excess of the White House's own projections. (The CBO's estimates proved to be far more accurate.)[37]

A feature of the budget reform designed to impose a measure of self-discipline on Congress in fiscal policymaking ended up as a powerful tool for the president. A process called *reconciliation* provided that after Congress approved its first budget resolution and after action was taken on all budget and spending bills, Congress would pass a second budget resolution reconciling changes with the original budget resolutions. If the second resolution was at odds with the first, committees might be instructed to alter their previous actions by rescinding or amending appropriations, by increasing or decreasing revenues, or by similar budgetary actions.[38] President Reagan used reconciliation to win massive budget cuts, enabling him to circumvent the time-consuming and far more politically treacherous course of going through numerous appropriations and program committees to get his cuts.

MONETARY POLICY

Lack of money is the root of all evil, according to George Bernard Shaw in *Man and Superman*. The lack of money is only one of the evils faced by presidents, however. The other is too much money. Control of a nation's monetary system is an essential ingredient in any economic policy, but governments find that controlling money is about as difficult as eradicating evil or controlling sin. The president has less influence over monetary policy than fiscal policy because regulating the amount of money available to the economy belongs to decision makers and forces largely beyond his control.

Monetary policy is based on the total amount of currency, bank deposits, and other forms of negotiable money such as checking accounts, credit cards, and savings accounts. Responsibility for managing the money supply is vested in the Federal Reserve Board whose seven governors are appointed for fourteen-year terms by the president, subject to Senate confirmation. Presidents are responsible for naming the Fed's two most powerful members: the chairman and vice-chairman, whose four-year terms overlap the president's.

The Federal Reserve Board oversees the Federal Reserve System, which was created by Congress in 1913 as a private-governmental banking system with authority to set banking policies and to regulate the amount of credit and currency available for circulation. There are twelve Federal Reserve Banks in the system, each located in a geographical district. The seven members of the Fed along with five Federal Reserve Bank presidents form the Federal Open Market Committee (FOMC), which is responsible for carrying out the monetary policies decided by the Fed.

The Fed attempts to regulate the money supply by controlling the size of bank reserves—commercial bank deposits required by the Federal Reserve System to be kept on hand and not circulated back into the economy in the form of personal or business loans or investments. The Fed affects monetary policy by setting the discount rate, that is, the interest charged to commercial banks borrowing from the system. The main power of the Fed is its control over the amount of nonborrowed reserves available to commercial banks. These reserves constitute the majority of a bank's total money reserves, and they are controlled through buying and selling federal securities such as Treasury bonds or short-term bills. These securities compete in the open financial market with private investors attempting to borrow for private or business needs.

The FOMC creates bank deposits either by buying securities (paying for the purchases with checks drawn on the Federal Reserve banks) or by electronic transfers. The seller of securities deposits the checks in commercial banks, creating additional reserves for credit or investment. The Fed—in short—pays for Treasury securities by adding to the bank's reserves. Whenever the Fed believes there is too little money in the economy, it buys government securities from banks, thereby releasing money into the system. When it thinks there is too much money, it allows banks to buy the securities. Money is not actually printed, but is created by a process of buying and selling securities.

The major difficulty with trying to control the economy through monetary policy is that money takes many different forms, and it is imprecisely defined. For example, only noninterest-bearing checking accounts were formerly included in the definition of the money supply, but now the Fed includes all of the newer interest-bearing checking accounts as well. Other measures of money include small savings deposits and savings certificates. The Fed has only a vague idea of how fast the money supply grows because the supply is subject to unpredictably sharp swings as a result of changes in the way people keep their money—in checking accounts versus money market funds, for example.[39]

Frequently the Fed pursues a "tight-money" policy by slowing down on the growth of money available for financial credit and business expansion in order to reduce inflation. Inflation is believed to result when the money supply, in whatever form it takes, grows over time faster than the GNP. This frequently pits the Fed against presidents, for while the Board is using the open money market to rein in inflation, administrations are more likely to be pursuing the politically expedient goal of priming the economy. The White House and Congress credit fiscal policy for all successes, but blame the Fed for any problems in the economy.

Democratic administrations are usually at greater odds with the Fed than Republican because the Board's tendency to pursue tight money hampers fiscal policies favored by Democratic Congresses and presidents. During 1961–1962 Fed Chairman William McChesney Martin was under frequent fire from the Kennedy White House because tight money policies and high interest rates threatened to choke off administration attempts to expand the economy. In 1965 the Fed adopted a tight-money line while LBJ was refusing to heed economic advice to raise taxes. President Carter was bitter toward the Fed in 1980 for restrictive money policies which, the White House charged, had fueled inflation by pushing interest rates to record high levels.

Republicans, usually more anxious to slow down inflation, are generally more comfortable with tight monetary policies, but even GOP administrations have their problems with the Fed. The Reagan administration blamed the Fed's "erratic management of the nation's money supply" for the continuing deterioration in the American economy in 1982, after Reagan's new economic policies had taken hold. Monetary growth had accelerated in late 1981, causing interest rates to rise because of investors' fears of renewed inflation. The Fed insisted it was the threat of even more horrendous federal budget deficits projected into the 1980s that caused interest rates to continue to rise in the face of recession. But White House economists asserted that Fed's procedures for controlling the growth of the money supply needed to be sharpened, redeployed, and made more precise.[40] Critics of the Fed's policies argued that the money supply was subject to such unpredictable swings because of the new forms in which people now held money. As a result of this development, not even Federal Reserve Banks knew how much was in circulation. With the economy mired in its worst downturn since the 1930s, the Fed in 1982 shifted from a tight- to an easy-money strategy, pouring more resources into banks to nudge interest rates down. This prompted some economists to worry that the Fed was more confused than ever about what to do, and that in response it was drifting back into a course that would be certain to reignite double-digit inflation.[41]

The fundamental weakness in any policy for dealing with the economy today is that fiscal and monetary policies rarely complement

MR. PRESIDENT... DON'T YOU UNDERSTAND? THIS IS REAL...
THIS IS ACTUALLY HAPPENING... WE CAN'T <u>CHANGE</u> THE SCRIPT...

Reprinted by permission of United Feature Syndicate.

each other. A congressional subcommittee studying the Federal Reserve System in 1964 at the time of the Fed's fiftieth anniversary declared:

> Since what the Federal Reserve does is perhaps the most important determinant of levels of employment, production, and purchasing power, the president cannot in any meaningful sense be held responsible for achieving the objectives of the Employment Act of 1946 as long as the Federal Reserve's independence of his views is preserved.[42]

OTHER PRESIDENTIAL TACTICS

When all else fails to arrest the upward spiral in wages and prices, presidents try to rally the public behind them in the hope that this will pressure business and labor to follow suit. Or the president may try to use budgetary resources to prod industries which fail to heed wage-and-price guidelines. The White House may attempt to use foreign-trade policies as leverage, or to raise the specter of regulation or deregulation. As a last resort, the president may seek authority from Congress to impose mandatory wage-and-price controls on the economy.

PUBLIC EXHORTATIONS

Going public via television may win a president support for economic policies when Congress is resistant. Kennedy used every available public forum or media event to publicize his tax-cut proposal in 1963, building a fire under Congress that eventually led to passage of the measure in 1964. Reagan made several televised appeals to the nation, urging people to contact their Representatives in Congress and recommend passage of his federal budget cuts and new tax program.

Mass appeals aimed at changing fundamental economic behavior or expectations are usually less successful with the public, especially when such appeals are unrealistic. Ford asked the people to fight inflation by making a list of ten ways to save energy and by sending a copy of their list to him.[43] The White House mercifully never revealed the results of the president's entreaty. But Ford did not give up easily. A few days later he presented a series of emergency proposals to Congress for dealing with inflation. The president urged Americans to "WIN"—that is, to "Whip Inflation Now!" WIN buttons suddenly cropped up on the lapel of the president and other administration officials. But in the end the White House did not win its battle against inflation.

Reagan was never at a loss for simple public remedies for complex economic problems. He suggested to reporters on one occasion that many unemployed workers might find work by perusing the help-wanted ads in the Sunday *Washington Post*. At another news conference he noted that the number of businesses outnumbered jobless workers in America, and suggested that if every firm hired just "one more person," the nation's serious unemployment problem would be solved.[44]*

JAWBONING BUSINESS AND LABOR

Pressuring business and labor—"jawboning"—can be productive because the president can threaten to publicly embarrass management or

---

Time (January 17, 1983, 36) counted 14.7 million businesses and 12 million unemployed, but more than 11 million of these businesses were small operations, involving members of a family or a few people.

labor if they refuse to go along with wage-price guidelines which are in the public interest. Kennedy used a televised news conference in 1962 to castigate U.S. Steel for its proposed hike in prices after the White House had helped negotiate a noninflationary settlement between union and management. Kennedy blasted "a tiny handful of steel executives whose pursuit of private power and profit exceeds their sense of public responsibility . . . [and shows] utter contempt . . . for 185 million Americans."[45] Other steel companies declined to raise prices, and U.S. Steel was forced to back down. Shortly thereafter, the Department of Justice and the Federal Trade Commission began to investigate the steel industry's pricing procedures for possible violation of antitrust laws.

Johnson's skills in arm-twisting and cajolery, which worked well for him when he was Senate majority leader, proved equally successful with business and labor. Working behind the scenes, LBJ countered a price hike of aluminum by the giant Alcoa Corporation with an order to the Defense Department to release on the open market 200,000 tons of aluminum stockpiled for the nation's military. Alcoa and other aluminum corporations rescinded their increases.[46] Johnson also intervened in negotiations to ward off a threatened rail strike in 1964 by promising management that he would pry loose from the House Rules Committee legislation providing greater flexibility in setting rail rates. He also promised that the Internal Revenue Service would allow depreciation for bridge and tunnel construction.[47]

Jawboning, however, succeeds only as long as the president enjoys reasonable credibility with both labor and management as well as public support. Economic conditions must be such that the president's guidelines or wishes can be realistically met. Carter criticized price increases by the oil industry as unconscionable, but he was unable to roll back prices because there was an oil shortage. Immediately after Reagan's budget and tax cuts went into effect, the president tried to jawbone American investors into reflecting greater confidence in the economy by buying stocks, but the stock market remained in the doldrums until interest rates began to fall.

WAGE AND PRICE CONTROLS

Wage and price controls are never popular, even in the most desperate times. Such measures are expected and tolerated during wartime, when savings accumulate because an economy with high employment lacks many civilian goods on which people can spend their incomes. Once controls are lifted, prices usually surge, making up much of the difference that might have occurred over time had controls never been in place to begin with. Inflation surged, for example, in late 1946 when World War II controls expired.

Most presidents are opposed to controls in peacetime because of the considerable difficulty in administering them and because of their questionable value. Johnson refused to institute wage and price controls when inflation worsened in the late 1960s, but Nixon, who opposed controls in 1970 when Congress voted him standby authority, surprised everyone by suddenly announcing the nation's first peacetime wage-price freeze in August 1971.

Nixon's controls included four phases. The first was a temporary ninety-day freeze on all prices and wages. Phase two involved the development of methods for monitoring prices and rents by a pay board and price commission, with wages limited to a maximum 5.5 percent increase while dividends, interest, and corporate profits were left uncontrolled. A cost-of-living council would oversee wage and price changes while the administration attempted to slowly remove controls during the last two phases.

Controls failed for several reasons. First, they did not address the underlying cause of inflation in the United States: the decline in the nation's productivity was not matched by a decline in consumption; in fact, consumption was continuing to increase. The controls lacked credibility because it was soon obvious to everyone—particularly labor—that workers were being asked to bear the brunt of controls which were haphazardly administered and which left many areas in the economy untouched. When legislation authorizing controls expired in 1974, the Democratic-controlled Congress declined to renew it, and both Ford and Carter preferred to jawbone rather than to seek authority for controls once again.

REARRANGING THE DECK CHAIRS

If the efforts of economists are really tantamount to rearranging the deck chairs on the *Titanic*, one might extend the analogy to suggest that the president *is* the captain. During the past fifteen years one president after another has gone under while trying to command an economy that was listing if not sinking. Failure to deal with the nation's economic woes unquestionably has been a major factor in the political demise of presidents.

One president after another has optimistically predicted that he would halt inflation and federal budget deficits, put people back to work, and restore the United States to its former high levels of economic performance. But all the while the economy has continued to deteriorate. Presidents shift from expansionary fiscal to restrictive monetary approaches and back again with such frequency that no one can be sure what the nation's economic goals will be from one week to the next.

All of this is a far cry from the mid-1960s, when it seemed that economics had "come of age," as Walter Heller, Kennedy's Council of Economic Advisers chair, put it.[48] *Business Week* proclaimed the first five years of the 1960s a time of "remarkable growth—and remarkable stability . . . rais[ing] the prestige of economists . . . to an all-time high."[49] President Johnson proudly declared in February 1966 that the United States was "now in the 60th month of record-breaking prosperity . . . and the Council of Economic Advisers has a lot to do with that amazing achievement."[50]

The chronic economic problems that followed this rosy forecast in part were unavoidable since they were influenced by global economic changes set in motion earlier. But the long-term reversal in the nation's economy also raised serious questions about the value and dependability of economic theory, as well as doubts about the competence of presidents to make economic policy. Economists themselves began to admit as early as 1970 that huge risks were involved in applying various theories to policymaking. Arthur Okun, a former member of the CEA, asserted that the economy had jumped the track of stable growth more often and more severely because of government actions than as a result of autonomous shifts in public demand.[51] Inflation and unemployment had become intertwined and combined in ways that economists found historically unexplainable. By the early 1980s high interest rates which persisted in the face of a deepening recession would also challenge traditional economic theory. Economists knew *why* the economy was in such a sorry mess, but they were far from agreement on what to do to restore it to robust health. On one point there was widespread agreement: our problems during the late 1960s stemmed from the Johnson administration's misjudgments.

Johnson's Folly

For all his new-found admiration for economists, LBJ could be indifferent to their advice whenever it suited his purposes. Johnson's chief economic advisers warned him in late 1965 that if he did not restrain government spending, he would have to raise taxes substantially or risk inflation.[52] The 1964 tax cut had sharply spurred consumer spending. Business invested heavily in new plants and equipment to meet rising demand. Government expenditures were rapidly rising to pay for the Great Society. And the escalation of the Vietnam War caused demand to far outpace productivity, setting off the spiral in wages and prices which would continue unabated until the early 1980s.

LBJ preferred jawboning with business and labor to halt the vicious cycle of wage-price increases. But by 1967 patriotic appeals to follow administration guidelines were mostly useless as the overheated economy raced out of control. The precise cost of war was hidden from Congress and the public, for as Johnson admitted to his biographer, Doris Kearns, it was impossible to estimate accurately the cost.[53] By 1967 Johnson was finally forced to accede to the CEA's advice, and he requested congressional passage of a surtax on income taxes. But it was too late—consumer and government spending had become uncontrollable, and the economy was set on a chaotic course from which it was unable to recover even after some fifteen years.

Nixon's Economic Stewardship: Expediency Over Theory

Richard Nixon attempted initially to employ the classic conservative solution of tight monetary and fiscal policies to reverse the course of the economy in 1969. Although these policies would result in an inevitable recession, the economy—after the cycle of rising wages and prices was arrested—should have left time for the administration to reverse course and return to an economy promising full employment and stable prices by the time Nixon sought reelection in 1972.

As predicted, a mild recession began in 1969 and continued into the next year, but with inflation *accelerating*, polls showed Nixon heading for certain defeat in 1972. So the administration decided to reverse course.[54] Nixon's first move was to freeze wages and prices, an action he promised would only be temporary since "our best days lie ahead."[55] The freeze was more an act of desperation than optimism, however, for it was aimed at forestalling further damage to his bid for another term. To improve his chances, wage and price controls were paralleled by contradictory moves by the administration to stimulate fiscal and monetary policies. These policies were directed at easing unemployment during the campaign.

The latter half of 1971 and all of 1972 were highly expansionary in terms of fiscal policy. Social security benefits were raised significantly, the investment tax credit was restored, excise taxes were reduced, and personal income-tax exemptions increased. As a result, the Treasury suffered a net loss of personal taxes of $8.5 billion in 1971. In 1972 a 20 percent increase in social security benefits just prior to the election and increased grants-in-aid were the major forms of fiscal stimulation. The budget, which was nearly balanced in 1970 during the fight against inflation, ran a deficit of $10 billion in 1971 and $12 billion in 1972.[56] Tufte notes that such fiscal policies were administered under the heavy-handed influence of the White House "Responsiveness Program," the aims and methods of which later became a part of the sleazy record of the Watergate hearings.[57]

Democrats who were unenthusiastic about four more years of Richard M. Nixon ironically proved to be strong allies in the stimulative fiscal policies benefitting his administration. Democrats in Congress were as eager as the administration to ease unemployment, but they mistakenly believed that government spending could be increased because controls had eased inflation.

The Federal Reserve Board pursued its own form of stimulative policy prior to the presidential election of 1972. The money supply increased by 7.9 percent, and by as much as 8.7 percent during the final quarter of 1972.[58] It was this temporary lull in the Fed's tight money policies which gave rise to charges of collusion between the Fed chairman, Arthur Burns, and Nixon's White House. The fact that the Fed reapplied the brakes soon after the election and that the expansion of the money supply slowed down to 5.8 percent did not help dispel suspicions.

Nixon's economic policies were successful in postponing until after the election further increases in the cost of living. Once controls were phased out, inflation resumed with a vengeance. Some of this was catch-up inflation, but a good deal of it was due to several economic events which occurred at the time. The United States experienced a poor crop harvest in 1972, and along with the impact of Nixon's huge grain deal with the Soviet Union, prices in the supermarket soared by 20 percent in 1973, compared to only 5 percent the previous year.[59] OPEC's hike in the price of oil led to a surge in gasoline prices of 39 percent between October 1973 and May 1974. Pressure on the dollar because of the heavy U.S. trade deficit also contributed to higher prices for imported goods.

The administration's response to this new burst of inflation was to revert once again to tight fiscal and monetary policies. The result was that the nation's GNP stopped growing in the final quarter of 1973; in the first three quarters of 1974, it actually began to decline in terms of real growth measured against inflation.[60] Even though the economy was shrinking, throwing more and more people out of work and creating idle plants and machinery, inflation would not stop. The administration watched as the Fed turned the screw even tighter on monetary policy to the point that by the end of 1974 credit was prohibitive and the economy was growing still more feeble.

Ford's Confusion: Inflation or Unemployment?

President Ford inherited an economy that was more depressed than any since the 1930s, for not only was inflation racing along at a near double-digit clip, unemployment was growing worse by the day.

Declaring inflation to be "domestic enemy number one," Ford vowed to trim federal spending through deferrals and recisions, mostly of congressional pork-barrel projects that had been added to the administration's budget. Singling out these congressional add-ons, Ford precipitated the same kind of confrontation that Nixon had earlier with his impoundments: the OMB was according a higher status and value to administration budget items than to those funded by public law. The new budget act required the White House to document any spending delays or terminations, but Ford interpreted it to allow more than a hundred policy impoundments. Recision proposals flooded Congress, where they were rejected virtually en masse.[61]

Ford's decision to deal with the economy in a traditional Republican manner not only led him to ask Congress to participate in clamping down on spending but it also prompted him to seek a 5 percent temporary income-tax surcharge on corporations and upper-income families. The government wanted to follow a contractionary fiscal policy, precisely at a time when the economy was tumbling into a dangerously deep recession—a complete reversal of the fiscal theories that had guided presidents since Roosevelt.

Ford held to his view for only a few months. By early 1975 the economy had deteriorated so badly that he conceded during a nationwide television address that the time had come to shift gears from fighting inflation to battling unemployment. Ford asked Congress to enact a $16 billion tax cut, including $12 billion for consumers through a rebate on 1974 taxes and a $4 billion slash for businesses in new investment tax credits. He called for a moratorium on new federal spending and threatened to veto any new spending proposals.[62] The final tax-cut measure approved by Congress was more than Ford had asked—$23 billion—and it was slanted in favor of low-income families.

The recession grew worse during 1975 in spite of the tax cut. By year's end the economy began to recover, aided by the increased dollars returned to consumers' and business hands. Unemployment peaked at 9 percent, and almost a third of America's productive capacity was idled, but the recession had one benefit: inflation slowed by the end of 1975 and continued to decline during the first half of 1976—a trend due as much to the depressed economy as to fiscal or monetary policies.

Ford could not restrain his optimism as 1976 began, a year when he would have to win the office on his own accord. "The underlying fact about our economy is that it is steadily growing healthier. My policies . . . are intended to keep us on that path."[63] Ford insisted that all trends pointed in the right direction, and that his administration would do better (presumably than that of any Democratic challenger's) in continuing to control inflation and to ease unemployment. In his 1976 budget message Ford asked for an additional tax cut of $10 billion which, combined with the 1975 cut, would produce a shortfall of $28 billion to the Treasury. He linked this cut to a $28 billion cut in spending, which Congress clearly opposed.

The fiscal policies pursued during the Nixon-Ford years led to the largest budget deficits since World War II. From under $10 billion in 1974 the deficit exploded to nearly $50 billion in 1975, and close to $70 billion in 1976. Fiscal policy proceeded in spurts, guided more by politics than by economic theories. The relationship between productivity and aggregate demand seemed to have never been of any relevance to those shaping economic policies.

Carter's Learning Experience

Carter's anti-inflationary strategy was the standard tight monetary-fiscal approach designed to create idle capacity. Whenever the economy threatened to expand, the screws were tightened to slow it down to create idle capacity in hopes that inflation could eventually be squeezed out of the economy. The only problem was that while the administration espoused such a theory, the government was busy pursuing policies which were building into the economy inflationary effects far into the future. Agricultural price supports were reintroduced, social security payments were made more generous, pricing policies were created to protect American industries against foreign competition, and the minimum wage was raised substantially to help low-income workers. The administration either went along with or acquiesced, creating new pressures on wages and prices.[64]

By 1979 inflation raged completely out of control, triggered in part by the massive increase in the cost of imported oil, but also by heavy consumer demands. Unemployment declined to a modest 5.6 percent by spring, and it remained under 6 percent until prior to the 1980 election when it shot up—to the discomfort of the Carter White House—to 7.8 percent.[65] Worse, an inflation mentality had overtaken Americans, destroying incentives to save or to defer purchases since it appeared that everything would cost more in the future.

Whatever influence the president once had to exert over fiscal policymaking went out the window during Carter's administration. Too many groups were exerting pressure on Congress and government agencies to protect their interests for the administration to succeed in restraining inflationary pressures on the budget. Carter had tried to implement zero-based budgeting in his first year to slow the inexorable pressure to increase spending by various agencies. While the ZBB system required agencies to justify their programs and to assign priorities, bureaucrats craftily circumvented the process. Important programs were targeted for extinction with full knowledge that neither Congress nor the White Houe would allow them to suffer. Less needed programs were placed on a high priority.[66] Few programs were not increased at inflation-adjusted levels, and the federal budget deficit continued to mount exponentially. By the end of the 1970s the government had become responsible for much of the extraordinary inflation which devastated the economy, and to some extent the government encouraged the declining competitiveness of American industry.

Reaganomics: Old Tonic in New Bottles

Every president comes into office believing *his* economic leadership will provide answers to America's problems, but no president ever displayed as much public confidence or had as clearly stated a program and ideology as Ronald Reagan. The nation's economic woes, Reagan insisted, could be simply solved by "getting the government off the people's back." Reagan promised an economic revival by reducing the size of the federal government, freeing business from excessive governmental regulation, and cutting personal and corporate taxes. He promised nothing less than the dismantling of many of the New Deal–Great Society programs and a restoration of private rather than public sector development through *supply-side economics*.

Supply-side theorists claimed that large-scale tax cuts slanted in favor of those earning higher incomes would ignite a burst of investment, providing business and industry with the capital necessary for expansion. The entire economy would benefit from such an expansion: workers would find employment opportunities enhanced, and the shortfall to the nation's treasury caused by tax cuts would more than be made up by revenues produced by a vigorously productive economy. Critics of supply-side economics argued that it was not new, but that it was the old Republican doctrine of giving tax breaks to the wealthy in hopes that some of the benefits would "trickle-down," an observation that was reinforced in the notorious *Atlantic* interview of Reagan's chief economic adviser, OMB Director David Stockman.

Reagan was successful in selling his economic plan to the public in 1981, and within six months of taking office he accomplished two extraordinary legislative feats: first Congress approved some $37 billion in program cuts in the 1982 fiscal budget, and then it passed the Economic Recovery Tax Act providing $750 billion in personal and corporate tax cuts over the next five years.

Not everyone suffered from the budget cuts, and the benefits of the tax cuts went mostly to those earning $50,000 or more. Significantly, beneficiaries of social security and other large groups receiving entitlements were spared budget cuts because of their political clout. Federal programs benefitting select constituencies in which members of Congress were especially vulnerable to pressure survived or even flourished while the poor, the young, minority groups, the unskilled, and students suffered the most. The tax bill ended up a gargantuan give-away for especially well-organized or politically influential interest groups. Corporations benefitted from liberalized depreciation rules so magnanimous that corporate income taxes appeared headed for extinction. Families earning $20,000 a year or less suffered from the across-the-board tax reductions because payroll taxes on social security continued to rise, taking a larger percentage from take-home pay and all but eliminating any benefits from the tax cut.

Americans tolerated Reagan's economic policies even though they were widely perceived as favoring the rich over the poor. If the president's promises of a new economic miracle could come true, who cared if some would be made richer than others? Patience is a desirable trait, but when it comes to one's personal economic well-being, patience is not an especially strong American virtue. Within weeks of the passage of Reagan's new economic program, stock and bond markets began to shudder, unemployment began to rise, interest rates edged upward, and the American public began to grow cynical once again. "Stay the course" became the battle cry of the administration as the 1982 congressional elections approached with prospects of disaster befalling Republicans, for the economy by then had plunged into a near depression.

Reagan's promise of a quick return to a "brighter future for all our citizens" had become a nightmare of unemployment, declining living standards, and bankruptcies by 1983. Inflation was partially wrung out of the economy, not by a regeneration of productivity but by our most severe economic downturn since the Great Depression.

Despite massive cuts in the budget, the federal government under Reagan continued to absorb a quarter of the nation's GNP because sizeable increases in defense spending and the ever rising cost of entitlements absorbed any savings achieved by budget cuts. The shortfall to the Treasury threatened by the tax cuts threatened to choke off any sustained economic recovery because record-high federal deficits would require extraordinarily heavy governmental borrowing, keeping interest rates from declining sufficiently to spark an expansion of business or consumer borrowing.

By mid-1983 the economy appeared to be rebounding and the Reagan staff was touting his economic policies as a proven success. But many European leaders and some economists were unconvinced that the economy was experiencing a sustained recovery after its dismal record of the past ten years. Not only did the threat of astronomical federal debts and continued high interest pose risks to future recovery but unemployment remained high and the nation's balance of payments continued to rage out of control. Whether Reagan benefitted from the economy or not depended on whether the slowdown in inflation and the turnaround in economic activity could be sustained on through 1984. A public opinion poll in 1983 concluded that voters with household incomes below $20,000 a year gave Reagan low marks on his economic leadership while those above $20,000 a year were generally optimistic about the economy and rated the administration positively.[67]

CONCLUSION

Americans continue to hold to the illusion that their country is blessed with an extraordinary economic destiny, and that prosperity and a bigger and better standard of living are our natural birthrights. Candidates for the presidency perpetuate this illusion, and presidents do little to dispel it. Instead, the hope is forever held out that our declining economic monopoly can be corrected by the right president, by new, improved economic advisers, or by the application of magical economic theories devised in the White House. No president can honestly afford to risk educating the public to economic realities, for to do so would run counter to the American dream, which has taken a firm hold on our consciousness and expectations since World War II.

The federal government has assumed a much more substantial role in the economy since the 1930s, and this has placed immense pressures on presidents to perform economic miracles. For a brief period during the 1950s and 1960s, when the United States led the world in productivity and economic growth, presidents generally benefitted from their overrated positions as economic leaders. Once our privileged position began to decline, however, it was the president who suffered most.

In reality, presidents have to contend with economic instability as a matter of course. The new global economic order emerging today makes economic policymaking tenuous, risky, and virtually impossible. No nation any longer exists as an economic island unto itself. Furthermore, the American economy itself has developed practices and trends that preclude any centralized form of control or planning. The American president consequently is at the mercy not only of unpredictable economic conditions at home but also of worldwide uncertainties and change.

NOTES

1. Lester C. Thurow, *The Zero-Sum Society* (New York: Penguin Books, 1980), 12.
2. Frank Kessler, *The Dilemmas of Presidential Leadership* (Englewood Cliffs, N.J.: Prentice-Hall, 1982), 240.
3. Richard A. Brody and Benjamin I. Page, "The Impact of Events on Presidential Popularity: The Johnson and Nixon Years," in Aaron Wildavsky, ed., *Perspectives on the Presidency* (Boston: Little, Brown and Company, 1975), 146.
4. Kim Ezra Shienbaum and Ervin Schienbaum, "Public Perceptions of Presidential

Economic Performance: From Johnson to Carter," *Presidential Studies Quarterly* 12 (Summer 1982).

5. Henry Kenski, "The Impact of Economic Conditions on Presidential Popularity," *Journal of Politics* 39 (1977): 764–73.

6. Robert Y. Shapiro and Bruce M. Conforto, "Presidential Performance, the Economy, and the Public's Evaluation of Economic Conditions," *Journal of Politics* 42 (1980): 49–67.

7. Edward Tufte, *Political Control of the Economy* (Princeton: Princeton University Press, 1978).

8. Morris P. Fiorina, *Congress: Keystone of the Washington Establishment* (New Haven: Yale University Press, 1977).

9. Alan S. Blinder, *Economic Policy and the Great Stagflation* (New York: Academic Press, 1979), 30.

10. Thurow, 3.

11. Ibid., 43.

12. *San Antonio Express*, November 22, 1982, 6C.

13. *Wall Street Journal*, December 31, 1982, 13.

14. Ibid., 1, 12.

15. Marshall A. Robinson, H. C. Morton, and J. Calderwood, *An Introduction to Economic Reasoning* (Garden City, N.Y.: Anchor Books, 1980), 245–48.

16. *San Antonio Express*, August 11, 1983, 15.

17. Simon Ramos, "The U.S. Technology Slip: A Political Issue," in Walter E. Hoadley, ed., *The Economy and the President* (New York: American Assembly, Columbia University Press, 1980), 159.

18. Barry Bluestone and Bennet Harrison, *The Deindustrialization of America* (New York: Basic Books, 1982).

19. Joint Economic Committee of Congress, Special Study on Economic Change, vol. 9 (December 1980), *The International Economy: U.S. Role in a World Market*, 345–57.

20. Theodore H. White, *America in Search of Itself* (New York: Harper & Row, Publishers, 1982), 143.

21. *Wall Street Journal*, December 21, 1982, 1.

22. *Today: The Journal of Political News and Opinion*, October 3, 1980, 14.

23. Joint Economic Committee of Congress, 351.

24. Thurow, 11.

25. Donald H. Haider, "Presidents as Budget Policymakers," in Thomas E. Cronin, ed., *Rethinking the Presidency* (Boston: Little, Brown and Company, 1982), 371.

26. Kessler, 254.

27. *National Journal*, January 1, 1983, 5.

28. Louis Fisher, "Developing Fiscal Responsibility," in Richard Pious, ed., *The Power to Govern. Proceedings of the Academy of Political Science*, 34 (1981): 64.

29. *Budget of the U.S. Government, Fiscal Year 1981*, 258–73.

30. Ibid., *Fiscal Year 1984*, 3–5.

31. James Fallows, "Entitlements," *Atlantic*, November 1982, 52.

32. Office of Management and Budget data, as reported in the *National Journal*, January 1, 1983, 7.

33. *Christian Science Monitor*, September 5, 1982, 16.

34. Haider, 377.

35. *Wall Street Journal*, December 21, 1982, 16.

36. *U.S. News & World Report*, October 4, 1982, 77–78.

37. Data from Office of Management and Budget and the Congressional Budget Office, as reported in *U.S. News & World Report*, November 1, 1982, 70.

38. Lance T. LeLoup, *Budgetary Politics* (New Brunswick, Ohio: Kings Court Communications, 1977), 133.

39. *Congressional Quarterly*, November 7, 1981, 2160–61.

40. *Wall Street Journal*, January 22, 1982, 16.

41. Ibid., December 16, 1982, 1.

42. U.S. Congress, House, Committee on Banking and Currency, *The Federal Reserve System After Fifty Years*, (88th Cong., 2d. sess., August 25, 1964), 22.

43. *Weekly Compilation of Presidential Documents* 10 (no. 40, 1974), 1208–9.

44. *Time*, January 17, 1983, 36.

45. *John F. Kennedy, Public Papers: 1962* (Washington, D.C.: Government Printing Office, 1963), 315–16.

46. Kessler, 265.

47. Merle Miller, *Lyndon: An Oral Biography* (New York: G. P. Putnam's Sons, 1980), 374.

48. Walter Heller, *New Dimensions of Political Economy* (Cambridge, Mass.: Harvard University Press, 1966), 1.

49. *Business Week*, February 5, 1966, 125.

50. *Weekly Compilation of Presidential Documents* 2 (no. 5, February 7, 1966), 156.

51. Arthur Okun, *The Political Economy of Prosperity* (New York: W. W. Norton & Company, 1970), 111.

52. Doris Kearns, *Lyndon Johnson and the American Dream* (New York: Harper & Row, Publishers, 1976), 296.

53. Ibid., 297.

54. Thurow, 43–44.

55. *Weekly Compilation of Presidential Documents* 7, no. 34 (August 23, 1971), 1172.

56. Blinder, 142.

57. Tufte, 52.

58. Richard Pious, *The American Presidency* (New York: Basic Books, 1979), 314.

59. Blinder, 36.

60. Thurow, 46.

61. Louis Fisher, *Presidential Spending Power* (Princeton, N.J.: Princeton University Press, 1975), 198–99.

62. *Weekly Compilation of Presidential Documents* 11, no. 3 (January 3, 1975), 42.

63. *Weekly Compilation of Presidential Documents* 12, no. 5 (January 30, 1976), 80.

64. Thurow, 46.

65. *Chicago Tribune Graphic*, as reprinted in *Today*, October 22, 1982, 3.

66. Kessler, 262.

67. *San Antonio Express News*, June 26, 1983, 2K.

Chapter 9

Media Celebrity

There never was a honeymoon with the press . . . just a one-night stand.

  Jody Powell, Press Secretary to Jimmy Carter

If you'd been more successful in the movies, you wouldn't have had to go into politics.

  Johnny Carson, to Ronald Reagan

The single most important factor in the mismatch between the image of the president and reality is the mass media. Reality for most people is filtered through the media, and the president of the United States is unchallenged as the nation's leading celebrity. He is produced by ABC, NBC, CBS, PBS, cable TV, several national radio networks, and a host of print journalists—all this with the help of an army of White House publicity flacks. No one monopolizes public space as much as the president, and no other political leader is as dependent on the media for the resources to govern.

A president must fit every aspect of his public and personal life to the demands of the media. A grasp of issues or knowledge about domestic or global affairs often matters less than the ability to project well on television. Experience in politics is less important than skill in using the techniques and tactics of mass communications. A president needs to be an actor, to display the talents and sense of timing congenial with the world of entertainment if he is to successfully negotiate his way to power today. His personal popularity and political influence depend on how well he plays not only in Peoria but from Portland to Portland.

This chapter will examine the critical role the mass media play in creating, sustaining, and then often rejecting popular images of presidents. We will consider the nature of the media-president relationship, especially how it has evolved in the era of electronic journalism. We will suggest that the media not only reflect and report on presidential politics but that they *cause* many of the problems and crises confronting the presidency today. No political institution in the United States is affected more profoundly by the media than the presidency, for the role is tailor-made for our national entertainment-based media.

NUMBER ONE CELEBRITY

No president can afford to ignore the techniques, style, and needs of the various communications media if he hopes to survive beyond four years. Truman once wrote his sister, "All the president is is a glorified public relations man who spends his time flattering, kissing and kicking people to get them to do what they are supposed to do anyway."[1] An aide to Reagan admitted as much years later: "There is a general misconception about how a president uses his time. The bulk of what he does is to communicate and reinforce messages, even to his own bureaucracy."[2] Carter's press secretary, Jody Powell, conceded that a major reason for Carter's failure as president was that he spent too much time bogged down in details and too little time thinking about how to sell his policies.[3]

Presidents cannot succeed without the media, but they have difficulty surviving because of the media, which make every president into a celebrity. Sustaining the public's interest and affection as a celebrity is no small challenge today. In the pre-electronic past, whenever a great man appeared in U.S. public life, people looked for some kind of divine purpose. Now they look to see who is his press agent or image adviser. Daniel Boorstin has suggested that there is a significant difference between greatness—the attribute of a genuine hero—and fame, which belongs to anyone who can gain celebrity status. Earlier presidents occasionally were considered heroes because of what they accomplished or did. Media professionals now have ways of creating instant fame by making someone into a celebrity through the national media. Celebrities become known because of *who* they are, not especially for *what* they have accomplished. They are recognized for their images, and their continued celebrity status depends on how well they can keep their images in the mass media.[4]

Celebrities may be created more quickly than ever before, but they also die more rapidly than in the past. Too much exposure wears out a celebrity image; consequently celebrities pass from the public scene almost as quickly as they appear and are then replaced by new faces.[5]

The mass media enable a president to "achieve an omnipresence in the general flow of news and awareness of the average citizen which in itself has vast implications for the shaping of both national opinion and public policy."[6] This media saturation of the presidency provides Americans with a staggering amount of news and information about the man in the White House, but it also creates a significant risk of overexposure. It is a rare day one does not see or hear the president in the national media. No photographs or television footage of President Reagan appeared for four days after he underwent surgery for a gunshot wound to his chest following the 1981 assassination attempt. The four weeks that Reagan did not appear on television at all was the longest time in the history of the medium that the tube failed to record a president.

PRESIDENTS AND THE MEDIA: A TEMPESTUOUS MARRIAGE

The relationship between the president and the mass media is comparable to a marriage between two parties who cannot get along with each other but who cannot stand breaking up. Rather than a marriage of passion, it is more one of convenience. The press needs the president because he is the star of political news, fulfilling important media needs for entertainment, personalization, oversimplification, and high drama. Nothing in politics or the news is better suited than the White House to satisfy the public's limited curiosity and interest in government. The media are essential to the president, for they constitute the conduits through which he reaches out to the public to build the popularity and influence needed for leadership.

Tensions are inevitable because presidents always attempt to use the media as extensions of their own White House publicity efforts. Reporters have a responsibility for maximizing the impact of their stories from the White House as well as in reporting, analyzing, and frequently criticizing the president's actions. The responsibilities of the media and the needs of the president clash because the public's right to know often runs counter to the president's need to preserve his image, protect his confidences, and enhance his flexibility.

The tension also stems from fundamental differences in the values sought by each of the two sides. Because our media are primarily profit-seeking enterprises, they must gear their coverage of politics to mass audiences normally apathetic about the subject. Consequently the leading imperative for journalists reporting on the White House is to magnify the presidential personality while providing news accounts which are exciting, dramatic, colorful, timely, and filled with conflict.

The president for his part is forced to concentrate on image and appearance, spending countless hours devising tactics to win over the

"Bea doesn't like to hear any criticism of Reagan because he's such a hunk."

media or to shortcut them. Nothing a president decides or does escapes the need to consider how the media will treat him. Because the president's powers are so ephemeral and are mostly based on his ability to rally public opinion behind him, the media factor usually is the single most important criterion in his decision making.

In recent years some observers have suggested that hostility or antagonism constitutes the dominant attitude reporters and presidents have had toward one another. In fact, there are many moments of mutual stroking. The president, his White House assistants, and managers of publishing and broadcasting enterprises try to avoid conflict whenever possible because each side has much to gain by cooperating with the other. "Those who lead the major news organizations as well as most of those who serve as senior advisers to the president will go to considerable lengths to attain and maintain cordial relations with each other," according to Michael Baruch Grossman and Martha Joynt Kumar, political scientists who have studied the White House–news media relationship.[7] The relationship seems destined to deteriorate, however, because of the frustrations and antagonisms that develop between the White House and press corps over the physical setup and organizational structure linking them, as well as because of conflicting goals. No president can permit the press the kind of intimacy it seeks with him, while the press cannot shirk its constitutional responsibility to be a watchful critic of government.

Each president, operating on the assumption that what the press does *not* know cannot hurt him, attempts to manage the news or to utilize the technology of mass communications to avoid embarrassment or revelations about his shortcomings. Nixon entered office with an innate hatred and distrust of the press but a realistic understanding of its power over the presidency. In his memoirs he wrote that he was prepared to do combat with the media in order to get his views and programs to the people. But he felt that despite all the power and visibility he would enjoy as president, the combat would not be between equals. "The media are far more powerful than the president in creating public awareness and shaping public opinion, for the simple reason that the media always have the last word."[8]

From the beginning Nixon was determined to damage the credibility of the national press before it could undermine his. He sought to intimidate and to harass the national networks and major print media through a series of carefully orchestrated public attacks by Vice-President Spiro T. Agnew, and by using such federal agencies as the Federal Communications Commission and the Federal Bureau of Investigation. The FCC indirectly threatened removal of licenses from television stations not providing "impartial treatment" of the administration, and the FBI was used to investigate CBS reporter Daniel Schorr under the pretext he was being considered for a job.[9]

Every president begins by believing that the public will gladly support him as long as it understands him, and that it will understand him so long as he can reach the public with the force of his personality and logic. The media are essential to his purpose, but when the media are seen as in the hands of adversaries, the president begins to limit his accessibility and to "hunker down," as Lyndon Johnson liked to put it, regarding journalists with the same distrust early western pioneers felt toward Indians circling their covered wagons.

A president feels compelled to deal with political problems he believes are the most important, at his convenience, and on his own schedule. The press insists on its prerogative to decide what is most important on the public agenda. The pressures of competition and newsworthiness force journalists to constantly seek information that is live as well as lively. News is a highly perishable commodity and what happened yesterday is history. The press consequently tries to uncover details and plans at a time when the Executive Branch is trying to formulate, bargain, negotiate, or build coalitions.

A president must proceed cautiously, secretively, and incrementally, working against innumerable roadblocks built into our fragmented governmental structures. Dealing with countless other decision makers, the president must act politically, bureaucratically, and manipulatively if he is to achieve any success. The press, meanwhile, is on the lookout for evidence that the president is acting out of political motivations, as if being political was one of the worst traits a president could possess. The media search and probe for stories which lend themselves to audience appeal, but in the process the president is inhibited in his freedom of action. The press is often responsible for tipping off opponents of the president to his strategy, for sabotaging confidences, and frequently for making life miserable for the White House.

A GROWING HOSTILITY BETWEEN PRESIDENT AND PRESS

The Grossman-Kumar study of White House–press relations found that coverage of presidents was generally favorable until the Johnson administration, but that a steady decline in the press-president relationship has set in since the 1960s. White House–media relations appear to have fallen into a predictable pattern in recent years in which each new administration starts out with a reasonably cozy relationship, but inevitably separation if not divorce follows.[10]

The most favorable coverage as far as the White House is concerned occurs during an "alliance phase"—the first few weeks and months of an administration, when it is enjoying a honeymoon with the public. Attention centers on the president as a personality, on his style, and on his family. The tone of the content is almost embarrassingly folksy. Excited by the newness of the celebrity in the White House, the press falls all over its typewriters and cameras to reveal that he does not beat his wife or servants, and that he really is a down-to-earth fellow.

As the president becomes embroiled in decisions or choices that reward some and penalize others, coverage shifts to a "competition phase" and the relationship turns adversarial. Reporters now concentrate on the president's involvement in conflicts among personalities and controversies over policies. Disputes between White House staff members and the cabinet begin to reveal the political side of the president, and cynicism—both on the part of the press corps and the White House—replaces cooperation.

The press and president enter a "detachment phase" during the last months of an administration, characterized by the press leveling off in its criticisms and the president increasingly delegating his press relations to surrogates. Detachment occurs because there is a limit to how long the media or the White House can allow hostility to continue since each needs the other. Consequently, relations are resumed but formally and somewhat awkwardly. The president meets with reporters a bit more frequently but in controlled settings; otherwise he avoids them.

White House staff members are more protective of the president than ever before because there has been a major shift in the past decade in the attitude of the press toward politicians, especially presidents. Journalists have grown more adversarial in their treatment of presidents as well as all other political leaders. Mass-communications scholar Paul Weaver suggests this is the result of a series of incidents since the 1950s in which politicians were caught deceiving the press and public.[11]

Throughout most of our history, a relatively cooperative relationship has existed between the White House and the press. But beginning with the Gary Powers–U-2 episode in 1960, that relationship started to erode. When Powers was shot down and captured while on a spy flight over the USSR, President Eisenhower initially told the press he knew nothing about the mission, but soon thereafter he admitted that he had been aware that such flights took place. Media confidence in the White House was further dimmed by the Bay of Pigs fiasco in 1961. The *New York Times* withheld publication of a story it had uncovered about a pending secret invasion of Cuba on an appeal from President Kennedy, who claimed national security would be jeopardized if the story were published. Kennedy later publicly chided the *Times* for *not* printing the story and thereby preventing what ended up as the worst foreign-policy fiasco in the Kennedy administration. The credibility gap between the White House and news media widened as a result of President Johnson's misleading or distorted pronouncements about Vietnam. Watergate, however, was the crowning blow, and any remaining vestiges of trust or respect for the presidency on the part of journalists were virtually destroyed.

Watergate provided all reporters with a new inspiration for muckraking in political journalism. Two *Washington Post* reporters, Carl Bernstein and Bob Woodward, became rich and famous as the result of their unraveling of the scandal. Reporters traditionally had been discreet about the private lives of political leaders. FDR was never photographed showing him crippled in a wheelchair, nor was his affliction ever mentioned in news stories. His secret meetings with Lucy Rutherford were never mentioned by journalists, even though many knew about them. But no longer would presidents be treated with kid gloves. After Watergate, every prominent political celebrity would be fair game for whatever peccadillos, gossip, or personal shortcomings a reporter could dig up.

The new adversarial journalism clearly has contributed to the public disenchantment and cynicism toward the presidency in recent years. Hamilton Jordan, President Carter's chief adviser, asserts in his memoirs that the changing attitudes of the White House press corps were mostly responsible for an enormous divergence between what Carter accomplished and how he was perceived by the public:

> *Jimmy Carter underestimated—as all presidents do—the aggressiveness and hostility of the White House press, although we did recognize and accept the basic adversarial nature of that relationship, realizing there had never been a president who was pleased with his press coverage. We did not, however, understand or appreciate the extent to which the Washington press corps had changed in the past decade.*[12]

Despite this trend, each new president starts his administration by courting the press as carefully as a bridegroom does a new bride, believing that *his* relationship will survive where others failed. The president hopes that by being open, frank, and courteous, he can win over the media and thereby succeed in getting his policy goals across to the public. When the ardor between journalists and president cools, the temptation is to then turn to in-house media professionals to sell the president. The president desperately *needs* the media, but if the Washington and national press corps does not respond to his charms, he will use his own professionals to reach the public.

Each president pays a steep price for this preoccupation with mass media forms, however. He must fit his political and personal style and actions to the demands of a communications system that is first and foremost geared to entertainment. As a result, each president risks acting less like a leader and more like a directed performer. Unable to trust his fate to an increasingly more cynical and inquisitive national press, each incumbent finds himself growing dependent on White House flacks whose press-agentry—as we noted in Chapter 5—feeds on itself.

The White House media establishment that has evolved during the past fifteen years dwarfs the news operations of most giant media organizations. An army of press agents, speech writers, public-relations professionals, and "image" experts now surround the president to fend off threatening attacks by the "killer press" (see the discussion in Chapter 5, pages 223 to 225). Nixon, who was more dependent on his own White House propaganda machine than any president before or since, has noted of this dependence:

> *In the modern presidency, concern for image must rank with concern for substance—there is no guarantee that good programs will automatically triumph. "Elections are not won or lost by*

programs," I once reminded Haldeman. . . . "They are won or lost by how these programs are presented to the country and how the political and public relations considerations are handled." I do not like this situation; I can remember a time in American politics when it was not the case. But today it is a fact of life . . . and anyone who seeks a position of leadership must master it.[13]

Ironically, the president's turn inward to his own media super-salespeople only serves to whet the appetite of journalists for revealing the nakedness of the emperor. Reporters complain that every president has immense resources in his speech writers, press secretaries, and propagandists on the payroll to disseminate the party line. The press can only counter this barrage of self-serving propaganda by concentrating on what is being concealed, evaded, denied, or distorted.[14]

TR: THE PRESIDENT AS PRESS AGENT

Concerns about image and press coverage did not begin with recent presidents or with television. The American press has been deeply involved in presidential politics from the start, and early newspapers were key agents in the development of mass-based political parties linking candidates to the electorate. Not until the turn of this century, however, would an incumbent president boldly and systematically attempt to manipulate the press to popularize his personal public image and to make his White House a "bully pulpit."

Three elements combined to make Theodore Roosevelt America's first media celebrity president. First and foremost was his colorful and irrepressible personality. Roosevelt's fearless charge with his volunteer Rough Riders up San Juan Hill during the Spanish-American war made him the most famous man in America, and "Teddy"—as he became known to everyone—could not resist reminding his fellow citizens of his heroic deed. Garbed in his Rough Rider uniform in public, TR cultivated a hero's image, which eventually carried him into the vice-presidency and then to the White House.

Republican leaders thought Roosevelt a madman because of his progressive ideas and his madcap behavior in public. But the news media and the American people never ceased to be intrigued and occasionally amazed by their unorthodox president. TR delighted the nation with such antics as climbing trees on the White House lawn for exercise, tumbling in the White House library with a Japanese wrestler, or swimming naked in the icy Potomac, accompanied by shivering and less enthusiastic members of his cabinet. On one occasion he hailed a horse-drawn cab on Pennsylvania Avenue, seized the startled horse, and mimed a knife attack on the confused creature. Once he surprised passengers on a trolley car by making grimacing faces at them from his presidential carriage.[15]

There was considerable method to Roosevelt's zany behavior. Presidents prior to TR rarely felt that the press needed to be catered to or the public wooed. Roosevelt, however, realized that his tenuous relationship with Republican party chieftains meant that his personal power and his progressive policy agenda depended on establishing a direct and personal appeal with the public. The growing interest of the press in the presidency offered Roosevelt the channels of political communication through which he could develop his personal influence and power. Richard Rubin, a student of media politics, notes:

> *Unlike his immediate predecessors, Roosevelt not only welcomed pervasive public exposure but also sought to deploy it for planned political advantage, hoping to instigate broad electoral support for himself and his policies* across *party lines.*
>
> *Roosevelt's direct cultivation of public opinion outside partisan channels . . . mark[ed] the beginnings of a partial but important* disengagement *of the president from party.*[16]

Roosevelt changed dramatically "the expectations of the press and public alike by establishing a new sense of what a president should be like, and how he should relate to both press and public."[17] The changing role of the news media in American life at the turn of the century afforded TR a perfect opportunity to advance his quixotic personality and conception of the role. Technical improvements in newspaper production along with a significant drop in the cost of newsprint made newspapers both profitable and readily available to masses of people who seldom had used them before. Mass-circulation dailies evolved which created interest in the national government for the first time for millions of people. Inevitably the presidency emerged as the prime source of news, partly because of the status of the office but also because the always fascinating TR occupied it.

TR rarely disappointed reporters. He provided reporters covering the White House with their first press room; he held news conferences in the Oval Office; and he leaked choice items to friendly reporters. News conferences were more like pep rallies or lectures; the president would beguile reporters with personal anecdotes on nature, big-game hunting, economics, politics, football, poetry, art, and literature. It was said that Roosevelt "discovered Monday" because he would release important statements to reporters on Sunday evening, fully aware that it was a slow news day and whatever he announced then would probably receive prominent coverage on Monday's front pages.[18]

Roosevelt did not gladly suffer reporters who crossed him or who wrote things with which he disagreed or who cast him in an unflattering light. He particularly disliked journalists prying into his personal life, and occasionally he banned individual reporters from the White House. In general, however, he usually enjoyed reporters and was frequently solititous for their comfort and needs. He established a pattern for press relations that continued until newer mass-communications technologies reduced the status of print media reporters.

None of the five presidents who followed TR proved as effective in dealing with the press or in mobilizing public opinion. Wilson inaugurated regular press conferences and hired the first full-time press secretary. But Wilson was too dour and aloof to make the White House into a "bully pulpit." Wilson's inability to rally public opinion behind the League of Nations became a personal tragedy as well as a public-relations and political failure. During the 1920s the White House sank to a twentieth-century low as a source of news, largely because of the insensitivity of Presidents Harding, Coolidge, and Hoover to the great value of manipulating the press. Not until Franklin D. Roosevelt would another president prove to be a consummate master of the media, and once again success was tied to a newly emerging technology in mass communications that enabled the White House to reach out to the nation.

FDR: THE VOICE IN THE LIVING ROOM

"When I became president, I found a country demoralized [and] . . . disorganized," Franklin D. Roosevelt declared during the 1938 congressional election campaign. "[A] great part of my duty as president has been to do what I could to bring our people together again."[19] Roosevelt was well aware he would need the press if he were to successfully reach out to the public, but he was also alert to the hostility of most of the conservative owners of the mass media. Roosevelt knew he had to win over the White House reporters and many editors who did not share the political convictions of the owners of the media. He also would have to reach over the heads of the press to the people directly if he were to get his message out.

FDR's early cultivation of the press is legendary. He was sensitive to the professional concerns of reporters, and he maintained friendly relations with them even as he sought to sabotage the credibility of their bosses. Roosevelt held wide-open, lively, and provocative press conferences twice a week, and they were usually filled with solid news and quotable quotes. Flamboyant, gregarious, and witty, Roosevelt enjoyed a certain give-and-take with reporters. He was never reluctant to act like an editor, suggesting how a story should be written, what the lead paragraph should be, and even the format of the story. Jack Bell, an Associated Press White House correspondent, had the following recollection of FDR's press technique:

> *He talked in headline phrases. He acted, he emoted; he was angry, he was smiling. He was persuasive, he was demanding; he was philosophical, he was elemental. He was sensible, he was unreasonable; he was benevolent, he was malicious. He was satirical, he was soothing; he was funny, he was gloomy. He was exciting. He was human. He was copy.*[20]

Given the opposition of the press lords, however, conflict with the press was unavoidable. Reporters could be irritated by FDR's patronizing manner. Through sarcasm he could humiliate any reporter he considered unfair or guilty of distorting the "facts." (He once told a reporter who had asked a prickly question to "go off to the corner and put on your dunce cap.")[21] After World War II broke out, Roosevelt's contacts with the press grew fewer and his personal ties with reporters less chummy, but he still managed to hold a total of 998 press conferences in just over twelve years. Roosevelt believed the proper role of the press was to be a channel through which information about government could flow to the public to keep it well informed. He held that government itself was the major if not exclusive source of facts, and any opinions added to these facts by the press were distortions.[22] Newspaper readers consequently should not believe unfavorable stories because they contained editorial or publisher biases, and Roosevelt's contempt extended beyond the bosses to include political columnists, even those generally favorable to his administration.

His attempt to manipulate the working press was only half of FDR's mass-communications strategy. The other half involved a carefully planned effort to control his public exposure on the relatively new medium of radio, which Roosevelt used to cast himself as the nation's chief political educator. If the press could never be relied on to provide the "facts" to the American people, the president would— through direct appeals over the airwaves.

In the 1930s radio tied together into nationwide networks people who had been separated culturally and regionally ever since the founding of the nation. Radio rivalled and later surpassed large daily newspapers and national magazines as the most profitable channel for advertising and merchandising. For FDR, radio represented the perfect marriage between personality and medium, for it permitted him to use his polished voice and ham-acting ability to get his message across to the entire nation without interference from publishers, columnists, or media kingpins.

Gifted with a patrician voice and a style of delivery that was never patronizing, Roosevelt had the unique talent of making listeners feel as if the president were personally *there* in the living room, speaking directly to them. For most of the generation that grew up during the Great Depression, their first memory of politics came while sitting beside the radio hearing *that* voice. According to journalist David Halberstam:

> *Most Americans in the previous 160 years had never even seen a president; now almost all of them were hearing him, in their own homes. It was literally and figuratively electrifying. Because he was the president, he had access to the airwaves any time he wanted, when he wanted. Because he was such a good performer, because his messages so bound the nation, the networks wanted him on more often regularly.*[23]

FDR managed to establish the identification of *his* personality with the national government so thoroughly that every president thereafter would be challenged to prove himself the master of the media or fall short of public expectations.

HARRY S. TRUMAN: A PLAINSPOKEN PRESIDENT

FDR's success proved to be a hard act to follow for Harry Truman, who was almost the antithesis of Roosevelt when it came to public relations. Brusque, direct, and short-fused in temperament, Truman frequently fired off public salvos that were personally embarrassing and seemed demeaning to the presidency. He was unable to change his image of a small-time, machine politician nor did he appear to go out of his way to charm the press or public. Although some reporters were close to Truman, he was cocky and combative toward most of the press. Truman believed that the press in general, and a number of columnists and reporters in particular, were unfair to him and his family. One of his most notorious public outbursts came after *Washington Post* music critic Paul Hume panned daughter Margaret's singing debut. Truman wrote Hume that he was going to flatten the critic's nose and kick him "in the nuts." On another occasion Truman called columnist Drew Pearson into the Oval Office to give him a tongue-lashing for a column in which Pearson claimed a special train had been dispatched from Washington to Independence, Missouri, to bring Margaret back to the White House. "Back where I come from, we put our women on pedestals," Truman told Pearson. "You see that drawer over there?" Truman asked, pointing to his desk. "I've got a gun in there and I'll blow your damn brains out if you ever write a lie like that again about my daughter or my wife," the president told an ashen-faced Pearson.[24]

Truman's image seemed not only a bit too crude for the presidency but it also suggested an uninformed and awkward man in public appearances. He was never as comfortable nor as polished as Roosevelt in using the radio. Truman believed that resorting to the radio was not far from demagoguery. "I hope it will never come about [that] the man with a sweet voice and great personality . . . could do things to this country if he could control the air[waves]."[25] Nor did Truman make much of an effort to utilize the brand-new and as yet poorly understood medium of television, although he made the first television broadcast ever from the White House.

EISENHOWER: AN AUTHENTIC MEDIA HERO

Many men find it difficult to appear presidential even after they have won the office with the approval of their fellow citizens. Occasionally, one appears to have been born to the role; Dwight D. Eisenhower was one of these.

Eisenhower was an authentic hero, the victorious commander of Allied forces in World War II, and the possessor of a remarkable instinct for leadership. He had warmth, but this was matched by sincerity, humility, and seemingly a lack of excessive ambition. He was as uncomfortable as Truman had been with the media technology available to the presidency. In public appearances Eisenhower often became bogged down in garbled syntax, sentences without ends, and a strange new vocabulary. (*Prioritize* and *finalize* were among his most notable contributions to the American language.) His lack of ease in public forums, however, only seemed to enhance his personal appeal for he appeared all-too-human, a man who could not be packaged no matter how slick the salesmanship.

Eisenhower's press conferences were formal and infrequent, but he received generally favorable press coverage because of James C. Hagerty, his talented press secretary. Hagerty provided reporters with a great deal of substantive news about his chief, thereby undercutting some of the frustrations White House reporters had in trying to cover a president who was not overly accessible.

Hagerty encouraged Eisenhower's use of television because the image that stood out indelibly was that of a sincere man doing his best to perform the awesome duties of the presidency. Significantly, Eisenhower was the first president to have his press conferences regularly televised, but not live. They were filmed and then edited by Hagerty before release to the networks.

CAMELOT ON TELEVISION: JFK AND THE MEDIA

Television may have increased Eisenhower's popularity, but for John F. Kennedy television was the vitalizing force behind his nomination, election, and conduct of the presidency.

Kennedy was a national political celebrity whose following was developed not within the channels of the old-fashioned political party, but via the channels of national network television. The decline of political party influence over the selection process and in government had begun long before Kennedy. But television, in tandem with the Kennedy administration's approach to the medium, combined to accelerate the rate of party decline.

Before Kennedy, television coverage of the White House had been relatively conventional: hard news about decisions, policymaking, political maneuvering, and conflict in the Executive Branch, or stories about the conflict between the president and Congress. Occasionally personal glimpses into the life of the First Family were offered, but television did not reflect the preoccupation with the personal life of the president that would come with Kennedy. JFK and his glamorous family came to dominate the screen as if they were the creation of a gifted script writer. Television seemed to "create more and more public curiosity about the man as more and more was written and broadcast about him," according to public-opinion experts Harold Mendelsohn and Irving Crespi. Eventually, some observers became concerned that an "overemphasis on the 'trivia' of the president's life might well divert the public from the pursuit of the 'serious' aspects of politics."[26]

Kennedy's White House staff reflected JFK's press-wise outlook because many of its members had media experience. Reporters enjoyed access to White House officials without prior clearance. Kennedy granted frequent interviews and numerous background briefings, and he maintained intimate friendships with several journalists. But he was aware that excessive reliance or overexposure on television could cheapen his image. Therefore, Kennedy used spontaneous televised press conferences more often than direct appeals. Holding the first live-televised presidential press conference in history, Kennedy appeared candid, informal, witty, well-informed, articulate, and quick—a virtually flawless television performer. "Hollywood could not have done any better in preparing a spectacular," mused *Time*'s White House correspondent. "In a sense, that's what it was."[27]

In fact, Kennedy's televised press conferences were instrumental in making the president a cult hero. Rubin asserts:

The press conferences elicit[ed] a tremendous mail response largely because of television coverage. . . . [T]elevision only par-

tially satiated the vast public curiosity about the president. This young man was a center of national attention virtually every day of his tenure in office. A substantial portion of the citizenry, their appetites whetted by all of the mass media, placed John F. Kennedy and his family in a hero-worshipping category formerly reserved for movie stars and the like.

Revealed to the nation was a terribly vigorous, aggressively dynamic, and yet deeply introspective personality. Television suited him well, and he seemed made for it—a true partnership of man and medium.[28]

TELEVISION'S LONGEST-RUNNING SHOW: THE PRESIDENCY

Newspapers at the turn of the century paved the way for a massive expansion of public interest in and information about national government. Television had a similar but much more exaggerated impact from 1960 on. Prior to Kennedy, television had had little or no great impact on politics, but after his election the three major networks would find the office irresistible. In 1963 the networks expanded their evening newscasts from fifteen minutes to a half-hour. The White House, glowing alabaster-white behind the network correspondent, became the best-known backdrop in America as each evening the president's day was described in measured, clipped, and authoritative sentences.

A majority of Americans know the president only through television. With an exposure frequency and a name identification that is the envy of any entertainment celebrity or film star, the president is provided with an immense amount of publicity. But this same massive media exposure also sets the president up as the focal point for ultimate political failure or frustration. Much like a powerful magnifying glass, television enlarges and brings the presidency into vivid relief. But a magnifying glass can burn or destroy if focused too intensely, and television overemphasizes the president at the expense of other political actors and institutions so much that few incumbents can measure up.

Television emerged in the 1960s as the public's dominant entertainment and information source at the same time that the presidency as a public leadership role was commencing its steady and disturbing decline. The costly nature of television programming time with the resulting need to generate national audiences forces the medium to overemphasize entertainment rather than information. As a result, Americans see and hear more about the president than ever before, but much of what they receive via television is froth rather than substance and titillation rather than enlightenment.

Most of the communications Americans receive about the president originate from the White House press corps, some sixty newspaper, newsmagazine, radio, and television correspondents who cover the president as a full-time beat. In addition, nationally syndicated columnists, network news anchors, and other prominent journalists enjoy limited access to the president and cover his activities because they are newsworthy. For many years the wire services, which represent hundreds of newspapers and news outlets, were the most important news organizations covering the White House, and wire-service senior correspondents were the most influential reporters in the White House press corps. But television has long since restructured the pecking order in the White House pressroom because of its near-universal dominance in American media-use patterns.

White House officials keep television in mind when they make up the president's schedule. Announcements and appearances are set to make the deadlines of the evening network news. Television cameras and lights create an atmosphere similar to a movie set. The networks keep a correspondent on duty throughout the day whenever the president is in the White House. A crew of technicians is on standby at all times for coverage of fast-breaking events, crises, or announcements.

Research confirms a strong relationship between press coverage of public issues and the salience of those issues in the public mind.[29] Television now sets the national political agenda because of its saturation of the media market and because it is a low-intensity medium that encourages mass audiences to fill in the details of fleeting images and situations. In requiring personalized involvement by the viewer, the medium brings a subjective reality to the images it projects, giving viewers the feeling of participating in dramatic political events without the effort normally required in understanding the serious abstractions or details involved.[30]

Political scientist Murray Edelman argues that "people for whom politics is not important want symbols and not information, dramatic in outline, devoid of detail and of the realistic recognition of uncertainties and of opposing considerations."[31] Television is ideally suited for such preferences because its coverage is condensed, vivid, uncomplicated, and focused on personality and style. This presents imposing challenges to a president because the test of his capacities for leadership is increasingly tied as much to the quality of his video appearance as to his political skills or acumen.

Network White House correspondents are especially influential because they define the president's image for millions of viewers. Gaining the attention of a network anchorman such as CBS's Dan Rather, NBC's Tom Brokaw, or ABC's Peter Jennings adds legitimacy and authenticity to the president's image because such news figures are themselves national celebrities who possess credibility with the people.

Since television virtually monopolizes our national attention, it can actually overwhelm reality and create the very events it is covering. During the coverage of the attempted assassination of President Reagan, CBS reported that White House Press Secretary James Brady had died of a bullet wound to his head, information reported by a CBS correspondent who had been told by members of Brady's staff that they had heard that he was dead. *Their* source was CBS news. The network reported a rumor it had itself originally started. (Fortunately for Brady, CBS was wrong!)

Television transmits images more successfully than issues or ideas because, as Marshall McLuhan has noted, in a highly visual culture "it is as difficult to communicate the nonvisual properties of spatial forms as to explain visuality to the blind."[32] Television facilitates a new and seemingly intimate relationship between the politician and audience, according to political communications scholar Bernard Rubin. "Impressions about a politician—images of personality, leadership, values, and successfulness—are now brought together visually."[33] The "perfect" president thus is he who best projects television's "cool" image.

Television effectively shapes the viewers' images of national political figures, both those in office and these bidding for office, providing "a new set of criteria which enable viewers to shape expectations of what an American president should be and [which] help them to make judgments of a particular president as he is."[34]

PRESIDENTIAL NEWS THEATER

Theater critic Robert Brustein has called the resulting impact of mass media on politics *news theater*—"any histrionic proceeding that results from a collaboration between newsworthy personalities, a vast public, and the visual or print media."[35] Celebrities like Norman Mailer, Truman Capote, Billy Graham, Carl Sagan, and Johnny Carson become participants in news theater because who they are makes what they say or do newsworthy. Some who would never make it in Hollywood or New York achieve a kind of news theater notoriety with dramatic, horrifying deeds—such as John W. Hinckley, Jr., for his attempt on Reagan's life, or Sirhan B. Sirhan, for killing Robert F. Kennedy. The president of the United States is accorded the nation's leading role in news theater not by any single action or his performance but on the basis of expectations generated by his position, visibility, and status.

If the president is unable to perform with reasonable consistency to the needs of the media, he risks losing his ratings in public-opinion polls or having his show cancelled in a reelection bid. The notion of news theater applied to the president suggests that any chief executive hoping to capture the attention and loyalty of the public must be concerned not only with the image he projects but also with how well he is performing on television. The medium requires certain standards or features if it is to go over with viewers. Above all else, television must be entertaining because audiences want to be entertained rather than educated or informed. If real life does not provide the needed elements of entertainment, "pseudo-events" must be created to replace reality. Television accounts need to be self-contained mini-dramas or stories with clear-cut beginnings and ends, a conflict between good and evil, and a sense of completeness. Video presentations must also be timely, providing a sense of immediacy and involvement in the events portrayed.

The White House Story

News reporters are first and foremost storytellers. The quest for news is a quest for all the elements that make an interesting story. Television sharply condenses stories to the dimensions of 30, 60, or 120 seconds—on rare occasions, perhaps several minutes. Television consequently is under considerable pressure to cast reality into highly condensed dramatic stories or episodes. The evening half-hour news program, minus commercials, leaves only 22 minutes for actual news content. A 2-minute story is long by such standards, for time is an extremely valuable commodity. Because of the constant need to make content conform to the constraints of program time as well as entertainment, television must convert untidy, confusing, and chaotic reality into greatly oversimplified dramas salable to mass audiences. Scenes must be ordered into sequences that have inner logic and consistency; as a result, what is shown reflects what television producers know to be important.

A favorite technique involves the use of what mass-communications scholars Dan Nimmo and James Combs have called *nowism*. This means finding in a single event a "pattern, trend, or moral encompassing past, present, and future."[36] Nowism enables television to communicate a sense of immediacy that is peculiarly and devilishly effective. For millions of Americans, "personal qualities come across in a way no other medium can match. [D]istance is narrowed and time condensed. [And] showmanship can be used to define or illustrate issues, or to confuse them."[37] Pronouncements are terse and charged with importance because the flow of events is compressed into highly abbreviated segments of 30, 60, 90, or 120 seconds. The television story must present, nonetheless, a *complete* theme or the impression of a completed action or idea.

The presidency is uniquely suited for such requirements on a systematic daily basis. The story format of television creates and reinforces symbols, making news into a series of morality plays—today's equivalent of the legends and myths of folk societies.

By sharply condensing complex and obtuse reality into manageable dimensions, television is implying that if the president acts properly or logically, he ought to be successful most of the time. Reducing the government to the dimensions of a single person enables television to pinpoint responsibility for inflation, for America's success in the world, or for the failure of the federal government to balance its budget. A president obliges by acting as if he were indeed responsible for leading political, social, or economic events and trends. He implies that with public support he could succeed.

Presidential Entertainment

Bleeding from a gunshot wound to his chest after an assassination attempt, President Reagan gave an Academy Award–winning performance in the tense aftermath of the drama that unfolded on the nation's television screens late in March 1981. Aware of the risk of some public hysteria or of the danger to national security if he appeared badly wounded or incapacitated, Reagan insisted on walking into the emergency room of George Washington University Hospital even though he had difficulty breathing and felt faint. Acting as if he were the least anxious person around about his condition, the president treated doctors and aides to a series of one-liners, which were repeated to the press and then to a nervous nation and world. To his wife, Nancy, Reagan quipped, "Honey, I forgot to duck." To surgeons about to operate, he asked, "Please tell me you're all Republicans." Awakening from surgery, he scribbled on a pad, "All in all, I'd rather be in Philadelphia," the classic movie line uttered by W. C. Fields when asked by vigilantes about to hang him if he had any last wish. Hearing from a nurse that she would spend the night in the recovery room with him, Reagan asked if his wife knew.

Reagan's performance was that of a seasoned actor, sensitively attuned to the needs of the audience at the moment. Public-opinion polls showed a sharp rise in his popularity and performance as president, largely as a result of the courage and humor he displayed at a point when his life was in danger. Falling back on the tried-but-true actor's tactic of "leave them laughing," Reagan showed that a president skilled in the art of entertaining can capture public opinion and by the force of personality, style, and performance win people over. Such a performance projects convincingly many of the images or illusions about presidential leadership that are part of the public's myths and expectations.

This show-business aspect of presidential leadership has led some Democratic party supporters to suggest that Robert Redford or Warren Beatty, two of Hollywood's handsomest stars, might be the party's answer to Ronald Reagan in a future election contest. The emergence of stars as presidential material is not surprising since television and politics are virtually made for each other. Walter Cronkite, in fact, was suggested in 1980 as a potential vice-presidential candidate, if not an exciting possibility for the top job itself. If the Founding Fathers had not created the presidency, television producers probably would have had to, for the role is a natural for the medium.

Television and politics are "soul mates who rely on contrived drama, anxiety-ridden rhetoric, and theatrical settings."[38] Presidents may not see themselves as in the business of entertainment, but if they accept Truman's dictum that the prime task of a president is to persuade people, and if the single most powerful tool available to persuade people is television, then no president can hope to survive without mastering the techniques of the entertainer.

This does not mean that every president must be facile at unleashing one-liners, or that he must look like Robert Redford or have the articulation skill of Lord Laurence Olivier. It does suggest, however, that other things being equal, the president or candidate with such talents now has a distinct advantage over one who lacks them. The average person has only so much attention span, and politics is not a vital part of that attention. In a culture in which our senses are bombarded with a bewildering array of messages from the real world and from the realm of illusion and mass merchandising, attention is even more difficult to attract, hold, and influence.

THE QUEST FOR THE KENNEDY COOL

Four presidents who followed Kennedy in the White House found that the Kennedy television mystique was difficult if not impossible to emulate. Because JFK performed so well on TV he set standards by which all subsequent presidents have been judged. Not until Reagan would one be found who was as talented as JFK in the use of the medium.

President Johnson on television reminded people of their least favorite Sunday-school teacher. Sanctimonious and heavy of countenance, LBJ would lecture in a thick drawl, shaking his finger at audiences as if he were a vengeful Old Testament prophet reproving sinners. His public image, however, was that of an old-fashioned political wheeler-dealer rather than a moralist, and his attempts to use television to appeal to public opinion often failed.

If Kennedy was the quintessential "cool" politician, Richard Nixon was the ideal representation of one who is "hot." During the 1968 presidential campaign, television producer Roger Ailes made the following observation on Nixon's image problem:

> *You put him on television, you've got a problem right away. He's a funny-looking guy. He looks like somebody hung him in a closet overnight and he jumps out in the morning with his suit all bunched up and starts running around saying, "I want to be president."*[39]

Nixon believed after his 1968 victory that he had mastered the medium, but he was mistaken. To Nixon, this meant using television to undermine his opponents, including members of the television press corps. It also meant advancing his policies without interference. He was successful for a time in his first administration in gaining public support for his Vietnam policy and other foreign policies. But in time Nixon found that to live by television can also mean to die by it. Televised news coverage of Watergate events and later the televised hearings of the Senate Select Committee on Watergate signalled disaster for his administration. Time and again Nixon appeared on television and tried to assure the public that he was innnocent of involvement in a coverup. Although he wore an American flag pin in his lapel, and had a bust of Lincoln prominently displayed on his desk, he still came across as the same old partisan, awkward politician whom the media experts had tried to restyle in 1968. Televised hearings of the House Judiciary Committee sifting evidence for impeachment charges ended with a vote to recommend impeachment proceedings to the House. Nixon's public image was damaged beyond repair. When the Supreme Court ordered him to hand over incriminating tape recordings to federal prosecutors, he was forced to resign.

President Ford assumed the presidency with immense goodwill and relief that, as he put it in his inaugural message to a joint session of Congress, "our long nightmare is over." But his pardon of Nixon one month later ended Ford's honeymoon with the public and press. He appeared on television as a likable man who was conventional, dull, and a bit slow. Not even the addition of a $40,000-a-year television joke writer to his staff could make Ford into a video star. An apocryphal line attributed to LBJ held that Jerry Ford was "so dumb he couldn't walk and chew gum at the same time." Ford seemed to live up to the image of a stumblebum during a televised debate with candidate Carter when Ford declared that the Polish people did not consider themselves under the heel of the Soviet Union.

Compared to Ford, Carter was dramatically different—a marked contrast to politically tainted presidents like Johnson and Nixon. Carter spoke to people as a modern-day reformer, a man of conscience come to set a disarrayed government in order by the force of his Christian example. He was entertaining because he was so different from the familiar and tired names and faces that had dominated presidential politics for almost twenty years. James Fallows, Carter's chief speech writer, said Carter owed his existence to television. His first weeks in the White House seemed to confirm the fact that Americans had elected a truly prime-time president. Barry Jagoda, his television adviser, predicted, "We've got the biggest star in television. Jimmy Carter may be the biggest television star of all time. . . . He looks normal on television, natural; most of all, he's *comfortable.*"[40]

On inauguration day Carter and his family repeated Thomas Jefferson's famous walk down Pennsylvania Avenue, signaling an unpretentious presidency. Carter held town meetings in hamlets in New England and the Midwest, conducted phone-ins for the public, and stayed in the homes of typical American families on occasional trips across the country. He was a real showstopper after the imperial presidents of recent years, coming across as soft-spoken and sincere. But after a half-year in office Carter retreated into the White House under a barrage of criticism over Bert Lance, a close friend whom he had appointed director of the Office of Management and Budget. After Lance was forced to resign as a result of criticisms of his personal financial dealings, the president reduced his exposure to the media and grew testy toward reporters.

Carter was perhaps one of the best presidential *candidates* to appear on television. But once elected president, he resumed a manner that was more comfortable for him—that of an engineer and meticulous planner. He seemed more concerned with keeping abreast of even the most minute aspects of his office than with entertaining the public. Carter *was* cool on television, but his coolness seemed to reflect the lack of self-image on his part. Often he seemed to be trying to discover who the *real* Jimmy Carter was. His speech did not project the slow cadences of a cool media personality. He was unable or unwilling to employ rhetorical flourishes or dramatic gestures that would excite people. Fallows later told how Carter and his aides resisted attempts to help the president develop a more effective way of speaking. They rejected speeches containing memorable phrases on the ground that such speeches might make Carter sound *too* presidential.[41] Late in his administration Carter engaged Atlanta publicist Gerald Rafshoon to make the president appear decisive and dramatic. But such efforts made the public even more unsure about who Jimmy Carter really was.

If Carter's television advisers at first thought that he was television's first presidential star, Reagan's advisers in the 1980 campaign *knew* that their candidate was a star. The fundamental strategy underlying their campaign was that *"Ronald Reagan is the best electronic media candidate in American history."*[42] Their approach was simple:

get Reagan in front of a television camera and have him talk directly to people whenever possible. Virtually the entire campaign was designed to maximize the differences between Reagan and Carter as political communicators and thus as political leaders. Reagan was comfortable with the strategy because it suited his entire life's experience. Before making his acceptance speech at the Republican national convention, Reagan attempted to quiet the cheering delegates by jokingly reminding them, "You're using up my prime time."

Carter always seemed to disappoint people on television, leaving the impression that the nation's problems were mostly the result of his own lack of forcefulness and decisiveness rather than of complex political forces. Reagan, on the other hand, used television as if it were a natural extension of his personality. Early in his administration, he dramatized with one simple but exceedingly effective gesture on television how inflation was shrinking the American dollar. Brandishing a dollar bill in one hand, he tossed a quarter, dime, and penny onto his desk, proclaiming that that was what the worst economic mess since the Great Depression had done to the once mighty dollar.

But Reagan's smoothness with television itself became the source of press cynicism and criticism. David Gergen, head of the White House Communications Office, admitted that as the White House became more and more a television stage, those managing the president's press relations tried to become stage managers. According to Gergen, "An enormous amount of time is spent trying to make the president look good. It is easy to become convinced that style is more important than reality." The tendency to "hype" events, which often results in accentuating crises or problems, may be good theater but it is terrible policy, Gergen conceded.

From the perspective of the White House communications staff, this situation is as much the fault of the media as of the White House. The media have focused an inordinate amount of attention on the presidency and forced the selling of the incumbent. Network news correspondents, however, lay the blame for staged presidential news on the White House. Reagan's White House press spokesperson, Larry Speakes, was irked by a reporter's criticism that Reagan was staging one phony media event after another while keeping the press at bay. Speakes snapped back, "Don't tell us how to stage the news, and we won't try to tell you how to cover it."[43]

WHITE HOUSE PSEUDO-EVENTS

The president may be television's leading news celebrity, but his activities usually do not rival normal television fare for excitement or drama. Either the medium or the White House must create the ele-

"DAMN MEDIA! YOU SHOULD KNOW BETTER THAN
TO REPORT ALL THE DOPEY THINGS HE SAYS"

WHITE HOUSE
SPOKESPEAK

Copyright 1983 by Herblock in the *Washington Post*.

ments that make for good television if they are not already at hand. However, what creates excitement or entertainment in television news may be threatening to the president, and coverage showing the president with his best foot forward may not meet television's criteria of a newsworthy story. As a result, television and the president spend much time and effort trying to inject color, verve, or drama into what comes out of the White House—partly to raise audience ratings, partly to generate favorable public-opinion ratings. A major tactic each side employs is to manufacture *pseudo-events*.

A pseudo-event is something not spontaneous but planned, an event that is deliberately designed to elicit a certain response.[44] Frequently public demonstrations, interviews, press conferences, or ceremonies designed to attract attention and fanfare are pseudo-events arranged for the convenience of the media (usually television). The success of such pseudo-events is gauged by how widely and extensively they are covered. The question of authenticity looms darkly over many pseudo-events, for whether or not they are real is often more significant than whether or not they are newsworthy. Normally pseudo-events are self-fulfilling prophecies, for their outcome must conform to the intention of their perpetrators. If not, control over the pseudo-events has been lost, and *real* news may result.

Presidents today dwell in a pseudo-eventful world. Almost constantly "on camera," they are caught in an ongoing performance that does not end as long as they inhabit the White House. An audience is always standing by to evaluate the performance. Some suggest this makes the White House a "goldfish bowl," but a more appropriate analogy is that the White House has become a permanent television studio. The strategy by which presidents attempt to upstage challengers to their office by conducting business in the White House rose garden symbolizes the use of pseudo-events.

Pseudo-events overwhelm spontaneous and real events because they satisfy the needs of television. Since pseudo-events are carefully planned, they can be more dramatic and easier to disseminate. They can become more vivid as a result of careful attention to their setting, timing, and participants. Pseudo-events can also be repeated to reinforce their impact, and they can be advertised or touted beforehand or designed for easy assimilation by mass audiences. Usually they are planned for prime viewing hours to gain maximum audience exposure. Pseudo-events spawn more pseudo-events until they come to dominate reality.

Many Americans are responsive to pseudo-events because they have matured with television as the dominant medium in their lives. Student protestors in the late 1960s and early 1970s, for example, often scheduled antiwar demonstrations for television as a demonstration staged in front of television cameras could dramatically confront and resolve political and social wrongs in full view of a mass audience.

The target of many such protests, Richard M. Nixon, had himself discovered pseudo-events during his quest for the White House. In 1968 Nixon supporters gathered in a studio with the candidate where they asked preselected questions which Nixon answered with the force of a home-run hitter being served slow pitches. Television dutifully recorded Nixon's rehearsed answers, giving the impression of a highly qualified candidate fielding tough queries with the skill and sureness needed in a president. Pleased with the success of such controlled use of television, Nixon continued the same approach after winning office. Sometimes after presidential policy speeches mass letter write-in campaigns to support Nixon were engineered by the White House staff. Staff members produced the letters, mailed them, and then reported their glowing results to a proud president!

President Carter also staged pseudo-events to bolster his polls throughout the 1980 campaign. Several times during the primary season he appeared briefly on television to announce progress in gaining release of hostages held in Iran. In late April he ordered a risky attempt to free the hostages, but the mission had to be aborted as a result of equipment failure. Eight men lost their lives. Critics charged that the mission was foolhardy, and that it had been staged to prove that Carter was trying to obtain the release of the hostages.

Another well-publicized pseudo-event during Carter's presidency involved the building of a tree house for daughter Amy. The White House press corps, television camera operators, and photographers were invited to follow the president over to the tree house to interview Amy and the president's twenty-month-old grandson, Jason. CBS news correspondent Ed Bradley later complained, "This is the sort of thing that eats up our time. Most of it doesn't mean a damn thing, but the White House grinds it out and we eat it up. The network wants everything we can give them on the president."[45]

Presidential press conferences—originally a means for obtaining hard news about the White House—have also become primarily pseudo-events, particularly with the advent of live television. The president prepares for hours, sometimes days, so as to be ready to field any question reporters might throw at him within the thirty minutes usually allotted. Typically the president sets the tone of the conference by taking the first few minutes to make a statement or to issue a clarification of some issue. Reporters clamor for attention—some primarily to be seen on television by their bosses—and ask questions which are rarely unexpected and even more rarely followed through with by subsequent queries.

Many if not most of the filming opportunities made available to television in covering the White House involve pseudo-events: ceremonies on the White House lawn welcoming a head of state; an address to a large gathering of union officials, business leaders, or professional group; or an award or citation to someone representing the handicapped, needy, or heroic. The White House is tempted to cast real events into pseudo-events because they promise less uncertainty and more potential for making the president look good than unplanned situations.

Occasionally the best-planned pseudo-event can go awry, as occurred when President Reagan conducted a White House "briefing session" for sixty Republican congressional candidates shortly before the 1982 election. A candidate from California suddenly rose to his feet as Reagan was speaking and shouted, "Mr. President, you have given us the largest tax increase in the U.S. history. . . . the Soviets get the wheat and the Americans get the shaft. . . . we have a Reagan-*mortis* setting into the nation's body politic."[46] (Aides quickly hustled the agitated man out of range of television cameras.)

Nothing is more crucial in show business than good timing, the sensitivity to know precisely what to say and do at the right moment. Political television requires an exquisite sense of timing not only for programmatic reasons but for scheduling as well. A well-developed sense of timing enables a president or candidate to propel himself or his policies into the very center of the public's attention, but only if the elements of drama, human interest, genuine news, or surprise are evident. A campaign aide to Candidate Howard Baker in 1980 observed, "Everyone wants 30 seconds of national exposure. The point is to come up with something different, not talked about, to get onto television. The question we keep asking is 'What can we do to get onto one of those evening time slots?'"[47]

Candidates for the presidency carefully plan the timing, setting, and day of major pronouncements to gain national television coverage because thirty seconds on network news is worth a considerable number of paid advertisements. The president must constantly be alert to the timing of decisions or actions, not only in terms of meeting the daily deadlines of network news but also for the impact he can have on public opinion. *When* a president acts often may be more important than *how* if he is dependent on rallying popular support behind him. President Carter, for example, did little to add to his personal credibility when he gave a pessimistic appraisal in late spring of 1979 of American energy resources, and the very next day told reporters that the nation had ample supplies of gasoline for summer vacation driving.

Despite his problems with the media, President Nixon in contrast to Carter had a keen sense of timing. His arrival in Beijing on his historic trip to China in 1972 coincided with prime-time Sunday viewing hours in the United States, and it preceded by a few weeks the New Hampshire primary, the first major test of Nixon's renomination bid. On the return trip, the presidential party laid over for nearly half a day in Anchorage, Alaska, ostensibly for refueling, but actually to enable Nixon to land in Washington during another prime-time television hour.

In June 1974, as the House Judiciary Committee was about to hold hearings on possible impeachment charges against the president, Nixon once again timed a state visit to show himself to good advantage on television. He made a triumphant visit to the Middle East, where he toured under the watchful eye of network cameras the Sphinx and pyramids of Egypt, and later Jerusalem. Television showed hundreds of thousands of Egyptians cheering Nixon as he was driven in a motor-cade from the airport into Cairo. This time, however, television was not enough to save the president's political life. The image of a president caught in a web of crimes had already been defined on the media, and Nixon's popularity among foreign peoples could not be transferred by the magic of global communications satellites to his own country-men.

PRESIDENTS AS WORLD CELEBRITIES

Television and new advances in mass-communications technology have not only influenced the way presidents act; they have also contributed substantially to restructuring the foreign- and domestic-policy environments. In domestic politics the media have reshaped the relationship between the president, Congress, political parties, and the electorate. In foreign affairs a "global village" has evolved in which images of leaders and peoples are communicated worldwide, and instantaneous news is spread from nation to nation and continent to continent into the most remote corners of the globe within seconds. Because the United States has the world's most extensive, advanced, and unrestrained mass media, the president enjoys advantages and disadvantages unmatched by any other leader.

National leaders concerned with protecting their country's security and advancing its interests among other nations must try to control the mass media. For the media constitute the most important means by which political elites can manipulate public opinion in support of foreign-policy goals in today's global village. Political leaders and the peoples of various nations respond to one another mostly on the basis of images, and modern mass-communications technology is the source of most images or perceptions.

Successful diplomacy and credible defense strategies in a nuclear world depend on the impression of will as much as of weaponry. As a result, leaders need secrecy, their governments must give the impression that political elites as well as the mass public are united behind their leadership, and they must frequently resort to bluffing adversaries and finessing opponents. Our mass media, unfettered by governmental controls and motivated by the quest for exciting, dramatic, and controversial stories, have converted the White House into an ongoing soap opera in which petty jealousies, intrafamily disagreements, and disputes are broadcast daily into the homes of millions of viewers. Indeed, the whole world is watching as differences, failures, and blemishes within the presidential policymaking establishment are communicated openly and systematically.

Foreign-policy news coverage increasingly has weakened the capacity of presidents to provide global leadership. Television, in particular, has created a vast, new inadvertent audience for foreign-policy news. Before television the public was largely insulated from a great deal of global news and largely disinterested in foreign affairs.[48] The launching of the first communications satellites in the early 1960s made instantaneous television transmission across oceans and continents possible, and a decline in the cost of transmission by the 1970s made it feasible. Major events such as Vietnam, the 1973 Middle East war, Sadat's peace mission to Israel, and the Iranian seizure of the U.S. embassy were brought directly into American homes. Such events— and others like them—were transformed into something much greater in political and historical consequence than the sum of their parts. For the first time millions of Americans became a part of important happenings in the world.[49]

This combination of new technology, cheap transmission, and dramatic news events all over the world led to a substantial increase in foreign news on all three major television networks, according to political scientist Michael Mosettig.[50] In 1976 "NBC Nightly News" carried 334 foreign stories transmitted by satellite; by 1979 that figure had more than doubled to 800. "ABC World News Tonight" telecast more than 900 foreign stories in 1979, compared to 530 two years earlier.

Foreign-policy news on television is overwhelmingly oriented toward conflict, criticism, or controversy. The public responds to this increased volume of generally depressing news by becoming more cynical, negative, and critical of their presidents and other decision makers. The president is particularly threatened by such coverage because the audiences that regularly follow foreign affairs on television tend to be largely uninformed and disinterested in foreign affairs. They traditionally hold weak opinions about global policies, but because what they see over television is new, dramatically presented information, they form new opinions that reflect the critical and negative tone of the coverage presented on the tube.[51]

The problem with the emergence of such a huge foreign-policy audience is that it further diminishes the president's control over foreign affairs. The normally noninternationalist public is less patient with presidential initiatives, it expects more dramatic results, and it basically does not see the point of many aspects of American foreign policy. The dramatic but negative news brought home to them each evening only sows cynicism and distrust.

Not only is the president damaged by the critical reporting and commentary in the American media but he is also the target of negative coverage by foreign journalists based in Washington, D.C., who, working in the midst of the American press, absorb not only the same values but also embellish them with their own nationalistic or ideological perspectives. Doris Graeber found that most foreign journalists covering American politics were leftists who were quick to view much of American foreign policy as interventionist.[52] In closed societies where news is carefully censored and foreign correspondents have far less latitude than here, less criticism and fewer negative images are communicated about the leadership and its policies. As a result, regimes like the Soviet Union deceptively appear organized and powerful while the United States appears far less certain and weak.

The American press frequently is a useful source of intelligence for other governments because of the excessive amount of news and gossip published about high-level decision makers and their problems. The president's flexibility in foreign and defense policymaking is seriously limited by such disclosures, for foreign policy among nations and national leaders requires patience, caution, discretion, and secretiveness. The news media, in contrast, are noisy, quick, imprecise, blatant, and prone to oversimplify complex problems or issues. Ivo Duchacek, a leading student of global decision making, has suggested that the media cannot avoid "using shorthand expressions that, in the form of headlines, try to reduce a complex problem of conflict and cooperation among nations into a few words."[53] James Reston has argued that press coverage of foreign policy is deeply affected by geographical and business constraints forced on newspapers and by severe limits of time in television. Foreign news may be published in greater length in major city newspapers, but it usually is trimmed in smaller newspapers in the rest of the country. This results in news stories in which startling, eye-catching events or pronouncements overwhelm the more typical, everyday course of foreign affairs, giving a distorted sense of what is really happening in the world.[54]

Stories focusing on conflict and violence or that play up sharp differences of opinion and opposition dominate over stories offering in-depth or well-reasoned discussions about foreign affairs. This creates a public thrust and counterthrust of criticism and defense of policymaking in the American system that is devastating to the president's credibility. "The more public officials' policies are criticized, the more time they spend on defending their policies until the words become as important as the acts and the defense of the policy takes on more meaning than the policy itself," Reston believes.[55] The energy devoted to public-relations aspects in foreign policymaking are beyond calculation, and little time is left for reflection or for anything except to react to the particular crisis of the moment.

So many prominent people now speak out on foreign policy or attempt to conduct their own diplomatic relations with other nations that presidential leadership appears to be in a chronic state of disarray or impotence. The news media pounce on any sign of dissension or disagreement within the White House over foreign policy because such a story contains the important elements of personality clashes as well as conflict at the highest levels of government. Carter's attempts to resolve the Iranian hostage crisis were constantly hampered by self-serving individuals trying to negotiate—in front of television cameras—with the revolutionary government. Reagan's administration was particularly undermined by press coverage of infighting among his top foreign-policy advisers and by his secretary of state's frequent allusions to "guerrilla warfare." An exasperated Reagan finally appealed to the patriotism of reporters, lamenting that the District of Columbia had become "one gigantic ear" when it came to the conduct of foreign affairs:

> [I] think it behooves all of us to recognize that every word that is uttered here in Washington winds up, by way of ambassadors and embassies, in all the other countries of the world. And we should reflect on whether it's going to aid in what we're trying to do in bringing peace to trouble spots . . . or whether it's going to set us back.[56]

Other nations are well aware of the porous nature of the White House. Reagan's chief counselor, Edwin Meese III, once described to the author how the Egyptian government withheld from the White House confirmation that President Anwar Sadat had been assassinated for more than four hours. If his death had been confirmed, the American press would have immediately learned about it and relayed the news to the Egyptian people before their government could stabilize the situation and prevent a possible coup d'état. Although American intelligence had alerted Reagan that Sadat was killed on the spot when Egyptian soldiers opened fire on him as he watched a military ceremony, Reagan appeared before reporters in Washington to report that he had heard that Sadat was not in danger of dying. He asked the people to pray for the Egyptian leader.[57]

Sadat's assassination suggests that the growing media visibility of national leaders may set them up for increased risks. Sadat was perhaps even more popular in the United States and western Europe than in his own country as a result of his frequent appearances on television and an overwhelmingly positive press coverage. Sadat's image was that of a courageous statesman, a man of peace; but that image made him the prime target of dissidents opposed to peace with Israel. Chief executives who symbolize national or international movements become likely targets of assassins as a result of their celebrity status because they symbolize the frustrations and grievances that motivate people to violence. Appearing frequently in public events recorded by the media, they become easy targets for individuals or groups seeking to change governmental policies or the status quo. Most assassinations or attempted assassinations now are caught live by television. This makes it possible to replay time and again the violent scenario for a world of viewers, and thus to reinforce the use of violence as a systematic tactic against authority.

The vastly heightened visibility of American presidents and other national leaders also encourages summitry because summit meetings are admirably suited for media coverage. Summit conferences, in fact, are invariably pseudo-events since most of the major negotiating has been done beforehand by subordinates, and any agreements between the countries reached long before the ceremonial visits take place. Summit meetings typically involve limited chats between the president and other leaders amidst the confusion of television crews and mobs of reporters—hardly a setting for serious statesmanship. Substantive talks rarely last long enough to achieve anything of great significance, the major event being simply that leaders met, shook hands, drank toasts, and exchanged ideas of a broad nature.

Presidents are well aware that a highly publicized summit meeting or trip abroad is worth gold politically; as a result, there is cooperation among the White House and networks and reporters whenever the president makes a foreign visit. When Carter visited Venezuela in 1978, television coverage became an obsessive preoccupation with the White House. Each network spent more than a half-million dollars covering the trip, and each had advance personnel in Venezuela for weeks planning for the visit and helping to shape the president's itinerary.[58]

Carter's 1979 Vienna Summit, during which the ill-fated SALT II agreements were signed, may have been the first time in history that the media dwarfed the participants in numbers and celebrity importance, according to one journalist. More than two thousand reporters, commentators, anchors, photographers, directors, scriptwriters, and producers were on hand to record every gesture and toast. Among them were the most famous U.S. media stars, individuals who seemed often to be of more interest than either President Carter or Soviet President Leonid Brezhnev.[59]

The ultimate power of television over presidential foreign policymaking was reached during the Vietnam War. Television brought the war nightly into the living rooms of American families, revealing discrepancies between what the president claimed was happening and what was actually happening. Never was the president's credibility tested more than during the Tet offensive of February 1968. President Johnson had publicly declared in his State of the Union address that progress was achieved and victory near when suddenly the Viet Cong unleashed the most violent offensive of the war, in the American command's front yard in Saigon and other major cities. Battles raged in full view of American television crews, suggesting that the Viet Cong were anything but defeated.

Later assessments of the Tet offensive indicated that LBJ had been right: the North Vietnamese and the Viet Cong *were* hurting, and Tet was a desperate, last-ditch effort to turn the war around, especially by turning American public opinion around. The offensive was actually a defeat for Hanoi: forty-five thousand enemy lives were lost, and the communist's matériel and supplies were so exhausted that it took the enemy more than a year to build up sufficient strength to renew the offensive. The media, however, never explored the possibility that Tet was really a desperate military maneuver by the foe, and that it might be a sign of the enemy's weakness. Tet helped to destroy Johnson not because of what happened but because of how the media portrayed it to the American public.[60]

One reason for this outcome was that CBS anchor Walter Cronkite was prompted by Tet to visit Vietnam, where he was appalled by what he saw. Cronkite was led to believe by CBS correspondents that the offensive had been just one more confirmation of the enemy's ability to persist and of American failure to build a strong anticommunist regime in Saigon. On his return to New York, Cronkite presented a special on the war in which he suggested that the war was not going well, that not even the addition of thousands of new American troops could turn it around, and that the United States needed to consider withdrawing. Cronkite's report may have been the straw that broke the Johnson administration's back. According to David Halberstam:

> It was the first time in American history that a war had been declared over by an anchorman. Lyndon Johnson watched and told his press secretary, George Christian, that it was a turning point, that if he had lost Walter Cronkite, he had lost Mr. Average Citizen.[61]

Nixon decided, not surprisingly, that if he were going to bring the war to a successful conclusion, he had to destroy the credibility of the media. It was too risky to directly challenge the popular Cronkite, but the Nixon White House went after CBS News and other well-regarded institutions of the media in an attempt to intimidate them in their coverage of the war.

DOMESTIC POLICY ENTERTAINMENT: THE PRESIDENT AGAINST CONGRESS

The mass media weaken presidents globally by broadcasting their weaknesses and by revealing chaos in the decision-making hierarchy. In domestic affairs the media undermine his authority by exaggerating his power and influence. The national media encourage the public to "think presidential" for virtually all major domestic problems or program needs. Paradoxically, the media magnify the president's domestic role at the same time they undermine him with constant revelations of his inadequacy and failures while minimizing the part that members of Congress play in the domestic policy process.[62]

A 1976 study of national television news found that about 20 percent of all network news was devoted to Congress, almost all of which was negative and focused on Congress as a single institution. Individual legislators, however, were all but ignored. Another study found that newspapers paid more attention to Congress while television was more attentive to the White House. What may be even more important, the study found that the "best stories about the White House [were] funneled through Capitol Hill."[63] Legislators and their staffs were more willing to talk to reporters than were Executive Branch personnel, and journalists seeking controversy were more likely to get their stories from legislative sources than from the White House.

This presents a clear danger for the president because the substantial growth in congressional staffs significantly increases the availability of news sources and material that cast the president in a bad light. Legislative staff sources often remain anonymous, particularly if they are plotting against the president's agenda or his political standing. Meanwhile, the White House staff—unable to embarrass individual members of Congress in the national media—must content themselves with attacking Congress or its leadership.

Michael Robinson's study of congressional press relations found a new, bloodthirsty, and adversarial treatment of Congress by the press since Watergate. While the media have damaged the institution of Congress, they have not done much to discredit individual members. In-house media have helped members of Congress negate much of the personal effect of the hardened press corps. Comprehensive new computer information systems have enabled members not only to keep abreast of legislation and numerous details but they have also encouraged incumbents to use the technology to reach out to the public and media in a variety of new and efficient ways. Every Senator or Representative has a staff of one or more press secretaries and media assistants. The campaign media around Congress have grown substantially also, and they mostly benefit incumbents, particularly those in the House.[64]

Meanwhile, members of Congress generally find that the media back home are "softer" on them than the national media is on the institution of Congress. Local newspapers and television and radio stations account for most of the favorable coverage and positive image individual members of Congress enjoy. Robinson suggests the discrepancy between the soft local media and tough national press has grown wider, and this widening gap goes a long way toward explaining why people may hate Congress but love their congressional representative. (U.S. Senators benefit from this local press advantage less than House members since a Senator must deal with the state as a whole, and few "state" media exist. Senators also attract more national coverage, particularly Senators seeking to put themselves into contention for the presidency. In this way they become more vulnerable to negative national news. Many Senators who had become national or international political celebrities because of their television appearances lost elections in the 1970s and early 1980s.)

This duality of media coverage of Congress means that while the institution may receive national press attention for its failures in policy, individual members rarely are singled out. Meanwhile, the national media focus on the president as the domestic policy leader because his office is the only one which represents the entire country and not a collection of 435 different districts or 50 states. The public is led to expect more of the president simply because they see and hear much more about him than about any individual legislator.

Because presidents are cast into this role, they increasingly attempt to use national media to encourage public support for their policy goals whenever Congress fragments into its many parts and resists their initiatives. Television has become the most favored medium, and only rarely is a president denied his request to use television to address the American people. (News directors from each of the three national networks decide on requests from the White House for free air time.)

The president does not have carte-blanche access to the airwaves, however. The networks have grown more cautious about granting requests for free time because of the tendency of the White House to use network television in a partisan manner. The fairness doctrine, which is part of the Federal Communications Act's equal-time rule, requires that equivalent time be granted for opposing viewpoints, and the networks are loath to lose expensive commercial time. CBS and NBC turned down a request in 1975 by President Ford to discuss tax-reform proposals because his speech was deemed political and the Democrats would have had to receive equal time for a response. The networks were reluctant to grant President Reagan free time before the 1982 election for a speech on the economy because he was expected to use the occasion to try to help Republicans running for Congress. Reagan nonetheless was granted time by two networks, and he did make a blatant political appeal for voters to "stay the course," implying they should elect or reelect Republicans. Angry Democrats were finessed out of equal time for a response.

The use of television to advance the president's domestic agenda frequently is as much a sign of weakness or failure as an indication of strength, for it often reflects his inability to convince Congress. The president, by going public, not only puts his influence on the line but he also places his neck on the public chopping block by identifying himself with an issue or program that inevitably will arouse opposition among certain groups of voters. His appeal may gain widespread national attention, but if it fails, the defeat is a personal one for the White House in the eyes of the public.

Congress resents such appeals because not only is the president going over the heads of legislators but by going public he suggests that Congress somehow is failing to serve the public's interest. Once alienated, Congress may prove more intractable toward the president's agenda. Indeed, most presidents are aware that there is a limit to how often such an approach will work. Most attempt to ration their media appeals so as not to weaken the impact by too frequent appeals on nationwide television.

What is significant about the president's use of national media to make national appeals is that the likelihood for consistent success is not very high given the built-in safety individual members of Congress enjoy through their dual media system. The national media may excoriate president and Congress for failure to meet national needs or to solve seemingly intractable problems, but only the president can be pinpointed for responsibility.

CONCLUSION

Two years after he left the White House, LBJ was asked by a television producer what had most changed in politics between his early days in Congress and the present. Johnson suddenly grew vehement as he shot back:

> . . . All you guys in the media. All of politics has changed because of you. You've broken all the machines and ties between us in Congress and the big city machines. You've given us a new kind of people. . . . They're your creations. Your puppets. No machine could ever create a Teddy Kennedy. Only you guys. [He's] all yours. Your product.[65]

The mass media have greatly magnified the presidential image. At the same time they have made it far more difficult for presidents to govern by creating unrealistic public expectations about the presidency. The media create illusions about political power which are accepted and readily believed by the mass public. Such illusions invariably serve as a script to guide the activities and public pronouncements of presidents.

Television especially has become the critical element in the conduct of the presidency. The White House is tailor-made for television because more than any other institution in government, it provides high drama, personalization, conflict, oversimplification, and symbolization. Television enables the president to reach out directly to the mass public to build a personal, private political consensus without having to seek the support of a faltering, fragmented political party.

Television along with our other national mass media enable modern presidents to extend their reach far beyond the wildest hopes of rulers in the past. But a terrible price is paid for this advantage. The media increase the president's visibility and potential for power and influence, but they also establish standards for performance and accomplishment that can only rarely be achieved in the present global and domestic political arenas.

NOTES

1. *New York Times*, April 19, 1981, A-1.

2. Ibid.

3. Ibid.

4. Daniel Boorstin, *The Image: Or What Happened to the American Dream* (New York: Atheneum Publishers, 1961), especially 47–70.

5. Ibid., 48–49.

6. Elmer Cornwell, *Presidential Leadership of Public Opinion* (Bloomington, Ind.: Indiana University Press, 1965), 4.

7. Michael Grossman and Martha Joynt Kumar, *Portraying the President: The White House and the News Media* (Baltimore: Johns Hopkins University Press, 1981), 15.

8. Richard M. Nixon, *Memoirs* (New York: Grossett & Dunlap, 1978), 355.

9. William E. Porter, *Assault on the Media: The Nixon Years* (Ann Arbor, Mich.: University of Michigan Press, 1976).

10. Grossman and Kumar, 273–98.

11. Paul H. Weaver, "The New Journalism and the Old—Thoughts After Watergate," *Public Interest* 35 (Spring 1974), 67–88.

12. Hamilton Jordan, *Crisis: The Last Year of the Carter Presidency* (New York: G. P. Putnam's Sons, 1982), 379.

13. Nixon, 354.

14. *Time*, November 22, 1982, 102.

15. Edmund Morris, *The Rise of Theodore Roosevelt* (New York: Coward, McCann & Geoghegan, 1979), especially the Prologue, 9–28.

16. Richard Rubin, *Press, Party, and President* (New York: W. W. Norton & Company, 1981), 84.

17. Ibid., 86.

18. M. L. Stein, *When Presidents Meet the Press* (New York: Julian Messner, 1969), 45.

19. *Public Papers of F.D.R., 1938. The Continuing Struggle of Liberalism* (New York: Macmillan, 1941), 520.

20. Stein, 86.

21. David Halberstam, *The Powers That Be* (New York: Alfred A. Knopf, 1979), 12.

22. R. Rubin, 131.

23. Halberstam, 15.

24. Diaries of Charles Ross, Harry S. Truman Library, Independence, Missouri.

25. Diaries of Eben A. Ayers, Harry S. Truman Library, Independence, Missouri, 373.

26. Harold Mendelsohn and Irving Crespi, *Polls, Television and the New Politics* (Scranton, Pa.: Chandler Publishing Co., 1970), 275.

27. Quoted in Stein, 133.

28. Bernard Rubin, *Political Television* (Belmont, Calif.: Wadsworth Publishing Co., 1967), 83.

29. See, for example, George Comstock et al., *Television and Human Behavior* (New York: Columbia University Press, 1978), 319-27.

30. Marshall McLuhan, *Understanding Media* (New York: New American Library, 1964).

31. Murray Edelman, "The Politics of Persuasion," in J. D. Barber, ed., *Choosing the President* (Englewood Cliffs, N.J.: Prentice-Hall, 1974), 157.

32. McLuhan, 290.

33. B. Rubin, 84.

34. Mendelsohn and Crespi, 266.

35. Robert Brustein, "News Theater," *New York Times Magazine*, June 16, 1974, 66.

36. Dan Nimmo and James Combs, *Subliminal Politics: Myths and Mythmaking in America* (Englewood Cliffs, N.J.: Prentice-Hall, 1980), 160-62.

37. B. Rubin, 33.

38. Dom Bonafede, "The New Political Power of the Press," *Washington Journalism Review* 2 (September 1980) : 26.

39. Joe McGinnis, *The Selling of the President, 1968* (New York: Pocket Books, 1968), 103-4.

40. Richard Reeves, "The Prime-Time President," *New York Times Magazine*, May 15, 1977, 17.

41. Personal communication from James Fallows, July 19, 1978.

42. Richard Wirthlin, V. Breglio, and R. Beal, "Campaign Chronicle," *Public Opinion* (February/March 1981) : 44.

43. Comments made at the Thirteenth Annual Leadership Conference of the Center for the Study of the Presidency, November 7, 1982, Minneapolis, Minn.

44. Boorstin, 7-45.

45. Anthony J. Lukas, "The White House Press 'Club,'"*New York Times Magazine*, May 15, 1977, 68.

46. *Time*, October 18, 1982, 25.

47. *New York Times*, January 1, 1980, A-17.

48. William Schneider, "Bang-Bang Television: The New Superpower," *Public Opinion* (April/May 1982) : 14.

49. Michael D. Mosettig, "The Resolution in Communications and Diplomacy," in Richard Pious, ed., *The Power to Govern, Proceedings of the Academy of Political Science* (New York: Academy of Political Science, 1981).

50. Ibid.

51. Schneider, 14.

52. Doris Graeber, *Mass Media and American Politics* (Washington, D.C.: Congressional Quarterly Press, 1980), 249–53.

53. Ivo Duchacek, *Nations and Men*, 3d ed. (Hinsdale, Ill.: Dryden Press, 1975).

54. James Reston, "The Press, the President and Foreign Affairs," *Foreign Affairs* (July 1966) : 553–73.

55. Ibid.

56. *Time*, November 23, 1981, 80.

57. Personal communication from Edwin Meese iii, October 15, 1981.

58. *Wall Street Journal*, March 28, 1978, 1.

59. *Time*, June 25, 1979, 19.

60. Peter Braestrup, *Big Story* (New Haven, Conn.: Yale University Press; abridged edition, 1983).

61. Halberstam, 514.

62. Michael Robinson and Kevin Appel, "Network News Coverage of Congress," *Political Science Quarterly*, 94 (Fall 1979) : 407–18.

63. Stephen Hess, *The Washington Reporters* (Washington, D.C.: Brookings Institution, 1981), 96–100.

64. Michael J. Robinson, "Three Faces of Congressional Media," in Thomas Mann and Norman Ornstein, eds., *The New Congress* (Washington, D.C.: American Enterprise Institute, 1981), 55–96.

65. Halberstam, 6.

Chapter **10**

A Reformed or Realistic Presidency?

There is nothing more difficult to take in hand, more perilous to conduct, or more uncertain in its success, than to take the lead in the introduction of a new order of things.
> Niccolò Machiavelli, *The Prince.*

Has the presidency become chronically unstable, or is it only suffering from a temporary downturn not unlike earlier cycles in which Congress dominated the Executive Branch? Is the decline of the office due to a succession of less qualified chief executives, or has the presidency become imperiled by a host of political and social problems at home and abroad that defy solutions? Can any president serve out a full term and still look forward to reelection, or is there no longer much hope that there is "life after inauguration"?

Deep misgivings about the presidency have surfaced during the past five administrations, paralleling a growing frustration and loss of confidence that have marked our nation at least since Vietnam and Watergate. A yearning for strong national leadership has long since extinguished fears about an imperial president. For Americans now seem to be less concerned about presidential abuse of power than they are by the inability of presidents to wield power at all.

Thoughtful observers of our politics grow uneasy over the chronic inability of the United States to develop stable, coherent policies to deal with domestic problems and global dangers. Chaotic swings in the political fortunes of one president after another raise serious questions as to whether *anyone* can manage the U.S. store. An increasing number of political experts now wonder if the office can ever function with reasonable efficiency *without* major reforms in the selection process and in the Constitutional powers of the presidency.[1]

Not everyone, of course, shares the gloomy view that the presidency is chronically ill. Candidates seeking the White House generally suggest that the presidency can be made to work effectively or else there would be little point to their seeking the office. Most presidential aspirants believe that they can translate good intentions into executive performance, and that the solution to the problems of governing the nation lies primarily in better organization.*

Candidates are not the only ones who believe that the presidency as we have known it for nearly two hundred years still has considerable potential. Some political scientists argue that improved managerial practices could make the presidency more efficient, even within the narrow limitations imposed by the Constitution. Every new president, in fact, attempts to reform the office to make it conform to a personal philosophy of administration and governance. The presidency is the most pragmatic institution in a government anchored in pragmatism.

Those who hold that there is nothing fundamentally wrong with the office believe that the presidency may regain a full measure of its honor and prestige and recapture the public's confidence as the memory of Watergate fades, as crises calling for decisive action erupt, and as Congress proves inadequate to fill the vacuum in political leadership.[2] The presidency itself is not impossible, but some of those elected were. Put the right man or woman into the White House, and the office will work with reasonable if not significant success. The reelection of President Reagan or of any future incumbent would be interpreted by those who believe that the right personality can make the office work as proof that the presidency is not beyond hope.

If the problems of the presidency can be solved by the election of better candidates or by reorganizing the Executive Branch, there might be reason to hope that the fortunes of the office will once again turn around. If, however, problems of the presidency are reflections of deeply rooted economic, social, and political forces affecting not only the United States but also countries worldwide, then *who* is elected or *how* the office is organized makes little difference. Instead, a host of intractable problems confronting a constitutionally weak executive might eventually force substantial changes on our political system. Otherwise, the United States may be doomed to an increasingly unsta-

---

*Asked why he thought that *he* could make the presidency work when the previous five incumbents seemingly could not, Walter F. Mondale, the Democratic party's front-runner for the 1984 nomination, responded that he would build a more effective personal staff to help him manage the government.

ble political future, characterized by an unending succession of failed presidents.

A persistent myth holds that the creativity of the Founding Fathers left Americans with "the frozen assumption that they had done what political thinking we need for all time."[3] The institutions and processes invented two hundred years ago have appeared so "self-evident" and perfect in conception that any suggestion they might be anachronisms in today's technologically advanced world is looked upon as heresy. The extraordinary reverence and belief in the "rightness" of the presidency is so strongly embedded that it is easier to believe that changing personalities is more desirable and functional than redesigning the Constitutional order to reflect modern conditions.

No ground swell of popular demand for major reforms of the political system has emerged, despite the growing incapacity of American institutions to address our pressing economic, political, and social problems. Whether or not Americans ever will demand an overhaul of their system may well depend on whether presidential failures appear to be chronic or merely temporary, and whether presidential weakness seems to worsen our economic woes or to jeopardize our national security.

Radical reform of political institutions has never appealed to Americans, in part because of the persistence of faith in our nation's exceptionalism. In addition, there is a lack of consensus over what our problems are and what we really expect government to do about them. Political scientist Norman C. Thomas has noted that the obstacles to major change seem almost insurmountable in the United States. "The diversity of American society and politics impedes the formation of majority coalitions for the passage of much substantive legislation and vastly increases the difficulty of building the sizable coalition required to amend the Constitution."[4]

Patchwork reforms of the presidency consequently are preferred to a major overhaul of the system. The most common involves reforming the selection process in an attempt to find "Mr." or "Ms. Right." Reorganization of the Executive Office in an effort to find techniques and administrative patterns that can improve accountability to the president is another perennial solution. Development of a "new, improved" congressional liaison and domestic-policy apparatus by every incoming administration is still another typical reform. As we have seen, most such reforms have failed to halt the decline in presidential fortunes, but new attempts continue to be made. Can the presidency work with minor reforms, or are major changes inevitable if the United States can hope to respond to the problems and challenges of the 1980s and 1990s?

CHOOSING THE "RIGHT" PRESIDENT: REFORMING SELECTION PROCEDURES

We now reform our presidential recruitment process as frequently as we reject incumbent presidents. Reforming the nomination system is an obvious tactic when the system appears to be producing unexceptional presidents. Since 1968 the selection system has undergone reforms every four years as both political parties attempted to meet new pressures and demands from the electorate while maintaining some semblance of party influence over the ultimate choice of a presidential candidate (see Chapter 2, pp. 58 to 63). In general, these reforms have failed to improve the *quality* of candidates or the success of those elected. In fact, the cumulative results of changes since 1968 have been to *increase* the likelihood for less experienced, independent, and autonomous candidates to win over politically seasoned veterans from either party. This development has further isolated the presidency from Congress and the mainstream of American politics. The party reforms of the late 1960s and early 1970s were aimed at democratizing the system in the belief that broader public involvement would help check the excessive influence of party organizations and party bosses. It was expected that such reforms would encourage a broader range of candidates offering choices and not echoes, and thus increase the chances for nominees with distinct policy positions. The shift to direct primaries and the increased involvement of rank-and-file voters in the party caucus system from 1972 on held out the promise of a truly democratic mass involvement. But as we saw earlier, the widespread participation reformers had expected never materialized. Rarely did more than a quarter of the eligible party voters turn out for primaries, and the turnout rate has been declining for the past thirty years.[5] The exaggerated importance of early contests such as New Hampshire's was more a reflection of the growing power of the mass media and campaign experts than of public involvement. Reforms consequently promoted more volatility and the "illusion of change" than democratic results. According to political scientist James Ceaser:

> The "open" nominating system . . . deinstitutionalized the entire nominating process, leaving the choice of the party nominee to the caprices of public opinion, especially as it is excited by the news media in its natural quest to emphasize the new and dramatic. . . . Deinstitutionalizing the nominating process opened the way to constant shifts in direction that follow the prevailing popular mood.[6]

All this occurred without notable improvement in the caliber of nominees at a time when the presidency was entering its prolonged winter of discontent. The electorate as well as party regulars obviously were not very happy with the quality of presidents produced by these reforms. While candidates and presidents were encouraged to arouse the public, the resources available to the White House were never sufficient to fulfill their promises.

By 1980 the original goal of reformers to open up the system through democratic objectives had been achieved—some would argue overachieved. The power of national conventions as deliberative bodies had been severely curtailed, and the influence of party chieftains was sharply limited if not almost destroyed. The new rules resulted, as we saw in Chapter 2, in the candidate picking his delegates rather than the delegates choosing the candidate. Personal campaign organizations replaced parties in linking the candidate to the electorate, as each presidential hopeful created his own personal majority.

The convention delegate who was a representative of the presidential candidate could not be a representative of the delegate's broad constituency, however. Nor were the new breed of presidential candidates in the business of building political coalitions. The decline of party influence in the electorate as well as in the government meant that the successful presidential candidate had to satisfy his personal majority and work with coalitions without the benefit of party organizations. This not only made things difficult for a new administration but it also confused individual voters who found it hard to understand what their votes for president meant in terms of public policy. The result was far less of a connection between what voters wanted and what they got. "Elected officials may mean to keep their promises. They may try to keep them. But they cannot deliver," according to political analyst Anthony King.[7]

The obvious disappointments and shortcomings of democratized selection procedures have led to a counterreform movement to reinvigorate political parties. The catchword for the latest wave of suggested reforms is *representative decision making*. A representative recruitment system would mean that delegates would retain much more personal discretion in the national convention; they would be free to bargain and negotiate for their support. This, it is argued, would strengthen political parties, particularly at the local and state levels, since wheeling and dealing for delegate support would have to begin before the national convention. Existing party organizations and leaders would become key agents in influencing this process. Additional reforms aimed at condensing the long nomination season, channeling funding through national parties, and reducing the impact of the mass media are also prominently suggested as remedies for the current ills of the system.

CAN THE PARTY BEGIN AGAIN?

Implicit in many of the party reforms after 1972 was the goal of reestablishing the presence of party regulars in the midst of the new legions of amateurs. Now reformers are more openly urging a direct frontal attack by party regulars to regain some of the ground lost since the late 1960s.

The most radical reversal of the present system has been proposed by Jeane J. Kirkpatrick, President Reagan's ambassador to the United Nations. Her plan would totally do away with direct primaries, replacing them with conventions consisting exclusively of party leaders and elected officials such as Representatives, Senators, governors, mayors, state party chairpersons and cochairpersons, as well as members of the national committee.[8]

A proposal developed by Everett Carll Ladd, Jr., suggests that two thirds of the delegates to the national convention be chosen in fifty state primaries—all held the same day—with the remaining third picked by parties and consisting almost entirely of ex-officio delegates, such as Senators, Representatives, governors, mayors, the national chairperson and vice-chairperson, as well as members of the national committee. Such delegates, numbering between 1000 and 1200, would be uncommitted to any specific candidate but would be free to bargain and negotiate over their support at the convention.[9]

A similar plan has been proposed by Terry Sanford, former governor of North Carolina and Democratic candidate for the presidential nomination. Sanford urges that both national parties develop rules requiring all delegates be chosen without previous commitments to a candidate. These delegates would be chosen from single-member districts either by party caucuses or by primary elections. But primaries would be merely "beauty contests," and delegates chosen through such elections would be representatives of their constituencies with considerable freedom to exercise their best judgment. . . ."[10] The popularity of a candidate in states holding primaries may or may not be considered in the delegates' final decisions, but there would be no provision for binding delegates as exists now in most states.

Sanford's main argument is that national nominating conventions need *thinking delegates* more than mere "messengers" for presidential candidates. Such a system would permit delegates time to meet with candidates before and during the convention, and allow constituents ample opportunity to communicate their preferences to the delegates before the final balloting at the convention. It would mean presidential primaries that guide and instruct but do not bind and distort.[11]

The President's Commission for a National Agenda for the

Eighties, which was established by President Carter in 1979, urged that between one fifth and one third of the delegates at each party's national convention be set aside for party officeholders and leaders. Both national parties currently are moving in this general direction. The Democratic party's 1984 rule changes require that about 14 percent, or more than 500 of the 3800 delegates, be "uncommitted" and chosen from among public officials and party leaders. Republican rule changes are targeted for 1988, and they are expected to resemble the Democratic party's attempt to reestablish a number of party professionals in the process.

The likelihood that parties will regain substantial influence over the selection process through the reforms already mandated, or that some of the more radical proposals will ever be enacted, is not promising. The Democratic party's rule changes for 1984 establishing a "window" for primary and caucus dates between March 11 and June 10 met with resistance from a number of states, and several exemptions were granted (New Hampshire, for one). Other proposals aimed at reestablishing parties as presidential power brokers have even less chance of being accepted.

Political parties in the United States were born as unmandated institutions responsive to a changing environment, Jeane Kirkpatrick has argued. Because parties are customary, permeable, and highly adaptive, they characteristically reflect the societies in which they exist, and they change with social change. Changes affecting parties in recent years have diverse sources:

> Some have been stimulated by events occurring outside the parties in the environment . . . , others have resulted from policies adopted by the parties; some have been desired, planned and deliberately undertaken, while others, willed by no one, have been the byproducts of social, cultural, or demographic developments or the unintended and often undesired consequences of reforms conceived with quite different intent.[12]

Almost all changes of the past two decades have been antagonistic to parties. At a time when the public visibility of the presidency was significantly increasing, the capacity of parties to sustain coalitions for governing and for connecting electoral politics to governing was being diminished. The growing disenchantment, distrust, and lack of confidence in political institutions paralleled a similar decline in regard for parties.

As Austin Ranney has noted, direct democracy devices such as the direct primary are considered highly legitimate. Thus any attempts to restore power to small groups of politicians or party leaders would be regarded as illegitimate, even though a system managed by insiders might be touted as the best way to provide a better breed of presidential candidate.[13]

Even if parties could reestablish their influence over the selection process, there is no reason to believe that party officeholders or leaders would be as effective as they once were. If party identification is weak from top to bottom among candidates, why should one expect that strong party interests will suddenly motivate their decision making at a national convention? The party-in-the-electorate has long since lost its linkage to the party-in-government, and every public official today is beholden to various networks of special interests and constituents. There would not be much of an imperative for such a politician-delegate to resist or check "popular" front-runners chosen in primaries. As one labor union chief warned members of the Hunt Commission, the Democratic party's latest rules reform commission, "Elected officials aren't grabbing for power, they're running for cover."[14]

Party leaders and elected officials, under the most recent Democratic party rule changes, win their seats as individuals and are not in a position to appoint or direct large blocs of delegates. Consequently there is little likelihood that they would be able to organize or negotiate with sufficient delegates to meaningfully influence the outcome. Not all governors, Senators, Representatives, big-city mayors, and party officials necessarily share the same candidate preference, and in all probability party professionals will be divided in roughly the same proportion as are the popularly elected delegates. Nor will appointing an elite minority of party regulars slow the momentum of a candidate with a strong showing in party caucuses and primaries. The national media would have a field day if there were any suggestion of a smoke-filled room of party professionals trying to deny a popular front-runner the nomination.*

If there were no clear-cut front-runner as a result of the democratically conducted primaries and caucuses, and if the nomination were up for grabs at the convention, reforms targeted at restoring party influence could cause considerable anguish for party delegates. It would be difficult for such officials or elected officeholders to exercise their franchise in a deliberative fashion because they would be under

---

*Attempts to limit the primary and caucus season to three months beginning with the 1984 nomination season have encouraged the evolution of yet another media phenomenon: the preseason straw poll. Straw polls are unofficial samples of party faithfuls as to who they would like to see nominated. Florida Democrats conducted a nationally publicized straw poll in November 1979, which pointed up Carter's strength and Senator Ted Kennedy's weaknesses, and Carter's renomination chances were improved. Wisconsin Democrats held a straw poll in the spring of 1983 in which Senator Alan Cranston of California upset the front-running Walter F. Mondale, leading the press to speculate that Mondale had peaked too soon and was on his way downward.

intense pressure from their own supporters—especially their financial backers—to vote for one candidate over another.[15]

Many reforms which would reinsert the party into the nominating process are incompatible with what has been happening to parties and to elections in general. Most candidates who emerge as front-runners now are independent of the party to begin with. Candidate-centered campaign organizations and political action committees (PACs) are more effective at raising funds than the parties. (Such organizations "are the wave of the future," President Reagan's political director observed.[16]) It would be difficult to reimpose an elitist structure on a process which has grown increasingly democratic because there is no longer much basis for party consensus on national problems. Nor do parties any longer have the discipline to convert principles or rhetoric into realistic, distinctive policy alternatives.

REGIONAL OR NATIONAL PRIMARIES

Those who favor even more democracy for selecting presidential candidates reflect a streak of realism in their views: if political parties have lost much of their ability to influence either elections or government, then why pretend that halfway measures to restore their powers will succeed? Conceding that mass public involvement in presidential politics is here to stay, the logical solution would be to eliminate the more glaring weaknesses and problems associated with direct primaries. This is the main argument of reformers who urge a system based exclusively or primarily on direct primaries. The present patchwork system of primaries would be systematically overhauled by three main variations that have been suggested: (1) holding primaries in monthly cycles by time zones; (2) grouping state primaries into regional contests; and (3) holding a single national primary.[17]

Time-Zone Primaries

The President's Commission for a National Agenda for the Eighties urged that four presidential primary dates organized on the basis of the nation's four time zones be held to select delegates to the national convention. Using time zones instead of the more traditional regional groupings of states would cut across some of the economic and political concerns that mark the various regions. Spacing out the primaries over a period of four months, with each primary date at least a month apart, might reduce the media's ability to create a New Hampshire bandwagon effect. The first set of primaries probably would still be interpreted as establishing the front-runner. But the longer period between each set of primaries would allow some of the media buildup to die down, the commission believed. This might enable more experienced national officeholders to compete better with candidates who are "unemployed" and whose campaigns have been full-time for an extended number of months.[18]

Regional Primaries

Several proposals for regional primaries have attracted attention, although none have gotten far in Congress. One plan would make primaries optional, but any state holding one would have to schedule it according to five regional primaries established by the federal government, each of which would be separated from the others by a month. A federal election commission would require that each regional primary list the major candidates, and delegates would have to be approved by the candidates to whom they are pledged. Delegates would be required to stick with their candidate for the first two ballots at the convention, or until the candidate's share of convention votes fell below 20 percent.[19]

A similar regional proposal permitting states a presidential primary option would establish four regional primaries spaced out over four months. Every candidate qualifying for federal matching funds would have to be listed. Each regional contest would include a presidential preference poll, and all candidates winning at least 10 percent or more of the preferential vote would be allocated a proportionate share of the delegates.[20]

The most extensive regional primary proposal would *require* every state to hold a primary. Each would be assigned to one or another of five regional primaries with the sequence to be determined by lot.[21]

Whether or not any regional plan would result in better-qualified candidates is questionable. Regional primaries would not dramatically change such basic features of the present system as openness, grassroots control, or direct candidate approaches to the voters, nor would it eliminate the national convention as the final formal nominating mechanism. The main attraction of regional plans is their potential for shortening and simplifying what is now an overly long and confusing process. Regional primaries also might reduce the "horse-race" atmosphere nurtured by the national news media in their coverage of the results of early, small, and unrepresentative state primaries. Any dramatic reversal of the media's influence in creating presidential candidate-celebrities or in defining candidate images is highly unlikely, however. This is because the media can still prove influential under a regional plan, and there would be added emphasis and excitement attached to each contest. (Indeed, media fascination with most of the primaries after the early ones tends to decline sharply.)

National Direct Primaries

Far more radical than any of the regional plans is one for mandating a single national direct primary in which any candidate receiving more than 50 percent of a party's vote would automatically become that party's standard-bearer. If no one received a majority, a run-off would be held between the top two vote-getters to settle the nomination. National party conventions would no longer have any responsibility for choosing the presidential nominees although conventions would be held after the primaries to write platforms and to select vice-presidential running mates.[22]

The national primary has enough popular support so that the possibility that Congress might someday create such a system cannot be totally ignored. A Gallup poll in January 1980 reported that 66 percent of the American people favored abolishing party national conventions altogether and replacing them with a system of choosing nominees by a single national primary. Only 24 percent favored continuing the present system.[23]

Advocates of a national primary spotlight its simplicity, openness, and directness. They argue that voter participation would rise significantly; participants would be more representative of ordinary party identifiers; votes would count equally; national issues would become much more important than local or regional issues; the distortion of bellwether states in establishing early favorites would end; and the influence of the media would be diminished.[24]

Veteran political analyst Richard Scammon defends the national primary on the basis that primary nominations for virtually all other elected offices at all levels of government have worked well over the years, and a single national primary would help parties by reducing the divisiveness created by a long series of bitterly contested primaries and party caucuses. "[A] single primary settles things. It's clear; it's public; it's open. The verdict is accepted. You don't have people arguing about caucuses being packed or conventions rigged."[25]

Opponents concede simplicity, but they strongly challenge assumptions that a national primary would in any way *help* parties or *reduce* the influence of the mass media. Austin Ranney argues that a direct national primary would "effectively remove the party organizations from any active role in the sifting and winnowing process," and the clear gainers would be the national news media:

*In a national direct primary . . . the only preelection facts rele-
vant to who was winning would be public opinion polls and
estimates of the sizes of crowds at candidates' meetings. . . . [A]
one-day national direct primary would give the news media even
more power than they now have to influence the outcomes of
contests for nominations by shaping most people's perceptions of
how these contests were proceeding.*[26]

Party leaders criticize the plan for other flaws. A national primary
would be far more advantageous to "celebrity" figures than less well-
recognized challengers. The field of candidates would swell considerably, fragmenting the vote and invariably necessitating a run-off.
Candidates from the fringes of the party, even extremists, as well as
single-issue candidates would be encouraged even more than they are
today in individual state contests. The task of unifying a party for the
national election after the nomination would be more difficult than
ever if a candidate outside the mainstream of the party were to be
nominated.[27]

Basing party nominations on a single national primary may curtail
horse-race political journalism, but it would almost certainly mean
that candidates would forget about grass-roots campaigning in favor of
staged media appearances designed to maximize viewer audiences.
Entire campaigns would be run by media professionals out of studios in
the major media centers, and the influence of the image makers would
be increased even beyond today's excesses. This would significantly
encourage the selling of the president, a major factor in undermining
the credibility of recent presidents and a source of unrealistic images
and expectations. Another undesirable outcome would be that the
influence of political action committees would probably be magnified
since campaigns geared to national or regional audiences would be far
more likely to attract the support of special interests than of localized
interests. In addition, the high costs of nationwide network media
time would force candidates to seek as many lucrative contributions as
possible from well-heeled political fund-raising groups.

Each of the suggested reforms in the nomination system might
resolve procedural problems in the selection of presidential candidates.
But they pose the risk of making the presidency even more vulnerable
to great shifts in public opinion, or they propose a return to an earlier,
less complicated past, which it is probably impossible to recapture.
Whether more democracy or rejuvenated parties would even lead to
more qualified candidates—and by implication more effective chief
executives—is itself highly problematical. Increased democratic participation in the nomination process and weakened parties were, after
all, reflections of broad social and political trends. The idea that a
heavier dose of either would somehow or other strengthen the presi-

dency is unsupported by any recent developments in American politics.

Nonetheless, the belief persists that improving the system for choosing presidents will improve the office. Linked to such notions is a perennial attempt to reform the electoral college system for electing presidents.

Electoral College Reforms

The recurring effort to restructure or to abolish the electoral college is motivated less by a belief such a move would produce better presidents than by the hope that it would provide greater legitimacy to those who win. The public is constantly reminded that the present electoral college system can result in a candidate winning a majority of the popular vote, yet losing the election because of coming in second in electoral votes. This has occurred only twice—in 1876 and 1888—but it almost occurred in 1968 and again in 1976. A shift of only 9250 votes in Ohio and Hawaii in 1976, for example, could have lost Carter the election in the electoral college even though he polled more than 1.7 million more popular votes than Ford.

The electoral college is not held in high esteem by the American public because it is difficult to understand and unwieldy. Opponents argue that it violates the one-man-one-vote principle because it reflects the unequal representation of states in the U.S. Senate. Others point to the possibility of the "faithless elector," the occasional case of an elector refusing to cast an electoral vote for the candidate entitled to it by having carried a state's popular vote.

A number of proposals for modifying aspects of the electoral college or for doing away with it altogether have surfaced. One plan provides for doing away with the winner-take-all provision whereby all the state's electoral votes go to the leading vote-getter. Another would automatically distribute electoral votes without the formality of having formal meetings of state electoral colleges, thus eliminating the opportunity for a faithless elector to renege. One plan would base electoral votes in congressional districts, with a bonus going to the candidate winning a majority of a state's vote. This plan is already in effect in Maine. A national bonus plan suggested by a task force of political scientists, journalists, and politicians would retain the present system but add a national bonus pool of 102 electoral votes (two for each state plus the District of Columbia) for the candidate winning the most popular votes nationally.[28]

By far the most popular reform is one calling for a Constitutional amendment that would abolish the electoral college and replace it with a direct national popular election of the president, a plan favored by a number of powerful organizations and many prominent politicians. As with a national primary, simplicity and direct democracy are the chief benefits that recommend such a reform. Direct popular voting for the president would, however, lead to many of the undesirable results feared by the Founding Fathers when they created the electoral college: individuals with burning ambition would be tempted to play to the sentiments and tastes of the masses in order to win election. The risk of demagoguery would be ever present. Third- or fourth-party candidates could drain away enough votes to deny the most popular candidate a popular majority. While most proposals for direct popular elections suggest a run-off between the top two candidates when no one gets 40 percent or more, the danger that the "wrong" candidate could win is substantially increased.[29]

The debate over the electoral college is not over whether the president ought to be elected by popular vote, but over *how* the popular vote should be aggregated: by states, as in the present system; or by the nation as a whole, as the reformers urge. "Aggregating votes in one national constituency would have major consequences for the structure and dynamics of American politics and for the parties through which they are conducted," according to Kirkpatrick.[30]

A single national electorate would favor a racial, ideological, and homogeneous aggregate popularly termed the *real* or *silent majority* or *middle America*. A president elected by such an electorate would be able to ignore the support and interests of controversial elements or minorities that did not contribute significantly to his victory. He would be far more responsive to the well-organized wealthy minorities that helped nominate and elect him. The national media would be all-important since national mass audiences would be the target of campaign appeals. National direct elections would probably sound the death knell of the two-party system since presidential politics would become a battleground for competing celebrities.

Direct national elections would magnify the shortcomings of direct national primaries. Both would give the impression that a genuinely democratic national decision was being made. But in reality presidential hopefuls would be completely abandoning any strategy for building a national coalition since each would have to construct his own coalition on the basis of personality and narrow issue interests. The result would reinforce the trend toward fragmented, directionless policymaking. The gap between illusion and reality would widen since voters—laboring under the myth that more democracy should lead to better leaders—inevitably would be disappointed time after time by presidents who had to juggle the demands of their personal coalitions against the interest of the national electorate.

INSTITUTIONAL REFORMS OF THE PRESIDENCY

The presidency may be one of the most reformed political offices in the world. This is because each new incumbent in the White House tries to reshape the role to make it more responsive and more functional. But the old dictum that the more things change, the more they remain the same holds especially true for presidential power. Major reorganizations such as Franklin D. Roosevelt's creation of the Executive Office of the President (EOP), Nixon's conversion of the Bureau of the Budget into the Office of Management and Budget, and Carter's creation of a Senior Executive Service have changed basic organizational structures. But the essential form of the presidency has mostly reflected the personality occupying the office rather than any substantial reorganization. Because the presidency is so personal, it is difficult to distinguish between permanent reforms and those that are only ephemeral.[31]

Every candidate promises dramatic reorganizations of the Executive Branch to solve the problems of an uncontrollable federal bureaucracy, and each new president begins office supremely confident of shaping an administration that will work. Public expectations may be temporarily encouraged by such optimism. But before long it becomes obvious that Americans have one more chief executive whose rhetoric exceeds his reorganizational skills, for there are distinct limits to just how much any president can rearrange the essential powers of the office.

The most apparent change over the years has been the inexorable swelling of the presidential establishment as new agencies and additional staff are added to the EOP to deal with increased demands and expectations on the president. To deal with the increased size and complexity of the EOP, policy-planning units, supercabinet councils, and revamped White House staffs have tried to coordinate presidential management with the permanent government and Congress. Such reorganizations are as predictable as the changing of the seasons. Predictable too is the inevitable retreat of the president and his assistants to the "Fortress White House" when attempts at reorganization fail to achieve results. The major problem with most such reforms is that they are oversold to the public, and each administration ends up believing that a set of large-scale reforms can resolve all long-standing problems of the office.

Most such reforms are ad hoc solutions to problems and conditions which existed before the administration took office and which will continue long after it has departed. Such reforms reflect the futile efforts of presidents to construct a governing majority centered in the White House. They invariably fly in the face of the very conditions which now prevent anyone or any institution from developing national policies or a collective consensus on national problems.

In rearranging the offices and agencies under his command, every president nonetheless is gamely trying to row against the current. The president attempts to develop stronger liaison with Congress, but Congress is itself hopelessly fragmented with power dispersed among many members. The president tries to best the iron triangles or triple alliances, but he is politically indebted to some of them himself. In addition, there are far too many of these groups whose power and influence with Congress and federal agencies are impenetrable. Many Executive Branch officials have been coopted by amorphous "issue networks." As "technopols" or specialists, they are beyond political influence from the White House or cabinet heads. The president attempts to appeal to party unity. But he finds little partisanship in his party to begin with, and he cannot afford to alienate members of the opposition who may end up providing even more support than the president's party. The president seeks help from his own staff, but often he is handicapped by their overzealous attempts to seal him off from controversy swirling around him. He turns to his own White House public relations to assist him in reaching out to the public over the heads of the mass media, but invariably he becomes the victim of overselling as the results seldom measure up to the glowing press releases of his staff assistants.

American politics is almost universally seen as the politics of coalition building, notes Anthony King. But coalition building presupposes that there are political formations—parties, interest groups, voting blocs, and factions—which can be brought together, and that some kind of structure of leadership exists within such formations that can make them function responsibly. Fewer and fewer cohesive blocs exist in the United States now, and the result is the increasingly fragmented, decentralized, specialized, and atomized politics that have grown more obvious over the past twenty years.[32]

Leadership has become much more difficult because "building coalitions in the United States today is like trying to build coalitions out of sand. It cannot be done," according to King. Politicians have no other option left but to try to create majorities out of this hodgepodge. But "each new majority has to be constructed out of new combinations of individuals and groups," while the "number of individuals and groups upon whom influence has to be brought to bear" grows larger.[33]

All of this means that efforts to impose efficiency, accountability, or any improved managerial techniques on the operation of the presidency are unlikely to succeed. If one president after another fails to make the office work satisfactorily, we can only conclude that a major reassessment of what we expect of presidents is in order. Or we may need to consider whether or not the political system itself can afford to stumble along with an ineffective if not impotent chief executive. If Americans decide they need and want a stronger presidency, major Constitutional reforms ultimately may be necessary. Recent presidents have begun to concede as much, and several have recommended suggestions for major changes in the presidency to make it more efficient, effective, and responsible.

CONSTITUTIONAL REFORM: A TIME FOR NEW IDEAS?

Major reforms of the presidency are not to be lightly suggested. Changes which would remove the most obvious impediments to the exercise of executive authority would not only challenge the very foundations of our Constitutional system but would also require a drastic restructuring of our governmental institutions and major alterations in the way Americans regard presidents. "To question the future of the presidency is to question the future of the entire American political order," according to political theorist Robert E. Denton, Jr.[34]

Reforming the presidency would mean changing the public's cognitions, attitudes, beliefs, and values. Thus any major reordering of the office would probably face considerable resistance. Americans may want efficient government, but they have never wanted their national government to be *too* efficient. Reforms designed to enhance the powers of the executive unquestionably would meet with fierce resistance, especially from the nation's political observers and commentators. (When more than thirty state legislatures called for a Constitutional convention to consider a balanced budget amendment to the U.S. Constitution, many opponents warned that this would lead to a much broader Constitutional convention in which major changes might be attempted. The consensus among many was this would threaten the U.S. Constitution's very existence.) Really significant changes in the office, consequently, are not very likely, although calls for reform have grown more vocal and numerous during the present decline in the presidency's fortunes.

A Single Six-Year Term

The most familiar and frequently suggested reform calls for a Constitutional amendment providing for a single six-year term. Former Presidents Eisenhower, Johnson, Nixon, and Carter have all voiced support for such a change, as have a number of other prominent politicians and students of the office. Public-opinion polls show that the American public either is mostly opposed or indifferent to such a reform.[35]

Proponents of the six-year term insist that it would free presidents from political constraints and enable them to concentrate on the important problems of government instead of worrying about reelection. Four years are insufficient for any administration to plan, carry through, and implement a president's agenda. This is because a new president needs at least a year to get a grasp on his office, and he is not fully responsible for the federal budget until at least his second year. Since presidential campaigns now begin at least two years before the next election—if not sooner—the White House is forced to constantly regard every challenge for what it means to the president's reelection chances.

Opponents of the proposal contend that if an incumbent is unable to succeed in four years, there is no reason to expect that two additional years will significantly enhance his fortunes. In fact, the country would be better off getting rid of an inept incumbent after four years rather than having to contend with him for two more years. A reasonably successful and popular president should have the opportunity to be reelected, both as a reward for his service as well as to provide him with four additional years to complete his policy agenda. An eight-year administration could go a long way toward reestablishing legitimacy to the presidency and stability to our nation's political system, opponents to a single term argue. The president *is* political, and by subjecting him to national reelection, the American people are able to communicate a judgment on his performance as well as to send signals as to the acceptability of his policies. One extended term would make every new president a "lame duck" from the start, reducing his political resources in dealing with Congress and federal bureaucrats, particularly during the final few years of his term.

Pairing Presidential and Congressional Elections

The political nature of the presidency might be significantly reinforced by a proposal for a Constitutional amendment combining election of the president with congressional elections. This would require extending the term of office for members of the House of Representatives from two to four years since each candidate for Congress would be listed on the ballot with the presidential and vice-presidential candidates of the same party. Voters in each congressional district thus would vote for a "package" of candidates, and as a result the presidential candidate with a majority of congressional district victories would also enjoy a majority in the House. Proponents of such a scheme argue that it would provide incentives for the president and Congress to work together after the election, thereby encouraging closer links between the White House and Capitol Hill. Representatives running for reelection with a president or a presidential candidate would be far more responsive to the president as their party leader, and might feel a stronger obligation to defend the president's record or to support him on key policy votes.[36]

Such a plan would also make members of Congress or candidates for a seat less dependent on the financial backing and less vulnerable to the pressures of political action committees or single-issue groups. (No one has proposed that U.S. Senators likewise be linked to the presidential ticket since Senators obviously would never agree to reducing their constitutional terms from six to four years.)

The major weakness of such a plan is that it ignores the social and political changes that have contributed to the decline of political parties. It ignores the fact that a new kind of congressional candidate—one who is often as independent-minded as the new breed of presidential candidate—has emerged in recent years. Instead of creating a new party cohesiveness, it would enhance the politics of individualism since the "coattail" effect would require congressional candidates willing to submerge their own political views with those of the top of the ticket. The decline of parties would not necessarily be arrested and, in fact, might even be hastened by the emergence of national "presidential parties" whose commitment is not to a broad-based coalition but to a single person.

Another possible danger in such a reform is that it could contribute to even more stalemates in the national government than exist under the present system of checks and balances. A president might find he has considerable influence with the House, but the House is not the same autonomously powerful body that the House of Commons is in the British system. When the president's popularity begins to slip, the temptation would be for members of Congress to move away from the White House rather than continue close ties with it. The Senate would probably become a major stumbling block to collective leadership even if the president's "own" party controlled a majority. Opposition to administration policies would inevitably become centered in the Senate, risking distortion in that body's constitutional duties and responsibilities.

Other Reforms Linking Presidents and Congress

Perhaps the most radical constitutional reform considered thus far would provide for a congressional nonconfidence vote on a president, or for the president to dissolve Congress and call for new elections. One amendment proposed in 1974 by Representative Henry Reuss of

Wisconsin proposed that Congress would be required to dissolve itself and face new elections along with a president. Other variations on this plan would include requiring the president to resign, to face a new election, or to run on his own record.[37] Lloyd Cutler, President Carter's chief counsel, would place such authority in the president's hands, as the French constitution does for the French president. Under Cutler's proposal the president would have the authority to dissolve Congress and to call for new congressional elections at least once during a four-year term.[38]

The rationale behind such proposals is they would enable either Congress or the president to break serious executive-legislative impasses, and permit voters to decide whether to support Senators and Representatives backing the White House or whether to oppose the president. More extensive consultation between the White House and Congress would obviously occur, and if the power to dissolve a government rested with the president, his influence over policymaking would be immensely enhanced.

Either way, proposals for dissolving Congress or calling for a new presidential election in midcourse stand almost no chance of adoption. Opponents of the Congress having the power to call for new elections believe such a measure would severely cripple the presidency without enhancing the capacity of Congress to lead.[39] More rather than less instability would develop as either Congress or the Executive Branch maneuvered for political advantage.

Another reform with little support would mandate congressional questioning of the president and his top executive aides, thus undermining the president's capacity to claim executive privilege for himself and his top appointees. Stemming from the Nixon-Watergate era, this reform ostensibly seeks to curb secrecy in the White House and clandestine military actions conducted without congressional knowledge. Critics have argued that such a procedure would encourage even more secrecy by the White House, or it could seriously erode the president's credibility and legitimacy.

A less extreme idea for advancing executive-legislative cooperation would require the president to select 50 percent of his cabinet from among members of his party in the Senate and House; these cabinet appointees would retain their seats in Congress while serving in the administration. Such a reform would require amending Article I, Section 6, of the U.S. Constitution, which prohibits anyone holding an office in the government from serving at the same time in Congress, but advocates do not see this as a major hurdle. They insist that more frequent contacts would develop between the Executive Branch and Congress, and that the cabinet would have a healthy mix of qualified presidential appointees from the outside as well as seasoned politicians from Capitol Hill.[40]

A variation on this plan would provide that the president form his cabinet from a joint legislative council created by both houses of Congress. Such a cabinet would be capable of controlling as well as supporting a president since its members would not be completely dependent on him, and they would represent a wider consensus than the president could form by himself.[41] A possible drawback to such an arrangement would be that it would increase the president's problem of gaining accountability.

It is significant how much these ideas are suggestive of a parliamentary-cabinet system. Each would establish linkages between the executive and legislative bodies that are distinctive features of parliamentary government. Yet most political observers insist there would be widespread public resistance to such reforms, and strong disclaimers are made that a parliamentary system could ever work for the United States.

The symbolic importance and almost religious reverence the American people accord to the U.S. Constitution, along with our highly inflated images and illusions about presidential power and greatness, almost guarantee failure for major constitutional changes in the existing order. Ironically, they would fail because such reforms would make the office more political and less symbolic even as they were making it more efficient and capable of fulfilling a greater number of expectations.

The American people would have to exchange an office invested with grandeur and inflated accomplishments for one of less pretensions but a more pragmatic political potential. This would require overcoming our almost instinctual distaste and distrust of politics as well as our traditional bias against strong, responsible, and collective government. Americans would be admitting that the presidency glorified by historians and magnified by the mass media mostly has been a myth and an illusion. The possibilities of the presidency would be revealed as exaggerations, and the actual role—in spite of its capacity for attracting and holding attention—would be recognized as weak in actual performance. If Daniel J. Boorstin is right that the "American citizen . . . lives in a world where fantasy is more real than reality, where the image has more dignity than its original,"[42] the prospects for major constitutional reform of the presidency appear no more likely than a more realistic appraisal of the existing office.

A REALISTIC PUBLIC: A REALISTIC PRESIDENCY?

Even in the best of times, presidents have rarely been as successful, dynamic, or powerful as we imagined them to be. Conditions during the 1980s and 1990s will probably be even less favorable for the presidency. Consequently either the office or the public image of the presidency must change if the United States is to avoid continued instability in its national leadership.

If Americans continue to expect more from the White House than it can deliver, few presidents can realistically avoid the frustrations of the American people or hope to survive more than four years in office. The public must become more realistic about the actual constraints facing not only the White House but political institutions in general if the presidency is to function with even moderate success.

The likelihood of a more rational perspective on the presidency is not promising, however. For it would require a better informed and more politically enlightened public. Developing a new, more commonsensical outlook toward the presidency probably would be even more difficult to achieve than Constitutional reform, for it would require our mass cultural institutions as well as the public to change behaviors and practices which are deeply ingrained and which have evolved over the years.

If this is the case, there would be considerable resistance to redefining the president's public role since changing cultural beliefs is never easy. It would require a number of challenges to long-held assumptions and expectations about our country's past, present, and future, and it would force individual Americans to make political self-evaluations that could be personally difficult for many if not impossible for some. One of the most difficult but important reassessments would challenge our ethnocentric views about American exceptionalism.

"Only in America . . ."

The myth of presidential greatness is inseparable from our belief in America's exceptionalism—the view that our nation is inevitably destined for economic and political greatness. This means, however, that when things do not go right, we attribute the problem to our own failure to uphold certain first principles of the country or to the fact that we have strayed from the straight path. We see the problems of the presidency as uniquely ours, and we tend to ignore the fact that political executives and governments worldwide are suffering from many of the same woes as our own. Such Western parliamentary systems as Britain, West Germany, Canada, France, Denmark, Greece, Spain, Sweden, and the Netherlands have all experienced frequent turnovers in governments in recent years as a result of public frustration with leadership. The general rule during the 1970s and early 1980s, in fact, has been for the "outs" to replace the "ins" with each successive electoral cycle.

Even the more efficient parliamentary-cabinet governments find it difficult, if not impossible, to build lasting coalitions today as a result of increasing economic uncertainty, continuing controversies over foreign policy and nuclear arms controls, greater fragmentation of national electorates, and a growing disenchantment with the ability of nation-states to resolve the problems of a new technological, interdependent world. Political leadership in other countries is seldom as functional as reformers in the United States would suggest, and rarely is successful enough to prevent instability or to promote national consensus on the new kinds of policy problems facing governments.

Presidents as News Makers and Newsbreakers

If Americans are ever to gain a more rational outlook on the presidency, there must be a substantial change in the present relationship between the news media and the White House. President Reagan's chief White House spokesperson, Larry Speakes, asked, "Can the modern presidency survive the modern media?"[43] The press for its part continues to wonder when, if ever, the White House will stop trying to manage the news by pseudo-events, by isolating the president from the press, and by distorting the prospects and accomplishments of the administration.

The media contribute to the failures of the presidency by creating an unreal world in which the president is the leading hero one moment but the national villain the next. The national media portray the president in such a way that he appears larger than life but falls short of expectations. The needs and biases of the commercially driven, entertainment-centered nationwide news media typically encourage a big buildup of a new president. Just as predictably this leads a few months later to the inevitable put-down of the president once he becomes a familiar figure involved in a series of unsuccessful or only partly successful political struggles. Presidents and their White House staffs insist that the media can make or break them, and that only by fighting fire with fire can an administration defend itself against the media.

Neither side wills this adversarial relationship because the media depend on the president as much as he needs them, but the mass media cannot resist the imperative to entertain, titillate, oversimplify, overdramatize, and personalize politics any more than the White House can resist using the media to enhance the president's image and influence.

Responsibility for improving the quality of information people receive about presidents consequently falls on both parties to the relationship. The national media—especially network television, the most powerful communication medium with the general public—should provide a more balanced coverage of national politics. It should avoid an oversimplification of complex political events and processes that suggests that the president is responsible for most of what occurs in American politics. This would require the media to give more emphasis and analysis to Congress, even to the point of emphasizing the role individual members of Congress play in key policies and decisions.

Members of Congress are rarely linked to policy failures (or successes) in the national consciousness, and they avoid accountability to their unquestioning local media, even though the ultimate success of the president depends on their individual actions. Greater attention by national media to the triangular relationships binding Congress to interest groups and federal agencies would go a long way to help the public understand why one president after another is unable to develop a national consensus or to achieve national goals.

Presidents, however, cannot ask for more balanced treatment from the press if they are not willing to be more candid in their dealings with the media and American electorate. Every president would be well advised never to exaggerate his weaknesses or limitations, but he would be equally well counseled to be more forthright with the press in assessing his policy proposals and accomplishments. Candidates for the presidency seem to believe that they must exaggerate the promises of the presidency to win the office. And it would be unthinkable for an incumbent president or a member of his White House staff to level with the media or the public by admitting that an administration does not have sufficient resources to accomplish presidential goals, or that proposals have failed because of misjudgments or mismanagement.

Journalists and television correspondents who regularly cover the White House understandably grow skeptical toward a chief executive who cannot admit to anything less than perfection. Reporters quickly tire of White House attempts to use them to sell the president's image at the same time that extensive efforts are made to keep the press at arm's length. One of the more obvious examples of White House manipulation of the media occurred early in 1983 when President Reagan called an impromptu news conference to read a statement claiming credit for lowering the nation's unemployment rate. Reporters started to question the president about his claim, and Reagan had answered a few of their inquiries when suddenly Mrs. Reagan appeared with a birthday cake. The cake-cutting ceremony and brief party— captured live on television—lasted for more than ten minutes before Reagan quickly departed, leaving a number of unanswered questions. "We were used," a network news correspondent later complained.[44]

There have been signs that both the media and presidents have become more sensitive about the problems each causes the other, although neither side has yet renounced old habits. National newsmagazines, syndicated national political columnists, and occasionally television have begun to examine the problems of the presidency with greater insight and understanding in recent years.[45] There is a growing awareness among many journalists of the fact that the media have been less than perfect in their objectivity and fairness in dealing with politicians, although old habits are hard to break. Former presidents occasionally have been able to be more analytical about shortcomings in their dealings with the media, although they have little forgiveness for the press's role in their problems.[46]

Public awareness may be growing about the real condition of the contemporary presidency. The inevitable decline in public support of every incumbent within a year of inauguration suggests that the electorate quickly tires of unrealistic optimism and unfulfilled promises. There are grounds for encouragement that as the "presidential story" focuses with greater frequency on the chronic shortcomings and frequent defeats of one incumbent after another, both the mass media and the White House may be forced to deal with presidential power as it really is, instead of as it once appeared to be.

Dealing with the office more honestly and objectively in political science texts and in government classes could likewise contribute to a more realistic presidency. And utilizing scholarship about the changing nature of the office might be helpful in inoculating a president-elect against unwarranted optimism or foolish press-agentry.

Political Education and the Presidency

Precollege textbooks and traditional civics or American government courses are major sources for the early idealization of presidents that has led to the growth of myths and illusions. College textbooks treat the presidency more realistically, particularly since Watergate, but there is little evidence that materials used in elementary, middle, or high-school social studies have changed much.[47]

Political education in America emphasizes a passive, "spectatorlike" relationship between the future citizen and the presidency. It offers few suggestions that an American has any obligation to make judgments about the quality of a president's decision making. Presidential greatness is accepted as the norm, and students rarely hear about the Pierces, Fillmores, or Hardings. Instead, they have a heavy dose of Washington, Jefferson, Lincoln, FDR, and, more recently, Kennedy. Little consideration is given to how much the presidency is dependent on or constrained by other decision makers. The implication is that a successful president will measure up to one or more of the past greats.

The role of political parties, interest groups, ideologies, socioeconomic forces, and trends is seldom discussed in connection with presidential power. The office, instead, is examined through charismatic personalities, major historical milestones, legalistic processes, and formal institutions.[48] American youth consequently are trained to regard presidents as omnipotent, even though the nightly news usually portrays the present incumbent as something less than extraordinary—"a Ford and not a Lincoln."

Misconceptions about the presidency are rampant in educational materials, and teachers as well as administrators reflect political values that do not deal with the political world as it is. There is a serious need for a more honest treatment of presidents and for all aspects of the political process if Americans are ever to relate intelligently and rationally to the demands and challenges of the real world. This would involve linking the problems of contemporary presidents to the deterioration of political parties, as well as a more accurate assessment of the limited authority available to presidents as executives, global leaders, and domestic policymakers.

Students should be required to examine more critically, analytically, and honestly the presidency in the context of other American political and social institutions. The possibilities for a more enlightened educational treatment of the office are not much better than for a more realistic relationship between the media and the presidency. But without changes in both these situations, our popular images and expectations will continue to be unrealistic and unfulfillable.

Educating Presidents

Newly elected presidents need a similar reeducation about the office even more than future citizens. The chief executive of most parliamentary democracies assumes office possessing considerable political knowledge about government as well as a wealth of experience in both politics and government service. The average length of parliamentary apprenticeship of a newly installed prime minister in Great Britain since 1945 has been twenty-eight years. American presidents since 1952 have increasingly been political innocents, at least insofar as experience in Washington, D.C., is concerned. (Eisenhower, Carter, and Reagan were all strangers or outsiders to the Washington establishment.)

Some will argue that serving as governor of a state or as the supreme commander of the nation's armed forces during wartime are forms of experience relevant to the conduct of the presidency, but they are not equivalent to the kind of executive or administrative experience undergone by almost every new prime minister or president in parliamentary-cabinet systems.

Since presidents increasingly are self-selected and self-employed, the political experience they and their associates bring to the White House relates more to running a campaign than to running a government. A president almost invariably has no previous experience of directing "a major federal agency," Richard Rose has noted. "No postwar American president has previously headed an agency in the executive branch, thus learning about the direction of government at first hand."[49] Recent presidents and their White House staff members have been neophytes when it comes to the national political arena. They often reflect an underdeveloped understanding of social, economic, and political forces exerting powerful pressures on both the United States and the global order.

Many of a president's unrealistic promises or exaggerated claims to power are made during the heat of campaigning or the first few months in office. Overblown campaign rhetoric may be a normal part of selling new-style independent candidates, but when a president-elect continues such rhetoric on into his term, we must wonder whether he and his staff have not been captivated by their own press-agentry.

There is no reason why an outsider or someone lacking national government or political party experience should possess the requisite skills or theoretical understanding of complex political problems or issues that would enable him to avoid pitfalls common to today's presidency. If he relies on a band of personal loyalists who themselves lack national governmental experience to help form a government, chances are that the president will end up with a decision-making structure that discourages new information, understanding, or accommodation. This is a major reason why the "Fortress White House" mentality invariably takes hold after the first half year of a new administration.

No president-elect would ever be foolish enough to concede how little he knows or how truly unprepared he is for the impossible challenge of being president. He banks on the illusion that an elaborate transition team is hard at work to make a smooth changeover, and that as soon as the new administration begins, the president will take charge of a structure that has logically evolved out of that of his predecessor. Presidential transitions, however, frequently involve outgoing, defeated, or tarnished administrations prepping amateurs. There is a high risk of losing the insights, skills, and knowledge gained by the existing White House crew since the euphoria of the winners is, "It can't really happen to us."

The nature of the presidential job is that it can only be learned through experience, but every new president makes the same mistakes of exaggerating his promises and of expecting more than he will realistically be able to accomplish. Neophyte presidents consequently might benefit from a more intense, substantive transition involving political party leaders, presidential scholars, economists, sociologists, foreign-affairs experts, journalists, and especially past presidents and members of their White House staffs. Such a transition could resemble a high-powered "cram course," a "retreat," or a series of seminars involving experienced individuals with the new president and his staff. Considerable emphasis could be given to the major pitfalls that await every incoming executive in today's rapidly changing political environment. Such a transition could be held under the auspices of one of the nation's leading think tanks, such as the Brookings Institution or the American Enterprise Institute. It could involve the Center for the Study of the Presidency as well as major universities, business leaders, and foreign-policy experts.

Every president-elect receives transitional assistance, but most of the energy of transition teams is directed toward the recruitment of key personnel, and the president-elect is not directly involved in an intensive learning effort. The expertise of predecessors, particularly if they are from the opposite party, is seldom taken as seriously as it should be. (After all, *they* lost the White House!)

The transition period is the ideal time for presidential learning because once the president is formally inaugurated, he or she becomes less and less advisable and approachable by anyone outside the president's immediate circle. Individuals who might be candid and informative in discussions earlier now may feel less confident in giving advice to *the* president. There is a strong likelihood that the president and his or her staff would be less open to information or recommendations that run against their preconceived notions or goals.

CONCLUSION

Paradoxically, reforms involving the presidency that stand the best chance of being adopted are the very changes that would most likely make the office even more untenable. Since national or regional primaries and direct national elections are perennially favored by a majority of Americans, pressures continue to surface for further democratization of our political processes. Congress may eventually accede to such reforms, thus subjecting the presidential race almost completely to the organizational and technical skills of the mass media and professional image makers.

Significant changes that might convert the presidency into a parliamentary-style prime ministership are increasingly suggested by reformers, who insist that the presidency will never function without political accountability. But there is almost no chance that we will ever convert our system of separated powers and checks and balances into a parliamentary-cabinet government. The U.S. Constitution was designed to prevent major changes, and there would be an extraordinary amount of opposition from many elements in American government as well as from the electorate to any sweeping reforms of the existing executive or legislative branches. Many powerful interests would resist restructuring the national government in such a way as to enhance the collective decision-making powers of the Executive Branch. For such a change would probably work against their present alliances with Congress or the federal bureaucracy. Americans would find it difficult to exchange the presidency for a political role offering only practical administrative qualities for one embedded in symbols, illusions, and myths.

Some students of the presidency suggest that instead of changing the illusions, we need to reduce the responsibilities of the presidency and to refocus our attention on other executives. We should look to leadership in local, state, and regional governments or in the corporate world or other fields. Returning certain functions to states and localities would decentralize the authority of the federal government and lower our expectations of presidents. A more limited presidency might be more successful in living up to public illusions and images, thereby stabilizing the power of the office.

The problem with this approach, however, is that just as it may be difficult to change human nature so that people seek substance and realism, so too it is difficult to reverse political, cultural, and economic trends. All important trends in political leadership point toward more rather than less emphasis on chief executives as the focal point of national policies and public aspirations. Nothing in our media-dominated culture suggests that this trend will be easily reversed.

Neither is there much likelihood that a new realism about the presidency will soon alter the way the mass media, the American public, presidential candidates, and presidents regard the office. The United States may be the most open, unstructured society in the world. Its political institutions, forms, and processes, which have evolved over time, remarkably reflect our society. The presidency has grown weaker and less relevant because authority of all kinds has become less potent and meaningful as a result of the ever present rivalry between the executive and legislature and because of the frequently conflicting agendas of individual members of Congress and the federal bureaucracy. Our existing Constitutional order offers few remedies for this state of affairs; in fact, it encourages it. The one institution which in the past enabled a president to occasionally rise above the serious limitations of his office—the political party—has been undermined by social, economic, and political changes. Attempts to resurrect parties as coalition builders inevitably fail because there is *no* national coalition.

On rare occasions a president may be sufficiently charismatic, skillful, and—most important—lucky to survive more than one term. But this is now the exception rather than the rule. When the challenger—a self-propelled "new face"—appears to be an even greater risk than the incumbent, a president may slip through to reelection (may even win by a landslide as happened in 1972). But reelection will rarely be a sign from the electorate that it is genuinely *pleased* with a president's performance, because there are far too many distorted public perceptions and expectations and too much distorted presidential rhetoric.[50]

The impossible presidency is not just a recent phenomenon. The office has always been exaggerated in the public mind and by individuals in the White House. What is disturbing is the growing gap between illusions and myths and the increasing inability of presidents to achieve much of anything. This is unfortunate for the American system and even dangerous. For this nation cannot afford a chronically crippled presidency, particularly if it is to overcome its fragmentation and diversity sufficiently to meet the challenges of a rapidly changing and uncertain world.

The problems of the impossible presidency are not just those of a single incumbent or even of an institution. They are the problems of an entire society. The president is every American's surrogate. His greatness and his accomplishments are reflections of the potential greatness and accomplishments of all Americans. His shortcomings and failures reflect the failures and shortcomings of all of us.

NOTES

1. See, for example, Lloyd N. Cutler, "To Form a Government," *Foreign Affairs,* Fall 1980, 126-43; Godfrey Hodgson, *All Things to All Men* (New York: Simon & Schuster, 1980); Richard E. Neustadt, *Presidential Power: The Politics of Leadership from FDR to Carter* (New York: John Wiley & Sons, 1980).

2. Dom Bonafede, "Presidential Mythology," *National Journal,* January 12, 1980, 61.

3. W. Wayne Shannon, "Mr. Reagan Goes to Washington: Teaching Exceptional America," *Public Opinion,* December-January, 1982, 58.

4. Norman C. Thomas, "Reforming the Presidency: Problems and Prospects," in Thomas E. Cronin and Rexford Tugwell, eds., *The Presidency Reappraised* (New York: Praeger Publishers, 1977), 341.

5. James W. Ceaser, "Direct Participation," in Richard Pious, ed., *The Power to Govern, Proceedings of the Academy of Political Science* (New York: Academy of Political Science, 1981), 133.

6. Ibid., 134.

7. Anthony King, "The American Polity in the Late 1970s: Building Coalitions in the Sand," in *The New American Political System* (Washington, D.C.: American Enterprise Institute, 1979), 392.

8. Jeane J. Kirkpatrick and Michael J. Malbin, *The Presidential Nominating Process:*

Can It Be Improved? (Washington, D.C.: American Enterprise Institute, 1980), 16–20.

9. Everett Carll Ladd, Jr., "A Better Way to Pick Our Presidents," *Fortune*, May 5, 1980, 132–42.

10. Terry Sanford, *A Danger of Democracy: The Presidential Nominating Process* (Boulder, Colo.: Westview Press, 1981), 133–53.

11. Ibid., 153.

12. Jeane J. Kirkpatrick, *Dismantling the Parties: Reflections on Party Reform and Party Decomposition* (Washington, D.C.: American Enterprise Institute, 1979), 20.

13. Kirkpatrick and Malbin, 3.

14. Robert Shogan, "The Gap: Why Presidents and Parties Fail," *Public Opinion*, August-September 1982, 19.

15. Ibid.

16. Ibid., 18.

17. See President's Commission for a National Agenda for the Eighties, *The Electoral and Democratic Process in the Eighties* (Englewood Cliffs, N.J.: Prentice-Hall, 1981); James Ceaser, *Reforming the Reforms* (Cambridge, Mass.: Ballinger Publishing Company, 1982); Thomas R. Marshall, *Presidential Nominations in a Reform Age* (New York: Praeger Publishers, 1981).

18. President's Commission for a National Agenda for the Eighties, 28–30.

19. Senate bill 1207, introduced by Senators Bob Packwood (Rep., Oregon) and Ted Stevens (Rep., Alaska). Several other bills quite similar in content have been introduced in both the Senate and House.

20. House resolution 4329, introduced by Representatives Morris K. Udall (Dem., Arizona) and John Ashbrook (Rep., Ohio).

21. House resolution 4519, introduced by Representative Richard Ottinger (Dem., N.Y.).

22. Kirkpatrick and Malbin, Preface.

23. Michael Nelson, "Two Cheers for the National Primary," in Thomas E. Cronin, ed., *Rethinking the Presidency* (Boston: Little, Brown and Company, 1982), 55–58.

24. Ibid., 59

25. Austin Ranney, *The Federalization of Presidential Primaries* (Washington, D.C.: American Enterprise Institute, 1978), 37.

26. Ibid.

27. James Ceaser, *Reforming the Reforms*, 130–42.

28. *Winner Take All: Report of the Twentieth Century Fund Task Force on Reform of the Presidential Election Process* (New York: Holmes and Meier, 1978), 3–15.

29. Ranney, 3–4.

30. Kirkpatrick, *Dismantling the Parties*, 25.

31. See Thomas, 323.

32. King, 390–91.

33. Ibid., 391.

34. Robert E. Denton, Jr., *The Symbolic Dimensions of the American Presidency* (Prospect Heights, Ill.: Waveland Press, 1982), 134.

35. *The Gallup Opinion Poll, Public Opinion, 1981* (Wilmington, Del.: Scholarly Resources, 1981), 41.

36. See Cutler, 139–40; see also Arthur M. Schlesinger, Jr., *The Imperial Presidency* (Boston: Houghton Mifflin Company, 1973), 386–88.

37. Thomas, 329.

38. Cutler, 140.

39. Thomas, 330.

40. Cutler, 140.

41. Edward S. Corwin, *The President: Office and Powers*, 4th ed. (New York: New York University Press, 1957), 297–300.

42. Daniel J. Boorstin, *The Image: A Guide to Pseudo-Events in America* (New York: Atheneum Publishers, 1980), 37.

43. *Washington Post*, February 18, 1983, 1.

44. Ibid.

45. See, for example, "The Presidency: Can Anyone Do the Job?," *Newsweek*, January 26, 1981, 35–51; Joseph Kraft, "The Post-Imperial Presidency," *New York Times Magazine*, November 2, 1980, 31, passim; Henry Graff, "Presidents: Hired, Mired, and Fired," *New York Times*, June 20, 1982, EY-23, as well as the articles by Cutler and Shogan.

46. See Richard M. Nixon, *Memoirs* (New York: Bantam Books, 1982).

47. Harold M. Barger, "Demythologizing the Textbook President," *Theory and Research in Social Education* 4 (August 1976) : 57–66.

48. Ibid.; see also American Political Science Association, Committee on Pre-Collegiate Education, "Political Education in the Schools," *PS: Newsletter of the American Political Science Association* 4 (1971); and Thomas E. Cronin, "The Textbook Presidency and Political Science," in I. R. Feszman and G. S. Poschman, eds., *The American Political Arena* (Boston: Little, Brown and Company, 1972), 294–309.

49. Richard Rose, "Government Against Sub-Governments," in R. Rose and E. Suleiman, eds., *Presidents and Prime Ministers* (Washington, D.C.: American Enterprise Institute, 1980), 318.

50. Denton, 135.

Bibliography

CHAPTER 1 THE IMPOSSIBLE PRESIDENCY
Illusions Versus Realities

Barber, James David. *The Presidential Character: Predicting Performance in the White House.* Englewood Cliffs, N.J.: Prentice-Hall, 1972.

Boorstin, Daniel J. *The Genius of American Politics.* Chicago: Phoenix Books, 1958.

Boorstin, Daniel J. *The Image: Or What Happened to the American Dream.* New York: Atheneum, 1972.

Boulding, Kenneth. *The Image: Knowledge in Life and Society.* Ann Arbor: University of Michigan Press, 1956.

Carter, Jimmy. *A Government As Good As Its People.* New York: Simon & Schuster, 1977.

Cronin, Thomas E. *The State of the Presidency.* 2d Ed. Boston: Little, Brown & Co., 1980.

Easton, David, and Dennis, Jack. *Children in the Political System.* New York: McGraw-Hill, 1968.

Edwards, George C., III. *The Public Presidency: The Pursuit of Popular Support.* New York: St. Martin's Press, 1983.

Gans, Herbert. *Deciding What's News.* New York: Pantheon Books, 1979.

Greenstein, Fred I. *The Hidden Hand Presidency: Eisenhower as Leader.* New York: Basic Books, 1982.

Hargrove, Erwin C. *The Power of the Modern Presidency.* New York: Alfred A. Knopf, 1974.

Hargrove, Erwin C., and Hoopes, Roy. *The Presidency: A Question of Power.* Boston: Little, Brown & Co., 1975.

Hartz, Louis. *The Liberal Tradition in America.* New York: Harcourt, Brace, & World, 1955.

Heclo, Hugh, and Salomon, Lester M., eds. *The Illusion of Presidential Government.* Boulder, Colo.: Westview Press, 1981.

Hess, Robert D., and Torney, Judith V. *The Development of Political Attitudes in Children.* Garden City, N.Y.: Anchor Books, 1967.

Hodgson, Godfrey. *All Things to All Men.* New York: Simon & Schuster, 1980.

Leuchtenburg, William E. *In the Shadow of FDR: From Harry Truman to Ronald Reagan.* Ithaca: Cornell University Press, 1983.

McGinnis, Joe. *The Selling of the President, 1968.* New York: Pocket Books, 1969.

Meltzner, Arnold. *Politics and the Oval Office.* New Brunswick, N.J.: Transaction Books, 1981.

Nelson, Michael, ed. *The Presidency and the Political System.* Washington, D.C.: Congressional Quarterly Press, 1983.

Neustadt, Richard. *Presidential Power: The Politics of Leadership from FDR to Carter.* New York: John Wiley & Sons, 1980.

Nimmo, Dan. *Popular Images of Politics*. Englewood Cliffs, N.J.: Prentice-Hall, 1975.

Novak, Michael. *Choosing Our King*. New York: Macmillan, 1974.

Roelofs, H. Mark. *Ideology and Myth in American Politics*. Boston: Little, Brown & Co., 1976.

Rose, Richard, and Suleiman, Ezra, eds. *Presidents and Prime Ministers*. Washington, D.C.: American Enterprise Institute, 1980.

Rossiter, Clinton. *The American Presidency*. New York: Harvest Books, 1960.

Shogan, Robert. *None of the Above*. New York: New American Library, 1982.

White, Theodore, *In Search of History: A Personal Adventure*. New York: Harper & Row, 1979.

CHAPTER 2   THE PEOPLE'S CHOICE
The Myth of the Nonpolitical President

Califano, Joseph A., Jr. *A Presidential Nation*. New York: W. W. Norton & Co., 1975.

Ceaser, James. *Presidential Selection*. Princeton: Princeton University Press, 1979.

Crotty, William J., and Jacobson, Gary C. *American Parties in Decline*. Boston: Little, Brown & Co., 1980.

Crouse, Timothy. *The Boys on the Bus*. New York: Ballantine Books, 1973.

Davis, James W. *Presidential Primaries: Road to the White House*. Westport, Conn.: Greenwood Press, 1980.

Daly, John Charles. *Choosing Presidential Candidates: How Good Is the New Way?* Washington, D.C.: American Enterprise Institute, 1980.

Delegate Selection Rules for the 1976 Democratic National Convention. Washington, D.C.: Democratic National Committee, 1974.

Delegate Selection Rules for the 1980 Democratic National Convention. Washington, D.C.: Democratic National Committee, 1978.

Delegate Selection Rules for the 1984 Democratic National Convention. Washington, D.C.: Democratic National Committee, 1982.

Kirkpatrick, Jeane. *The New Presidential Elite*. New York: Russell Sage Foundation and Twentieth Century Fund, 1976.

Ladd, Everett Carll, Jr. *Where Have All the Voters Gone?* New York: W. W. Norton & Co., 1978.

Lazarsfeld, Paul; Berelson, Bernard; and Gaudet, H. *The People's Choice*. New York: Columbia University Press, 1968.

Lengle, James I., and Shafer, Byron E. *Presidential Politics*. 2d Ed. New York: St. Martin's Press, 1983.

McGinnis, Joe. *The Selling of the President, 1968*. New York: Pocket Books, 1969.

Miller, W., et al. *The American Voter*. New York: John Wiley & Sons, 1960.

Nie, Norman; Verba, Sidney; and Petrocik, J. *The Changing American Voter*. Cambridge, Mass.: Harvard University Press, 1976.

Page, Benjamin I. *Choices and Echoes in Presidential Elections*. Chicago: University of Chicago Press, 1978.

Patterson, Thomas E. *The Mass Media Election*. New York: Praeger Publishers, 1980.

Patterson, Thomas E., and McClure, Robert D. *The Unseeing Eye: The Myth of Television in National Elections*. New York: G. P. Putnam's Sons, 1976.

Polsby, Nelson. *Consequences of Party Reform*. New York: Oxford University Press, 1983.

Rubin, Richard. *Press, Party, and Presidency*. New York: W. W. Norton & Co., 1981.

Sabato, Larry J. *The Rise of Political Consultants*. New York: Basic Books, 1981.

Sanford, Terry. *A Danger of Democracy*. Boulder, Colo.: Westview Press, 1981.

Schramm, Martin. *Running for President: The Carter Campaign*. New York: Pocket Books, 1977.

Scott, Ruth K., and Hrebenar, Ronald J. *Parties in Crisis: Party Politics in America*. New York: John Wiley & Sons, 1979.

Wayne, Stephen J. *The Road to the White House*. 2d Ed. New York: St. Martin's Press, 1983.

Winograd, Morley, Chairman. *Openness, Participation and Party Building: Reforms for a Stronger Democratic Party*. Washington, D.C.: Democratic National Committee, 1978.

CHAPTER 3 THE GRAND LEGISLATOR

Barber, James David. *The Presidential Character: Predicting Performance in the White House*. Englewood Cliffs, N.J.: Prentice-Hall, 1972.

Congressional Quarterly. *Congress and the Nation*, IV. Washington, D.C.: Congressional Quarterly, Inc., 1978.

Downs, Anthony. *An Economic Theory of Democracy*. New York: Harper & Row, 1957.

Early, Stephen T., Jr., and Knight, Barbara. *Responsible Government: American and British*. Chicago: Nelson-Hall, 1981.

Edwards, George, III. *Presidential Influence in Congress*. San Francisco: W. H. Freeman & Co., 1980.

Evans, Rowland, and Novak, Robert. *Nixon in the White House*. New York: Vintage Books, 1972.

Fenno, Richard J. *Congressmen in Committees*. Boston: Little, Brown & Co., 1973.

Fisher, Louis. *The Constitution Between Friends: Congress, the Presidency and the Law*. New York: St. Martin's Press, 1978.

Goldman, Eric F. *The Tragedy of Lyndon Johnson*. New York: Alfred A. Knopf, 1969.

Hargrove, Erwin C., and Hoopes, Roy. *The Presidency: A Question of Power*. Boston: Little, Brown & Co., 1975.

Hodgson, Godfrey. *All Things to All Men*. New York: Simon & Schuster, 1980.

Holtzman, Abraham. *Legislative Liaison*. Indianapolis: Bobbs-Merrill, 1973.

Jewell, Malcolm. *Senatorial Politics and Foreign Policy*. Lexington: University of Kentucky Press, 1962.

Kearnes, Doris. *Lyndon Johnson and the American Dream*. New York: Harper & Row, 1976.

King, Anthony, ed. *The New American Political System*. Washington, D.C.: American Enterprise Institute, 1979.

Kingdon, John W. *Congressmen's Voting Decisions*. New York: Harper & Row, 1973.

Koenig, Louis. *The Invisible Presidency*. New York: Holt, Rinehart & Winston, 1960.

Light, Paul C. *The President's Agenda*. Baltimore: Johns Hopkins University Press, 1982.

Mansfield, Harvey, ed. *Congress Against the President*. New York: Praeger Publishers, 1975.

Meltsner, Arnold J., ed. *Politics and the Oval Office*. San Francisco: Institute for Contemporary Studies, 1981.

Mowry, George E. *The Era of Theodore Roosevelt*. New York: Harper & Row, 1958.

Neustadt, Richard. *Presidential Power: The Politics of Leadership from F.D.R. to Jimmy Carter*. New York: John Wiley & Sons, 1980.

O'Brien, Lawrence F. *No Final Victories: A Life in Politics from John F. Kennedy to Watergate*. New York: Ballantine, 1974.

Oleszek, Walter J. *Congressional Procedures and the Policy Process*. Washington, D.C.: Congressional Quarterly Press, 1978.

Pious, Richard M. *The American Presidency*. New York: Basic Books, 1979.

Polsby, Nelson W. *Congress and the Presidency*, Englewood Cliffs, N.J.: Prentice-Hall, 1976.

Schlesinger, Arthur M., Jr. *The Coming of the New Deal: The Age of Roosevelt*. Vol. 2. Boston: Houghton Mifflin, 1958.

Shull, Steven, and LeLoup, Lance. *The Presidency: Studies in Policy Making*. New Brunswick, Ohio: King's Court, 1979.

Sundquist, James L. *The Decline and Resurgence of Congress*. Washington, D.C.: The Brookings Institution, 1981.

Watson, Richard A., and Thomas, Norman C. *The Politics of the Presidency*. New York: John Wiley & Sons, 1983.

Wayne, Stephen J. *The Legislative Presidency*. New York: Harper & Row, 1978.

Wicker, Tom. *J.F.K. and L.B.J.: The Influence of Personality Upon Politics*. Baltimore: Penguin Books, 1968.

Wildavsky, Aaron, ed. *Perspectives on the Presidency*. Boston: Little, Brown & Co., 1975.

CHAPTER 4　THE CHIEF EXECUTIVE
Illusion of Bureaucratic Responsibility

Califano, Joseph A., Jr. *Governing America*. New York: Simon & Schuster, 1981.

Cater, Douglas. *Power in Washington*. New York: Vintage Books, 1964.

Cronin, Thomas E., ed. *Rethinking the Presidency*. Boston: Little, Brown & Co., 1982.

Cronin, Thomas. *The State of the Presidency*. Boston: Little, Brown & Co., 1980.

Early, Stephen T., Jr., and Knight, Barbara. *Responsible Government: American and British*. Chicago: Nelson-Hall, 1981.

Fenno, Richard T., Jr. *The President's Cabinet*. Cambridge, Mass.: Harvard University Press, 1959.

Fritschler, Lee A. *Smoking and Politics*. Englewood Cliffs, N.J.: Prentice-Hall, 1983.

Heclo, Hugh. *A Government of Strangers*. Washington, D.C.: The Brookings Institution, 1977.

Hess, Stephen. *Organizing the White House*. Washington, D.C.: The Brookings Institution, 1976.

King, Anthony, ed. *The New American Political System*. Washington, D.C.: American Enterprise Institute, 1978.

Lowi, Theodore J. *The End of Liberalism*. New York: W. W. Norton & Co., 1979.

Meltsner, Arnold, ed. *Politics and the Oval Office*. San Francisco: Institute for Contemporary Studies, 1981.

Nathan, Richard P. *The Plot That Failed: Nixon and the Administrative Presidency*. New York: John Wiley & Sons, 1975.

Polenberg, Richard. *Reorganizing Roosevelt's Government, 1936–1939*. Cambridge, Mass.: Harvard University Press, 1966.

Ripley, Randall, and Franklin, Grace. *Congress, the Bureaucracy and Public Policy*. Rev. ed. Homewood, Ill.: Dorsey Press, 1980.

Rose, Richard. *Managing Presidential Objectives*. New York: The Free Press, 1976.

Rose, Richard, and Suleiman, Ezra, eds. *Presidents and Prime Ministers*. Washington, D.C.: American Enterprise Institute, 1980.

Rourke, Francis E., ed. *Bureaucratic Power in National Politics*. Boston: Little, Brown & Co., 1972.

Seidman, Harold. *Politics, Position and Power*. New York: Oxford University Press, 1980.

Sorensen, Theodore. *Decision-Making in the White House*. New York: Columbia University Press, 1963.

White, Theodore H. *America in Search of Itself*. New York: Harper & Row, 1982.

Woll, Peter. *American Bureaucracy*. New York: W. W. Norton & Co., 1963.

CHAPTER 5 THE MIRROR-IMAGE MACHINE
The Presidential Establishment

Anderson, Patrick. *The President's Men*. Garden City, N.Y.: Doubleday, 1968.

Califano, Joseph A., Jr. *A Presidential Nation*. New York: W. W. Norton & Co., 1975.

Cronin, Thomas E., and Greenberg, Sanford, eds. *The Presidential Advisory System*. New York: Harper & Row, 1969.

Grossman, Michael, and Kumar, Martha Joynt. *Portraying the President*. Baltimore: Johns Hopkins University Press, 1981.

Heineman, Ben W., Jr., and Hessler, Curtis A. *Memorandum for the President: A Strategic Approach to Domestic Affairs in the 1980s*. New York: Random House, 1980.

Hess, Stephen. *Organizing the Presidency*. Washington: The Brookings Institution, 1976.

Hoxie, R. Gordon. *The White House Organization and Operations*. New York: Center for the Study of the Presidency, 1971.

Janis, Irving L. *Victims of Groupthink*. Boston: Houghton Mifflin, 1972.

Johnson, Richard Tanner. *Managing the White House: An Intimate Study of the Presidency*. New York: Harper & Row, 1974.

Koenig, Louis. *The Invisible Presidency*. New York: Rinehart, 1960.

Medved, Michael. *The Shadow Presidents*. New York: New York Times Books, 1979.

Nathan, Richard. *The Plot That Failed: Nixon and the Administrative Presidency*. New York: John Wiley & Sons, 1975.

Parmet, Herbert S. *Eisenhower and the American Crusades*. New York: Macmillan, 1972.

Reedy, George. *The Twilight of the Presidency*. New York: Mentor Books, 1970.

Sorensen, Theodore. *Decision-Making in the White House*. New York: Columbia University Press, 1963.

The White House Transcripts. New York: Bantam Books, 1974.

Tugwell, Rexford. *The Enlargement of the Presidency*. New York: Doubleday, 1960.

CHAPTER 6 LEADER OF THE FREE WORLD
Imperial or Imperiled President?

Almond, Gabriel. *The American People and Foreign Policy*. New York: Praeger Publishers, 1960.

Crabb, Cecil V., Jr., and Holt, Pat. *Invitation to Struggle: Congress, the President and Foreign Policy*. Washington, D.C.: Congressional Quarterly Press, 1980.

Duchacek, Ivo. *Nations and Man*. Hinsdale, Ill.: Dryden Press, 1975.

Etzold, Thomas E. *The Conduct of American Foreign Relations*. New York: New Viewpoints, 1977.

Farrell, John C., and Smith, A., eds. *Images and Reality in World Politics*. New York: Columbia University Press, 1967.

Halberstam, David. *The Powers That Be*. New York: Alfred A. Knopf, 1979.

Hoopes, Townsend. *The Devil and John Foster Dulles*. Boston: Atlantic–Little, Brown, 1973.

Jordan, Hamilton. *Crisis: The Last Year of the Carter Presidency*. New York: G. P. Putnam's Sons, 1982.

Kessler, Frank. *The Dilemmas of Presidential Leadership*. Englewood Cliffs, N.J.: Prentice-Hall, 1982.

Kissinger, Henry. *Nuclear Weapons and Foreign Policy*. New York: W. W. Norton & Co., 1969.

Kissinger, Henry. *Years of Upheaval*. Boston: Little, Brown & Co., 1982.

Miroff, Bruce. *Pragmatic Illusions: The Presidential Politics of John F. Kennedy*. New York: David McKay, 1976.

Mueller, John E. *War, Presidents and Public Opinion*. New York: John Wiley & Sons, 1973.

Pious, Richard M., ed. *The Power to Govern*. Proceedings of the Academy of Political Science, 1981.

Purifoy, Lewis McCarroll. *Harry Truman's China Policy*. New York: New Viewpoints, 1976.

Roseman, Cyril, et al. *Dimensions of Political Analysis*. Englewood Cliffs, N.J.: Prentice-Hall, 1966.

Rosenau, James N., ed. *International Politics and Foreign Policy*. New York: Free Press, 1969.

Schell, Jonathan. *The Time of Illusion*. New York: Vintage Books, 1975.

Schlesinger, Arthur M., Jr. *The Imperial Presidency*. Boston: Houghton Mifflin, 1973.

Sheehan, Neil. *The Pentagon Papers*. New York: Signet Books, 1971.

Sorensen, Theodore. *Kennedy*. New York: Harper & Row, 1965.

Spanier, John, and Uslaner, Eric. *How American Foreign Policy Is Made*. New York: Praeger Publishers, 1978.

Stoessinger, John G. *Crusaders and Pragmatists*. New York: W. W. Norton & Co., 1979.

Truman, Harry S. *Memoirs*. Vol. 2. New York: Signet Books, 1957.

White, Theodore. *Breach of Faith*. New York: Atheneum, 1975.

Wicker, Tom. *J.F.K. and L.B.J.: The Influence of Personality on Politics*. Baltimore: Penguin Books, 1968.

Wildavsky, Aaron. *Perspectives on the Presidency*. Boston: Little, Brown & Co., 1975.

CHAPTER 7 UNATTAINABLE EXPECTATIONS
Presidents as Domestic Problem Solvers

Heineman, Ben W., Jr., and Hessler, Curtis. *Memorandum for the President: A Strategic Approach to Domestic Affairs in the 1980s*. New York: Random House, 1980.

King, Anthony, ed. *The New American Political System*. Washington, D.C.: American Enterprise Institute, 1979.

Ladd, Everett Carll, Jr. *Where Have All The Voters Gone?* New York: W. W. Norton & Co., 1978.

Light, Paul C. *The President's Agenda*. Baltimore: Johns Hopkins University Press, 1982.

Lowi, Theodore J. *The End of Liberalism*. New York: W. W. Norton & Co., 1979.

Miller, Merle. *Lyndon: An Oral Biography*. New York: G. P. Putnam's Sons, 1980.

Pious, Richard, ed. *The Power to Govern*. Proceedings of the Academy of Political Science, 1981.

Ripley, Randall, ed. *Public Policies and Their Politics.* New York: W. W. Norton & Co., 1966.

Sundquist, James L. *Politics and Policy: The Eisenhower, Kennedy, and Johnson Years.* Washington, D.C.: The Brookings Institution, 1968.

Wayne, Stephen J. *The Legislative Presidency.* New York: Harper & Row, 1978.

CHAPTER 8   ECONOMIC MASTER MECHANIC

Blinder, Alan S. *Economic Policy and the Great Stagflation.* New York: Academic Press, 1979.

Bluestone, Barry, and Harrison, Bennett. *The Deindustrialization of America.* New York: Basic Books, 1982.

Cronin, Thomas E., ed. *Rethinking the Presidency.* Boston: Little, Brown & Co., 1982.

Fiorina, Morris P. *Congress: Keystone of the Washington Establishment.* New Haven: Yale University Press, 1977.

Fisher, Louis. *Presidential Spending Power.* Princeton: Princeton University Press, 1975.

Heller, Walter. *New Dimensions of Political Economy.* Cambridge, Mass.: Harvard University Press, 1966.

Hoadley, Walter E., ed. *The Economy and the President.* New York: American Assembly, Columbia University Press, 1980.

Kessler, Frank. *The Dilemmas of Presidential Leadership.* Englewood Cliffs, N.J.: Prentice-Hall, 1982.

King, Anthony, ed. *The New American Political System.* Washington, D.C.: American Enterprise Institute, 1979.

Miller, Merle. *Lyndon: An Oral Biography.* New York: G. P. Putnam's Sons, 1980.

Okun, Arthur. *The Political Economy of Prosperity.* New York: W. W. Norton & Co., 1970.

Pious, Richard. *The American Presidency.* New York: Basic Books, 1979.

Pious, Richard, ed. *The Power to Govern.* Proceedings of the Academy of Political Science, 1981.

Robinson, Marshall A.; Morton, H. C.; and Calderwood, J. *An Introduction to Economic Reasoning.* Garden City, N.Y.: Anchor Books, 1980.

Thurow, Lester C. *The Zero-Sum Society.* Baltimore: Penguin Books, 1980.

Tufte, Edward. *Political Control of the Economy.* Princeton: Princeton University Press, 1978.

White, Theodore H. *America in Search of Itself.* New York: Harper & Row, 1982.

Wildavsky, Aaron, ed. *Perspectives on the Presidency.* Boston: Little, Brown & Co., 1975.

CHAPTER 9   MEDIA CELEBRITY

Barber, J. D., ed. *Choosing the President.* Englewood Cliffs, N.J.: Prentice-Hall, 1974.

Bell, Jack. *The Splendid Misery.* New York: Doubleday, 1960.

Braestrup, Peter. *Big Story: How the American Press and Television Reported and Interpreted the Crisis of Tet 1968 in Vietnam and Washington.* New Haven: Yale University Press, 1977.

Comstock, George, et al. *Television and Human Behavior.* New York: Columbia University Press, 1978.

Cornwell, Elmer. *Presidential Leadership of Public Opinion.* Bloomington: Indiana University Press, 1965.

Duchacek, Ivo. *Nations and Men.* Hinsdale, Ill.: Dryden Press, 1975.

Gans, Herbert. *Deciding What's News: A Study of CBS Evening News, NBC Nightly News, Newsweek, and TIME.* New York: Pantheon Books, 1979.

Graeber, Doris. *Mass Media and American Politics.* Washington, D.C.: Congressional Quarterly Press, 1980.

Grossman, Michael, and Kumar, Martha Joynt. *Portraying the President: The White House and the News Media.* Baltimore: Johns Hopkins University Press, 1981.

Halberstam, David. *The Powers That Be.* New York: Alfred A. Knopf, 1979.

Hess, Stephen. *The Washington Reporters.* Washington, D.C.: The Brookings Institution, 1981.

Jones, Alfred H. *Roosevelt's Image Brokers.* Port Washington, N.Y.: Kennikat Press, 1974.

Jordan, Hamilton. *Crisis: The Last Year of the Carter Presidency.* New York: G. P. Putnam's Sons, 1982.

Mann, Thomas, and Ornstein, Norman, eds. *The New Congress.* Washington, D.C.: American Enterprise Institute, 1981.

McLuhan, Marshall. *Understanding Media.* New York: New American Library, 1964.

Mendelsohn, Harold, and Crespi, Irving. *Polls, Television and the New Politics.* Scranton, Penna.: Chandler Publishing Co., 1970.

Minow, Newton N.; Martin, J. B.; and Mitchell, L. *Presidential Television.* New York: Basic Books, 1973.

Morris, Edmund. *The Rise of Theodore Roosevelt.* New York: Coward, McCann & Geoghegan, Inc., 1979.

Nimmo, Dan, and Combs, James. *Subliminal Politics: Myths and Mythmaking in America.* Englewood Cliffs, N.J.: Prentice-Hall, 1980.

Pious, Richard, ed. *The Power to Govern.* Proceedings of the Academy of Political Science, 1981.

Porter, William E. *Assault on the Media: The Nixon Years.* Ann Arbor: University of Michigan Press, 1976.

Rubin, Bernard. *Political Television.* Belmont, Calif.: Wadsworth Publishing Co., 1967.

Rubin, Richard. *Press, Party, and President.* New York: W. W. Norton & Co., 1981.

Stein, M. L. *When Presidents Meet the Press.* New York: Julian Messner, 1969.

CHAPTER 10   A REFORMED OR REALISTIC PRESIDENCY?

Ceaser, James. *Reforming the Reforms.* Cambridge, Mass.: Ballinger Publishing Co., 1982.

Corwin, Edward S. *The President: Office and Powers*. New York: New York University Press, 1957.

Cronin, Thomas E., and Tugwell, Rexford, eds. *The Presidency Reappraised*. New York: Praeger Publishers, 1977.

Denton, Robert E., Jr. *The Symbolic Dimensions of the American Presidency*. Prospect Heights, Ill.: Waveland Press, 1982.

Hodgson, Godfrey. *All Things to All Men*. New York: Simon & Schuster, 1980.

King, Anthony. *The New American Political System*. Washington, D.C.: American Enterprise Institute, 1979.

Kirkpatrick, Jeane J. *Dismantling the Parties: Reflections on Party Reform and Party Decomposition*. Washington, D.C.: American Enterprise Institute, 1979.

Kirkpatrick, Jeane J., and Malbin, Michael J. *The Presidential Nominating Process: Can It Be Improved?* Washington, D.C.: American Enterprise Institute, 1980.

Marshall, Thomas R. *Presidential Nominations in a Reform Age*. New York: Praeger Publishers, 1981.

Neustadt, Richard E. *Presidential Power: The Politics of Leadership from FDR to Carter*. New York: John Wiley & Sons, 1980.

Nixon, Richard M. *Memoirs*. New York: Bantam Books, 1982.

Ranney, Austin. *The Federalization of Presidential Primaries*. Washington, D.C.: American Enterprise Institute, 1978.

Rose, Richard, and Suleiman, E. *Presidents and Prime Ministers*. Washington, D.C.: American Enterprise Institute, 1980.

Sanford, Terry. *A Danger of Democracy: The Presidential Nominating Process*. Boulder, Colo.: Westview Press, 1981.

Schlesinger, Arthur M., Jr. *The Imperial Presidency*. Boston: Houghton Mifflin, 1973.

Winner Take All: Report of the Twentieth Century Fund Task Force on Reform of the Presidential Election Process. New York: Holmes & Meier Publishers, 1978.

Index

NOTE: Page numbers in *italics* indicate that
information is presented in a figure or a table.